BATTLE
FOR THE
NORTH

BATTLE
FOR THE
NORTH

The Tay and Forth Bridges and
the 19th-Century Railway Wars

CHARLES McKEAN

Granta Books
London

Granta Publications, 2/3 Hanover Yard, Noel Road, London N1 8BE

First published in Great Britain by Granta Books 2006

A CIP catalogue record for this book is available
from the British Library.

1 3 5 7 9 10 8 6 4 2

ISBN-13: 978-1-86207-852-9
ISBN-10: 1-86207-852-1

Typeset by M Rules

Printed and bound in Great Britain by
William Clowes Ltd, Beccles, Suffolk

CONTENTS

ACKNOWLEDGEMENTS

I am enormously indebted to Bill Dow for inducting me into the subject of the Tay Bridge. I am also grateful to Aileen Black, Donald Cattanach, Mal Clark, Rob Duck, Ian Flett, Bob Harris, David Kett, Alex Marshall, Christine Matthews, Alan Macdonald, John McGregor, Richard McKean, Eileen Moran, Richard Oram, John Rapley, Derek Reid, Ted Ruddock, Jim Tomlinson, Chris Whatley and Iain Boyd Whyte for the information, assistance, advice and suggestions they provided. I also owe an enormous debt to Dundee City Archives, and the Wellgate Library; Pat Whatley, Caroline Brown and Mary Young at Dundee University Archives; the St Andrews Preservation Trust Museum; Steve Bell and Jan Merchant at Perth and Kinross Archives; the Institution of Civil Engineers, particularly Mike Chrimes and Robert Thomas; Stirling Council Archive Service, and to the staff of West Register House and General Register House, Edinburgh, particularly Linda Ramsay and Leanne Swallow. John Saddler inspired this book, and Sara Holloway and Bella Shand were charmingly merciful editors. My family has been very patient.

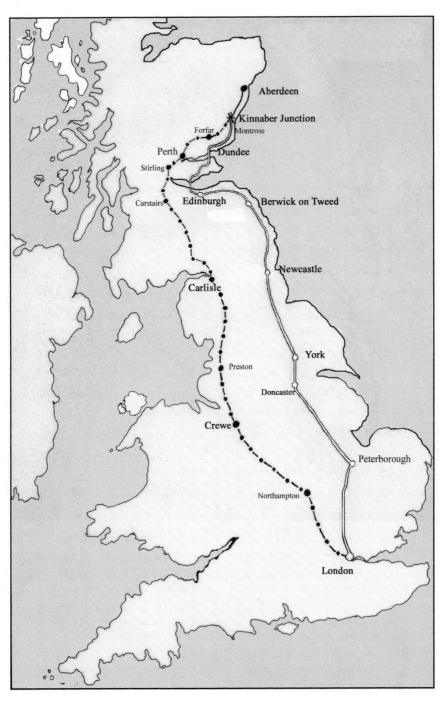

East Coast line (North British north of Berwick on Tweed) and
West Coast line (Caledonian north of Carlisle).

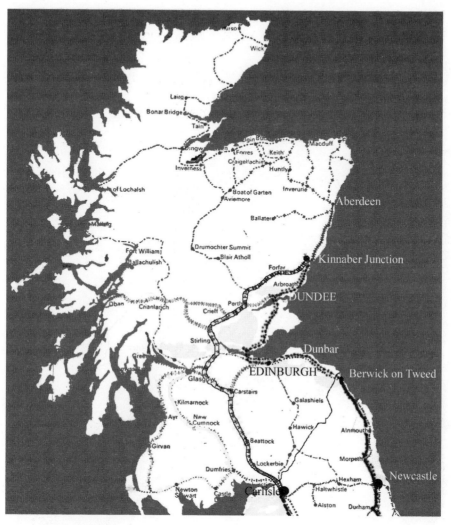

The Scottish network. The North British Railway's principal trunk route (dotted) connected with the English east coast lines (solid) at Berwick on Tweed, ran up to Edinburgh, across the Forth and the Tay to Dundee, then north-east to Aberdeen. The Caledonian Railway's trunk route (hatched) ran from Carlisle to Stirling and Perth, sharing the track with the NBR from Kinnaber Junction on its last leg to Aberdeen.

Left: London to Aberdeen: the west and east coast railway routes of Britain, completed by 1890

PROLOGUE

On Sunday, 28 December 1879, Maggie Pirnie, the admired general servant and cook in the service of the Rev. J. Edgar Hill, left her employer's house in Albany Terrace, high above the town on the slopes of Dundee Law, and walked downhill to Dundee's Tay Bridge station, to meet her fiancé coming by train from Edinburgh. It was the day after the Feast of St John, patron saint of Freemasons, when each Lodge in the town of Dundee customarily made a ceremonial visit to each of their brother Lodges in a parade of stately standards led by a band of musicians. Christmas festivities now over, Maggie Pirnie was about to begin a new life. She had met Robert Culross, a carpenter with the North British Railway in Leith, and they were to be married on 6 February.[1] She was marrying late by the standards of the time, and her meeting with Culross had been fortunate – not to say passionate, given that he had visited her every weekend. She had handed in her notice and had spent all and more of her savings in making 'a lot of purchases for the marriage'.[2] Culross was coming to collect her to take her back to Edinburgh, bringing additional funds to cover the debts she had incurred. Her place in the household had been awarded to another.

Albany Terrace was a row of new villas of variegated design stretching across the brow of Dundee Law, the volcanic plug that rises sharply behind the town about half a mile inland from the shoreline of the River Tay – sufficiently high to be above the smoke level of the multiplying textile factory chimneys, and Maggie Pirnie's employer was typical of the substantial bourgeoisie who occupied that hillside suburb. Offering incomparable views of the estuary, Albany Terrace lies well above the snow-line, and the steep walk down to the town centre would have been very tricky in the snow of earlier that month – so cold indeed that large ice-floes had endangered shipping on the river.[3] A partial thaw now meant that the streets might not have been so slippery. The unseasonable warmth, however, brought wind. A south-westerly gale was massing for attack, and there had been heavy showers of sleet in the early evening.[4]

As she was making her way downhill, the wind was turning blustery, expelled in short severe gusts,[5] but Maggie Pirnie would not have noticed it particularly, since the deepening blasts were narrowly concentrated in the river plain. Houses up the Law and the factory chimneys clustering around its bottom remained unscathed. Nor would she have felt it as she passed through the town centre. Long adapted to its tempestuous location, the form of Dundee's medieval market-place had evolved to exclude such wind. Only once she had passed out of its shelter, down onto the Shore and neared the railway stations would she have felt its blasts, or noticed glinting in the sporadic moonlight the white horses of the growing waves that extended two miles across the Tay estuary. The river, observed one retired sea captain, was 'a sheet of foam'.[6] Passengers on the train that had just arrived had spotted that foam flying about in the dark, eighty-eight feet above the sea at the level of the railway viaduct itself.[7] The only shelter from that foam at the west end of Dundee's Shore was snug inside one of Dundee's railway stations.

Robert Culross was on the 4.30 train from Edinburgh, travelling by roll-on, roll-off boat between Granton and Burntisland, then north through Fife, through Leuchars Junction to the tiny new rural halt at St Fort. He would probably have been in the third-class carriage. It was neither a full nor a very fashionable train: servants and workmen, mostly, travelling home ready for work on Monday morning. Lady Baxter's personal maid, perhaps carrying the Baxter family jewels,[8] a man rushing to his father's funeral – but nobody travelling in first class. With steely commercialism, the North British Railway Company had persisted with Sunday travelling in

spite of the repeated efforts to block it. A motion to prohibit train
services being scheduled to run on a Sunday had been defeated in
1844, the Company's very first year of operation, but
Sabbatarianism, much more supported in Scotland than in
England,[9] arose annually, Lazarus-like, at shareholders' meetings
thereafter. From the sophistication of London, *The Times* was tickled at the condition of Scotland. 'Calm and observant men, not
given to exaggeration, have said, from time to time, that Scotland
is the most priest-ridden country in Europe.'[10] The North British
survived its Sabbatarian ambushes, pleading that Sunday was the
only day when the poorer sort could visit relatives or take outings,
and its Sunday train services had continued.

When Culross's train reached St Fort, the south-westerly wind
was gathering its full force. Captain Pryde, in charge of the Pile
Lighthouse out in the estuary, felt the lighthouse shake more than
it had ever done before: 'Worst night I have ever experienced. We
were afraid that the Pile would come down itself.' The night had
become drier. Clouds scudding across the moon intermittently illuminated the spume from the river so dense that onlookers
compared it to mist. The Aberdeen express in front was running
slightly behind schedule, and since it was customary to hold the
local trains back to let the express get through,[11] Culross's train was
four minutes late.[12] Doubtless its engine driver intended to accelerate, as was the custom, as he passed over the Tay Bridge to make
up time.[13] It left St Fort with perhaps seventy-two passengers (the
figure is still disputed),[14] and slowed down by the cabin at the
entrance to the bridge at 7.13pm, to collect from signalman Barclay
the trainstaff – the baton – that signified the train was safe to cross
the longest railway bridge in the world.

The records show that the first-class carriage was empty, so
David Jobson, one of the few Dundee dignitaries on the train, was
probably sitting in second. Scion of a dynasty of Dundee banking
and Russian flax merchants over the previous two centuries, Jobson
was a paint and oil merchant in West Dock Street, living with his
wife and five children in a simple house in Airlie Place. As town
councillor and guild brother, he had been a guest at the banquet to

celebrate the opening of the Tay Bridge on 31 May just over eighteen months earlier. Fiercely critical of the inefficiencies of the British railway system as compared to those on the Continent, he had suggested that it was high time that the railways should be nationalised.

Provost Robertson was watching the train from the comfort of his house in Newport on the south bank as he always did. His son worked in a blacksmith's shop in Dundee, and began work so early in the morning that he preferred to travel back to Dundee on the Sunday night, usually taking the 6.30pm from Burntisland. The Provost did not have a clear view since, at certain points, the train was concealed behind the roofs and chimneys of neighbouring houses. His habit was to watch as it appeared and disappeared behind a landscape of roofs and chimneys. The provost watched the train disappear as normal, at 7.16pm, but no matter how he stared, he could not make it out emerging on the other side.

Two miles north across the estuary, the wind was causing anxiety. Chimney stacks had been blown over, tiles lifted and the glass roof of the semi-underground Dundee Tay Bridge station had been broken by a crashing chimney. Some stationary laden coal wagons had been driven by the gale back along their tracks half way from the bridge to the goods yard.[15] By 7.23pm, the Dundee Station Master James Smith was becoming uneasy at the late arrival of the Burntisland train; and when he tried to telegraph signalman Barclay in the south cabin, the cable which ran along the bridge no longer worked. He set out toward the bridge to investigate, accompanied by the locomotive superintendent, James Roberts. When they met people coming the other way with alarming tales of having seen the bridge tumble into the river, he bound them to silence. Smith continued only 'as far as it was necessary to see'; whereas Roberts pressed on 'with great difficulty' onto the bridge, crawling out until its last eight or nine yards. There he could discern the railway tracks periodically illuminated by the moon trailing down toward the sea. The Station Master then ordered all entrances to the station be barred, and asked the growing press of people to leave the station – ostensibly for their own safety since glass was still falling from the station roof. He telegraphed the North British Railway Company Headquarters in Edinburgh, and ordered up a steamer from the harbour.[16] At this juncture, nobody knew whether the bridge had gone down before the train had reached it or while it was crossing.

Barely a minute after leaving Barclay's cabin on the south shore, passengers on the train had probably felt an unusual jolt or bounce – a very sharp one in the case of the second-class carriage at the rear of the train – and then perhaps a dragging motion accompanied by the squealing of wheels against rails. The second-class carriage then came to an abrupt halt, smacking into a girder tie-bar, and was immediately annihilated by the heavier Guard's Van behind, which mounted up over it crushing David Jobson and his companions to death. The force caused the cast-iron columns below to fracture, and the bridge to begin to topple downstream into the foam. Robert Culross probably drowned with the remaining passengers and crew minutes later, knocked unconscious by the impact of the carriage hitting the sea – so colossal that it had broken many of their limbs.

Maggie Pirnie remained outside Tay Bridge station, in the cold of Lower Union Street, until 8.45pm. The shock, as her minister later informed the North British Railway Company's Appeals Committee, had made Pirnie unfit to work. She had lost her job, her house, her fiancé and her future. She was duly awarded £17.[17]

What or who was responsible for the death of Robert Culross and his fellow travellers? Blame moved quickly from the unexpectedly ferocious gale – and thereby from an 'Act of God' – to human error; and, for the last 120 years, it has been heaped on the head of Sir Thomas Bouch, design engineer of the bridge. The Inquiry held in 1880 to investigate why the bridge collapsed encouraged lurid tales of inefficient construction practices, untried design and inadequate supervision. Bouch alone was its scapegoat, and for the next century he became an object lesson and an acute embarrassment to the engineering profession.

It suited the times to claim that Bouch retired meekly, humiliated, to die of melancholy, but he was not such a milksop; and although the realities of typical Victorian construction were indeed laid embarrassingly bare at the Inquiry (shocking to those who have believed the Victorians' portrayal of themselves as responsible, careful and clever constructors, but less shocking to those who watch the realities of human nature), the evidence was not unequivocal.

Moreover, to look at the Tay Bridge in isolation gives a distorted perspective, for it had never been an end in itself. Bouch was also the designer of a pioneering Suspension Bridge across the River Forth for the same railway company at the same time. Construction of these two bridges over the Forth and Tay estuaries was central to the fifty-year trunk railway war waged by the North British Railway Company to achieve parity in the battle for Scottish railway business with the Caledonian Railway Company; and over that half-century, the Caledonian would do what it took to prevent the NBR succeeding in that objective. The Caledonian had the advantage. It controlled the principal inland railway route from Carlisle through central Scotland eventually north-west up to Aberdeen –

'The Spirit of the Storm'. This cartoon of the catastrophe, subtitled 'Veni, Vidi, Vici', reflected the view that, in the building of the Tay Bridge, man had overreached himself.

known as the West Coast line. The NBR had the short straw for, unless it used the Caledonian's own track, its route to Aberdeen was blocked by the sweeping estuaries of the rivers Forth and Tay. So long as the rivers remained unbridged, the Caledonian would hold the NBR to ransom in a deep and enormously wasteful rivalry.

The adversarial British parliamentary system only made things worse. It exacerbated the companies' native belligerence to the extent that any potential for competitive co-operation was replaced by 'war to the knife' as *The Times* was to put it in 1866. Economic historians view the outcome as a success: namely that Britain cleverly achieved a railway network built from the pockets of the wealthy without any state investment.[18] The reality is that the eventual Scottish railway network was far from ideal and consumed grossly disproportionate resources in its making.

From the story of the Scottish trunk railway war can be inferred much of the story of the modernisation of North Britain. Preternaturally large companies could bully town councils, conceal their true finances from their shareholders, influence Parliament, and yet be so inefficient in the running of their business as to lead to repeated calls for their nationalisation. *Plus ça change* . . . They were enormously powerful, almost unstoppable (save by each other), and presented towns large and small with the vision of exponential trade expansion. In the highly competitive world of Victorian urbanism, town councils were usually desperate to get a railway since they deeply feared being marooned by progress. Only once they appreciated the likely consequences of the railway companies' heedless attitude to the historic identity of their town, did they demur. It was usually too late, and railway companies transformed nineteenth-century Scotland and its cities profoundly and permanently.

There are always victims from the processes of modernisation. The dead of the Tay Bridge disaster, fewer than the number of workmen or 'briggers' dead from working below and above the rivers Tay and Forth, were as much the victims of the time as they may have been of defective construction, inadequate design, inadequate track maintenance, or inadequate supervision. For they were the victims of speed – of the inexorable pressure to build quickly – too quickly – to conform to the wildly over-optimistic construction programmes that had been necessary to persuade the railway companies in the first place. The Inquiry into the Tay Bridge collapse, however, obscured all that. It skewed our perception of why the bridge was built in the first place, the conditions of its construction and why it fell; it ignored the Tay Bridge's importance relative to the Forth Bridge, and the role that these two huge structures played in the intense mid-Victorian commercial battle between the North British and Caledonian Railway Companies.

Railway company chairmen and managers (though not the Ordinary shareholders) happily regarded the railway warfare in Scotland as the condition that kept them in power, and their enthusiasm permeated all ranks. It extended, legendarily, to occasional fisticuffs between rival ticket collectors on the shared platforms of Perth railway station. Even once the trunk routes were complete, that same warfare underlay both the great railway race of August 1895 when sleek engines streaked at dawn along opposite banks of Montrose Basin panting to reach Aberdeen first, and the competitive hotel construction at either end of Edinburgh's Princes Street. Only five years before the century ended, the railway footsoldiers could still scarcely be restrained from seeking to disrupt the business of their rivals whenever possible.

That, therefore, was the context within which the North British, a relatively small railway company by British standards, was driven to build the longest railway bridge in the world over the Tay, and the largest railway bridge in the world over the Forth – on a route which, in world terms, was hardly connecting one major centre of population to another. Its traffic would be lucky to cover the cost. Why and how such a perverse ambition was achieved is the purpose of this book.

CHAPTER ONE

THE ENGINE OF MODERNISATION

The railways are, next to printing, the most powerful instrument of civilisation which the genius of man has been able to create, and it is difficult to foresee and assign the consequences which one day they will bring to the lives of nations.

DIRECTOR OF THE FRENCH BUREAU OF BRIDGES
AND ROADS, 1837[1]

For all their achievements, and their reputation for thoroughness, efficiency and engineering excellence, the Victorians were as prone to anxiety, indecision, self-contradiction and bad practice as we are today, and nowhere was that more evident than in the evolution of the railway network.

Railway companies had been granted the necessary powers of compulsory purchase of land for their tracks by Parliament, in return for which Parliament protected competition and the public interest through an ineffective and onerous licensing procedure. Special Committees of both Commons and Lords vetted route, capital and timescale for each railway. They would approve the 'running rights' of one railway company to run trains upon the lines of another; and, occasionally, determine which routes should be designated trunk lines or not. Parliament regarded competition as a good in itself since it would force rival companies to offer better, prompter and more luxurious services, always at a lower cost. In a policy of controlled laissez-faire, it left it up to the market to assess where lines might run, retaining only the right to approve them or not. The avidity with which people attended railway hearings, the length at which they were reported in the press, and the combats in the correspondence columns thereafter, imply that this belief in competition had deeper atavistic roots. This was a spectator sport with railwaymen as gladiators.[2]

For all its apparent power, Parliament was not prepared to involve itself in anything so sordid as monitoring the cost or effectiveness of its licensing activities. If one railway company held a rival company to ransom over running rights by either extortionate cost or physical obstruction, Parliament remained aloof despite the bluster of the 'railway interest' – the coven of MPs who had been retained by the railway companies. If a railway company needed to use the lines and stations belonging to others, there was no guarantee that it could do so, whatever agreements were in place. For example, at the periodic meetings of its senior operational officers, the North British managed its business, set rates, received applications for special service, appointed carriers, and examined operational difficulties. It was reported to one such meeting in 1866 that, whatever agreements had been negotiated, the company was unable to negotiate delivery of any goods into any Liverpool station in its own carriages. The goods had to be transferred to others' carriages if they were to be delivered at all.[3] That was not what Parliament had intended to happen.

The costs of presenting railway bills to Parliament, however ineffective the consequence, and of fighting off all opposition, were so great that, if aggregated, they would amount to billions at current values. In 1844, it cost the embryonic Caledonian Railway Company £75,000 to win the 'long and arduous contest excited, conducted and paid for by other railways' just to persuade Parliament to permit its very birth,[4] to which must be added the aggregated costs of all the Scottish railway companies incurred in trying to abort it. When a Bill for a new railway from Edinburgh was presented in 1863, sixteen adverse petitions were lodged by individual objectors, four rival railway companies, a bank and four burghs – each bearing the cost of its own legal representation.[5] The procedures of parliamentary committees were not just slow and expensive, but amateur in operation. They entertained evidence from those with only marginal railway experience. In 1863, a naval Captain, summoned as expert witness to comment upon a North British proposal, judged the construction estimate as insufficient, and questioned the financial viability of the railway company itself.[6] Inexpert hearsay by a naval captain on the financial viability of a railway company was perfectly acceptable to a Parliamentary Special Committee. Moreover, newspapers were full of allegations that such Committees were biased in line with their respective chairmen. No wonder railway business became a lawyers' paradise.

In the belief that market forces would properly determine where railways should run, in contrast to the State-designated system in France, Parliament confined its role to ensuring that local interests were kept in balance through its licensing procedures, with the addition of setting maximum fares, and insisting upon the intro- duction of cheap ones. On their part, railway companies felt betrayed by Parliamentary procrastination, ambivalence and fudge. A bitter petition from the Scottish Midland Junction Railway Company alleged that it had only invested in a principal section of the route from Carlisle to Aberdeen on the explicit 'reliance on the traffic which it was the intention of Parliament to guarantee them'. It was deeply unfair that Parliament would even countenance a proposal that could only diminish their guaranteed traffic.[7] Fairness did not come into it. Only the consulting engineer expert wit- nesses, the railway and parliamentary lawyers, the counsel, and the proprietors of London hotels benefited from the repeated appear- ances before Parliament. Most of the British railway system owed its existence less to an efficient strategy than to what can only be called *adhocary-pokery*.

Constructing railway lines was an enormously ambitious and complicated undertaking, and railway companies conceived of themselves in terms of noble organisations undertaking heroic acts of national significance. The invitation to the opening banquet of the Forth Bridge in March 1890 suggested a railway encircling the world: from Aberdeen across the Tay Bridge, across the Forth Bridge, down to London, through a Channel Tunnel, across Eastern Europe, thence through Siberia to Alaska and down to New York.[8] It was not possible then, and is not possible now. The North British was signalling that, with the completion of the Forth Bridge, it was bidding to be admitted to the pantheon of world railway companies alongside the Union Pacific, Central Pacific or Canadian Pacific railroads: those giants who strode across the land-scape in the pursuit of national objectives, their engineers remedying the inefficiencies of nature that lay in their path.

Any North British jealousy of the Union Pacific, Central Pacific or Canadian Pacific Railways' achievements would have been jus-tified. The latter had been conceived for nation-building purposes and endorsed by governments which funded them with bonds and by grants of swathes of countryside more valuable than the entire costs of construction. The later reputation of the two American railway companies as corrupt, with the payment of incredibly lavish dividends to a small *coterie* of insiders whilst refusing to pay their contractors and attempting to impose ransom-level fares upon the public, were coincident with rather than integral to the process that had been followed. The Pacific railways, however, all enjoyed polit-ical influence far more powerful than the British 'railway interest' appeared to muster. No British Prime Minister, for example, was a noted railway lawyer like Abraham Lincoln.[9] Lincoln had been so committed to a transcontinental railroad as a means of binding his country together that he found the time during the Civil War, only a month after the battle of Shiloh, to support the Pacific Railroad Bill through the House of Representatives, confiding to one Congressman 'that he would hurry it up so that when he retired from the Presidency, he could take a trip over it, it would be the proudest thing of his life that he had signed the bill in aid of its construction (*sic*)'.[10] He did not live that long. But the railroad streaking west from Omaha after the end of the Civil War con-verged so rapidly upon the railroad streaking east from Sacramento, to be joined at Promontory Point, Ogden, Utah, that

The cover of the invitation for the opening of the Forth Bridge in March 1890. Beneath Edinburgh Castle, the engine steaming out of Waverley boasts *Progress*, and its carriage offers a through trip over the Forth and Tay Bridges, then round the world.

nearly 2000 miles of track were completed and opened in the same six years that it took for the notion of a railway bridge across the River Tay in the Old Country to move from outline concept to a building contract.

The Canadian Pacific Railway was the means by which the emerging Dominion of Canada indulged in nation-building, for its construction was required if a reluctant British Columbia were to be persuaded to join the new Dominion.[11] British Columbia was separated from America merely by a boundary line and the Puget Sound, whereas it was isolated from the rest of Canada by the massif of the Rockies. The largely British-financed Grand Trunk

Railway, which had been formed to link eastern Canada with the Pacific, ran for large stretches within United States' territory, and unless the railway track lay entirely within Canada, it could not be regarded as national, inviolate in times of conflict. Without a railway, communications between British Columbia and the east were infinitely more difficult than communications with America to the south. Furthermore, bullish American newspapers like the *San Francisco Chronicle* were suggesting that British Columbia should not be given the choice. It campaigned for British Columbia to be annexed to the United States – by force if necessary – on the grounds that it was a back door through which evil infected Americans. It argued that through British Columbia, drugs poured into America, along with unstoppable Chinese immigration (ignoring, conveniently, the 7000 Chinese workers imported by the Central Pacific Railroad without whom it could not have been constructed).[12] Worse, unless the Americans took British Columbia over, the newspaper warned of a serious threat from armies of ferocious Esquimaux.[13]

Successful completion of the Canadian Pacific Railway ensured that threats of American expansionism remained just rhetoric. The government in Ottawa had decreed that the railroad – some 2000 miles of line through uninhabited (unowned in the western meaning) prairie and wilderness, the obdurate plateau of the Shield, and over the heights of the Rockies to Vancouver – had to be complete within ten years. In February 1881, within a fortnight of the Bill receiving royal assent, the Canadian Pacific Railway company had established itself in temporary headquarters in Winnipeg. Its General Manager William Cornelius van Horne completed the railway – the last spike driven on 6 November 1885 where the eastern and western arms met at Craigellachie – in only five years.[14] *That* was heroism. *That* was nation building.

Railway construction was infinitely more complicated in the Old Country. For prairies with no legally established owner, substitute parks. There was no question of processing, as the Central Pacific had through Sacramento in 1862, with placards saying: 'Little Indian Boy. Step Out of the Way for the Big Engine.'[15]

Every square inch of Scotland was owned by a Scottish landowner, his lawyer brandishing a writ in anticipation. Railway companies faced endless negotiation, threats and being held to ransom, and during the two decades of principal railway development in Scotland, at least 25% of Scottish railway costs were spent on land and compensation.[16] When they tried to buy their way through such thickets, they did so with financially disastrous commitments, believing that once the railway was open and revenue was pouring in, everything might be afforded retrospectively. Old Country landowners could afford to wait for the best price, and land purchase costs soared far beyond railway companies' calculations. They swiftly realised that they had to keep their routes secret for as long as possible for, as one agent confided of a particular country gentleman: 'He is rather a ticklish hand at bargain making, and if he discovers that it is a railway company who wants to buy his land, he will probably try to back out and vie in his demand. I have thought it best therefore to avoid letting him know until he is fully committed to the price.'[17] When the Central Scotland Railway attempted to bring its line into Perth through the grounds of the King James VI Hospital, the price of land was described as 'one of the most extravagant claims that has ever been set up even amongst the many attempts that have been made to extort money from railway companies. The idea of claiming two thousand pounds per acre for land which had previously not yielded annually . . . as many half pence is truly absurd.'[18] The great English railway contractor Sir Morton Peto attributed his downfall and bankruptcy in 1875 partly to the fact that 'the land cost *three* times as much as was calculated on'.[19]

It was much easier for the Canadian Pacific Railway. General Thomas Rosser, chief engineer, approached the first settlers in Grand Valley, the MacVicar brothers, with a view to buying up their farmstead to lay out the proposed town of Brandon upon it. A lucrative deal was apparently reached (the details are disputed), but John MacVicar changed his mind overnight, thinking he could get more from the railway company if he held out. Rosser promptly moved town and station two miles further west, leaving

MacVicar to a life of subsistence farming rather than luxury. It was a public warning that the CPR would not be held to ransom.[20]

Scotland offered few opportunities for railway heroics on the North American scale. There was the occasional chasm, the inconvenient mountain, the soggy peat bog, but the more difficult the terrain the fewer the inhabitants and the less pressure for railway construction. There were two exceptions. To reach England to the south, some railway lines had to negotiate the Southern Uplands, the bleak hilly moorlands between Hawick and Carlisle. The second challenge offered to the railway engineer were the country's fjords and river estuaries: particularly the firths of the great rivers Tay, Clyde and Forth. Sensible people did say (as the Dundee poet William McGonagall was to put it) that such river firths were best bridged upstream and, being simpler and cheaper, that was the initial strategy. Railways brought enormous commercial benefit to those ancient towns and cities that occupied historic upstream crossing points – Glasgow on the Clyde, Stirling on the Forth and Perth on the Tay. It might have remained thus, leaving downstream crossings solely to the imaginations of the engineers, had it not been for railway competition.

The first Scottish railway initiatives were fundamentally local affairs with origins in coal rather than in passengers. Horse-drawn wagons had heaved coal along fixed track from the pitheads to convenient ports or markets since at least the mid-eighteenth century. Wemyss of Wemyss had thus transported coal from his Wemyss collieries for export through his West Wemyss harbour. This combination of individual enterprise and piecemeal approach had led, by the 1820s, to a few small railways delivering coal to ports or to the major cities of Glasgow and Edinburgh. Nobody could forecast in the 1820s and 1830s which of these small operations might grow to become mighty enterprises or which others would be eaten up by them. So when the first railway boom in England was peaking by the mid-1830s,[21] railway movement north of the Border, whilst extensive, remained small scale and unadventurous.

Building a railway appeared so much simpler in Scotland than in the New World. British tunnels were generally short and simple when compared to the twelve lengthy tunnels blasted by some 8000 mostly Chinese workers through the Sierra Nevada in 1866,[22] or the extraordinary horseshoe tunnels that provided the only means whereby the Canadian Pacific Railway could reach the requisite height at Kicking Horse Trail in the Rockies. Railway builders had to blast out routes from the sides of New World canyons by suspending workers in wicker baskets to drill the holes, insert explosive, and set the fuses. Yet whether the railway was hundreds of miles across the Sierra Nevada or but a few miles through rural Perthshire, its impact upon the country through which it passed was profound. Engineers refashioned nature according to their needs, the railway lines blocking the migration of herds of wild buffalo in Canada and the customary movement of disobedient sheep in Scotland. Railways levelled the landscape by inserting embankments and viaducts, and the effect inspired artists such as David Octavius Hill. He sketched the wild beauty of the gorge in the ancient estate of Ballochmyle, Ayrshire, in the process of being tamed by a gigantic masonry arch, the centrepiece of a long, arched railway viaduct. It appeared far more heroic during its construction, for once complete it neutered the romantically savage Ballochmyle landscape – like scribing a perforated plank across a Constable.

Railways blocked ancient tracks, rights of way and roads. Small bridges throughout rural Britain signal the location of livestock passages from pasture to farm that had to be protected when the railways were built. Owners were prepared to accept the 'injury and damage occasioned by severance, level-crossing access or otherwise', provided they were paid handsomely at a rate set by an agreed arbiter.[23] The benefit was that proximity to a convenient railway came to be a significant inducement in the marketing of a country seat.[24] Interruption to ancient tracks was a tangible sign of the modernisation that the railways brought to the countryside, even more than the distant whistle, the clanking noise or the plumes of smoke.

Amongst the losers were the longer-distance carriers, horse-drawn carriages and carters, who had initially enjoyed a lucrative swansong transporting goods and passengers to and from railway halts; but as the network extended its tentacles, they found themselves out of business. In their wake closed a number of other industries like urban stabling. Coaching inns gave way to railway hotels. The coastal shipping businesses of smaller ports were likewise threatened when the railway arrived. Perth's seaborne trade reduced by over 80% between 1854 and 1875 as ships got larger and more difficult to navigate into the smaller harbours, and goods moved to rail.[25]

As the railways took hold, the principal institutional losers were probably the Trustees responsible for the country's turnpike roads. During the previous forty years, Scotland had been transformed by these new roads, which had sometimes required both towns and country estates to laboriously re-orientate themselves towards them; and their Trustees were required to pay for their upkeep by charging tolls. Railways now cut people off from access to the turnpikes and severed the turnpike routes themselves. As railways seduced traffic away from the turnpikes, their toll revenue – their only source of income – was drastically reduced. Faced with reduced income, reduced access, and their new roads severed by the iron track, Turnpike Trustees had to sue and the railways had to pay.[26]

Railways were obliged to ensure that their passage caused no damage. In some countries, fields were set on fire by sparks from the engines, and the Central Pacific's smokestacks were specially modified to reduce the risk. Scotland's climate ensured that it was a less common occurrence there.[27] The companies also had to maintain surveillance against broken fences which could lead to the slaughter of livestock. ('Bracksie lamb' is the old term for nicely matured roadkill mutton found on a railway or roadside, best eaten with capers.) Seeing the Caledonian Railway as a promising source of revenue, two farmer brothers by the name of MacFarlane repeatedly sought compensation for dead sheep. Caledonian staff were despatched to investigate. They concluded that the problem lay in the wayward nature of the beasts. 'The fence turns out to be a four-foot-high dry stone dyke. We observed the sheep jumping over the walls in all directions with apparently little difficulty. MacFarlane with his dog herds them; but when he is at one place, the sheep jump over the fence at the other.' Perhaps, the inspectors concluded, the height of the fence was insufficient.[28] The slaughter of horses and sheep, and of the occasional cow, remained prominent in railway accident books for decades – but, numerically, by far the most frequent victims were humans. Alongside the occasional trespasser or drunk on the line, the numbers were made up of railway servants (as employees were invariably called) crushed by engines that had failed to stop correctly, or by victims of accident after accident.[29]

By providing a fertile ground for spurious claims, railways also assisted the growth of the insurance industry. A Captain Tennant sought recompense for losses incurred after his servant boarded the wrong train; and a John Johnston sued for injuries he had sustained whilst trespassing in front of a train.[30] In 1876, the Caledonian was sued by two cheesemongers of Stranraer after the special cheese they booked to exhibit at the Staleybridge Show failed to arrive promptly. Whereas a sympathetic magistrate awarded the two a modest £8.10 each, an appeal judge held that there was no evidence that the Caledonian had guaranteed that the cheeses would arrive on time.[31] The Caledonian had won a crucial judgement: for it escaped a precedent that might have compelled reliability and punctuality upon it.

Whilst railway companies expanded at the expense of others, perversely they prospered mostly at the expense of their own Ordinary shareholders. Railway companies needed Ordinary shareholders to subscribe the initial capital; and in the early part of the nineteenth century, a great deal of it had been available. In the 1820s, as the *Edinburgh Weekly Journal* observed, 'Never was the capitalist so much at a loss how to turn his money to account, and live decently on the produce.'[32] As the century progressed, some investors were thought to be looking for a substitute as investing in slavery was no longer an option and they turned – 'sleepers not slaves' – to railways. Whereas speculators regarded railway shares as a means of making a quick killing, particularly during the 1840s, 'small capitalists' – the vaunted clergymen, widows and orphans –

looked to this new industry as a source of guaranteed income, and as each new company offered Ordinary shares, they were eagerly bought. Investors were reassured (foolishly) by the belief that since Parliament controlled the plans and finances of railway companies, their finances should surely be as stable as Consols themselves, even though offering a much higher rate of return than the latter's 3%. Dividend forecasts could rise to 12–15%, and some railways – the Lancaster & Carlisle for example – 10–12%.[33]

A railway could only generate profits, unfortunately, once its lines were open and generating income, and as the consequence of chronic underbudgeting, they usually found that their initial capital was wholly insufficient to complete the project long before that. To make up the shortfall, railway companies then offered preference shares and debentures, payment of whose dividend took priority over the original Ordinary shareholder. So the only benefit left to the Ordinary shareholder lay in the potential rise in value of the stock. More often than not, it was negative. In 1842, an Edinburgh stockbroker had warned that railways were 'at best hazardous ventures, and we would advise capitalists to be on their guard when they embark in them',[34] but capitalists were not listening. The promise of juicy dividends proved too tempting to generations of investors and they continued to pump money into railways.

Dundee, fearful of being bypassed by the new railways, became an early centre of Scottish railway activity. In the fifteenth to seventeenth centuries, Dundee had been second only to the capital Edinburgh in size and importance, its wealth deriving from its port and a spacious sheltered 'shipping roads' or anchorage, but it since had fallen behind Glasgow and, periodically, Aberdeen. Its leading citizens were not kings, churchmen or landowners, but international merchants. For the previous half-century, Dundee's main income had been from importing flax from the Baltic, transforming it into cloth, and shipping it out via London to Charleston and the West Indies. In the 1830s it had become the principal linen town of Britain[35] and its skills in mechanical engineering were transferring easily to the manufacture of railway locomotives.

Dundonians were alert to both the potential of transport modernisation and the dangers of being bypassed. In 1810, an engineer had proposed a canal from Perth north-east along the fertile valley of Strathmore to the harbour of Arbroath, eighteen miles to the north-east of Dundee, leaving Dundee isolated. To combat any repeat of this act, Dundee Town Council established a committee to consider a railway running northwards into the Strathmore valley, subscribing a large amount toward the cost of the survey.[36] Since most of Scotland's myriad small railways were initiated by small groups of local gentry, industrialists and civic dignitaries, the pivotal role of Dundee Council was unusual. The survey was undertaken by the Dundonian engineer Charles Landale (who had earlier drawn up colliery railway proposals for both Wemyss and the Earl of Elgin), and duly delivered to the solicitor and town clerk Christopher Kidd's young assistant, James Cox. Cox, later to become Dundee's principal jute manufacturer, was also to be the proud chairman of the Tay Bridge Undertaking when the bridge opened fifty-four years later.

Landale thought a railway to Strathmore would be comparatively simple and highly profitable, returning not less than 10%. But Dundee was not separated from Strathmore just by the broad Sidlaw Hills. It was jammed right up against the river by Dundee Law with its hill fort. Landale proposed to haul trains up the steep slopes of the Law by cable, like a funicular, into a tunnel dug through the Law's shoulder, before letting it canter out northwards across the Sidlaws and down to the tiny rustic hamlet of Newtyle on the southern slope of Strathmore. This inland terminus was probably selected because its owner, Lord Wharncliffe, was one the principal subscribers to the railway.[37] (Wharncliffe's name became synonymous with the compulsory presentation of a railway proposal to the company's shareholders before submission to Parliament.) The Newtyle railway was novel in that it was not a railway from a coal-mouth down to a town or harbour, but was devised as a general trading proposition. Farmers in Strathmore needed lime, coal (from Dundee's harbour), dung (from Dundonians), iron, grocery goods and timber (from Dundee's merchants); and the spinners and weavers of Coupar Angus, Alyth and Blairgowrie needed their flax. Dundonians would take finished cloth, yarn, freestone, potatoes, grain and agricultural produce in return.[38] Passenger income was entirely omitted from the calculations; the profit would lie in the movement of trade inward and outward.

In 1825, steam engines had yet to prove themselves as suitable for railways and Landale intended the railway carriages, save where being tugged up the inclines, to be horse-drawn. He recognised their potential, however, writing 'I have had in view the use, at a future time, of locomotive engines in case it be considered expedient to employ them. I propose that all the bars shall be of the size necessary in a Railway where such engines are used, and I have made my estimate accordingly. There is good reason for believing that such machines will work at much less expense than horses.'[39] It was probably the first published use of the word 'locomotive' for a steam-powered railway engine.[40]

The Dundee–Newtyle railway was typical of early British railways. Its estimated cost was wildly adrift because landowners sold their land for four times the estimate. The costs and difficulties of tunnelling through Dundee Law had been underestimated significantly, and the optimistic trade projections were never realised.[41] Wharncliffe had taken the opportunity of the railway's arrival in Strathmore (just as Andrew Carnegie was to do in America with such profit later in the century) to lay out a new town around its terminus at the hamlet of Newtyle. But its location in a low density agricultural valley, near nowhere and poorly provided with roads, meant that neither the railway nor the New Town of Newtyle ever flourished as anticipated. Moreover, the ad hoc nature of the enterprise was symbolised by the fact that the Company's carriages were converted horse-coaches.

Only in one respect did the railway outstrip expectations. It had not budgeted for passengers, and yet passenger traffic proved its mainstay.[42] Travellers raved with enthusiasm. One anonymous woman wrote to a friend: 'You can't think how delighted I was last week with the ride from Dundee to Newtyle in the railway coach . . . the sudden movement of sixty human beings by an unseen power upwards like a flock of geese in the air and onwards by horse at full gallop – the light and shade of the tunnel through the Law . . . flying through a mountainous region, the atmosphere of which is as cold as the Arctic regions – the sudden bursting on us of the warm rich Vale of Strathmore – all contributed to my amusement'; but she much disliked having to sit beside a dandy smoking a foul cheroot.[43] You could stop the train simply by putting out your hand, as for a bus. Despite its popularity, the Newtyle Railway also provided a warning of the disdain with which railway companies would treat ancient towns. As it descended from Dundee Law toward the harbour, its track blithely sliced across two of Dundee's principal streets, causing enormous disruption. Its trucks trundled insouciantly a few feet in front of the western façade of the church of the Blessed Virgin Mary, Dundee's mother church and the largest medieval parish church in Scotland.

Making a profit from a railway running over the top of some of the highest hills in the region to debouch into an agricultural hamlet was problematic, and the Dundee–Newtyle railway soon needed to refinance itself, just when English railway mania was moving toward its second peak.[44] Undeterred, the Scots, particu-

In 1825 carriages were drawn by horses, but the Dundee to Newtyle railway track had been laid for easy conversion to locomotives. Sketched by the railway's engineer, Charles Landale.

larly those in the hinterland of the larger towns and cities, were picking up the contagion, and plans for four different railway companies were announced on the same day in 1835 in the *Perthshire Courier* [45] and all for the same region: two from Perth to tiny towns or hamlets, one from Perth to Dundee and the other from Dundee north-east to the port of Arbroath. With the Newtyle Railway, Dundee had launched its strategy of pre-empting any bypass through the easy lands of Strathmore to the north.

The Newtyle Railway complete, Dundee turned its attention to the Arbroath line. Promoted by a group of landowners, MPs and businessmen typical of the smaller railway, it was designed by the principal Scottish railway engineers Grainger and Miller to feed to and from Dundee, the largest regional port. It was inaugurated on 6 October 1838 with a smooth forty-five-minute ride from town to town, coasting through rich farmland and scenic coastline at a rapidity of twenty-five miles per hour. The following year General Ulysses Grant was mightily impressed by a railway trip from Harrisburg to Philadelphia, enthusing, 'I thought the perfection of rapid transit had been reached . . . We travelled at least eighteen miles at full speed, and made the whole distance averaging as much as twelve miles an hour. This seemed like annihilating space.'[46] The Arbroath train had been considerably faster.

The Dundee–Arbroath Railway Company had been fortunate that the principal landowner, the Earl of Panmure, had been so enthusiastic that he had sold them fifty acres of land at a nominal cost. His generosity was one of the reasons why the railway had cost only £6000 per mile to construct as compared to the cost in England of up to £54,000. Amid the mutual congratulations at the 'most sumptuous dinner' in the Seamen's Fraternity Hall that followed the trip, Patrick Chalmers MP observed how easily and cheaply the railway had passed through Parliament. Nobody had felt threatened by it: there had been no competitors and, as a result, legal costs remained low. For 'many of the railways which were contested, the expense of passing the bill was enormous, forming a large percentage of the work'. To the accompaniment of loud cheering, the Paisley MP described his vision of how the new railway to Arbroath would industrialise and urbanise this neuk of beautiful, unmodernised, ocean-bounded countryside. 'This line of railway . . . induces me to look forward to the time when between this town and Arbroath will be one continuous field of weaving, spinning and every other description of mechanical industry.'[47] Mills did indeed sprout in unlikely hamlets like Carnoustie, but Chalmers's vision was happily not entirely realised, and the trip remains beautiful in parts, even now.

The Provost of Arbroath had refused to attend the banquet. Perhaps he had objected to the thoughtless reformatting the railway had forced upon his town, and resented the town's own pusillanimity when faced with the power and impetus of the railway companies. In Dundee, it was not much different. The Arbroath railway initially stopped at Stannergate, in the east, but it was extended in 1840 on piles across the low-tide flats to a new station by Dundee's wet dock. All those living or working in the Seagate of Dundee – the whaling quarter with its blubber boiling yards and private jetties – were marooned. Their piers were cut off from the sea, useless save to young fishermen trying their best in what became a stagnant lagoon, noisome with sewage and dog corpses. Some businesses moved, others went bankrupt, and Dundee lost its ancient port character. A similar process emerged nine years later with the construction of Dundee's third railway, the Dundee-Perth railway.[48] As it approached Dundee, it was driven through the tidal flats isolating the town's renowned beaches. Stripped of its riparian character, Dundee forgot that its entire *raison d'être* during its most glorious period – the Renaissance – had been as a seaport. Although small beer compared with the urban haemorrhage caused by railway construction in London, recorded, amongst others, by Charles Dickens,[49] the impact of railways was cumulatively more damaging upon smaller communities.

It has been suggested that nineteenth-century railways did not make a critical difference to the British or American economy.[50] This conclusion was reached by calculating how much railway traffic would have travelled by road or canal if the railways had not been constructed – concluding that most of it could. Leaving aside the technical challenge and likely costs of constructing canals across searing deserts or roads over the almost impassable Rockies, the question is, rather, what contemporaries themselves regarded as important. Railway companies were importuned endlessly by British towns and villages seeking their own branches, a station or country halt, or even additional services at commuting time. They feared isolation, and considered a station, or at least a halt, as essential in the competitive drive for modernisation and survival. To attract railway companies, concessions – particularly aesthetic concessions – had to be offered.

Although the towns they ran through enthusiastically sought out a partnership with the railways, the railway companies usually failed to appreciate that they shared any common interest with them. They did not form the partnership that one might have expected, and usually displayed an alienating arrogance. The danger faced by the city of Perth, a pro-railway town that aspired to become the railway capital, a York of Scotland, provides a salutary example. For a short while the capital of medieval Scotland, Perth controlled the lowest bridging point of the River Tay. Quick to appreciate the commercial advantage of railways, it became a promoter of railway companies, and suitor for the attentions of over half a dozen of them. Its position was like that of a spider at the centre of an iron-railed web, whose tendrils extended south-east, east, south, west, south-west, north and north-east. As county town, Perth was also the centre of wealthy estates and great families, with a gracious architecture and a genteel character to match. Its physical setting was particularly splendid. Set low in the flood plain of the Tay with fine views bounded by the highland hills north and west, it was flanked on the east by the great river, and by the North and South Inches – formerly islands but now pleasant and open riparian greensward – framing the town to north and south. Although Oliver Cromwell had built his fort on the South Inch, the Inches remained the town's glory, the feature most admired by respectable visitors.

Where, then, to place Perth's railway termini? Moreover, given that lines and companies were proliferating, was there to be a single joint station or several individual ones? Where should the railways cross the Tay? With the river lining the town to the east, the natural location for such a station was on its western fringe, and the Perth citizens naively believed that a mutually beneficial opportunity was in prospect. But had they recalled how the new railway in Stirling blocked access to its harbour on the Forth, they might have been more alert. The Dundee–Perth Railway Company planned to do the same to Perth as had happened at Stirling: shipping on the Tay would be prevented from entering its harbour by a low-level bridge constructed across its mouth. Perth's interests never appear to have been considered. When a further railway company proposed to build its terminus upon the precious South Inch, the City Council had finally had enough, and it appealed to Parliament for protection. Its ancient privileges were now in such danger, that even its guilds – like the Incorporation of Glovers – laid aside funds to object.[51] The Board of Trade intervened, stopped the attempt to 'intrude upon and destroy the Inch',[52] and insisted upon a single General Terminus for all railway companies on the west side, paid jointly by all the companies using it.[53] This bitter and entirely needless campaign lasted three years, and reveals what little value the railway companies must have put upon a cooperative partnership with their host councils. Where lesser issues and smaller communities were concerned, there would be no contest at all. The Edinburgh, Perth & Dundee Railway disliked the name of the village 'Ferryport-on-Craig' (already modernised from Partan Craig – or crab rock), since it was too long for its signs and timetables. So they shrunk it to Tayport, as it remains today.[54]

Whereas the early lines were spawned by local interests, what is less clear is why Parliament allowed the draining of so much of the railway companies' resources in fruitless competition with their rivals. It would have been unnecessary had it adopted a rail strategy comparable to France. The French Government had centralised decision-making about railways. It determined what lines were needed, allocated suitable construction companies and railway operators to build and operate them, and then guaranteed a minimum statutory interest/dividend.[55] Parliament had no doubt that the British approach was superior. 'It appears decidedly best to leave Railways in Great Britain, like all other undertakings, to be decided upon according to the judgement and interest of those who are willing to embark their capital in them.'[56] One MP considered that 'it was much better to leave these great works to private capital, and not mix up the government in them as was the case in France'.[57] The dividend-free Ordinary shareholders in British Railways might not have agreed. The cost of the British way of doing things becomes clear when you realise that the guaranteed French dividend was more than double the maximum that the North British offered as dividend to its Ordinary shareholders for much of the nineteenth century.

Initially, railways were short, sponsored by local interests for local purposes. But short local lines do not require, and could not pay for, world-scale bridges. Whereas a little line to Little Dunkeld might bring farm produce into the town, or an extension of the Kirkcaldy and Newburgh line might be useful for importing coal and lime (the shipowners still unaware that their ships would be made redundant by railways), some railway lines began to emerge which were of sufficient national importance as to attract support and investment from throughout the kingdom. The first hint of such a railway company in Scotland came in 1835. Edinburgh and Glasgow, claimed the prospectus, were now the only important cities in Great Britain situated within fifty miles of each other not connected by a railway, and 'they afford the most tempting facilities'.[58] So, that same year, the city council of Perth, with its merchants, bankers, shipowners, manufacturers and other inhabitants, was persuaded to join other towns in petitioning the House of Commons in support of a railway between Edinburgh and Glasgow. The line – the first major passenger route in Scotland – was opened three years later and its promoters' optimism proved correct.

The Edinburgh & Glasgow Railway Company displayed the combination of pragmatism and ruthlessness that came to characterise railway development, particularly in its use of short-term expedients. When its original route was opposed by the parallel

canal company, it opted to enter Glasgow down a steep slope from
Cowlairs, but it had to avoid incurring excessive expense for engineering works before its income stream developed. So it used a
cable to winch the trains up out of Glasgow on the return trip.
Such temporary expedients, hastily built with a short life, were not
as common in Britain as they were in America, where timber trel-
lis bridge structures with only a five-year life were used as a matter
of course. It gave the railway companies a chance to test both routes
and structures before finalising them, and get the lines open and
income moving before committing full expenditure. Though visitors noted how trains rattled across the early timber bridges used
on the first North British line from Berwick upon Tweed,[59] temporary experimental expedients were less frequently used in
Scotland than in the New World. Nonetheless, for a number of
people it was to prove an appropriate frame within which to consider the bridge that collapsed into the Tay.

The Edinburgh–Glasgow Railway proved ruthless when it came
to planning its route through Edinburgh. To bring traffic from
Glasgow through to the east side of Edinburgh, at what is now
Waverley, the railway puffed its way through the formal pleasure
gardens and canal that had been laid out between Edinburgh Castle
and the New Town and crashed through one of Edinburgh's principal medieval suburbs, causing the demolition of some of its most
venerable structures including Trinity Hospital (so similar to its
counterparts in Bruges), and the soaring late medieval Trinity
College Church. The historic past was being crushed by modernity, as the memorialist Lord Cockburn protested:

> The last and finest Gothic fragment in Edinburgh, though
> implored for by about four centuries, will disappear for the
> accommodation of a railway! An outrage by sordid traders, vir-
> tually consented to by a tasteless city, and sanctioned by an
> insensible Parliament . . . It is said that the edifice is to be
> replaced *exactly as it is* in some better situation . . . These people
> would remove Pompeii for a railway, and tell us they had applied
> it to better purpose in Dundee.[60]

Ancient Edinburgh removed for a railway. The suburb of charitable
hospitals that clustered around the magnificent Trinity College
Church (left) was demolished for Waverley Station and its
approaches. Drawn in the 1840s.

Even had such modernism been necessary, it was carried out in a
deplorably heedless and wasteful manner, as Sir Patrick Geddes, the
founder of town planning, opined:

> This railway system has not been the utilitarian success it still
> pretends itself, but has been, not merely half-ruinous to the
> beauty of Edinburgh, but structurally bungled and economically
> wasteful to all concerned.[61]

The public outcry in Edinburgh served as due warning to other
towns had they only been prepared to listen. Unless town councils
could organise themselves to withstand this new power, the arrival
of railways carried as much danger to their heritage as it did opportunity for increased trade; and Edinburgh was under particular threat
since most major railway companies still wanted their own terminus
there. When, in 1848, the North British sought to purchase land for
its own station, the only suitable land left was Shakespeare Square

and the Theatre Royal at the eastern end of Princes Street – which the Council was not prepared to cede. The railway company then, according to the Council, attempted to prejudice 'the public against the proceedings of the Town Council' and even tried 'to intimidate the members of that body' by inundating the city with lawsuits – presumably in the hope of grinding the Council down financially. The Lord Provost lamented, 'In their conduct, they [the North British] resemble the Russians, Prussians and Austrians with regard to Poland. They want to gobble up everything.'[62] With their growing economic muscle, and the Zeitgeist of modernisation on their side, railway companies could purchase influence both locally and in Parliament, dispense largesse, and appoint key local figures as their agents. For the town councils, it was comparable to a town facing the depredations of a ruthless multinational today.

The reverse of the Menu Card for the opening banquet of the Forth Bridge.

CHAPTER TWO

THE BATTLE FOR SCOTLAND

Railroad iron is a magician's rod to evoke the sleeping energies of land and water

RALPH WALDO EMERSON

A belief in the benefits of competition dominated nineteenth-century governments in Britain and America. In its encouragement of competition between the Central Pacific and the United Pacific railroads, the American government had failed to establish where exactly in Utah the two should meet. Both railway companies were being rewarded by the government for each mile they laid, so there was competition not only to build faster, but also to reach further into Utah than their rival. They began to compete for how many miles of track each could lay in a day. The United Pacific had achieved an astonishing four and a half miles of completed track, but that was challenged by its rival on 7 April 1869. The Central Pacific's entire end-of-line[1] had been organised and provisioned with military precision so that they laid, from scratch, over ten miles of track in a day: approximately 1,000 men laying 240 feet of line every seventy-five seconds. An army officer observed to the contractor, Charles Crocker, 'I never saw such organisation as this; it is just like an army marching across over the ground and leaving a track built behind them.'[2] The ludicrous side of the competition was that the two railway construction gangs soon passed each other building parallel tracks, bridges and embankments in opposite directions, close enough to hear each other speak, whilst the government dithered over where the junction should be placed.

Parliament regarded competition as the most efficient means of curbing any abuse of the railway companies' monopoly. A railway company would be held up to obloquy if it showed contempt for its passengers by providing a dreadful service – allegedly as the result of a monopolistic *lack* of competition.[3] When a passenger complained to the North British that a ticket from Edinburgh to Derby cost 18% more than one from Edinburgh to the more distant Birmingham, he was informed that 'there was competition to Birmingham . . . but not to Derby'.[4] But as the effort, obstructions, delays and additional costs that were proving inseparable from the British way of building railways became apparent to newspapers and public alike, they became wary of the undiluted benefits of competition, and moved to a position of ambivalence. At one time, the *Scotsman* considered the main advantage of a proposed Scottish railway was that it was 'totally free from anything in the shape of competition'.

Despite the endless reports from Parliamentary committees and commissions, Parliament took no action to deal with the malpractices arising from competition. A critical matter were the rights that one company might enjoy to run their trains over another company's track ('running rights'), for Parliament established no agency to enforce that the running rights it granted could be reasonably exercised. Operational risk remained a matter for the railway companies and their shareholders; and the consequences borne by Ordinary shareholders and railway users. Yet so ruinous were the costs of competition, that it became customary for railway companies to make periodic non-aggression pacts where 'neither company should this year apply for any branches or extensions involving a competition of interest'[5] followed by a tense period waiting to see who would be the first to break it. The Scottish Trunk Railway War was the product of such a system, and competition would eventually force railway companies to duplicate their rivals' lines if they were to avoid the problem.

During the 1830s, the potential market between Scotland and England beckoned to the emerging railway companies of England, in particular the Grand Trunk railway which had constructed the route from London to Carlisle, England's former frontier town guarding the Scottish Border. An extension from Carlisle north of the Border into Scotland was only logical, and in 1836 the Grand Trunk's engineer, Joseph Locke, suggested that it would be entirely feasible to take a line up to the city of Glasgow, on the River Clyde, then undergoing rapid industrial expansion. Locke's preferred route lay to the west, via Dumfries, the county town of Dumfriesshire, and Kilmarnock in the manufacturing heart of Ayrshire; but that was hotly contested by rival landowners.[6] Although Locke's route had the advantages of passing through the principal settlements of Dumfriesshire and of Ayrshire, it was seventeen miles longer than the straighter one following the valley of the River Clyde due north, which he had deliberately avoided since it required hauling the line up and over the 314-metre high Beattock summit in the Southern Uplands.

At this point, no railway company yet existed to pursue the idea. The proposal lay fallow after the slump of 1836–7, but when it was revived in 1839, its route had moved away from Ayrshire and followed the ancient English invasion route of the Clyde valley after all – past Lockerbie, Howcleuch, over the Beattock summit, through Elvanfoot to Crawford and into central Scotland (and thereafter over land to Stirling, Perth and Aberdeen). Although technically more difficult, its shorter length, at the then 'modest' average construction cost of £16,000 per mile,[7] meant a saving of £272,000. Moorland would be much easier to purchase than the nightmarish complications implied by land purchases in low-lying and prosperous agricultural areas. The railway would bifurcate at Carstairs – one line north into the iron and coal heartland of Scotland, and the other branching eastward toward Edinburgh. Glasgow itself would be reached by buying out existing lines.[8]

Coincidentally, a trunk railway up the east coast from London through York and Newcastle to Edinburgh was being mooted by Scottish-dominated interests. A public meeting in Berwick's Town

House in 1838, chaired by Richard Hodgson, MP for Berwick upon Tweed, agreed to promote a 'Great National Line of Railway from London northward to Edinburgh'.[9] The following February, a prospectus, *The Great North British Railway*, was issued seeking £2 million in capital. Its committee, headed by Edinburgh's Lord Provost, included the chairman of the Edinburgh & Glasgow Railway, industrialists like the Cadells of the Carron Iron Works, and a good smattering of country gentlemen and businessmen. George Stephenson, who had surveyed the English section of the line, was enthusiastic: 'I may say that, in the whole course of my experience, I never examined a country for the line of railway of the length this will be, where the works to be executed were of an easier description, or the levels of inclinations of a more favourable character.'[10] The promoters confidently forecasted a return of 11%. However Locke, who had surveyed a number of the sixteen competing suggestions for the railway route across the Border, including the Great North British, concluded that the Scottish market could not sustain both: 'Two great lines from Scotland to England cannot pay.' He recommended a Commission be established to select the single best route.[11]

When railway construction was reaching its first peak in December 1838,[12] England had built 497 miles of railway to Scotland's 49.[13] So there was some catching up to do. Making a slight exception to its laissez-faire position, Parliament appointed a two-man Commission (Sir Frederick Smith and the engineer Prof. Peter Barlow) to review all sixteen possible railway routes between the two countries, the three frontrunners in detail. As the *Scotsman* reported: 'Readers must have been astounded and disbelieving when they read about these speculations about laying railway lines across untouched country', comparing them to 'jokes about tunnels beneath the Alps and a railway crossing of the Channel'.[14] Reporting in May 1841, the Commission endorsed Locke's static view of the Scottish economy that the market would bear only a single line, and chose the western route running down to Carlisle and the west coast of England.[15] In Scotland, this route line would easily connect into a Trunk Route running via Perth and Stirling to Aberdeen, avoiding 'the east coast navigation estuaries'.[16] The scale of the eastern estuaries of the Forth and Tay rivers – a total of almost five miles of tidal water – was deemed beyond the reach of railway bridges as they were then conceived, and so long as there was to be only a single trunk route between England and Aberdeen running overland through central Scotland, no imperative existed for bridging them. The seas could be left untamed in their pristine state. And that was where matters rested when an economic slump in 1841 caused any development of a Scottish trunk route between Scotland and England through Carlisle to cease.

On 8 January 1842, the supporters of the eastern trunk route, the Great North British Railway, that the Commission had rejected, met in the Edinburgh & Glasgow Railway Company's boardroom to discuss reviving an eastern railway line to London now that the western one had stalled; this was followed by a three-day meeting in Edinburgh's Waterloo Hotel chaired by Edinburgh's Lord Provost. It was attended by a throng of 'respectable' and genteel modernisers including lairds,[17] the Provost of the port of Leith, the Merchants' Company, baillies, councillors, advocates, bankers, the author Sir Thomas Dick Lauder, and the journalist, publisher, campaigner and future Lord Provost William Chambers. They selected 'The North British Railway Company' as the title of the company, Learmonth of Dean (who was chairman of the Edinburgh & Glasgow) as its chairman, and devised a grand plan.[18] The plan, in point of fact, was not so grand: barely thirty miles of railtrack running eastwards from Edinburgh to the ancient port and fortress of Dunbar (just where the coastline curves southwards towards England).[19]

The only advantage a line to Dunbar might have brought to Edinburgh was fish. Most likely, the proposal was a surreptitious way of slipping past a somnolent Parliament the rejected 1839 eastern trunk line from Edinburgh to London disguised as a local branch proposal. This short line needed only £500,000 capital (£25 shares requiring a deposit of ten shillings per share), and each North British Board member in Edinburgh had to dispose of at least one hundred shares themselves, having been allotted a sector of the city to canvass. Only 25% of the shares were to be sold in Scotland, the balance to be sold by brokers Robertson & Co in the large towns of England – particularly in Liverpool where so many of the Edinburgh–Glasgow railway shareholders were based.[20] Liverpool held a particular attraction for Scottish industrialists – particularly Dundee industrialists – since fast communication to Liverpool meant faster communication to America.[21] The route of combined railways that gave a speedy transit across Scotland and down the west coast to Liverpool was regarded with particular favour. For such reasons of mutual benefit, a large investment in Scottish railway companies had been made by Lancashire merchants.[22]

It took the North British a further two years to bring its line to Parliament. Its route to Berwick ran through the prosperous plantations along the south bank of the Forth. Fertile and near to the capital, East Lothian was dense in aristocratic estates, giving an unusual number of grandees a proprietorial interest in the railway's route. Lords Dalhousie, Lauderdale and Melville, the Duke of Buccleuch, and even the Queen herself at Holyrood (as represented by her Commissioners for Woods and Forests), had all to be placated. This lengthy operation was successful, for when the railway prospectus was finally issued in 1844, it was endorsed by seventy-one landowners, professionals and Members of Parliament. There was some opposition attributable to commercial rivalry. The diminutive Edinburgh & Dalkeith Railway (the 'Innocent Railway,' as Robert Chambers termed it), which quietly chugged coals to the capital, regarded the North British as a threat but was neutralised when the NBR bought it up. Opposition also arose from those whom the route ignored, like East Lothian's county town of Haddington which was not just left stranded, but its function as a major coaching town under threat. The town rose to oppose the entire venture, and was only pacified by the NBR constructing a connecting branch.

Aristocrats who had not been included in the initial canvass, because it had been anticipated that they might prove difficult, took their fight to Parliament. The Marquess of Abercorn and the Earl of Wemyss won enhanced compensation; whereas Sir Charles Fergusson was placated by the track being shifted a little further from his house. The Queen, represented by a Mr Miller, opposed a high-level railway viaduct about 100 yards north of Holyrood Palace on the grounds that it would render the palace 'unfit for an occasional royal residence'. The architect William Burn, not a man blessed with enormous sensitivity, concluded that the proposed railway viaduct would do no damage to the environs of the royal palace, but that if noise proved a problem, the railway could always be boxed in with wood for a short stretch opposite it, rather like the Britannia Bridge.[23]

The North British selected excellent engineers – Grainger and Miller[24] – but appointed them on condition that if the line failed to win Parliamentary approval, they would be paid costs only.[25] Making its engineers work at risk like this was a cheeseparing tactic: Brunel would have refused the commission. The company's stingy attitude also applied to track construction, and became one of its recognisable characteristics in its early years.

By 1844, however, it was ready to place before Parliament a proposal for a railway between Edinburgh and Berwick upon Tweed, thus pre-empting the promoters of the preferred western route. Despite the Commission's recommendation against it, Parliament approved the Bill, and thus the North British Railway Company was born. When the western route's promoters caught up in the following session, Parliament approved it as well – without undertaking any new investigation of whether the market could now stand both. Thus began a bitter and ruinous railway competition between the two trunk railway routes that would last for at least the next forty-five years.

The character of the two rival railway companies was implicit in their names. The name of the eastern line, the North British Railway Company (modestly dropping the 'great'), conveyed the unionist overtones of the eighteenth-century Scottish Enlightenment when the Scots, styling themselves North Britons, had sought to be the modernisers of the Union, operating to mutual benefit. It was a good name for a railway company tying the capital of Scotland to that of England. The western line, with a fine nationalist flourish, called itself the Caledonian Railway Company and took up the motto of Scotland 'Nemo me impune lacessit', meaning nobody harms me with impunity or – as traditionally translated into Scots – 'Wha daur meddle wi' me?' Whereas early Board meetings of the North British dealt with practicalities such as fundraising and lobbying, early meetings of the Caledonian were devoted to strategy and rhetoric. Its minutes reveal a bullish sense of national destiny:[26]

> Their conviction [is] that the undertaking in which they have embarked linked and united as it is with other Great Lines both in England and Scotland, cannot fail to realise the most favourable anticipation of its promoters both as an important national work, and as a profitable investment . . .

After all, the 1841 Commission had offered them a trunk monopoly between Scotland and England, and whatever Parliament might have decided since, the Caledonian was not minded to change its strategy. It intended to become the national Scottish Trunk Railway accommodating the 'whole of Scotland' into what it called 'the Caledonian system', and it would brook no rivals.[27]

Upon receiving Parliamentary assent, the Caledonian Railway Company appointed a Board of a very similar composition to that of the NBR with the addition of two each of colonels, bankers and MPs. With offices in Edinburgh's Princes Street (as befitted the national Scottish railway) and promising an 8% dividend, it contemplated no mean operation. It conceived itself as a great river from England to central Scotland, with extensions north to Perth and ultimately to Inverness and the West Highlands,[28] and feeder lines to either side with which it intended to capture all Scottish–English trade. Unlike the NBR, the Caledonian had no intention of constructing everything itself: just the 122 miles where no suitable track already existed. 'In every legitimate way' it would encourage existing lines to connect with it, or otherwise come to an accommodation through purchase, negotiation or partnership.[29]

Its expectation of goodwill between it and existing railway companies was disingenuous. Most were distinctly unenthusiastic about such a newcomer in a small country. Far from agreeing that the Caledonian should be a single mother railway from whose udders they could feed, they smelt a rival. Since the finances of the NBR had likewise been predicated on capturing the same English–Scottish trade, it moved to opposition as well. The resulting 'long and arduous contest excited, conducted and paid for by other railway companies' cost Caledonian Directors £75,000.[30] Huge legal and Parliamentary costs incurred before a railway could even start were not unusual, and they often rose beyond 10% of the total construction cost of a line, to which a company would have to add its legal and engineering costs.[31] In 1853, the contractor Thomas Brassey observed that he had completed the entire railway from Turin to Novara 'for about the same money as was spent in obtaining the Bill for the railway from London to York'.[32]

Since the profitable 1838 Edinburgh & Glasgow Railway straddled Scotland east to west, both rival companies wooed it ardently. Having an expansion strategy of purchasing other lines of its own, the E & G was attracted to neither. Given their conviction that their own company was the 'great national work', the Caledonian directors were hurt by such an unpatriotic response. 'In its infancy, the Caledonian was met by the Edinburgh & Glasgow in a spirit of hostility. It offered uncompromising opposition to every measure proposed.'[33] It warned that any railway company with an attitude like that would become a legitimate target for hostile action or take-over. It was their 'sincere desire to maintain a friendly relation with other Railway interests in Scotland. But should other companies attempt any measures tending to divert traffic legitimately belonging to this Company, our interests demand that every means should be adopted to defeat such design.'[34] In the end, the Edinburgh & Glasgow failed to expand or remain independent. It was gobbled up by the NBR in 1865.

Those who were not part of the Caledonian's solution were part of its problem. The resulting railway warfare was characterised by allegations of ransom, blackmail, wilful obstruction on the track, ruinous fare cutting, physical violence, and agreement breaking. The Caledonian's hostility was not directed solely at the North British: it was extended promiscuously to any other railway that appeared to threaten its ambition. As the saddened chairman of Glasgow, Dumfries & Ayr Railway perceptively reported to his shareholders: 'They had done everything they could to come to amicable terms with the Caledonian Company but with little effect. He thought the latter would not rest satisfied until they possessed themselves of the entire of Scotland.'[35] Just so.

During its first decade, the Caledonian Railway seemed likely to achieve its ambition and become the dominant railway company of Scotland, principally because its route up through the west and centre of Scotland was logical and easier, and avoided any major river crossing. Its first 122 miles of construction lay between central Scotland and Carlisle where it would join up with the Lancaster & Carlisle Railway. The line was designed by the engineers Joseph Locke and John Errington (whom Locke had taken into partnership in 1840). Locke had been an outstanding pupil, then assistant, of the great railway engineer George Stephenson, and had made his reputation with the construction of the Grand Junction Railway. At his death in 1860, *The Times* was to refer to Joseph Locke, Isambard Kingdom Brunel and Robert Stephenson (son of George) as the 'triumvirate of the railway world'.[36] Locke and Errington were the original surveyors of the proposed line over Beattock, so the Caledonian saw no need to go elsewhere for an engineer when their line became a reality. One of Locke's abilities was to select the right contractors, and although there was no competitive tender, the Caledonian's files purred with its contentment at the organisation and professionalism of Locke's appointed contractor. Perhaps that was perhaps not surprising given that the contractor was Thomas Brassey.[37]

Unusually for a railway contractor, Brassey was the son of a landowner, well-connected within both the railway and financial sectors. He had been a minor developer in Birkenhead before Stephenson and Locke encouraged him to shift to civil engineering contracting. Brassey developed a reputation for ingenuity,

efficiency and organisation in an extraordinary career in which his
firm constructed 1900 miles of railway in Britain, 3000 miles in
continental Europe, and 1550 miles further afield, including the
Grand Trunk Railway in Canada. He fostered a reputation for
integrity, organisation and efficiency, and was so well backed that
he was able to finance the running of railway companies, manage
their traffic, and invest in the lines he was building. He was rare in
being prepared to admit and pay for his own mistakes.[38] The
Caledonian started out with as good an engineer and as good a
contractor as it was then possible to find.

It was different on the sixty-mile-long North British line from
Edinburgh to Berwick. Whereas its engineers were good, its line
was hastily constructed by twelve indifferent contractors at a cost
per mile well above average. Despite the investment, the NBR
took possession of a line 'that was in many places badly built, and
in some positively dangerous'.[39] In autumn 1846, only a year after
construction, much had to be rebuilt after being washed away by
torrential rain.[40] James Bell, the future NBR chief engineer, would
later lament how 'for many years past, every new station has been
opened with the smallest possible expenditure' as a consequence of
the railway company's financial position. The company thought
cheap and built cheap.[41]

Work on the rival railways began when the greatest Victorian
railway mania was moving towards its peak; 405 railway lines were
opened between 1845 and 1850, mostly short – at an average of
only 10.5 miles in length.[42] Fifty-six further railway companies
were sanctioned that never materialised (twelve, more than double
pro rata, in Scotland), and many investors suffered acutely. The
Illustrated London News caught the frantic mood well:

> *Railway Shares! Railway Shares!*
> *Hunted by Stags and Bulls and Bears –*
> *Hunted by women, hounded by men –*
> *Speaking and writing – voice and pen –*
> *Claiming and coaxing – prayers and snares –*
> *See the world mad about Railway Shares.*

The frenzy of London, however, was a world away from the realities of railway engineering. Brassey's arrival north of Carlisle to begin the Caledonian Railway coincided with the February floods in the marshes of the Solway lying to the north of the River Eden. For centuries, these lands had been known ironically as the Debateable Lands, from the time when their allegiance between Scotland and England was disputed, and the debates were undertaken by passage of arms between Scots and English Border freebooters. The marshy terrain that had made it tricky to control politically was equally challenging to railway engineers. Yet by August, Brassey's workmen were ready to begin the two most difficult parts of the line: the Beattock summit and the Debateable Land bridges. All it wanted was better weather. The Lancaster and Carlisle workers had now joined the workforce, and the 10,500 workers had completed five miles of track in six months, a temporary bridge now crossed the Eden, cottages for platelayers and gatekeepers would be ready before winter, and the necessary animal-proof fence was almost complete. Locke was confident that the line would open, on schedule, in March 1848.[43]

There being no chance of local accommodation for workers in the desolate upland landscape, Brassey first pegged out the Beattock route, then erected workmen's huts, and ordered up highly expensive iron rails and 'chairs' (the fixings of the rail to the sleepers).[44] Once the Lancaster & Carlisle Railway was complete, materials and gangs of well-trained workmen moved from it to these new construction sites on the Caledonian. Railway construction sites brought together a heterogeneous and occasionally explosive mixture of nationalities. Almost 50% of those who had built the Edinburgh & Glasgow were Irish, and the Irish were by far the largest ethnic group on parts of the North British network.[45] Brassey's Beattock site for the Caledonian was generally more peaceful and better provisioned than the standard remote navvy construction site, and he liked to encourage self-development amongst his men through evening classes and religious instruction held in the small nearby village of Lockerbie.[46] Lockerbie, however, was also where over 1000 men received their wages each month,

and the natives of that small douce community were scandalised at
their drunkenness and lewd behaviour. The essayist Thomas
Carlyle, who hailed from nearby Ecclefechan and represented for
many the moral voice of the Victorian era, was profoundly unim-
pressed by these manifestations of progress. 'Our great Caledonian
Railway passes in this direction, and all the world here, as everywhere, calculates on getting to Heaven by steam! I have not in my
travels seen anything uglier than that disorganised mass of labour-
ers, sunk three-fold into brutality by the three-fold wages they are
getting. The Yorkshire and Lancashire men, I hear, are the
worst . . .'[47] On one occasion, a mob of some 400 navvies, probably a contingent from Yorkshire and Lancashire, attempted an
armed attack on their Irish counterparts, and had to be restrained
by magistrates.[48]

Scottish railway construction sites never developed the mobile
and volatile shanty towns – known as 'hell on wheels' – of the
Union Pacific's 'end-of-line', but not every company looked after
its navvies quite as well as Brassey. Over to the east, on the North
British main line, conditions were different. Alexander Ramsay
described the navvies' huts there to a Parliamentary Select
Committee in 1846 saying: 'In many of those places connected
with the railways, a humane man would hardly put a pig into
them.'[49] So whereas Brassey's sites generally avoided the not infre-
quent sectarian riots amongst railway navvies, it may have been
poor living conditions on the North British's Edinburgh to Hawick
line, so much worse than on Brassey's site at Beattock, that triggered the savage riot on the NBR line in February 1846. Northern
English navvies, supported by local coalminers, sought revenge for
the death of a policeman by beating the Irish navvies and their families from their huts and then burning them down.[50]

While Brassey's navvies were fighting floods near Carlisle and
cutting into the hard stone of the Beattock summit by hand, the
directors of the newly born Caledonian were plotting to spend
their unallocated capital on expanding their empire. They agreed to
acquire two railways (one into central Glasgow, another between
Glasgow and Edinburgh to challenge the Edinburgh & Glasgow),

lease a third, amalgamate with two more, and to construct fifteen branches extending from the main line with such stations as might prove necessary.[51] They then issued 51,000 new shares of £25 for each existing one of £50 (in other words, an injection of a further 50% of their original capital[52]) and, thus lubricated, contemplated a further *eleven* bills (of which Parliament approved six); and proposed agreements with two other railways. All this activity required interminably long appearances before Parliament, and the bottomless expenses of lawyers. Indeed, in its first year, the Caledonian's Parliamentary and legal costs outstripped all other items of expenditure.[53] But the railway was not doing so well. Railway mania was beginning to cause alarm and, for the first time, some shareholders demurred. Brassey was also encountering unforeseen engineering problems between Carlisle and central Scotland of such intractability that they were threatening the collapse of his entire business.[54] Fortunately, Locke persuaded the Caledonian Board to cover some of Brassey's additional costs.

Whilst most of the capital of major Scottish railway companies had been raised in England, their headquarters had remained in Scotland and barely a token Englishman had made it on to the Board of Directors. Not surprisingly, when things went wrong, those most likely to stir things up were aggrieved English shareholders. 'Nine-tenths of the shares were held in England', a disgruntled investor told a London meeting, but 'the whole of the patronage of the line was in the hands of the directors who were, with one or two exceptions, natives of Edinburgh and Glasgow'.[55] The spark for a shareholders' rebellion was usually a reduced or an unusually low dividend, and would generally take the form of a motion that a Committee of Shareholders should undertake a financial investigation.

The Caledonian's first taste of such insubordination was at a hot meeting in London's Euston Hotel in November 1848, when shareholders demanded an explanation of why the Company's proposed dividend was so low and suggested an investigation. The Board dismissed their request.[56] Although high-handed behaviour like this would invariably prove counterproductive, Railway

Boards would never learn. The following February, over 70 share-holders packed into Edinburgh's Gibb's Royal Hotel, to hear Thomas Thornborrow Fawcett condemn the Company for the technically impermissible use of its capital to purchase shares in subsidiary railway companies. Fawcett deployed 365 proxy votes on behalf of absent shareholders, and moved the establishment of a Committee of Shareholders.[57] The Board remained obdurate, holding enough votes to prevail a second time – and again a third time at an Emergency Meeting the following May. But each time, the votes deployed by the disaffected shareholders crept closer toward parity with those wielded by the Board, and on 27 September 1849, the rebels finally smelt victory. The meeting opened with unpropitious reports of cholera reducing railway traf-fic in Glasgow, branch lines opening late, and the construction programme lagging seriously behind. Moreover, in an act damag-ing the reputation of the company, Thornborrow Fawcett had referred his complaint about the misapplication of shareholders' funds to the Lords of the Court of Session in Edinburgh. The Caledonian Company had finally run out of funds, preventing the issue of any dividend, so a Committee based in London was inevitably appointed to investigate on behalf of shareholders. Its findings were presented in February.

The findings were bleak: terminal improvidence by the Board. Bills due within the following fortnight amounted to £74,000 but its 'Treasury was absolutely and literally empty', and the Company was beset by lawsuits. 'In no instance in Railway history has an undertaking been so deeply immersed in all the calamities of gigan-tic obligations in the hands of so many and so conflicting claimants'.[58] Preferential claims greatly exceeded 'the existing and even any rational estimate of the future income of the Company'. Procedures had been bypassed. Some agreements had never been approved by the Board 'but smuggled in',[59] and the Bank's head lease could only have been authorised by a suspension of the Caledonian's own Standing Orders. Despite its enormous floating debt, most of the Company's potential profit had been unwisely guaranteed to the shareholders of the lines which the Caledonian had leased or taken over, the levels 'based on great misrepresenta-tion'. One branch line which held out to earn 10.5% earned half that. With only a tiny minority against (including a certain John Stirling of Kippendavie), the meeting removed the Board.

The Caledonian retrenched, went through an accelerated matur-ing process, and negotiated its way out of its crisis. With a revenue of only £6,134 per week, the Directors refused to authorise pay-ment of any bill without first submitting it to legal scrutiny. Assets were sold, every contract renegotiated, and settlement on all law-suits agreed. Outstanding work was hastened, problems of 'imperfect accommodation and insufficient plant' addressed, and salaries and costs reviewed. The leased branch lines were aware that if the Caledonian trunk route were to go down, they would go down with it, so they were willing to negotiate. These measures worked over the following two years as the Caledonian returned to profit: passenger traffic increased by 75%, carriage of beasts by 67%, and of parcels by 6%.[60] Second-class passenger receipts also showed a healthy increase, but they were completely outclassed by a surge of 206% in third-class travel. The Board's proposed dividend of 4.4% in 1852 may have fallen short of the originally promised 8%, but it was a considerable advance on bankruptcy.

Once railway mania had cooled, and many of the workmen had left for the Antipodes,[61] Scotland was now covered by a plethora of small, short railways; but there were still communities frantic to achieve railway access even if only to import cheap coal and lime or export their produce to the urban markets.[62] The railway system entered a new evolutionary stage in which, like the game of *Monopoly* with railway branches instead of houses, a very few large railway companies would become powerful by eating up smaller ones. By 1892, for example, the North British Railway would be operating a network that had once been in the charge of forty-nine separate railway companies.[63] The trunk lines gulped down the branches in a series of large banquets. In December 1864 alone, six larger Scottish railway companies digested sixteen smaller ones.[64] Some had been mere adjuncts, and it was never very clear whether, as *The Times* put it, they were 'suckers and not feeders to the

trunks', [65] i.e. had they really been as profitable as originally estimated, or were they, in fact, a drain?

Of the lesser railways, the Edinburgh & Glasgow Railway was the
most significant, since it controlled the profitable traffic between
Scotland's two principal cities. Importunate railway companies eyed
it hungrily. The Caledonian was first, proposing amalgamation in
June 1852, since it had a shorter and more efficient line than their
own one. When the E & G proved unenthusiastic, the Caledonian
had tried a shotgun marriage by cutting its own rates between the
two cities, and the Edinburgh & Glasgow (already in a price war
with the Forth & Clyde Canal Co.) retaliated. Travellers briefly
enjoyed windfall fares as low as 1/- as the companies steamed
toward bankruptcy. Forced to treat for peace, the E & G agreed to
amalgamate, and it appeared that the Caledonian had finally won.
But when the two companies presented their amalgamation Bill to
Parliament, fear of a monopoly led to 'formidable opposition from
the public in Edinburgh and Glasgow'.[66] The North British, which
also coveted the Edinburgh & Glasgow, argued that since the
Caledonian would sooner or later win control of the trunk line
north-east to Aberdeen by amalgamation or by partnership, its possession of the Edinburgh & Glasgow would give it a dangerously
monopolistic power in Scotland. That appealed to Parliament's
competitive mentality, and the proposal was rejected.

At this stage, the NBR was in no position to bid for the
Edinburgh & Glasgow itself. It was, as a newly elected director,
Richard Hodgson, would describe it, 'a beggarly group of unproductive lines in miserable condition though extravagantly
constructed, unsafe for traffic and offering no prospect to the proprietors but that of hopeless ruin'.[67] Richard Hodgson of Carham
Hall, Coldstream, MP for Berwick, was elected a director of the
North British in 1853, becoming chairman in 1855. He appeared
every inch a country gentleman, and there was never any question
of personal gain in how he drove the North British.

Bizarrely, the British railway system had spawned two railway
chairmen who were both MPs, and both nicknamed 'King
Richard' by the press.[68] Richard Hudson MP was the first. Known

as the Railway King, Hudson had worked his way up to railway pre-eminence from beginnings as a Yorkshire drapery merchant, and his empire was centred upon four principal railways in the north, midlands and east of England, transforming York into a prominent railway nexus. He had been brought down in 1849 once committees of shareholders revealed that, whatever he had done for railways and for York, he had embezzled money, sold shares to his companies at much higher than the market rate, and paid money due to others into his own account.[69] The accounting of his companies was equally seriously adrift. In particular, the healthy 8% dividends paid out to keep his shareholders sweet had never actually been earned by his companies. By allocating revenue costs to capital, 'the presentation of the accounting statements was subordinated to the payment of dividends that would make the company look far more successful than it had been'.[70] The dividend was the thing: the company's reputation, and its ability to develop and expand, depended upon it. In times of competition, it was the most tangible signal of power.

There were no standard accounting methods to prevent railway companies from finagling their accounts to deceive their shareholders, and one did not emerge until a regulatory Act was passed in 1868.[71] So it was impossible to compare the success of one company against another. There was 'scarcely an account, abstract or statement . . . which is paralleled by a corresponding account, abstract or statement in the report of another company'.[72] By concealing inconvenient revenue costs in capital or other accounts, directors could make railway operations appear far more profitable than they really were, and therefore jack up the dividends accordingly. But whereas the jacked-up dividend was generally directed to the preference shareholder, the Ordinary shareholders were left with only any money that remained.

Hudson and Hodgson knew each other, not only as fellow MPs, but because Hodgson had been closely involved as the local MP in the Great North British Railway from Berwick to Edinburgh in 1838, which had depended upon Hudson developing the connection from Newcastle northward to join up at Berwick. Hudson had also played a minor but significant part as a member of the NBR's provisional committee at its conception in 1843–4. Few investors had been tempted to buy shares in a line that ran only from Edinburgh to Dunbar, and it was Hudson who had proposed that the line should be extended from Dunbar southwards to Berwick on Tweed. He offered to revive the Newcastle & Berwick line to meet it,[73] thus providing a through route to the south.

Hudson's offer had not been philanthropic. Once the Newcastle & Berwick line was complete and the Royal Border railway bridge over the River Tweed well under construction, Hudson viewed the North British as a tasty morsel, and declared his hand in 1847. He first sought to dent its directors' confidence by emphasising all its problems – floods causing tremendous interruption of traffic, unfinished stations, limited means of carrying goods and passengers, and incomplete connection with the southern lines. He then offered to shoulder all these burdens through lease, amalgamation or purchase – offering, in return, a guaranteed dividend. Privately, he wrote to Hodgson (who was not yet directly involved in the NBR other than as an influential shareholder) pointing out what sense such an arrangement would make: 'At the moment your traffic is suffering so severely, whilst ours is static.'[74] To depress the North British share value, Hudson broadcast his sentiments in the Newcastle newspapers, and then dispatched emissaries to Edinburgh to negotiate.

He offered the demoralised directors to take over the NBR for a guaranteed return of 8% on North British share capital.[75] The directors were much tempted, although they would have preferred 10%. When the agreement document arrived, however, the terms were nothing like as generous, and the North British Directors, embarrassed and angered, appealed directly to their shareholders to stand by them in rejecting it.[76] Whatever Hudson might claim, passenger traffic was approaching target, revenue promised 'to exceed the most sanguine expectation', and the completion of the line would open Scotland up to London. They urged shareholders 'not to be misled by the temporary depression in revenue'. They were not. The Railway King of England had received a sharp Celtic repulse.[77]

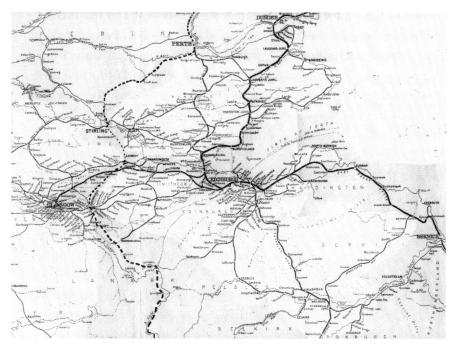

Making sense of the early railways in central Scotland. The North British route (solid) runs up the east coast to Edinburgh, with the Edinburgh & Northern taking it north through Fife to Dundee. The Edinburgh & Glasgow, the principal line linking Edinburgh to Glasgow, joins it to the Caledonian (hatched) line running up on the west.

In the early 1850s, the Caledonian was in a far stronger position than the NBR since its trunk route overland from Aberdeen to London was working almost optimally, despite uneasy and shifting alliances and broken pledges between the collaborating railways. The North British's weakness was not just the poor quality of its line down to Berwick. Under Hodgson, it was growing rather grander ambitions. His 'one constant comprehensive plan'[78] was to build up sufficient strength to challenge the Caledonian, and he began to expand beyond the North British's original remit of routes between Edinburgh and London. The ultimate destination of the Caledonian was Aberdeen, so Hodgson began to look north, initially building up partnerships with existing companies, and then slowly purchasing minor railways. When he paid over the odds, there was usually an underlying long-term logic. He justified offering a 4.5% dividend to shareholders in one railway when it was only producing 3.5% – at a time when Ordinary North British shareholders were receiving nothing – on the grounds that once the entire network was complete, traffic would increase exponentially, and that was when the real income would be made. It required only faith to wait for the entire system to lock into place.[79]

In Hodgson's mind, 'the entire system' included running a line along the east coast up to Aberdeen, but five miles of river estuary of the Forth and Tay lay obdurately in the way. Passengers from England disliked crossing them by ferry for reasons of inconvenience, delay, unpredictable weather and fear of seasickness, and this forced the NBR to take up its running rights on its rivals' overland track through the centre of Scotland.[80] Opposed to the NBR's northward expansion, the Caledonian imposed as high a toll as it could in order, Hodgson reasoned, to try to put the NBR out of business. The North British Company, he declaimed to his shareholders, had been 'fighting for its life' between 1856–6, forcing him to a policy, as *The Times* was to put it, 'of war – just and necessary no doubt ... but war to the knife with those rival Companies who would not amalgamate or allow a fair division of territory or traffic'.[81] His wartime strategy needed a deep war chest, and it was to force Hodgson, like Hudson before him, to stray far from the paths of economic prudence or probity.

He had so won the trust of his shareholders that the motion to re-elect him chairman in 1864 described to great applause how 'he had given heart and soul to the company, and almost sacrificed his own health to its interests ... they could not have a better chairman'.[82] Two years earlier, he had made his first major strategic break to the north in buying the Edinburgh, Perth & Dundee Railway Company. The E, P & D had earlier absorbed the Edinburgh & Northern, the company that had controlled railways north of Edinburgh through Fife, and its lines were essential to the NBR if it was to fulfil Hodgson's new strategy of building a rival railway route up to Aberdeen running along the east coast of

Scotland. With its Board of naval captains and great landowners like Sir John Gladstone of Fasque (father of the President of the Board of Trade and future Prime Minister, and largest investor in the Lanarkshire coal railways), and chaired by the Earl of Leven, the Edinburgh & Northern, however, had originally been constructed as a collier railway, to distribute coal from the 217 square miles of rich Fife coalfields north, west and south. Because its line specification was based upon lumbering coal wagons, trains cannot travel high-speed, even today, through the tunnel in and out of the cliffs at Kinghorn, Fife.

The Edinburgh & Northern provided a single-track railway running northwards from the Burntisland ferry to bifurcate west to Perth, and east to Ferryport-on-Craig which connected with a further ferry across to Dundee. Since it was trapped within the sea-girt peninsula of the County of Fife, this local working line presented little threat to other companies since it could never be remunerative. That did not stop existing railway companies from severely opposing its construction in Parliament – because that is what one had to do.[83] Nobody dreamt that these little tracks would one day form part of a national express network.

Opponents pointed out that steamboat communication between Aberdeen and Edinburgh was not only cheaper than by rail, but took only eight hours.[84] Whilst the new railway was clearly 'a local line of great advantage to Fife', it could never provide a serious challenge to the inland trunk route 'owing to the interruption of the Ferry'. It was, thought the *Scotsman* (unusually partisan for a British newspaper in its championing of railways[85]) – 'a hopeless undertaking, offering no advantages as an investment and none to the public in terms of real convenience'.[86] Any route which 'avoided the interruption, delay and expense incurred in crossing two arms of the sea' was to be preferred,[87] for 'a line of railway interrupted by two arms of the sea can never be a successful speculation'.[88]

On the other hand, from its inception, the Edinburgh & Northern had been 'deeply impressed with its great national importance,[89] and in 1844 it offered investors the 'moral certainty that [the railway] cannot fail to prove a most advantageous investment to those that may embark their property on the undertaking'.[90] Shares were oversubscribed by 40%. Taking the lines to the banks of the Forth and Tay, and having to depend upon ferries thereafter was frustrating. So one of its directors, Patrick Matthew of Gourdiehill, proposed that the Tay would be better crossed by a low-level swing bridge at a site about halfway between Dundee and Perth, using Mugdrum Island as a stepping stone. Perth's shipping interests, and anxiety that such a bridge would cause flooding of the low-lying estuarial lands by interrupting the river flow, stopped the plan. That, however, was the first plan for a rail bridge across the Tay.

The next was a 'chain bridge' across the mouth of the Tay estuary between Ferryport-on-Craig and Broughty Ferry, likewise abortive; and a third proposal – for a bridge with a northern landfall just to the east of Dundee at Stannergate – was never developed.[91] Anything that blocked the commercial shipping travelling upstream to Newburgh and Perth would be more trouble than it was worth. So, in September 1845, the Board agreed to take all necessary steps to construct a bridge at a high level, located substantially upstream from Dundee.[92]

In January 1849, thirteen years before Hodgson bought it out, the Edinburgh & Northern had appointed a young Cumbrian, Thomas Bouch, as its chief engineer and manager. Born in 1822, one of two engineering sons of a sea captain who had retired to Thursby in Cumbria, Bouch had been stimulated by an enlightened schoolmaster to study the physical sciences. It appears that he first went into mechanical engineering manufacturing, but finding it not to his taste, he moved to civil engineering, and spent his first four adult years as an assistant to George Larmer, who ran Joseph Locke's Carlisle office on the Lancaster & Carlisle Railway,[93] followed by four further years spent as a resident engineer on the Stockton & Darlington Railway.[94] Whilst his elder brother William left for Russia to be chief engineer to the Russian navy, Thomas Bouch came north, where he developed the ambition to bridge the Forth and Tay estuaries, his claim to be remembered as one of Britain's railway engineering heroes.

Sir Thomas Bouch.

Engineers occupied a special place in the Victorian mindset. Just as initial investment in railways had been given a moral dimension by diverting capital away from slave plantations, so did the engineer provide a peacetime equivalent to the soldier hero. William James, brother of the novelist Henry James, codified this idea when writing in 1906: 'Not in clanging fights and desperate marches only is heroism to be looked for, but on every bridge and building that is going up today.'[95] This ethos infused much of the contemporary and subsequent writing about engineers, underscored by frequent use of military analogies. Samuel Smiles provided role model engineers in his *Lives of the Engineers*. A railway employee himself,[96] Smiles wanted to guide the working and skilled classes to better their lot through self-development. Clever, observant and aspiring young craftsmen, like the wheelwright John Sturrock of Dundee,[97] could never hope to be an army officer, but might yet become an engineer.

Smiles's ideal engineer could be someone of humble origins but required the same personal qualities that Thomas Carlyle did of his heroes in his book, *Heroes, Hero-worship and the Heroic in History*: namely steadfastness, probity, moral perspective, leadership and a religious life. An engineer also required personal bravery. Smiles described the eighteenth-century lighthouse, bridge and harbour engineer John Smeaton, being rowed steadfastly into the storm, and leaping onto the Eddystone Rock to survey it in defiance of wind and rain.[98] Isambard Kingdom Brunel had proved his bravery in the construction of the Thames Tunnel, that left him permanently weakened;[99] and Washington Roebling's insistence on remaining down in the caissons with the Brooklyn Bridge excavators far beneath the East River in New York triggered eleven years of disabling illness.[100] Whilst it would be perverse to characterise the entire engineering profession by such people, the public imagination conceived of engineers as heroic, and the professionals did nothing to disabuse them.

An engineer was also expected to show creative inventiveness, practicality and application. William Arrol, for example, who was to become perhaps the greatest contractor of the later nineteenth century, constructing the Tay, Forth and Tower Bridges, 'held that before all things, practical experience was an essential to success, and he had a great contempt for the armchair engineer who would not make his hands dirty if the necessity arose'.[101] They should also be able to take rapid practical decisions as the occasion demanded – the very leadership qualities admired by Carlyle in kings. 'Mr Brassey', wrote his biographer Sir Arthur Phelps, 'was fortunate enough to possess this "two o'clock of the morning" courage in a high degree. If called up suddenly in the middle of the night upon some urgent peril or difficulty, he met the alarm with perfect coolness.'[102] Engineers were fortunately not all quite as self-conscious as Brunel, who confided to his diary 'I am afraid that I shall be unhappy if I do not reach the rank of Hero . . .', when aged only twenty-one.[103] But a strong sense of predestination emerges from the biographies of the Victorian engineer.

Because of their heroic stature, engineers, like architects, were accorded special dispensation from observance of budgets and timescales. Brunel's Great Western line cost over two and a half times the budget, and he lost £400,000 in his unsuccessful experiment to create an atmospheric railway (engines powered by compressed air that produced much safer and much smoother travelling conditions) in South Devon. The retrospective view is that his great achievements validated his failures, as argued, for example, in Brunel's entry in the *Oxford Dictionary of National Biography*. 'Even his disasters tended to assume epic proportions, however, and none of them did serious damage to his reputation.'[104] Contemporaries, at whose expense the work had been undertaken, were less forgiving. These experiments had been 'not at his own expense, but at that of others, the expense of persons of small means, widows and others who had invested all their savings and who could ill afford his playing in such a manner with their property'.[105] In an engineer's view, the pain of an overrun budget might soon be forgotten, but the glory of achievement would last for ever.

Thomas Bouch undoubtedly saw himself in the mould of the heroic engineer. His ambition manifested itself in the grandeur of his designs for the Tay Bridge and the Forth Suspension Bridge – the longest (Tay) and largest and tallest (Forth) railway bridges in the world. The designs themselves showed innovation, daring and originality; but they depended upon precise and careful construction: and that was probably Bouch's Achilles heel. Many of his fellow engineers had training or experience in workshops, foundries, or in the mud of construction. Bouch, however, had been in a consulting engineers's office virtually from the very start, and remained remote from the business of fabricating things. In mid-life, he would spend much time in London as an expert witness or arbiter,[106] which implies that he was, perhaps, more a managing than a practical engineer. His method was to determine a philosophy for a given project and then select the right people to design the engineering work and do the calculations for him. He developed, as a consequence, a remote approach to construction, with only sketchy personal involvement in site works, rather out of step with the idealised Victorian image of the truly hands-on engineer.

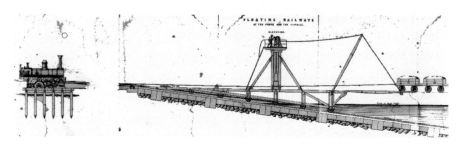

Bouch's first invention in 1851, a roll-on, roll-off machine that allowed entire trains to steam onto the Forth or Tay Ferries (most famously the *Leviathan*), whatever the state of the tide.

Judging by the volume of his work, and the money he made from it, Bouch was undoubtedly a successful engineer. Of his bravery, there is no evidence of the kind of dedicated personal valour shown by Smeaton on his storm-tossed rock, or of the Brunel foolhardiness in taking unnecessary personal risks, but it cannot have been negligible since he must many times have walked high over half-built structures. No question was ever raised about Bouch's probity or his religious observance. An engineer of typically undimmed self-confidence (as his portrait implies), Bouch was, however, was prone to be short with those who disagreed with him, particularly when answering questions before Parliament. His characteristic rejoinder, 'the thing speaks for itself and is common sense', implies someone unaccustomed to dialogue.[107]

Bouch made his name as an inventor with an intriguingly ingenious and enormously successful plan for the roll-on/roll-off railway ferry over the Forth for the Edinburgh & Northern between Granton and Burntisland (and later between Ferryport-on-Craig and Broughty Ferry). Prior to the arrival of the railway, 'passengers were taken across in small boats, which were sometimes rowed and sometimes sailed, just so as the weather suited. There were also small lighters for carrying cattle, carts etc'.[108] In Bouch's design, a train ran from its fixed track out onto rails fixed to the top of a sixty-foot long timber platform on wheels. Once the train was on the platform, the platform descended the slipway until at the same level as the rail track on the boat. The train steamed off the one onto the other, and similarly off on the other side. Since the platform could descend to meet the ship at any height of the tide, trains were relieved from tidal delay.

The vessel that carried the train across the Forth was the *Leviathan*, built by Robert Napier in Glasgow, and the trial run to test its safety in January 1850 successfully carried a trainload of 400 tons of turnips.[109] Duly reassured, the Directors' passenger train steamed onto it at Burntisland, returned across the Forth, and disgorged them at Granton thirty-five minutes later. So pleased were the Directors with this clever device that they ordered up another such device for the Tay Estuary, between Broughty and Ferryport-on-Craig. When carpers pointed to the similarity between Bouch's invention and one apparently proposed by Robert Stephenson in Egypt, Bouch was defended by no less than the President of the Institution of Civil Engineers, George Parker Bidder, who pointed out: 'There was little merit in the conception of this kind, as compared with a work practically carried out in all its details and brought to perfection.'[110]

After only two years as railway manager, Bouch left the company in 1851 to establish a successful engineering consultancy from offices in Edinburgh's George Street, and he speedily gained contracts for designing six smaller railways in Fife to feed into the Edinburgh & Northern Trunk Railway. This was followed by six further commissions in Scotland, four larger ones in the North of England, and the Sevenoaks to Maidstone Railway. Some of his engineering concepts were even utilised in the development of London's Underground District Line.[111] Bouch's brother William returned from Russia to become Locomotive Superintendent of the Stockton & Darlington, and much of Bouch's activity thereafter followed family influence, being focused upon the North of England. He became prosperous upon railways,[112] investment and foundries; and was appointed engineer of the South Durham & Lancashire Union Railway, shareholder in the Darlington

Railway, and shareholder partner in the Darlington Forge.[113] Whilst working for the South Durham, he designed tall iron viaducts at Belah and Deepdale. The Belah viaduct, whose foundation stone was laid in 1857, was 196 feet above ground level at its highest, and there were neither injuries nor fatalities during its construction. The contracting company was the firm of Gilkes Wilson, directed by Edgar Gilkes, which may be the first time that Bouch had worked with him. During the Belah viaduct construction, it was discovered that the foundations needed to be deeper than Bouch had designed, which cost 300% more than budgeted, and the railway company eventually had to offer Gilkes an inducement for accelerated completion.[114]

Bouch's strengths and weaknesses were exposed in the design of the smaller Fife lines. Impatient with the 'excessive cost and wastage of capital in construction',[115] Bouch was a pioneer of what he called 'cheap railways' as an alternative to over-designed railways. Through appropriate design, railways could be constructed of lighter materials and more quickly – hence more cheaply. A revealing instruction sent to one of his resident engineers stated 'you will, of course, consistent with safety, make the works as light as possible'.[116] His first cheap railway was the 4.5-mile line to St Andrews, inaugurated on 29 January 1850 at a small meeting of townsfolk, chaired by Provost Hugh Lyon Playfair. Bouch offered to undertake the engineering design for £455 – a rate of £100 per mile including preparation of plans, superintending of works, all expenses incidental with the Engineering Department, and free travel for himself and his assistant till the line was complete.[117] The line used lightweight iron and had its sleepers more widely spaced, and it cost only £3000 per mile to construct. But it could be used only by light engines 'run at a moderate speed'.[118] From Stephen Stoker's 1851 *The Opening o' St Andrews Railway*,[119] (penned 'in a dream of coming glory') modernism arrived in St Andrews as a burlesque:

> *When down the Lane*
> *O' gapin' men, the beast and train*
> *Like a mad tornado roared and swept*

Straight 'God help's a!' A gleg wife wept
And wild confusion raised a howl.

However, the bitterness of poor quality lingered long after the sweetness of lowest price had been forgotten. The light rails were broken up by the Edinburgh & Northern's heavy engines (the 'insufficiency of the permanent way' as the minutes put it), and the timbers of the line's two wooden bridges rotted because they had not been tarred with preservative.[120] The station at Leuchars Junction had not been improved from the original village halt, and the gentlemen and ladies' waiting rooms were 'despicable': 'a more ill-provided junction does not exist on this line'.[121] Heavy maintenance was required from its opening year, and the track had to be largely renewed after only eight years' service.[122] The St Andrews' line can be seen, retrospectively, as exemplifying Bouch's professional life. His ideas were probably sound if not adventurous, but the workmanship had been indifferently supervised.

Bouch's dealings with other small Fife railways were consistently problematic. The six-mile-long railway to Leven, further south, was beset by difficulties caused by Bouch's failure to attend meetings, reply to letters, produce drawings in time, or to inspect the construction. When it was inspected for the Board of Trade prior to opening for passenger traffic, the railway was found, in terms of curves, gradient and specification, to differ enormously from the one approved by Parliament. The Leven Railway's secretary was driven to write to his chairman: 'Mr Bouch's want of attention to our present interests in the matter is beyond comprehension.'[123] The Leven Railway's Board had already been made aware of problems with level-crossing gates and a grossly delayed engine shed, but the Inspector's report had revealed much more fundamental problems. Exasperated, the directors challenged Bouch about 'the defective condition of the works', variations from the plans 'of the most disgraceful nature', and why work had not been executed according to contract. Since 'special instructions given for their improvement had not received your attention' the directors, 'while implicitly trusting you . . . have been grievously disappointed'.

Bouch was dismissed, and warned that the company 'had strongest claims on you for relief of the consequences'.[124] There is no evidence, in fact, that claims were made. The probability is that Bouch had taken on too many projects, and was too immersed in his growing work in England to give adequate time to piffling local lines in Fife. Yet these small lines fed into the Edinburgh & Northern, which was absorbed by the Edinburgh, Perth & Dundee, which, in 1862, was absorbed by Richard Hodgson into the North British Railway's imperial strategy for a trunk railway line north of Edinburgh to Aberdeen.

That same year, the North British Railway Company began what might be called its courtship dance with the Edinburgh & Glasgow, beginning slowly with joint agreements, mutual partnerships, shared timetables, leading eventually to full nuptials in 1865. Previous attempts at expansion having failed, the E & G had realised that it was too small to remain independent any longer; and since Parliament had rejected its merger with the Caledonian, the North British was the default partner. From the latter's perspective, however, Hodgson had worried that 'if they had not been with us, [they] might have been absolutely against us'.[125] Instead, there was 'perfect harmony' and there was an immediate joint project to build a bridge across the River Forth. In autumn 1863, they appointed the engineering firm of Stephenson and Toner (the firm of the late Robert Stephenson) to design the bridge.[126] Unaccountably, the project moved to Thomas Bouch six months later. It is likely that proximity played a large part.

People had long been tempted to cross the Forth at the narrows of the Queen's Ferry – by tunnel or by suspension or chain bridge – but given the involvement of the Edinburgh & Glasgow, the Queensferry Narrows (where the Forth Bridge would eventually be constructed) were rejected in favour of a location further west, upstream, where the Forth broadened to two miles wide. The bridge would cross the wide and safe, if mostly shallow, 'roads' or anchorage, much used as a haven for shipping – particularly naval vessels. The railway line was to branch north, just east of Linlithgow, pass through the ancient demesne of The Binns, descend to the coast by Blackness Castle (the state prison of Renaissance Scotland) on its peninsula, and then stride over the river on a hundred arches, rising from forty to sixty feet above low tide to eighty-seven to a hundred feet above low tide in the central thirty long navigation spans. Two miles distant across the sea, land-fall was on the indistinct low slopes of the coast of western Fife, near the Earl of Elgin's principal seat at Broomhall. The Elgins were ancient industrialists only momentarily distracted by their Marbles. The landfall of the proposed bridge was, to Elgin's enthusiasm, right beside one of their most prosperous ventures, the exporting lime works at Limekilns.

A special shareholders' meeting was held on 22 May 1864 to consider a proposal to establish a separate Forth Bridge Railway Company (or undertaking), sponsored jointly by the North British and Edinburgh & Glasgow. Hodgson announced that when assessed against the cost of constructing the new piers and jetties required for the recently authorised new ferry crossing, a bridge made better economic sense. 'If the bridge be practicable, and be capable of being constructed at anything like the expense to which we should be put in constructing the piers and ferries and working the ferries . . . I say we should be very unwise not to retrace our steps and substitute that which would be of much greater accommodation to the public.'[127]

However, whereas sea traffic to the upper Tay and to Perth was mainly residual (ships were becoming too large for the narrow twisting Tay and its high tidefall) shipping in the upper Forth still flourished, and the ports of Grangemouth (at the eastern terminus of the Forth and Clyde Canal) and of Alloa were planning to expand. With that tunnel vision that seems to afflict professionals in pursuit of their clients' interests, and prevents them from appreciating opinions that differ from their own, Bouch does not appear to have accorded such river users with much consideration when designing his bridge downstream from them. By apparently posing a huge obstruction to their vessels, his design was calculated to inflame river users. An alternative scheme, simultaneously put before Parliament (whether by Bouch as well is unclear), had fewer spans but much more ambitious ones of 600 feet long rising 125 feet above high water of a spring tide. Two adjacent spans at the same height were to be 390 feet in length.

For over half this second bridge's length, it would be 125 feet above the sea, and it had fewer piers to obstruct traffic. The difference between the two was simple: the navigation spans of the first bridge extended to over two-thirds of its entire length, but with more columns and almost forty feet less clearance, whereas the navigation spans in the second – much higher and less obstructed – extended to barely half the bridge's length. Objectors claimed not only that there would be a 'great and objectionable interference with the navigation', but that the 130 piers of the first bridge would 'probably cause serious injury by the formation of shoals in the stream'.[128] Although these first two designs resembled neither what Bouch nor Benjamin Baker were subsequently to design to cross the Forth downstream at Queensferry, they were undoubtedly the genesis of the design for Bouch's Tay Bridge.

The first step in devising the Forth Bridge was to determine upon foundations. In November 1864, Bouch instructed a contractor to lay an experimental caisson from a steamer named after one of Scotland's greatest architects (and great grandfather of one of the NBR Directors), the *William Adam*. A caisson was an iron cylinder from which water was forced by compressed air, to allow navvies to excavate the seabed inside it until it sunk down to the right height. This one differed from the norm. After the water had been pumped out, rather than excavate the seabed, the contractor loaded the caisson's interior with 120 tons of iron to achieve a loading weight of five tons per superficial foot. Once it settled in the silt, they were going to measure whether it moved. It surprised everyone that Bouch did not turn up to observe the result of his experiment.[129] A lack of curiosity in his own inventions was unexpected in a Victorian engineer.

When Hodgson addressed his usual shareholders meeting in March 1865, he was in bullish form. The joint agreement with the Edinburgh & Glasgow had worked so well that it was time to consummate the marriage of the two companies. Test bores instructed by Bouch across the Forth riverbed had 'demonstrated the excellence of the substratum for the foundation of the piers'. All else, he continued airily, 'is a question of arithmetic'.[130] Hodgson, however, had been misinformed. The 'excellent substratum had turned out to lie beneath 200 feet of mud.[131] The survey of the riverbed of the Forth had been inadequate or inaccurate, and Bouch's caisson had proved unstable – probably because too narrow – and was abandoned.[132] Moreover, beyond funding exploratory work, the North British's own commitment to undertake the construction of Bouch's Forth Bridge was cast into doubt when Hodgson informed his shareholders that he 'did not at present intend to go with the Forth Bridge scheme *unless hostile measures . . . should render it necessary* [my italics]'. The time might come when, in his opinion, 'it would be expedient to go on with it, not as a measure of defence, but simply as a means of developing their own resources'.

So Hodgson, at least, did not regard the River Forth as a piece of nature overdue for taming at his shareholders' expense. Any bridge would have to justify itself as a commercial venture and that, up to a point, depended upon the attitude of the Caledonian Railway Company to the NBR's running rights over its lines. But if Bouch's very public experiments in testing foundations in the Forth were a form of engineering sabre-rattling funded by Hodgson to bring the Caledonian into negotiations, they called his bluff.

CHAPTER THREE

BOUCH'S BRIDGES

Let the Designer aim simply to supply a construction to fulfill the services required with the means and material at his disposal

WILLIAM HOSKIN, *THE PRACTICE AND ARCHITECTURE OF BRIDGES* 1843

Bridges have their own aesthetic. The great Renaissance architect Andrea Palladio recommended applying the same aesthetic rigour to bridges as to buildings: 'Bridges ought to have the self-same qualifications as we judge necessary to all other buildings, that they should be commodious, beautiful and lasting.'[1] There was enormous nineteenth-century controversy over whether or not they could be classified as art. Walter Scott described the twelve stone arches of Thomas Telford's Pontcysyllte canal aquaduct over the Dee near Llangollen as 'the most impressive work of art I have ever seen'. Bridges spanning water have a particular beauty, as their reflection in calm water twins their appearance, enhances their rhythm and provides an aesthetic contrast between the masculine solidity of the structure, and the moving fluidity below, 'sparking, soft, unpredictable and feminine'.[2]

Although approximately 25,000 bridges were created during the railway age – mostly small and stumpy and mostly inland, few British river estuaries would escape the ambitions of engineers.

Some of the greatest icons of the nineteenth century were bridges high over sea or river – such as Telford's Menai Bridge, Stephenson's Britannia and Berwick bridges, Brunel's Clifton Suspension and Saltash bridges, Eads's St Louis Bridge and Roebling's Brooklyn Bridge. A clear, coherent design is most likely to produce the most attractive bridge, and the poetry of a bridge often derives from how simply, logically and efficiently its design suits its purpose with the optimum economy of means. However, the effectiveness of the spectacle could depend partly on how the bridge joined the landscape on both sides, or otherwise how it might be framed, like Brooklyn's, by the towers of its own structure. One difficulty faced by any designer of the bridges across the Forth and Tay in their first locations was the breadth of the estuaries and the immensity of their landscape. In both cases, the distance from one shore to the other was over two miles, and whatever man might intrude into that landscape was likely to appear puny, with the far shore invisible. That was also a design challenge.

It appears that the pattern in Dundee was for a group of its ambitious citizens to meet privately to discuss the future of the town, and devise a plan which would then be proclaimed in the *Dundee Advertiser*, as a prelude to summoning a public meeting to take action upon it. The origins of the Tay Bridge lay in just such a meeting. It was organised by Thomas Thornton, a local solicitor, who had invited the Provost, the newspaper editor and various Dundonian businessmen to his chambers to discuss whether the town should take the initiative to bridge the Tay.

The term 'local solicitor' is a woefully inadequate way of characterising Thomas Thornton. The most influential professional figure of Victorian Dundee, this 'remarkable publicist' (as his obituarist described him)[3] had trained, like James Cox, the jute baron with whom he was to work so closely, in the office of Christopher Kerr,[4] the solicitor who had performed a similar function for the Dundee & Newtyle Railway almost forty years earlier. Opening the Dundee legal practice of Pattullo and Thornton, solicitors, in 1857, in fashionable new chambers in Dundee's Royal Exchange Court, Thornton grew it into one of the largest in Scotland by the time of his death.[5] His contemporaries attributed the evolution of Dundee during the last four decades of the nineteenth century to him alone. On his death, the city's Provost Moncur wrote: 'We cannot help acknowledging that behind all [those great works and improvements which have been carried out, in and around Dundee during the last quarter of a century] there was a master-mind planning and a master-hand guiding all to a successful completion. We all rejoice that during such an eventful and important period in the history of Dundee, there was such a man at the helm of affairs in our principal Boards.'[6]

Those many Boards directed the progress of the town. If Thornton had wished at any time to consult the Clerk, Secretary, Legal Adviser or Law Agent for Dundee's Harbour Commissioners, Police Commissioners, Gas Commissioners, Water Commissioners or Improvement Commissioners or the School Board, County Prison Board or Lunacy Board, all he had to do was cross his room to talk to himself. Although he claimed to be aware of the pitfalls of the inevitable conflicts of interest, distinctions in practice become very difficult where the interests of his various bodies failed to coincide. 'Masterful in word and action, and endowed with a measure of self-confidence that brushed aside difficulties standing in the way', Thornton's growing influence culminated in his appointment as Dundee's Town Clerk in 1893. Yet the power he already wielded implied that his new title was almost honorific. During the negotiations over the height of the Tay Bridge, he wrote confidently to the Town Clerk of Perth asking whether he could deliver 'your people' of Perth – for he, Thornton, could certainly deliver Dundee.[7]

His attitude to the members of his Boards was 'rather more didactic than was to be expected', for Thornton resisted any interference with the policies he so carefully devised 'with all the force and *brusquerie* that characterised a masterful nature'. It is not entirely clear, from this, whether his obituarist was an admirer or not. A similar ambivalence emerges from a memorial volume dedicated to him. Whereas his sense of humour, kindness, generosity and good fellowship (as well as fondness for charades) was quite patent, a formidable personality also emerges from descriptions of his 'furious rage and malediction' at blundering clerks;[8] his pride at being considered brusque, 'If I wasn't brusque, I'd be of no use';[9] and his strange, Nietzschean worship of strength: 'I like to have strong men about me,' he was accustomed to say, 'I hate weak men.'[10] It was not in Thornton's nature, observed his obituarist, to harbour petty spite. 'His enmities were on a colossal scale.'[11] Thornton's portrait by William Quiller Orchardson, funded by grateful subscribers in 1891, depicted the man behind the obituary: a brisk, compact figure of clear vision, serene confidence, implied impatience and awesome authority.

Thornton expressed his belief in hard work and temperate behaviour when lecturing on such topics to Working Men's Clubs and educational establishments. He was not sentimental. Regarding 'political action as a machinery for increasing the sum of human happiness and human virtue',[12] he believed that human happiness was only achieved by the right kind of progress. Railways signified appropriate progress and when a young lawyer in Edinburgh, he had become a significant shareholder in the North British, and later was a close personal friend of its General Manager, John Walker. As solicitor to the Oregonian Railway Company, established in America with Scottish finance, he represented the Scottish shareholders when the operating company repudiated its lease. The North British Railway Company had chosen well when it appointed such a man as its agent in Dundee.

Thornton and his fellow conspirators had perceived that if they wanted to accelerate a bridge across the Tay, it would be up to Dundonians themselves to take the initiative. Richard Hodgson's grand ambition to expand to the north remained in its infancy, and a bridge over the Forth, much nearer to Edinburgh, would naturally take higher priority in North British thinking than any bridge across the distant Tay. Convinced that there was sufficient economic value in the untapped Fife coal market and the undeveloped passenger market (constrained as they were by the ferries) to make a bridge over the Tay viable in its own right, the meeting agreed that Dundonians should not have to wait upon Edinburgh for their bridge, but should establish their own company to build it.

In an editorial in the *Dundee Advertiser,* John Leng, its campaigning young owner and editor, then went to work. 'Most
literally, he wrote, 'our town is on a siding, far away from the main
route southwards. To reach London from Dundee, or Dundee from
London is the pursuit of progress under difficulties.'[13] His editorial
was the first blast of the campaign to accelerate the construction of
a bridge across the Tay, and Thomas Bouch, then working in the
region on more railways in Fife, reassured them that the technical
challenge was inconsiderable. That encouraged Leng to declaim
confidently, 'in the presence of the great things that have been done
in tubular and suspension bridges in America and in Wales, we can
see no serious difficulties in the way of bridging the Tay . . . If the
Americans, in their half-cultivated country, have achieved so much,
[why should] we, in this old and rich and compact little island, hes-
itate to throw a bridge across the Tay?' Any bridge, however, would
have to be at such a height that ships could sail unimpeded below,
as concluded sixteen years earlier by the Edinburgh & Northern
Directors.

A public meeting endorsed the creation of the Tay Bridge &
Dundee Union Railway and the need to finance and build the
bridge themselves. Bouch, the natural choice as engineer, had characteristically underestimated the cost at £180,000. The company
set about trying to raise £350,000, to cover approach lines and station, in £25 shares.[14] The bridge design, now the *fourth* project for
a railway bridge across the Tay (after the low-level one at
Mugdrum, a chain bridge proposal at Broughty, and a bridge at
Stannergate), was the first one developed in detail, and it was
exhibited in both the Dundee Town House and in the Royal
Exchange in October.[15]

For the Tay, Bouch had adapted his Forth Bridge design of different lengths of girders sitting on different heights of piers with
which he was already comfortable, producing a drawing of both
bridges with one outlined above the other for comparison.[16] The
bridge was planned to cross the Tay between Newport and Craig
Pier in Dundee's harbour, downstream from the eventual site; sixty-
three spans, a hundred feet above the level of high tide over the

The strategists of Dundee. James Cox, lawyer-trained and a railway buff. A young (if balding) John Leng in 1851, who turned the *Dundee Advertiser* into a campaigning newspaper. The formidable solicitor Thomas Thornton in confident command of his portrait and, indeed, of everything else.

navigation channel, reducing in height as it approached the northern shore. The character of the Tay's foundations was assumed but remained to be tested. The *Advertiser* urged expedition in raising finance and obtaining the necessary Parliamentary approval. If Dundee let this opportunity slip, the town would remain on a siding, unable to enjoy easy to access to Edinburgh or benefit from the wealth of the coalpits of Fife.[17] As the mouthpiece for this coterie of Dundee strategists, Leng waxed enthusiastic about taking the opportunity of the bridge to rationalise all Dundee's railway termini into a single 'Grand Central Passenger Station', a *Hauptbahnhof* on the Continental model. This should be constructed at the dock end of the old town, exactly where the proposed bridge was expected to landfall, obliterating the densest part of medieval Dundee – the ancient seamen's quarter in the historic streets and wynds lying between the Market Place and the harbour.

Bouch's Tay Bridge fared little better than his design for the Forth. It was opposed by the city of Perth and its shipping interests, and by rival railways that suspected that such a massive engineering investment could only pay its way if it were part of a trunk route – which they were not prepared to tolerate. Thornton soothed those who feared they might lose business; and mollified the merchants and shipowners of Perth with the promise of a sufficient clearance of a hundred feet above high tide, sweetened by an annual subsidy. But the damage the railway would cause to Dundee itself ultimately forced Dundee Town Council, the organisation that would naturally have been the bridge's strongest supporter, into opposition. It established a special committee 'to watch over the interests of the burgh and the community', and commissioned expert advice from the former harbour engineer, James Leslie. Leslie advised that the central span height of a hundred feet above high tide would be too low for navigation upstream; but, even so, since the bridge would be crossing the Tay at a high level, it would hit the town twenty-five feet in the air. Trains would be running along a continuous high earthen viaduct that would form 'a high screen against free air and free view'.[18] The bridge's structure would also interfere with the river flow causing tailbanks (as they termed sandbanks created by the piers of bridges).

With casual brutality, the proposed viaduct would have sliced through the dense venerable closes around Fish Street and Greenmarket, the six-storeyed medieval tenements behind the Town House, as well as the recently built classical Castle and Union streets. The narrow arch with which Bouch proposed to cross each Dundonian street was wholly insufficient for its normal harbour traffic. So, by unthinking design, even Dundee's very own railway company was thoughtlessly projected into an unnecessary war against its own Town Council,[19] driving it to petition Parliament against the bridge – and thereby against its own entrepreneurs. The project ended in a costly rejection. An unexpected result, however, was that the NBR had taken note. Unenthusiastic about the Dundee Union Railway Company interpolating into its projected trunk route to Aberdeen, and to prevent the Dundonians from trying a second time, the North British agreed to adopt the Tay Bridge proposal as a high priority, on the condition that the

Dundee Union remained responsible for raising at least half of the capital itself.[20]

It was in the boom period between 1864 and 1866 that the lineaments of the struggle between the two rival lines dominating the Scottish railway network became manifest. The North British, using as it transpired funny money, bribed Edinburgh & Glasgow into amalgamation, and the Caledonian swallowed the remaining companies on its inland trunk route, thereby commanding the entire line from Carlisle to Aberdeen. Now that the two railway companies had achieved apparent equivalence, Richard Hodgson considered the first phase of his strategy to be fulfilled. If his shareholders cast their eye over the map, he informed them, 'all at once, they found themselves likely to get at peace with all the world, and the railway system in Scotland likely to settle itself into the normal condition from which it ought never to have been diverted'.[21]

However, for all that he spoke of peace and benefits of a free market, Hodgson's mindset was that of protectionism and war. In his victory speech to approximately 1000 shareholders in August 1865 to celebrate the completed amalgamation of the North British with the Edinburgh & Glasgow and the Monklands Railways, he said that 'these battles had not been won without a severe struggle, without some adventurous flights – that had, at times,' he would not say 'dismayed the North British shareholders, but had astonished those against whom they had fought, and fought with success'. He was presenting himself, like Oliver Cromwell, as a Protector of the vulnerable. The Edinburgh & Glasgow 'fought for compromise, but could never fight for victory ... The Monklands were even less capable of defending themselves.'[22] Now that the NBR had become sufficiently strong to withstand any 'poaching on our district' by the Caledonian, and the company had a short route between Edinburgh and Glasgow, Hodgson concluded briskly that it was time to turn attention to the trunk line up the east coast. Bridges were in prospect once more.

North British Ordinary shareholders had had enough. During its first decade, Ordinary shareholders, promised a return of 8% per annum, had received an average dividend of just over 2% for six of those years, and nothing at all in the remaining four.[23] During the following decade of battles and amalgamations, their return remained equally paltry, and Hodgson had become prone to take them for granted. Now that he needed their support for bridges, they turned on him. Arklay of Ethiebeaton, an outspoken laird from Angus, could not bear to contemplate his dividends being squandered on needless bridges. Nor did he believe Hodgson's protestations that the railway war was over, for, as he pointed out, it was not in Hodgson's nature. The chairman would not be satisfied 'with a termination at Glasgow. He would extend his lines to Aberdeen and John O' Groats.' Why, he enquired slyly, if a bridge over the Forth had been abandoned, were engineers sounding out the depths of the River Tay at that very moment? That, Hodgson riposted grandly, had nothing to do with the North British Railway. It was the business of the entirely independent Tay Bridge & Dundee Union Railway Company – which, at that time, it still just was. By the subsequent meeting, however, his specific commitment to build a bridge across the Forth at Charlestown had been renewed, and his previous position had slipped the chairman's memory. 'I never for a moment contemplated the abandonment of the works.'[24] Hodgson's confidence concealed the fact that Bouch's experimental, iron-weighted caisson had proved a failure,[25] and that he had persuaded the Company to invest up to £18,000 to test an entirely different type of foundation.[26]

Meanwhile, the NBR placed another Bouch design for a Tay Bridge before Parliament, at a location slightly upstream from his previous one.[27] It differed little from the previous design, and met with a similar reception, being opposed once again by Perth, two rival railway companies, and the Town Council and three public institutions of Dundee (Thornton, uncomfortably, was Secretary of each as well as agent for the railway). The company's counsel, George Bidder (son of engineer G.P. Bidder), informed Parliament that Bouch did not judge the bridge to be 'work of considerable engineering difficulty – only magnitude of length'. Now that it was admitted that the bridge was intended to transform the east coat line into a trunk route, the Caledonian's counsel attacked it on the grounds of unfair, injurious and prejudicial competition, as well as on the grounds of danger to public safety.[28] It was likewise opposed by the then chairman of the Aberdeen line John Stirling of Kippendavie, since its construction would substantially reduce their own revenue. Once again, the proposal was unsuccessful.

Posturing with great bridges had obscured the North British's worsening financial position. Its shopping spree in buying the Edinburgh, Perth & Dundee, and then the Edinburgh & Glasgow, had left it dangerously vulnerable, and both directors and shareholders had been kept ignorant of how the takeovers had been funded. After the North British General Manager had retired, his successor John Walker wrote to Hodgson in February 1866, alarmed that 'the prosecution of further new lines will cause embarrassments which may overpower us'. After forecasting a grave revenue shortfall, Walker worried that the likely costs of the Forth Bridge 'would hang like a dead weight on us', concluding that 'the only way, by which, in my humble opinion, we can rapidly and easily improve our position is to come to terms with the Caledonian' so as to bring a halt to their wasteful and costly rivalry.[29] He wondered if members of the Finance Committee were fully alert to the Company's position. Rather than being grateful, Hodgson regarded Walker's intervention as impertinent. Any sign of treating with the Caledonian would be taken as weakness and thereby damage the Company, and in his opinion, the likely Forth Bridge costs had been greatly exaggerated. He concluded:

> As to the *knowledge* of the Finance Committee, a little knowledge is a dangerous thing, and in some cases much knowledge would be much more dangerous. I think they know quite enough . . .'[30]

The patrician contempt for his fellow directors thus implied by his letter probably brought him down when it was published in the inevitable shareholders' report later that autumn.

Economic problems in early 1866 in the British railway industry were accelerated by the failure of the old established London bank of Gurney, Overend in May, with debts of over £10 million.[31] The resulting panic caused Brassey's occasional contracting associates, Peto & Betts, to go bankrupt, and even he encountered 'an amount of financial difficulty and trouble which was sufficient to overwhelm almost any man'.[32] In that climate, it would have been almost impossible to raise capital, and by June, Hodgson had no capital left. Since his revenue had been grossly overstated anyway, he had no leeway there either. His search for savings finally forced him to treat for peace with Col. Thomas Salkeld, chairman of the Caledonian Railway. He proferred a ten-year treaty 'with a view to terminating and preventing strife between the North British and the Caledonian Railway Companies'.[33] The savings would be made principally through not having to run competitive train services between the same locations, nor having to fund the enormous costs of fighting railways bills in Parliament. Salkeld returned a prompt response: such an agreement would be against the public interest and interfere with the Caledonian's own business.[34] After reflection, Salkeld wrote again, to insist that he had long wanted good relations, but that the North British 'daily and wantonly' violated earlier agreements, and that he had been given no earnest assurance that any new one 'would be better observed'. Accusing him of being childish, Hodgson challenged Salkeld to provide evidence of such violations. Chairman-level negotiations had hit the buffers.

Adam Johnston, solicitor for the North British, thought that a meeting of solicitors might be more productive. He wrote to his counterpart warning that 'already I find speculative lawyers and engineers devising aggressive schemes and seeking to trade on the conflicting relations of the companies'.[35] A meeting between them in August produced a three-year peace agreement that no Scottish bills should be put forward to Parliament by either Company without prior consultation. Nonetheless Caledonian staff were complaining only the following week that North British staff were trespassing into Caledonian territory, and vice versa. Despite such a high level of paranoia, the two Companies concluded the peace treaty on 5 September 1866.[36]

On the afternoon of 14 June 1866, cocooned from finance and politics, Bouch launched his next experimental bridge foundation for the Forth. It was an enormous timber raft of Memel logs, eighty foot by sixty foot by seven foot thick (Brooklyn caissons, by contrast, were 168 foot by 102 foot). An iron caisson was bolted onto its top, its purpose being to protect the bricklayers from the sea as the raft sank below water level beneath the weight of brickwork which they were to build up inside it. Six iron columns looking very much like funnels were fixed to the raft's top which would be filled with 10,000 tons of pig-iron, intended to press down the structure sufficiently deep into the mud for its surface to be level with that of the silt.[37]

The launch, described by the *Scotsman* as the 'beginnings of the North British Railway company's greatest enterprise, and perhaps the greatest railway enterprise that has yet been undertaken', took place at Burntisland in a carnival atmosphere, because it had coincided with the summer fair holiday. Crowded trains and steamers converged on a harbour jammed with small boats, all waiting for the three o'clock high tide. Every pier, every jetty, every rock was thronged with people gazing at the 'horrid monstrous bulk', willing it to move. Bouch's 'unshapely structure' of 32,000 cubic feet of timber lay on greased planks on a steep incline; and once the tide was high and the chocks (or dogshores) knocked away, it was expected to slide down into the sea. Like Brunel's *Great Eastern*, however, it stuck fast. A hawser from *Leviathan* was wrapped round it, to tug it off, but it remained steadfast, and the hawser snapped. The platform began to move at a second attempt, slid down into the water and rode high, whilst celebrants clambered on board to wave flags. Characteristically, Bouch does not seem to have been present.[38] The platform was then moored in the harbour pending adjustments. It never reached its destination, for the Directors stopped the project.

It was Hodgson's *Götterdämmerung*. The beginning of his end came on 29 September 1866.[39] The Directors' earlier report to shareholders contained the first announcement of a possible peace treaty with the Caledonian, and had been as full of work stopped as of progress maintained. Despite Walker's advice that there were no funds to do so, Hodgson nonetheless insisted on proposing a dividend. Walker then discussed his anxiety about the Company's finances with other Directors, and one of them passed it on to an obdurate shareholder, James White of Overtoun. The shareholders arrived at the September meeting already uneasy that rumours of financial difficulties had caused the North British share price to collapse by over 15%.[40] So when Hodgson tried to play them with his customary mixture of flattery, bravado and promise, he had probably misjudged the mood. 'I have been checked in my aspirations', he informed them, but if they would only trust him for another twelve months, they would then see the fruits of his strategy. Although the formation of a Shareholders' Committee was virtually foregone, he thought that he could talk them out of it. However, in a lengthy peroration well worthy of Shakespeare's speech by Mark Antony over the dead body of Julius Caesar (repeatedly emphasising how the chairman was indeed an honourable man) White of Overtoun carefully destroyed the credibility of the management of the Company. 'I would rather', he declared, 'have a 1% dividend honestly earned with honestly stated accounts than 3% of a dividend with cooked accounts and falsified statements.'[41] The three-and-a-half-hour marathon, during which shareholders suggested that 'the Board of Directors consisted of the Chairman alone', and that the Directors should be prosecuted, ended only when White won unanimous approval for his Committee of Shareholders.

The Committee reported a month later, and when the shareholders met to discuss its findings on 14 November, the resignations of the chairman and the entire Board had already been received.[42] Regional meetings of shareholders had been staged in many towns[43] and delegates from them joined the 2000 shareholders thronging into Edinburgh's Music Hall. White treated them to a two-hour statement for the prosecution of Hodgson. Like Hudson sixteen years earlier, Hodgson had maintained dividend payments by means of 'a careful and most ingenious fabrication of imaginary accounts' to show a surplus revenue 'which was not in existence and was known not to have been earned'.[44] He had managed, artificially, to make revenue expenditure appear lower than it had been either by charging it to capital, or by disguising it in various other accounts. North British operations had therefore been presented as much more profitable than they had been. For example, 80% of the huge £260,000 bill that Directors had squandered on parliamentary expenses over the previous four years had been hidden as 'construction' or capital, solely 'for the purpose of concealing from the shareholders the real cost to the Company of their Parliamentary contests'.[45] When the chairman peremptorily instructed the accountant to amend the accounts, the accountant customarily complied. The auditors reported only to the chairman, and had not 'pointed out the deceptive nature of the Journal entries'. The Committee had concluded: 'The conduct of the chairman has been so unjustifiable as to preclude the possibility of his being allowed to retain any official position in the company.'[46] The company's deficit was little short of £2 million. In the eyes of the shareholders, everything to do with Hodgson was tainted, including the bridge over the Forth which a Committee member Sir Graham Montgomery, kicking a dog when it was down, described as 'one of the most foolish things ever projected'.[47]

Shareholders could tolerate vainglory, bombast, or even short-cutting from Hodgson, but not the deliberate deception that had brought the Company to the edge of insolvency. They had short memories. Hogdson had done nothing that had not been done by Hudson before him, and he had been considerably less self-interested. Yet the media, heretofore largely uncritical of Hodgson, now turned on him. It was, claimed the *Spectator*, 'without parallel even in that long register of energy and villainy, the railway history of Great Britain'.[48] The *Daily Telegraph* thought it was time to end the fierce competition between railway companies that had led Hodgson to such a ruinous policy. 'As a railway director, he is one of the daring, dashing, ambitious class with whom we are all familiar – a man who appears to look on shareholders as mere tools and puppets of an imperial will.'[49] Only the *Scotsman* approached the truth. Hodgson 'understood credit better, saw like a statesman that if he could but make his lines seem to yield a steady unfailing dividend, capital would come fast enough – and he did it . . . It may be deception, but it is scarcely fraud.'[50] Sorrowfully, *The Times* judged the North British Company as 'a sad rake': within seven years, the burdens on its revenue had increased by 900%, whereas its capital had increased by barely 25%.[51]

The new North British Board was faced with near disaster, and on 21 December 1866, it invited John Stirling of Kippendavie and Kippenross, a laird with an estate near Dunblane, Stirlingshire, and a scion of the ancient family of Stirling of Keir, to become its chairman. He had been selected because he, in the role of company doctor, had so successfully rescued the Scottish North Eastern. Chairman of three railway companies,[52] he had supported ceasing traffic on Sundays in one, and had opposed the construction of the Tay Bridge in another. As chairman of the North British, he would be equally at home doing the opposite. Typical of a modernising Scots landowner, he was an enthusiastic agriculturalist – committee member of the Highland and Agricultural Society, purchaser and exhibitor of pedigree cattle – and a keen businessman as chairman of the North British Canadian Investment Co. Kippendavie understood that the North British needed time to recover. It could not contemplate, at least in public, funding either the longest or the largest railway bridges in the world. The initiative passed back to the Dundonians.

Indeed, the North British Company's financial position worsened so much over the next six months that by mid-1867 it was virtually bankrupt, not just unable to pay any dividends, but unable to meet fixed interest payments. Dissatisfied creditors threatened to seize its rolling stock.[53] *The Times* held that Parliament was at least partly responsible for the mess. After all, it was the regulatory body. Lord Kinnaird proposed that since the current muddled position was unsustainable, railways should either be brought wholly under Government control or be entirely free from it. Railway companies, he wrote, had been the favoured investment of 'small capitalists', yet they – the least able to do so – were put to enormous expense in having to propose or defend their lines before

Parliament in its guise as the protector of the public good. Parliament, in his view, had signally failed. Take the Edinburgh & Glasgow Railway, 'which for many years paid a fair dividend, and was considered a perfectly safe dividend'. It was now leased to a company [the North British] 'which has become bankrupt, to the ruin of hundreds of people – officers, clergymen, widows and orphans'. The House of Lords Committee on Railways, on which he sat, had recommended that Britain be divided into districts with a railway company allotted to each, on the French model, but the Commons had rejected it, leaving Britain 'with the worst of both worlds'.[54]

The engineering community widely shared this view. Both Stephenson and Brassey much preferred the French system, which the latter judged not only 'more calculated to secure the interests of the shareholders, but . . . more favourable to the public'.[55] 'We must confess', wrote his biographer Sir Arthur Phelps, 'that neither in the promotion of railway schemes, not in the investigation of those schemes by Parliamentary Committees, not in the subsequent administration of railway property, has anything like the skill and intelligence which were manifested in their construction been exhibited. In fact, there has been a deplorable want of organisation in all railway affairs, with the sole exception of the skill exhibited in their construction.'[56]

The Caledonian Railway must have felt triumphant at the North British's collapse. Its enemy had stopped foundation work on the Forth Bridge, had ceased any activity on the Tay Bridge, had been held up to public scorn, and was now virtually bankrupt. The Caledonian, by comparison, joyously paid out a dividend of 7⅜%. Indeed, at that lengthy, bitter North British shareholders' meeting on 14 November, Caledonian probity had been held up by White as a model of how a railway company should be run. When the Caledonian Railway had been in a similar financial position back in 1849, he stated that 'their accounts, I admit, were not cooked, or their statements dishonest'.[57] White's judgement, so far as the Caledonian's behaviour in 1866 was concerned, was entirely wrong. The Caledonian had been on a very similar shopping spree to the NBR, having swallowed the last two major railways on the inland trunk line only recently, and it had discovered that it had insufficient money to pay the huge dividends agreed with the shareholders of those absorbed companies. The principal components of the Scottish railway network were virtually bust by Christmas 1866.

A Committee of Caledonian shareholders found that what had been necessary for one railway had been equally necessary for its rival. In order to crush the North British, the Caledonian had adopted equally fraudulent policies. The Company's accountants had confused what might be charged to capital and what to revenue, and had permitted far more to be paid out in dividends than had been earned.[58] The dividend paid out in 1866 had been about 40% higher than it should have been, and 55% higher in 1867. Temporary timber bridges on its lines were overdue for replacement with stone ones, its engines were in a state of disrepair, and its terminus in Edinburgh was overcrowded and crumbling. Given the miserable condition of the track of the Companies that the Caledonian had bought over, the Committee even queried whether they had been inspected before purchase. Parliamentary expenses, the majority caused by its rivalry with the NBR, had risen by 50% over the previous two years. The Committee excoriated both Directors and General Manager:

> They were guided too much by that spirit of rivalry and competition which has proved so disastrous to railway shareholders, they have led the Company into most unprofitable transactions and projects, which have proved most detrimental and distracted attention from the proper development and regulation of the traffic to the best means of defeating and injuring other railways . . . Such policy and tactics lead to much that can scarcely be too strongly condemned.

The Caledonian shareholders, however, had no James White of Overtoun, and although its Directors offered to resign, matters were more genially resolved. On 1 February 1868, a new non-aggression pact with the North British came into force,[59] providing 'a solid and lasting agreement' which nothing should be allowed to inhibit.[60] The position of both railway rivals had turned out to be very similar, despite the considerably greater media attention attracted by the travails of the North British. Perhaps newspapers were aware that the unusually combative eloquence of the NBR's shareholders would never leave them short of copy.

The financial crisis of 1866, and the reorganisation of the two rivals thereafter, brought to an end the swashbuckling pioneering phase of railway expansion, and the companies matured operationally. A Traffic Committee would deal with drunkenness, and a Law and Claims Committee with passengers smoking in a non-smoker (fine £1), assault, theft, breaches of the peace and throwing stones at trains. There were some thirteen convictions from the North British Railway per fortnight. Prison waited for those travelling without a ticket (a three-day spell) or jumping off a moving train (ten days). Rolling stock was modernised, as Third Class carriages were ordered from the Lancaster Wagon Company (probably on hire purchase), pioneering sleeping cars were approved by the Board, and trucks were adapted to carry corpses. A novel method of deodorising its water closets and urinals would be tested by the workmen of the engine manufacturing works at Cowlairs, near Glasgow, as the experimental test bed.[61] NBR livery was olive, with cord or moleskin trousers, and blue overcoats.

Accidents, however, were such common occurrences that the public was fairly inured to them, and Companies budgeted to pay out c. £10,000–£20,000 per annum in injury claims and lawsuits.[62] The frequency of train collisions is surprising – sometimes with three collisions being referred to a single Board meeting.[63] Between November 1869 and May 1871, the North British suffered nineteen accidents in which eighteen humans and eighteen livestock (predominantly sheep which may have strayed on the line) were killed.[64] In October 1872, the Caledonian Railway paid out £34,000 in claims over an accident at Kirtlebridge,[65] and whilst 4% went on medical fees, 6% went to lawyers. In 1874, it paid out another £12,000 to twenty passengers injured in a single collision in Greenock, and there were ten collisions and twenty-nine other miscellaneous accidents the following year. Sorting out the claims absorbed enormous time, and given that compensation was far from generous, these figures imply extensive injury. So fatal rail accidents – crushed, smashed, severed, rolled over – were hardly unknown before the Tay Bridge disaster. Drowning was novel.

After a year of Kippendavie's leadership, the North British had recovered its nerve and was ready to renew its attempt to cross the River Forth. This new attempt was fourteen miles further upstream from the 'great Forth bridge' proposed for Charlestown, near the town of Alloa. Given that it was still out of the question for the North British to raise capital for new schemes, this new bridge proposition would only be possible if entirely funded by businessmen in the Alloa district. Another Bouch conception, it was a short swing bridge 500 yards long, only seventeen feet above high tide. Alloa citizens had been quick to raise three-quarters of the capital,[66] and the North British would simply work it for them.[67] Yet it was hardly a substitute for the great Forth Bridge Bouch had originally conceived and, as Bouch admitted to a Special Committee, it would be much less convenient to the national network. The proposed abandonment of the great bridge at Charlestown drew the wrath of the town of Dunfermline, since it now stood to be isolated from the trunk railway system. As its Provost declared bitterly to the Special Committee, 'From first to last, we have been made the tools, and I will add the fools, of the great railway companies.'[68] The North British's General Manager, John Walker, tried to excuse the change of strategy on the grounds of the Company's continuingly parlous state, but the Provost of Dunfermline riposted cuttingly: 'I think it is very bad for a company like yours, complaining of insolvency, to be coming to Parliament, as you are doing, and spending such a large sum in the promotion of new bills.' The Special Committee took little time in rejecting the Alloa Bridge,[69] and Bouch instructed his assistant Thomas Peddie to begin design work for a new bridge over the Forth at a site downstream, at Anderson's original location across the narrows of Queensferry.[70] So, under conditions of subterfuge, Bouch's final design to bridge the Forth began to take shape.

The design for the Tay Bridge, in the meantime, was nearing completion, and so two of the largest pioneering bridge projects of the 1860s – the Tay Bridge and the Brooklyn Bridge – finally went out to contractors to tender in autumn 1869. Throughout that summer, long before authorisation was received from the shareholders, the Bouch office (save Peddie) had been commissioned to work full tilt preparing details and schedules of quantities for the Tay Bridge, and showing prospective contractors around the site. The North British Board preferred to have precise contractor's prices in hand prior to seeking Parliamentary or shareholder approval,[71] whereas designs for Roebling's Brooklyn Bridge had been approved two years earlier, and the documents were only now ready for pricing. In all respects save the scale of engineering challenge, the two projects were utterly different. The Brooklyn Bridge was intended to avoid delay to commuting traffic between Brooklyn and New York caused by ice stoppages on the East River, whereas the Tay was to provide a shorter route from one part of a country to another free of seasickness and the Caledonian Railway's excessive tolls. Conceived by Henry Murphy, the Brooklyn Bridge was a profitable investment in itself, whereas the Tay Bridge was a means to an end. Whereas the Brooklyn's goal was for substantial profit, the profit in the Tay Bridge lay not in the bridge itself, but in the enhanced performance of the east coast trunk line running across it.

Raising capital for construction was also very different. The Brooklyn Bridge Act permitted both the cities of New York and Brooklyn to become major shareholders, and to bring New York on board, Murphy duly presented himself at Delavan House, the seat of power of the Boss, William Tweed, Grand Sachem of Tammany Hall, whose network of dependants and bribery then controlled operations in New York. In return for, so it was alleged, a personal inducement of between $55,000 and $65,000, Boss Tweed delivered New York and its investment.[72] No such civic option was available for the Tay Bridge. Town councils in Britain do not appear to have purchased shareholdings in major railway projects. The North British would naturally look to its own shareholders, but they were suspicious, impecunious and resentful. As a result, the bridge needed to be financed through an entirely separate Tay Bridge Undertaking.

If the Americans were less scrupulous about the funding, they were considerably more choosy about how to select an engineer. In early 1869, a 'Bridge Party' of twenty-one people had set out to inspect the bridges of north-eastern America with a view to selecting the engineer for the Brooklyn Bridge. They visited the Jacobs Creek bridge at Greensburg, the Smithfield and Allegheny bridges, Pittsburg, the Ohio Bridge at Cincinnati, and the International Suspension Bridge over the Niagara.[73] Only thereafter did they confirm the appointment of John Roebling, an innovative German immigrant, as designer. Roebling planned to build the then largest suspension bridge in the world over the East River to Brooklyn using his own patented plaited steel wires. During early site explorations of one of the towers, Roebling, showing that unfortunate single-mindedness characteristic of the hero-engineer, refused to move from a jetty when a ferry approached, and his foot was crushed. With that solipsist self-absorption that had characterised Brunel who, although ill, travelled on the maiden voyage on the deck of the *Great Eastern* and there dropped of a heart attack to die soon afterwards, Roebling refused adequate ministration or medicine. He contracted tetanus and died on 22 July 1869.

His son, Col. Washington Roebling, had also impressed the Bridge Party. Roebling Junior was no callow youth. He had enlisted during the Civil War, designed a number of suspension bridges (swiftly destroyed by the Confederates), and was the hero of the critical military action on Little Round Top, on which the Battle of Gettysburg is believed to have hinged. Having risen to the rank of Colonel and married his general's daughter, he had afterwards joined his father more as a colleague than a son, and succeeded him as engineer to the Brooklyn Bridge.[74]

In the old country, the question of a selection process for the engineer of the longest railway bridge in the world was never raised. Bouch seeped into the appointment by osmosis, by being on the spot. Had any directors studied his previous bridges, they would have discovered that he had built nothing remotely as large or in that type of estuarial location. His most distinctive bridges were those of Belah and Deepdale in northern England: inland, miniature by comparison, and of a completely different structure from the one Bouch was proposing to the Tay. But Bouch had now been identified with the Tay Bridge for over five years, so no effort was made to look elsewhere.

Finalising the Tay Bridge design in October, Bouch wrote to Lt Col. William Yolland, Chief Inspector of Railways, seeking guidance on wind pressure. Was it necessary, he enquired 'to take the pressure of wind into account for spans 100 feet plus, or for spans exceeding 200 feet'?[75] Yolland breezily replied from Guernsey: 'We do not take the force of the wind into account when open lattice girders are being used in spans under 200 feet' – which patently did not answer the question, but satisfied Bouch since, at that stage in the evolution of the bridge's design, no spans of the bridge were longer than 200 feet. Bouch saw no need for further investigation and forgot to revisit the question four years later when he lengthened the central girders by 25%. It is impossible to say whether this oversight contributed to the collapse, but it is further evidence of Bouch's lack of follow-through.

The North British decided to award the contract in advance both of its Board meeting and of the necessary Act of Parliament, believing that this was the only way it could present reliable contractor's costs to both.[76] But Bouch thought that to do so would result in higher tender prices.

> I much regret that we should be called upon to let a contract of this magnitude under the extremely disadvantageous circumstances which we are called upon to do . . . No competition brought to bear, prices likely to be at least 25% higher than if let in the ordinary way. I am doubtful about what the tenders may say owing to the lukewarmness of those invited.[77]

If all they needed for Parliament were accurate costings, he suggested that a target price of £237,000 be inserted (although the bridge, approach lines and station could probably be done for

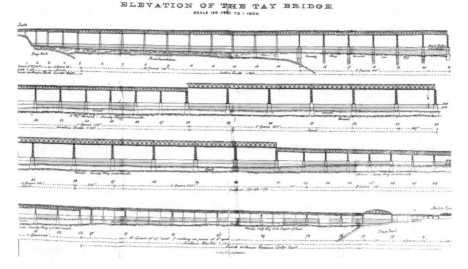

ELEVATION OF THE TAY BRIDGE.
SCALE 160 FEET TO 1 INCH.

The first Tay Bridge, designed by Bouch, drawn by Albert Grothe.
It is difficult to make a bridge that long seductive in elevation. Note
how the structure changes from brick piers 'like opera glasses' to
iron lattice work where the bedrock sank unexpectedly. The High
Girders are those at the centre with the sea lanes beneath.

£50,000 less), and the tender process withdrawn.[78] The
Parliamentary committee that had scrutinised his second scheme
back in 1866 had been advised by 'the most eminent engineers of
the day including Mr Hawkshaw and Mr Cochrane', and their
concurrence was sufficient proof that his estimates were correct. He
was probably correct. Nonetheless, after Bouch visited Leeds to
suggest that Butler and Pitts submit a revised tender,[79] they were
awarded the contract for £229,000.[80]

Pleading for 'calmness, reasonableness and absence of exaggeration' at a packed but uneasy Extraordinary General Meeting held a
fortnight afterwards in Dundee,[81] Kippendavie asked shareholders
to approve the construction of the Tay Bridge by a Separate
Undertaking. The obstreperous NBR shareholders were not
appeased. Since the original investors in the Dundee Union
Railway needed to be reinvigorated to finance the new Tay Bridge

Undertaking,[82] the Dundee jute baron, James Cox, already a Director of the North British, was proposed as the Undertaking's Chairman; and on that note, the motion was passed.

It was an astute choice. From his early days as apprentice solicitor in Kerr's office, Cox was one of three brothers who ran perhaps the largest jute works in the world – the Camperdown Jute Works, concealed just behind the north-western shoulder of Dundee Law, adjacent to the company town of Lochee.[83] Cox brothers had begun shipping jute directly to Dundee from Calcutta in 1840, introduced steam power five years later and, by the 1860s, employed 5000 hands with an annual wages bill of £150,000. Camperdown, which ran its own school for its 400 half-time children (they worked the other half), was virtually a separate principality from Dundee.[84] The Cox brothers were also very heavy investors in the American railroads.[85]

Most large textile complexes evolved organically, adding new buildings as they expanded. By contrast, the twenty-five-acre Camperdown Works was unique in that it was planned *a priori* around its own railway junction and cooling ponds. The Works' sixty-four furnaces consumed 26,000 tons of coal annually, their smoke being sucked through interconnecting underground tunnels leading into a single, soaring red- and yellow-patterned brick chimney nicknamed Cox's Stack. This 280-foot-tall chimney, designed in homage to an Italian campanile, square at the bottom and octagonal on high, was sufficiently tall for it to be seen over the Law's shoulder by those approaching Dundee by ferry. The Stack was an advertising tower and its construction in 1868 celebrated the completion of the Camperdown Works as a whole.

That Cox was 'an enthusiast in all mechanical and engineering details' was obvious from the Camperdown Works, but he was also highly efficacious.[86] To seek his participation in civic government, a deputation of 'the leading gentlemen of the town' toiled up to the Camperdown Works in 1868 to persuade him to stand for the Town Council, because membership of the Council had 'got under the status', as Cox put it, 'that Governors of the Town should be'. He refused. Another deputation – this time of working men – met with the same response. However, when only an hour before nominations closed he was ambushed by two more (legend has it that they were his own) working men, he finally conceded.[87] Working men's insistence that the town's largest industrialist should become its provost tends to contradict Dundee's reputation for industrial-class warfare in the nineteenth century. One of the very few jute barons to become involved in local politics, Cox introduced managerial change to Dundee's government, and was subsequently elected Provost in 1872. It was probably due to him that the Council passed its City Improvement Act in 1871, and then employed its first construction professional – William Mackison – as city engineer to implement it. With Cox its Chairman and Thornton its Secretary, the Improvement Commission began the process of 'improving' into oblivion what was then the most coherent surviving pre-modern town centre in Scotland.

Kind and deeply religious, Cox was 'full of good humour, and always [with] a joke and cheery word to buyers', and particularly interested in worker morale. In his manuscript autobiography, he commented: 'I never heard of a Frenchman singing at his work – they wear an anxious, careworn look' – which implies that, despite the clattering of the looms, singing was encouraged at Camperdown. What endeared him to railway people was that he seemed to know every one of them by name.[88]

By the time of Cox's election to chair the Bridge Undertaking, the North British's prospects had greatly improved. The 1868 profit of £71,000 on Dundee traffic alone was an increase of over 40% as compared to 1865. Nonetheless, Kippendavie presented the North British to shareholders as trapped both economically and geographically: the Tay Bridge Undertaking was still *absolutely required*. Economically, because the NBR could not raise the capital from its own shareholders; and geographically, because any growth in traffic depended upon both weather and elderly ferry boats over the river, and they cost over £10,000 a year to run. With 219 square miles of coalfield in central and western Fife just waiting to be exploited,[89] this natural market between 'the pit mouths in Fife and the furnaces and ships' hatchways in Dundee' could not be further developed since weather-dependent ferries could not guarantee a certain delivery.[90] The purchase of a third ferry would only aggravate rather than solve the problem. Above all, operations were being 'taxed to the utmost'[91] by the Caledonian, whose levy for the NBR's running over the 3.5-mile line between Broughty Ferry and Dundee on the north shore[92] had risen 50% over the previous two years to £10,000 – and it was still rising. If the bridge could be built for an annual cost of less than £20,000, it would therefore pay for itself. The Undertaking should yield a dividend of 5.5%, and if more than the target of £350,000 capital was raised, the North British would pay guaranteed interest on the excess at 5% (which, by the then level of dividends, was a good screw).[93]

Barely a year after the Caledonian and the North British shareholders had condemned the wastefulness of internecine competition, their hard-won peace agreement was unravelling. The ransom required for the Broughty Ferry line was one thing, but the NBR Board was increasingly dissatisfied 'at the numerous cases of reduction of rates and deviations by the Caledonian Railway Company and deviation from the agreement'.[94] The catalyst for a renewal of open hostilities might have been the Tay Bridge project, since the Caledonian would be well aware of how much it stood to lose if the Bridge went ahead. The North British would need to use far less of their running rights over Caledonian lines, and the latter's ransom income would decline sharply. The NBR dispatched a deputation to settle breaches of the peace agreement with the Caledonian but got a dusty answer. Unsurprisingly, the Caledonian moved to oppose the Bridge bill.[95]

The Tay Bridge Undertaking was no simple branch line funded by local subscribers for their own purposes. A major railway company was proposing to place the future of its primary route in the hands of a local consortium because it was itself unable to go back to its own shareholders for the capital. Neither Kippendavie's gloss, nor Cox's appointment, could quite mask the evidence of the North British's continuing weakness.

Kippendavie assured shareholders that despite the control of the Bridge falling outside NBR direct control, there would be no unnecessary risk to the project, and paraded Thomas Bouch before them as the guarantor of engineering reliability. Bouch, with the bushy-bearded, high-domed physiognomy of the successful Victorian, explained that a swing bridge would have posed unacceptable delays to both shipping, which was absolutely dependent upon the high, sweeping and often ferocious tide fall of the Tay, and to rail operations. To construct the towers of a large suspension bridge three-quarters of a mile out into the sea presented enormous difficulty. So he had designed a continuous girder bridge, with a raised portion at the centre – later known as the High Girders. The new design, he observed confidently, would be remarkable only in its length: two miles from the high bank on the south to the much lower level of the northern one. Its location would be 300 yards downstream from his previous design since, shorter by half a mile, it would reduce construction costs. One consequence was the sharp curve with an unusually steep slope of 1:74 as the line approached the northern bank, so train drivers would have to be cautious.

Shareholders were divided. George Kinloch, who was also a Caledonian shareholder, distrusted Bouch's estimate and worried about 'the hurricane the Tay Bridge was bound to encounter. Let them imagine that a ferry, or rather such a spider bridge was constructed as here proposed, and that any damage should arise to it from a gale, or floating ice, or an iron ship. The necessary consequence would be total suspension of all traffic – a serious matter even for a single day.'[96] Others worried, correctly, lest the bridge would be perceived as 'an aggression upon the Caledonian Railway Company and a commencement of the old state of warfare'. The North British should be 'at peace with itself, at peace with the Caledonian Railway Company, and abandon all unnecessary work'. If there were a genuine railway peace between the two companies, bridges over the Forth and Tay would be superfluous. Predictably, that obdurate anti-bridger Arklay of Ethiebeaton rose once again, to loud barracking, to protect his dividend. 'The whole state of affairs for the last few years has been most disgraceful. There has been nothing but spend, spend, spend, irrespective of what the poor shareholders were suffering [cries of *No, No, Retract*, and much hissing].' The directors riposted that each year without the bridge, the company would lose between £60,000–100,000. The figures showed that the bridge needed to generate a minimum profit of only £18,375 a year to pay a dividend upon the proposed capital cost – and that the combined savings on the ferries and the Caledonian's toll were more than sufficient to do so.

Arklay was unconsoled. He would rather have received his dividend. He warned that though the great ship *North British* was now sailing in smooth waters, 'soon they might pilot the ship through rocks and quicksands; and it might be that the gallant vessel, which had weathered many a storm, might strike upon a sunken reef and go to the depths of the ocean'.[97] His metaphor was picked up by Patrick Matthew of Gourdiehill – the man who had originally proposed a railway swing bridge crossing the Tay upstream at Mugdrum Island. In 1870 Matthew, a substantial fruit farmer near Errol whose 1831 book on arboriculture was admitted by Darwin as the first enunciation of the theory of natural selection,[98] was a constant correspondent of the *Dundee Advertiser*, and dispatched five letters bearing upon the Tay Bridge, probably triggered off by reports of the NBR shareholders' meeting. The editor John Leng had described him as 'a venerable, crotchety old man with a head stuffed with old-world notions, quite unsuited to the present age of progress', but he shrugged that off.[99] He had a remarkably analytical mind, for his series of warnings identified virtually all of the crucial aspects in the future history of the bridge. He first warned shareholders to require the engineers to calculate what the cost might be if the bridge had to be removed (as indeed proved the case). Next, he cautioned that the use of long girders and continuous track would lead to an 'eel-like motion', claimed that cast-iron had dangerous proclivities, and forecast likely difficulties with foundations. 'The foundations of the piers will, we may expect, be very unequal, very unsafe, or very costly; some of them standing as firm as the rock itself, others as false as the foundations of the Royal Exchange' (Dundee's Royal Exchange foundations having indeed sunk into a marsh).[100] In the case of accident, he wrote, and of one girder slipping off 'by the centrifugal impetus of a heavy train, would not the jerk and connected flooring bring the whole down like a pack of cards?'

The bridge, in his view, would absorb disproportionate resources much better applied to solving 'the fetid slums of Dundee'. 'Is half a million sterling to be sunk upon a bridge at Dundee when one tenth of the sum would suffice to erect a bridge where it ought to be? [Mugdrum] . . . It is injudicious, it is wrong − is it not so far criminal? − to divert so large an amount of capital away from where in utility, in humanity, it is so much needed.'[101] He warned shareholders against being 'too much in the hands of scheming engineers whose love of fame has interfered with their better judgement and prudence', − and against the vanity of the leading men of Dundee who were seeking 'a trophy of constructive powerbeating creation − an imposing magnificent object in the vista, reflecting grandeur upon the city'. The Wormit bridge (as he called it) was 'so high and top heavy' that it might be easily upset, and he forecast that should it topple over with a train atop, 'the whole of the passengers will be killed. The eels will come to gloat over in delight the horrible wreck and banquet.'[102] He would be validated, retrospectively, as the 'Seer of Gourdiehill'.

Some subconscious doubt in the Directors' minds, arising either from the immensity of the bridge or from Bouch's reputation for ineffectiveness, is suggested by their decision (while loudly protesting that they retained 'every confidence in the Company's Engineer'), to refer his design, specification, schedules and appointed contractor's tender for detailed scrutiny by 'the eminent and experienced engineer' Thomas Harrison.[103] One of the most distinguished engineers in England, Harrison was engineer to the North Eastern Railway Company, involved in both the Berwick line and the Berwick Bridge. Sir William Cubitt had said of him: 'Tom Harrison is one of the soundest and most honest men I ever knew.'[104] The directors claimed that they had been forced into this action by people 'too ready to give credence to exaggerated and detracting statements industriously circulated by rival interests'.[105] Tom Harrison's report on Bouch's bridge design and Butler & Pitts'

tender was entirely satisfactory, so, on 29 December 1869, the
NBR Board wrote to all its shareholders. The Tay Bridge
Undertaking would be complete by 1872 at a maximum cost of
£229,000, and it was time to collect the promised subscriptions.

The bridge was only the centrepiece – the metal buckle – of the
larger project to connect the trunk route from Dundee to northern
Scotland with the railways to the south, at Leuchars Junction, near
St Andrews. It required a connecting line down from the low-level
Tay Bridge railway station on the north, through a railway tunnel
behind Dundee harbour wall, to regain ground level beyond on the
east side of the town, eventually to sweep north to Arbroath and
Montrose. Linking railways were needed in the south to connect
the bridge to Newport and Leuchars. The non-bridge works were
to be constructed under a different contract under the direct
responsibility of the North British by the immensely practical
Edinburgh contractor John Waddell, later to be renowned for constructing the tunnel beneath the Mersey at Liverpool. The entire
scheme, including compensation for the compulsory purchase of
land, would cost £349, 515.16.2d of which the bridge cost was just
under £230,000.[106]

The Board of the Tay Bridge Undertaking met for the first time
on 13 July 1870. According to the circular, both Cox and Bouch
had pledged £10,000 each as a sign of confidence in the project,
whereas the record shows that Cox pledged £20,000 and Bouch
ten times less.[107] Cox badgered friends, colleagues and business
associates to raise, between them, 10% of the capital required, the
balance being raised elsewhere, and in the pursuit of saving
£100,000, the company decided to build a single-track structure
only. Preparations in Bouch's office were now almost complete.
William Wylie had been asked to update the test borings of the Tay
river bed he had made in 1866,[108] although it does not seem that
each new location or alignment was tested separately. Crucial to
Bouch's team was the resident engineer William Paterson, with
whom he had worked on and off since 1854, and whom he
regarded as a man 'of very large experience'.[109] Paterson was currently employed by the Caledonian as the engineer of the General

Station in Perth at a salary of £500.[110] It seems that Paterson, who established an office in Broughty Ferry, thought that he could do both jobs simultaneously.[111]

Once it was appreciated that only a single-track bridge was likely to be built, an exasperated John Leng attacked it for 'an exceedingly mean erection' since, 'in advocating a Bridge across the Tay, it never occurred to us that any engineer would think of running such a spider's web over the river as this is to be. If Mr BOUCH [*sic*] thinks that the comparison does injustice to his plan, then we will concede that the Bridge will in the distance have the appearance of a clothes-line stretched over a long row of clothes-props . . . If anyone supposes that the Bridge as now planned will be a magnificent and imposing object – an addition and improvement to the noble scenery of the river – he is very much deluded. Architecturally, it is excessively bald and commonplace.' Leng considered that a single-track line would brake the development of rail traffic; and he thought that the failure to seek additional funds in England for what he called 'the great north–east Coast route' had been a disastrous error.[112] Railway travel across the Tay, he concluded, will be little more than a gymnastic feat attractive to those 'who love something sensational in the way of adventure'. As rail passengers were to discover.

A complaint to the Board of Trade soon after the bridge opened proved the justice of Leng's case. The single track required trains to slow down at a cabin as they approached the bridge, pick up a trainstaff from one signalman to confirm that it was the only authorised train on the bridge at that time, and return it to the signalman on the far side. Running six minutes late on a Saturday's bleak winter dusk, R. Dempster's southbound train had just entered onto the bridge when he heard a fellow passenger gasp: 'Lord Save Us! There is a train coming from the opposite side.' All in the compartment, wrote Dempster, rushed to the carriage window 'and sure enough I saw a cloud of steam from the approaching train blowing from between the High Girders'. The guard learnt that the signalman had mistakenly given the driver permission to cross by handing him the wrong object. The northbound train spotted

Dempster's and stopped in the High Girders, then reversed all the way back along the viaduct to Wormit. The signalman was dismissed.[113] No real cause, perhaps, for alarm. Maybe not, but the single-line track was wholly inadequate for the trunk line with which the North British still hoped to topple the Caledonian.

When, despite the non-aggression pact, the Caledonian decided to oppose the bridge in June 1871, Leng was tickled that its grounds of objection included nothing negative about the bridge design itself. He argued that the reason for this oversight must be that the Caledonian had realised how absurd a single-track bridge was. 'Their astute advisers would see that a Bridge on this plan was not likely to divert much traffic from the Caledonian . . . In this light, the silence of the Caledonian . . . was much more ominous than encouraging.'[114]

The logical solution to the ruinous railway wars was full amalgamation of the two companies. Railway historians tend to regard this suggestion as somehow unworthy and ignoble,[115] but the competition had been largely artificial. Many people held shares in multiple railway companies and disliked seeing their dividends being squandered on unnecessarily competitive empire building, or paying for the enormous structures it seemed to require. It was entirely understandable for Kippendavie to explore whether the North British and the Caledonian might merge.

The idea probably arose in autumn 1871, from a revival of the notion of constructing a Central Station, a *Hauptbahnhof*, over narrow closes and tall medieval tenements of Dundee's seamen's quarter. The two termini of the Dundee, Perth & Arbroath railway were separated by a long windy dockside at the east and west end of its harbour, and the company had failed to end 'this great inconvenience of having its several stations sundered so far apart', before being taken over by the Caledonian.[116] The North British likewise had a terminus at the east, and planned another at the west end for the proposed bridge. As soon as the Dundee City Improvement Act was passed, the Harbour Commissioners (its secretary was Thornton) organised a conference to discuss how the powers of the Improvement Act might be used to create a single joint station down by the harbour. Four designs were commissioned,[117] but the station discussions faltered because they were overtaken by a more radical idea.

Kippendavie had been chairman of three of the railway companies now absorbed into the Caledonian, and he now led the discussions about an amalgamated station in Dundee on to the advantages of broader amalgamation of the railway Companies themselves. He obtained the unanimous approval of both Boards, but when he took it to his own shareholders, the proposition caused outrage. Although amalgamation was far from essential, he told them, the North British urgently needed to cut costs to offset the sharp rise in coal and iron ('and everything else'), and the single most effective way of doing so would be to stop running trains between Edinburgh and Glasgow competitively with the Caledonian. But so long as they remained separate companies, they were obliged to do so. The Scottish travelling public would be better served by a complete amalgamation of the two Companies, through a much more efficient use of rolling stock, integrated timetables, and the easy ability to travel simply throughout the network. There was a sure prospect of a 3% dividend even for Ordinary shareholders. Presciently, Kippendavie's underlying reason was his fear that the North British would find it difficult to remain an independent Scottish enterprise because of its size: 'At my time of life, a few years will probably see me done with railway work; but as a resident in Scotland, I should be extremely sorry to think of the management of our railways being consolidated in England . . . Depend upon it, in the long run, the management would go to the head of the concern, wherever that may be. Either the Scotch railways will be amalgamated into a large concern, or we shall be cut up and divided among the English lines.'[118]

Perhaps he should have given greater emphasis to the absurdities of railway competition. The Caledonian refused to arrange for North British trains to run on Caledonian lines. They ran their own trains in front of them at the same hour, detained North British trains on the grounds of testing their wheels or on 'other unreasonable pretexts', refused to recognise North British tickets, and started connecting services minutes before North British trains were due to arrive. They refused statutory accommodation to North British staff, stole its goods traffic, manipulated invoices and kidnapped North British goods. Five times the North British had taken the Caledonian to arbitration, and five times it had won. Five times the Caledonian had ignored the arbiter's judgment, and five times Parliament had done nothing. Amalgamation should bring such futility to a halt.[119]

When the Amalgamation Bill was placed before the House of Commons, his *volte face* astounded shareholders and public alike.[120] Some of his shareholders and indeed some of his directors reacted with disbelief. They were strong supporters of the North British and, in particular, of the Tay Bridge. The proposal took the outside public by surprise, and seriously undermined trust in what the Directors had been saying over the previous four years about the Company's regeneration. The reaction in Dundee was particularly strong. If shareholders were unable to overthrow the measure, threatened Provost Yeaman of Dundee, they would go to press and Parliament to do so. Being in the pay of the North British, Thornton was quizzed about his loyalties, and replied to say that he had refused all employment connected with the amalgamation, despite deputations and visits to do so. He offered his services against the amalgamation 'without fee or reward',[121] denouncing it as 'wholly indefensible and in breach of [the Company's] obligations'.[122]

Both Companies held SGMs, and both sets of shareholders were persuaded that their pockets should benefit substantially from enhanced dividends if the amalgamation went through. Beyond that, the debates differed according to the character of each Company. Caledonian shareholders were concerned lest a joint company with a monopoly would cease to provide a good service, becoming inefficient and objectionable instead. The North British shareholders, by contrast, regarded the matter rather in terms of snatching defeat from the jaws of victory since they had only recently been promised imminent victory over the Caledonian. John Leng, original champion of the Tay Bridge, speaking for the latter, claimed it was a capitulation, and he would oppose it step-by-step and inch-by-inch. 'The proper duty of the directors was to manage the affairs of the company and not to sell it to another which had been so long hostile to its welfare.'[123] Dundee Town Council, threatened with a railway monopoly, issued a circular to the four major Scottish cities and all town councils and chambers of commerce in Scotland, asking them to unite in opposing the bill.[124]

Assessors appointed to advise Dundee's Guildry concluded that 'the amalgamation was opposed to the interests of this country' and recommended that it should join with other public bodies in opposition.[125] Town Councillor David Jobson, who was to be one of the bridge's victims, lamented 'how far the railways in this country were behind the railways on the Continent in their good and cheap service', and urged the Government to take the main lines of the country into its own hands so that Britain might enjoy the reliability and cheap fares to be found in Europe. In a hugely revealing comment about the distrust in which railway companies were now held, Jobson concluded: 'Monopolies should be held by the people themselves and not by private companies, because if held by the latter, they were sure act injuriously on the public at large.' Once a Committee of Shareholders was established within the North British to oppose it, and two out of three English railways united against it, the chances of getting any Amalgamation Bill passed through Parliament began to recede.[126] Suddenly, the North British withdrew from the negotiations. *Railway News* suggested that it had discovered the Caledonian's books to have been cooked as the result of systematic overcharging of its customers rather than lowering its rates in accordance with the relevant Acts of Parliament. The Caledonian denounced the story as a monstrous lie, but *Railway News* observed that the last time such a story had emerged, it had been proved correct.[127] The identical allegation was raised in the Board meetings of both Companies without proof either way. With hurt dignity, the Caledonian declined 'to enter a newspaper controversy', but any possibility of amalgamation was now dead.

In the meanwhile, the contractors Butler and Pitts withdrew

from the Tay Bridge contract. Pitts, the man responsible for raising the necessary capital, had died and Butler felt unable to continue.[128] Luckily, only preliminary works and installing an engineering plant on site had taken place so far. Within a fortnight, Bouch had negotiated a new contract for the Tay Bridge with Charles de Bergue & Co. almost £12,000 cheaper than Butler and Pitts.[129] A call went out to shareholders for deposits for the Tay Bridge Undertaking to be lodged and, on 8 May 1871, the contract to build the bridge was signed.

The Tay Bridge had undergone a difficult and extended birth. Who wanted it? Was it necessary? Was it the right type of bridge? Was it on the right site? It lacked the self-evident logic of the Brooklyn Bridge, and certainly lacked Brooklyn's political muscle. It was also enormously cheaper. Everybody had taken Bouch at his word, namely that the only significant aspect of the bridge's construction would be its length.

A small ceremony was held on 22 July at Wormit on the fifty-foot bluff overlooking the estuary. Once the Sheriff had proposed a toast to the success of the bridge, young Master Paterson, son of Bouch's newly appointed Resident Engineer, tapped the first stone into place. They were observed by a newspaper reporter with de Bergue's two principal managing engineers, Messrs Grothe and Austin. No Cox, no Undertaking directors, no NBR directors and, characteristically, nobody from the Bouch office.[130]

CHAPTER FOUR

THE LONGEST AND CHEAPEST RAILWAY BRIDGE IN THE WORLD

Having a peculiar genius for the work, Mr Grothe, under the control of Messrs Hopkins Gilkes, has brought the bridge to the position in which we now see it. (Applause). It is a triumph of design; it is a triumph of execution; and it has been completed in such a manner as I hope you will all be able to bear testimony as to its stability.

SIR JAMES FALSHAW, LORD PROVOST OF EDINBURGH, PROPOSING A TOAST TO THE CONTRACTORS BEFORE FORMER PRESIDENT GENERAL ULYSSES GRANT, 1 SEPTEMBER 1877.

Had the amalgamation of the North British and the Caledonian Railways gone through, neither the Tay nor Forth railway bridges might ever have been built. Rail routes would have been rationalised and expenses reduced. Shareholders might have received the level of dividend they had been promised back in the 1840s. Sleek railway lawyers, who had done so very well from assiduously promoting the rival interests of the Caledonian and the North British before Parliament and its Committees, would have had to retrench. Occupancy rates in London hotels would have declined. But once the railway amalgamation had failed, the estuaries now needed crossing.

The Tay, thanks to the efforts of the Dundonian entrepreneurs, was the first. The sources of the River Tay lie upwards and westwards in distant Highland Perthshire, and by the time it finally sweeps out into the North Sea past Broughty Castle (on a promontory acting rather like an upper lip constricting its mouth), the river discharges the greatest amount of fresh water into the ocean of any river in Britain. Since the estuary, which separates the coastlines of Angus and Perthshire on the north from the shores of Fife on the south, has a very narrow mouth, the widening sweep of water that one normally anticipates of a great estuary occurs not out to sea but, perversely, *upstream* to the west. It forms a natural reflective bowl for the central Highland landscape – a magical mirror for the Perthshire mountains – and enjoys a geographically limited microclimate that can be as benign (hence the Botanic Gardens in Dundee) as it can be savage. The estuary is celebrated for its outstanding and romantic scenery, but its topography can metamorphose its breezes into howling gales.

Sweeping up from the south-west, compressed between the Fife hills on the south and the Sidlaw Hills on the north, a Tay estuary gale can be awesome. Sir George Airy, Astronomer Royal, observed how a storm would 'fill' the Tay Valley more completely than the shallower valley of the River Forth.[1] It can suck the windows (particularly cheap twentieth-century windows) of Dundee buildings in and out. Water surges up in spouts from the river, the spume so thick that it seems like mist rising to the height of the Tay Bridge, and fearsomely high waves appear to try to clutch the cliff-side communities of Newport and Wormit on the south bank and drag them into the sea. For centuries, the credulous have believed that in just such a storm, fifty ships seized by General Monk from Dundee Harbour after its siege and sack during the Cromwellian invasion of Scotland in 1651 were sunk – all struck down 'within sight of the harbour'.[2] It was a sure sign, wrote Monk's contemporary biographer, of God's displeasure. Two centuries later, newspapers periodically recorded tempests. Bouch selected a spot about halfway up this watery amphitheatre for his bridge, where it was only a few feet short of two miles in width.

It was the fourth time that his office had attempted a rail crossing over the River Tay,[3] and at long last the realisation of an ambition that he had first expressed in 1854. It was to be part of his claim to engineering immortality. His remuneration for supervising its erection was 3% of the construction cost, which approximated £10,500 excluding costs and parliamentary expenses,[4] from which he had to pay all of his staff working on the project. When he dismissed the task of bridging the Tay as 'of no great moment', however, it seems that he took the Tay topography for granted. It was to challenge such engineering bombast.

The new bridge contractor, Charles Louis Aimé de Bergue of London, had settled in England only in 1834. Inducted into engineering in France by his godfather, Prince Louis de Broglio (a rare pedigree by the standards of British engineering contractors, even if Brassey had come from the ranks of the minor gentry), his bent appears to have been the invention of machinery. From his first engineering works in Manchester, where he devised rail track that could withstand high temperatures (and then proceeded to build it between Barcelona and Tarragona[5]), to the establishment of an office in London and a new works in Cardiff in 1861, he developed an international reputation for bridge building. On being awarded the Tay Bridge contract on 8 May 1871,[6] he formed a team partly made up of engineers who had been building bridges for him in Russia and Java.

One was Albert Grothe, whom he appointed Supervising Engineer. Grothe was a German born in Westphalia (he always referred to the North Sea as the 'German Ocean' and never lost his Teutonic approach to English[7]), who had trained in Utrecht, and been bloodied in the Dutch army. In 1869, when he was twenty-eight, he quit the military for engineering contracting, and moved to Russia to construct bridges for de Bergue on the railway between St Petersburg and Moscow.[8] He must have impressed de Bergue since he was put in charge of the Tay Bridge at the age of thirty-two. In a reversal of normal practice whereby the consulting engineer became the public face – the 'hero' – of construction projects, it was Grothe, the contractor's man, rather than the reclusive consultant Thomas Bouch, who represented the first Tay Bridge. It was a role in which he revelled. He adored giving lectures and demonstrations about the bridge and the technicalities of its construction to societies and working men's clubs. Sometimes he lectured for fundraising – as when raising money for victims of the floods in Holland in March 1876. Grothe thus brought the world of engineering to small local halls, and wowed his audiences with descriptions of the purposed Channel Tunnel, the Suez Canal, the Mont Cenis tunnel and other contemporary engineering works; always designed to show that the Tay Bridge would be a wonder as great if not greater than any other. His lecturer's tricks included a miniature caisson to illuminate how the foundations would be sunk.

> In a small glass tank half full of water, he placed a circular piece of wood, into which was fixed a lighted candle. Covering these with a glass cylinder closed at the top and sunk to the bottom of the tank he, by means of an air pump, removed the water out of the cylinder, and by the light of the candle, the piece of wood was seen gradually to sink as the water was forced out.[9]

The influence he exerted upon his listeners was considerable. General Ulysses S. Grant recorded that 'he scarcely knew which had given him most pleasure – his inspection of the wonderful structure [the Tay Bridge] or the brilliant and suggestive conversation of its superintending Engineer'.[10]

Thanks to the Tay Bridge's collapse, we have an enormous quantity of detailed evidence on the management of its construction that emerged from the subsequent Inquiry. There were clearly doubts about the quality of Grothe's leadership, albeit that most of the evidence comes from Frank Beattie, the general mechanical engineer on the bridge and Grothe's subordinate, who loathed him. Beattie described Grothe more as a showman rather than engineer, obsessed and isolated from the practicalities of the bridge, preparing abstruse papers in his office and fiddling with his precious models rather than exerting his authority on site. Beattie was later to write: 'Had it not been for the good feeling and sense which animated his staff and caused them to work well together, I don't

No known photograph exists of Albert Grothe. However, the launching of the major Mark 2 caissons onto the Tay was clearly an event of great moment, and Grothe is likely to have been one of those in this photograph – perhaps the lone, bearded, hatted man in the left foreground.

know how the bridge would ever have been built.'[11] At the Inquiry, workmen referred to Grothe's presence and influence on site so rarely as to support Beattie's opinion. Much the same could be said about Bouch.

In Grothe's eyes, it was certainly Grothe's bridge. In Bouch's eyes, it was never other than Bouch's bridge. But whereas Bouch was typically preoccupied with many other projects – including an 1873 scheme for introducing tramways to Dundee which failed since it did not address the local topography adequately,[12] Grothe had but the single project – which Beattie unkindly suggested was not so much the bridge as Grothe himself.[13] Whereas Bouch would remain steadfastly absent from any ceremonial occasion to do with the bridge, Grothe, equally steadfastly, would represent himself as its embodiment. Grothe, moreover, regarded himself as much a design engineer as a contractor. He badgered Bouch with suggested improvements to the bridge design, commented on the design of the Forth Bridge in his talks, and – after the Tay Bridge collapse – worked up designs for its replacement. Bouch accorded Grothe's suggestions for the Tay Bridge not the slightest attention, and Kippendavie instructed him to desist from commenting on the Forth.

Bouch's office had drawn out the Tay Bridge on twenty-eight contract drawings. It was a minimalist design, emerging from the mathematical genius of Bouch's structural consultant Allan Duncan Stewart who had applied contemporary structural analysis methods from Germany.[14] Stewart had been resident engineer for the Caledonian Railway before establishing his own consultancy, and would be responsible for much of the structural analysis of the Tay and Forth bridges. He would later assist Benjamin Baker and William Arrol with their succeeding Forth Bridge, and James MacLaren with Britain's response to the Eiffel Tower – the Wembley Tower in London. The Tay Bridge was a thin thread of eighty-nine girders in spans varying in length from 27 to 200 feet, mostly sitting upon piers founded on the rock that Bouch believed lay not far below the seabed. Each pier comprised of two circular brick columns tied together in the middle like stacks of brick opera glasses, in Leng's words, and had a caisson for its foundation. The track at the centre over the navigation channel was initially planned to rise to one hundred feet above the high-tide mark (but later reduced to eighty-eight). Bouch termed his design 'a sort of composite bridge' – very much a hybrid, with spans of differing lengths, a higher section at the centre, and the northern columns sitting upon cast-iron rather than brick, with rather ungainly raking columns projecting westwards at the curve to counteract the centrifugal force of the trains sweeping round eastwards into Dundee. If neither symmetrical, balanced nor picturesque, it would be practical, swift and economical to erect.

The bridge contract was worth £217, 099, construction had to be complete by November 1874, and the penalty for late completion was £250 per week. The quality of construction was to be to Bouch's 'entire satisfaction',[15] and 10% of the contract value was to be retained against any remedial works.[16] Any disputes were to be submitted to the arbitration of engineers Thomas Harrison or John Hawkshaw for judgement – both well known to Bouch and the North British, and both already well acquainted with this project. The contractor and his men were also strictly forbidden from giving in to the temptation to interfere with or disrupt the running of the Caledonian Railway whose lines ran closely parallel to the North British ones on the north bank. Where the bridge curved round toward Dundee, a longer span with a bowstring arch allowed Dundee Town Council to extend their proposed public park – the Esplanade – beneath it westwards into Magdalen Green. It was to be built up with the material excavated from the seabed.[17]

The base of each pier of the bridge sat on its caisson: a hollow metal cylinder sometimes lined with brick for ballast, 8 feet 6 inches in diameter, that was sunk to the seabed to sit on rock. The small scale of these chambers compared curiously with the elephantine caisson created to support the tower of the Brooklyn Bridge on the East River, New York, which, at 168 feet by 102 feet, was almost twenty times greater. Compressed air forced the seawater out of the caisson once at the bottom; and into the void thus created, eight workmen (compared to the 112 men of the Brooklyn day shift)[18] would scramble down through an airlock each day, to dig out the seabed until the caisson had sunk to the required depth. The spoil was sucked out by a tube and spewed into 'receivers' sitting in barges which took them over to the northern shore for the esplanade. After work, Roebling's excavators emerged onto dry land. Those on the Tay emerged into a little iron island in the sea, waiting to be plucked out.

The caisson was, in effect, a pressurised chamber, for it was only air pressure that prevented the water coming back in. An understanding of what such pressure could do to the human body – what became known as 'the bends' – and the need for controlled decompression, was just beginning. There is very little record of caisson working conditions for the men working below the Tay, so we depend on E.F. Farington, Roebling's Master Mechanic on the Brooklyn Bridge, to understand what it might have felt like:

> Everything wore a weird, unreal appearance. There was a confused sensation in the head, like the 'rush of many waters'. The pulse was at first accelerated and then fell below the normal rate. The voice became faint unnatural and it became a great effort to speak. What with the flaming lights, the deep shadows, then confusing noise of hammers . . . one might . . . get a realising sense of Dante's Inferno.[19]

In January 1872, Dr Andrew Smith began studying the effects upon workers on the Brooklyn Bridge – extreme pain, perspiration, rapid pulse – the most notable victim of which was its own Chief Designer, Washington Roebling.[20] As Edgar Gilkes was to observe, when he became contractor on the Tay, the pressure on the excavators depended upon the depth of the cylinder,[21] and the 18-foot depth of the Tay caissons was three atmospheres less than the 78-foot depth of the New York one.[22] It is interesting to consider that by 1877 Bouch, too, was suffering from some unidentified illness, that eventually may have killed him. It is most unlikely, however, that Bouch had the bends. He was far less hands-on than Roebling.

Once a vexatious lawsuit by Wedderburn – the farmer who owned the site at Wormit and claimed that the compulsory purchase of his land for a railway had not covered its use for workshops, furnace and ancillary buildings – had been trounced, the work went ahead swimmingly and the bridge snaked out from the south shore of the Tay into the expansive tidal amphitheatre.

The quality of the piers' brickwork was supervised by Henry Noble, a well-respected brick man Bouch had met in London during the latter's nine years working with Joseph Bazalgette on the London sewers and the Thames Embankment. He came highly recommended as 'an exceedingly careful man'.[23] The first four piers rose, as forecast, from a bed of red sandstone. The foundation of the next five, however, changed to a mixture of stone and clay, and the following five on clay alone. They went up slightly ahead of programme.

Barely a year into the contract de Bergue became insane and speechless,[24] and died a year later.[25] His obituarist was to claim later that the pressure of preparing calculations for the Tay Bridge contract had softened his brain. Whereas the Tay Bridge might well have triggered his madness, it was unlikely that those original calculations alone caused the damage. Rather, it was the emerging disaster that was about to overwhelm the Tay Bridge, for its foundations had begun to fail as the bridge stretched further from the shore.[26]

The survey of the seabed commissioned back in 1866 had been undertaken by Wylie, who did the borings, and Charles Ower, one of Bouch's assistant engineers, who interpreted them.[27] Ower reported bedrock not far beneath the surface extending right across the estuary. You might have thought that Bouch's unfortunate experience with the foundations at both Deepdale and his Forth Bridge experiment would have cautioned him against relying too unquestioningly on such surveys. Not so. When the contractors had reached Pier 15 of the Tay Bridge, they could only obtain a foundation at double the required depth, and even then only by piled foundations.[28] Thereafter, the seabed ran, as it were, down a cliff – nothing beyond but fathomless sand and gravel. Ower had been deceived into thinking a hard bed of gravel some 3–5 feet thick was bedrock which in reality sank down to 157 feet below at the centre of the river.[29] Just at the point that Bouch was finalising his *third* scheme to bridge the Forth for launch to the public, his Tay Bridge had hit catastrophe, and the contractor had gone mad. De Bergue's company, now owned by his wife and sister, was managed thereafter by the Supervising Engineer Albert Grothe. He was only thirty-four. For the next year, he diverted the workforce to the shallower waters and sandbanks of the northern shore where the original design of caissons with a lighter iron structure above was still appropriate. It was no less dangerous. At 2.30am on 27 August 1873, the caisson of Pier 54 was rammed, possibly by a coal barge driven by a violent easterly gale.[30] The caisson tilted, cracked open and flooded. Five excavators at the bottom were drowned, four men and the boy who had been manning the pumps on top scrambled to safety, but a fifth was killed, crushed by the tumbling air pump.

The Railway Company was informed of the delay only in a gnomic report, and shareholders not at all. So they were unusually sunny when Kippendavie addressed them on 28 March 1873 (interrupted every few minutes by cheers, hear-hears, and laughter). The year's work on the bridge had been 'tolerably good', albeit held back by storms and weather: 'I believe the contractors are very well satisfied that before the end of next year (1874) they will have their work completed.'[31] There was no mention of the complete redesign now having to be undertaken. Happy with the Tay Bridge, shareholders were nonetheless concerned lest the company become financially over-extended, and Kippendavie was quizzed sharply over rumours of NBR involvement in a bridge across the Forth. Genially, he replied that the North British was 'not liable for one shilling of the expense, nor under one shilling of liability so far as the Forth Bridge has gone at present'. He was being economical with the truth. The North British had pledged up to £100,000 toward the Forth Bridge's capital,[32] and had been funding Bouch's office to prepare designs for a bridge on the Queensferry site over the previous four years. Kippendavie, like Hodgson, was becoming prone to keeping his shareholders in the dark.

Three months later, the Bouch office completed the designs for the Forth River Bridge (as it appears in Bouch's timesheets). Judging from the delay in redesigning the Tay Bridge's structure, completing the Forth had been given priority. Bouch, again using

Allan Stewart, proposed a soaring suspension bridge – or rather two suspension bridges 100 feet apart braced together in mutual support – rising 550–600 feet into the sky.[33] Two gigantic eight-column piers braced together in mutual support would rise just where the banks shelved down into the river on each side, with another two on the central island of Inchgarvie. Enormous steel chains taken over their tops would suspend parallel permanent railway tracks 150 feet above the Forth at high tide. Despite its shorter length, the Forth Bridge's other dimensions dwarfed the Tay's. The widest span in the Tay Bridge was 240 feet whereas each Forth Bridge span would be 1500 feet, and the Forth's height was five times greater. The approach to the bridge on either side was along twin viaducts of 147-foot span, light lattice girders, 18 feet wide and 16 feet apart, sitting on circular brick piers very similar to those at the north end of the Tay Bridge. It was a design of unprecedented scale in Britain and, had it been completed, it would have confirmed Bouch's place in the engineering pantheon.

In June, the NBR submitted the Forth Bridge design to scrutiny by George P. Bidder, John Hawkshaw and Tom Harrison, and to William Barlow and Dr William Pole for a detailed analysis of its 'general system of construction'. Pole had particular experience of building bridges in Japan. Barlow had been resident engineer on the Midland Railway, in which capacity he had designed the soaring train shed at St Pancras. He had assisted Joseph Paxton with calculations for the Crystal Palace, and had completed Brunel's Clifton Suspension Bridge in Bristol with Hawkshaw. A brilliant theoretical engineer who had been elected Fellow of the Royal Society when only thirty-eight, Barlow had recently taken out a patent for improvements to beams and girders, and was a member of a Government committee examining the use of steel for structural purposes.[34] Bouch could not have had a better peer review.

Barlow and Pole took evidence from Allan Stewart,[35] Barlow's own father, Peter, who had studied methods of preventing lateral movement in suspension bridges, and the Astronomer Royal, Sir George Airy. Airy advised that the bridge would be able to withstand wind pressure of 10 lbs per square foot. Noting that such a

Thomas Bouch's magnificent conception for the Forth Suspension Bridge, over 600 feet tall. Although it was derided retrospectively, it had passed the scrutiny of the best in the engineering profession, who had admired its courage.

design for carrying heavy railway traffic at ordinary speeds had no precedent, Pole and Barlow concluded that the Forth River Bridge would be more than sufficiently rigid, adding, as a curious codicil, that they would not commit themselves 'to the opinion that it is the best possible'. Provided that sufficient care was taken in its construction, and that good maintenance prevented corrosion, Pole and Barlow judged the Forth River Bridge a project:

> which, for boldness in conception and design, has no parallel in the present age . . . As a monument of commercial enterprise and constructive skill [it] will be an honour to the British nation.[36]

Greatly reassured, the Forth Bridge promoters moved to winning hearts and minds using roughly the same arguments that had been deployed to promote the Tay Bridge. They emphasised the savings to be made in ferry costs, the ease and convenience for travellers, the blessed absence of seasickness, the cutting of one-and-a-half to two hours from the journey between Edinburgh and Aberdeen, and a projected bonanza in trade. Those investing in the Forth Bridge would be certain of a 4% return (perhaps they were learning: the Tay Bridge guarantee had been 4.5%),[37] and the enthusiastic response from correspondents to the *Scotsman* implies the public concurred. The Act for the bridge was duly passed in August.

The Forth Bridge Company began inauspiciously. Its inaugural meeting called for 3 November 1873 had to be abandoned as inquorate, as was another the following day – because there were very few shareholders (indeed, the shareholders' register was never completed). The Forth Bridge finances were based on securing agreements with operating railway companies to guarantee an income sufficient to pay off the capital. Both the Midland and the North British railway companies guaranteed a net annual payment of £75,000 each, representing a 6% return on capital; but only on condition that the other east coast railway companies would do likewise.[38] Save for the raising of capital, any distinction between the North British and the Forth Bridge companies was illusory. Kippendavie was its chairman, James Falshaw, James Cox and James Yeaman MP were directors (the Board was soon to be joined by the contractor John Waddell), the engineer was Bouch, the solicitor Adam Johnston, and the Secretary George Weiland. Whatever the shareholders were informed, it was the North British by another name.

Sixty miles north, Grothe continued to manage the Tay Bridge construction. De Bergue had died on 10 April 1873, and by the time Bouch and Stewart had completed the redesign of the bridge's central structure, the de Bergue family relinquished the contract, because it had been running at a substantial loss 'owing to the extraordinary increase of the cost of materials and labour' following the foundation difficulties. A new contractor was needed to take over. Bouch approached an old colleague, the iron-master

Edgar Gilkes of Middlesbrough, who had been the third lowest bidder for the bridge contract. The suggestion was that Gilkes should complete the Tay Bridge, taking on all the staff, men, machinery and materials on site as a going concern.

Edgar Gilkes, whose obituarist described him as the founder 'of the engineering trade of the Tees',[39] had assisted Robert Stephenson in locomotive manufacture in Newcastle, before establishing the Tees Iron Works and then moving into iron-bridge construction. He had built bridges for Tom Harrison and Henry Law, and had successfully constructed for Bouch the two iron bridges at Deepdale and Belah without any fatality. He admired Bouch's stripped-down, economical designs, 'muscle without flesh' as he called them, praising the Deepdale and Belah viaducts as 'material in the right place . . . muscular strength versus adipose bulk'.[40] Bouch's brother William, the locomotive manager for the Stockton & Darlington Railway, not only had a substantial shareholding in Gilkes's firm, but also was a director of it.[41] Gilkes's contract for the Tay Bridge was based upon a schedule of rates,[42] and Bouch recommended that reasonable rates could be agreed once de Bergue's accounts had been audited.[43] Far from the Tay Bridge suffering from under-investment,[44] the contract was not much different to a blank cheque.

On 26 June 1874 the North British announced the transfer of the Tay Bridge contract to the 'large firm' of Hopkins Gilkes, iron-founders and engineers of Middlesbrough, on the condition of accepting the bridge team as a going concern. Given de Bergue's high reputation, Gilkes probably considered it safe to take over the contract, site, building team, premises and machinery, lock, stock and barrel. As Grothe put it later (with typical immodesty), 'Hopkins Gilkes were fortunate to get into their service Mr A. Grothe to be manager to them'[45] – failing, characteristically, to include his fellow manager, Austin (to whom the successful pre-fabricated approach to the bridge's construction was attributed), the erection engineer Gerrit Camphuis, or the general mechanical engineer Frank Beattie who had the greatest and longest practical experience of them all. Other engineers included de Breugn and

Templeton, and two young Dutch aristocratic brothers called Delpratt, who were training on site.[46]

The grizzled Beattie disliked the 'gross and discreditable business'[47] of appointing such 'schoolboys' to positions which 'perhaps more than any others required the supervision of experienced practical men'. Beattie regarded Camphuis, though older, as 'still a learner in practical works'. Their responsibilities included overseeing the sinking of the caissons and erection of the superstructure (Camphuis and de Breugn), and the erection of piers and spans (Delpratts), and to some extent all that work came under scrutiny at the Inquiry. Beattie's negative perspective was conditioned by the circumstances in which he had quit the Tay Bridge, and was written after the bridge had collapsed.

Site meetings in the contractor's office in Wormit normally comprised the resident engineer down from Perth, William Paterson, Bouch's two assistant engineers who came down from Edinburgh[48] and Allan Stewart. They would be joined by Albert Grothe and, from time to time, Edgar Gilkes who would make a three-day visit from Middlesbrough. The team would meet sometimes weekly, and sometimes fortnightly, and although Bouch claimed to have been there weekly, neither his diary nor Inquiry evidence supports that.[49] Occasionally Bouch or his assistant Wemyss would travel to Middlesbrough themselves to select samples of iron to dispatch for testing by David Kirkaldy, an expatriate Dundonian engineer based in London. Kirkaldy had invented machines for testing metals by, as he wrote to Bouch, 'pulling, thrusting, bending, twisting, shearing, punching and bulging', and he was much in demand as an expert witness. 'Outspoken and fearless as a Viking . . . Kirkaldy was the terror of so many persons, that it is probable that at one time he was the best hated man in London.'[50] His terror was duly applied to testing more Tay Bridge iron after its collapse.

If Ower and Wylie's seabed survey had been accurate, Bouch's Tay Bridge would almost certainly be standing today – spindly, inelegant, inconsistent in design and only single track; for its structure would have been brick rather than cast-iron, and more solidly based upon twin columns. But fathomless sand and gravel rather than bedrock meant that Bouch had to lighten the bridge's weight. So he extrapolated from his Deepdale structure to use cast-iron columns, and single, wider dimensioned caissons, thereby reducing the weight of each pier by 50%. Although he claimed that the bridge was not only materially stronger but also one that could be erected in half the time;[51] it was also lighter, and the pairs of piers on separate caissons were replaced by single piers on single caissons. As a structure, it was more vulnerable to a sharp blow from the top – since it was more top-heavy – and its cast-iron was prone to fracture if sharply hit. To protect the iron from salt-water rust, the inside of the columns would be filled by cement and the outside painted every three years.

The use of scaffolding in that expanse of tormented tidal water would have been difficult and expensive, so the bridge components were prefabricated on shore, and floated out in large units to be bolted together in open water. Riveting was also done on the fore-shore to simplify quality control. At the foot of the bluff at Wormit, Gilkes created what became an artificial bay, bounded on the east by a special pier for the fabrication of the girders, with a wide, level concrete-floored platform on the foreshore, in front of which the thirty-one caissons were put together. Each mark 2 cylindrical cais-son, 31 feet in diameter, 28,000 cubic feet in volume and weighing 200 tons, would be amongst the largest in Britain, and Grothe hap-pily compared it to an 'artificial rock'.[52] They were made of malleable iron plates riveted into a cylinder 20 feet high, lined internally with brickwork for ballast. During construction, they were extended 24 feet upwards as a sort of coffer dam to protect divers from the sea waters when the caisson was towed out and then sunk into it. Bouch never lost his fear that the scouring of the river might weaken his bridge's foundations, and decided that the caissons had to be sunk much deeper than originally planned if they were to be safe from the current and the shiftings of the tide.

To haul such an enormous object out to sea (it resembled, thought Grothe, 'a huge gasholder') was a challenge. The caisson would be fixed between barges at low tide to wait until lifted by the

Tay Bridge caissons in the middle of the river were much simpler and smaller than where rock excavation was required. Sand and gravel were sucked into 'receivers' and dumped on the north shore of the Tay, to build up the new esplanade.

rising tide ready to be towed out. Grothe observed that it was a 'curious and interesting sight to see such a ponderous mass handled with as much ease and precision as if it were a small model'. Once the caisson had reached its destination, a hydraulic apparatus lowered it to the seabed where it would be pumped full of concrete. With a seabed of only sand and gravel, they had no need of the teams of rock excavators who had had such a fearsome time in excavating a foundation for the Brooklyn caisson. Pumps were all that were really required.

The floating equipment, sinking equipment and hydraulic lifting equipment were all invented by Frank Beattie and Frederick

Reeves who then patented them,[53] together with the sand pump that voided the caissons of seabed sludge. The pump, which could be handled by a lone diver using four suction pipes, extracted the sand and gravel from within the caisson and deposited it in the four 60-cubic-feet metal receivers in a barge sitting alongside. Each receiver, which took one to three minutes to fill,[54] was then emptied onto the proposed esplanade. Once the caisson was deep enough, concrete was lowered by bucket inside it and spread level by the diver. Each caisson was programmed to be sunk in a fortnight, but constant bad weather meant that it took twice as long as expected.[55] By setting a contract period predicated on reasonable weather, Bouch had incautiously overlooked the climate of the Tay basin. Nature would not be mocked. When the first of the large caissons was floated out in August 1875, a three-day gale blew up and hurled both caisson and its supporting barges well out to sea.[56]

When Benjamin Baker, whose Forth Bridge would eventually oust Bouch's, came to witness the sinking of the caissons, Grothe showed him the plans and took him onto the Tay estuary to watch. Baker was impressed.

> It is hardly necessary to tell an engineer that if the staff had not been a very efficient one, they could not have carried out these foundations. It was one of the most difficult engineering works in the country sinking these foundations in a stormy estuary, and the processes throughout were entirely novel. At every stage they had to invent something to meet a new difficulty . . . The ability of the staff made a great impression on me.[57]

Yet these caissons were child's play compared to those Baker would have to design for the Forth Bridge.

When each caisson was in position and filled with cement, a heavy hexagonal cutwater, 27 feet long, 16 feet wide, and 22 feet high, weighing some 200 tons, was fixed on top so that the feet of the bridge's cast-iron columns (or piers) were lifted above the high water mark to keep them from rusting. Constructed like a hollow brick box for ease of transport,[58] each cutwater would reach just

above a *low*-water mark when it was first fixed to the caisson, but was then built up to a level just above the *high* water mark. Its hollow core was then filled with Portland cement, and sealed off with a stone lid of four courses of ashlar stonework, which then acted as the platform for the two-foot-thick cast-iron base plates of each pier.

Stewart's structural analysis might have been particularly sophisticated, but the erection of the bridge required other more contingent decisions relating to the site, to the method of erection, and to the demands of economy; and success also depended upon the skills of the workmen and the quality of their supervision. Although what happened during the erection of the Tay Bridge may have been unexceptional by mid-nineteenth-century standards, it all looked rather more alarming when paraded in public as possible reasons for the disaster.

Bouch's revised lightweight structure comprised a group of columns made up of hollow, cast-iron tubes bolted together, and strapped to each other by wrought-iron tie-bars or straps in lattice fashion. Each pier comprised six tubular columns, arranged diamond-fashion in two pairs of three (see p. 215). The four inner columns were 15 feet in diameter, whereas the two outer, 18 feet in

The Tay Bridge from the sea, from *Fife News*, October 1877.

diameter, were gently raked inward for lateral support. Bouch had used strongly raking outer supports at Deepdale, but the limited size of the Tay Bridge caissons did not provide that opportunity, so the rake on these outer columns was so shallow as to offer virtually no additional support.[59] Much was to be made of the inadequacy of these columns in resisting lateral thrust at the Inquiry. On grounds of cost, Bouch left out the frame to bind the tops of the six columns of each pier together into a composite whole that he had used in Deepdale. Its omission would increase the risk of the pair of triangular groups of columns in each pier moving independently from each other, particularly if a vibration should set up, or any of the bracing that tied the columns together lower down begin to fail.[60] It is unlikely that this, of itself, brought about the bridge's collapse, but it may well have contributed to its weakness.

Each column was bolted through its base plate by enormous, five-foot-long bolts sunk deep into the stonework below and fixed with cement grout. For speed of erection, they were filled with cement only after all tiers of the columns had been bolted together right to the top,[61] whereas better practice would have been to fill up each stage as it was erected. The cracking of some of the columns was attributed to filling the entire column all at once which put great pressure on the bottom tier. Grothe was very proud that his cement 'had become so hard as to make the whole mass as strong as if it had been hewn out of stone'. The Inquiry's expert witness, Henry Law, differed: 'The concrete was so uneven in quality that no dependence could be placed upon its being of proper strength.'[62] Given, however, that only the High Girders at the centre collapsed in the disaster, and that the remainder of the bridge stood defiant resisting the extraordinary pressures to topple seawards with the rest during the disaster, Grothe's confidence seems more credible than Law's doubt. Bouch then compensated for the increased cost of his new structure by lengthening the central girders to 245 feet, thus requiring fewer piers. Contradictorily, given that he had originally intended to lighten the load on the foundations, this meant an increase in the weight put upon each pier.

Benjamin Baker considered the superstructure of the Tay Bridge largely unexceptional: 'ordinary, every-day work'.[63] The piers supported a box formed of wrought-iron lattice girders which ran beneath the railway track for most of the bridge. But to provide the required clearance of 88 feet over the shipping lanes, the thirteen 245-foot-long central girders were raised higher and the railway line ran within them as through a lattice tunnel. These were known as the High Girders. The centre of gravity was now alarmingly high, and Bouch was concerned about how the bridge would withstand wind pressure. He reassured himself with the advice he had received from the Astronomer Royal, Sir George Airy, and from Tom Harrison, relating to his Forth Bridge structure – namely that there was no need to withstand a wind pressure of more than 10lbs per square foot, save in exceptional and localised circumstances. Although his redesigned girders were now significantly longer than the 200 feet specified by Yolland, perhaps he assumed the 500–900% factor of safety which Stewart had calculated was sufficient to compensate.

Bouch's decision to change from a brick to a lighter iron structure following the foundation failure required adding a foundry to the contractor's yard. The great girders would still be manufactured in

Middlesbrough, but Beattie suggested that since they had to re-cast 500–600 tons of cast-iron from the abandoned structure already on site, a local foundry would save the bother of shipping the iron south to Middlesbrough,[64] and casting of iron columns could just as well be done under local supervision. Grothe added a tall 92-foot-long foundry to the bridge construction site at Wormit, where he had already erected offices, workshops, stores and a kitchen, dining room and dormitory for the briggers, high on the bluff above the Tay. This workaday brick shed, with its travelling crane and an engine room on the very cliff edge, was inaugurated by the casting of the first of twenty-three columns on 4 September 1874.[65] A fortnight later, Bouch reported to the Board that a new foundry would 'facilitate the works by giving command of the castings', adding ruefully, 'I had anticipated much greater progress.'[66]

So did the North British shareholders. According to the original programme, the bridge should have been within two months of being opened, but only about a third of the bridge was complete. Reverting to type, shareholders' meetings reverberated with their former ill-tempered boister (interruptions, continued hissing, considerable uproar, booing and cries[67]). Tay Bridge difficulties may have been corroding the slender trust that Kippendavie had built up with them, but their anxiety found voice about the Forth Bridge. Whereas the *Scotsman* trumpeted that a Forth Bridge might be the only thing to save the North British from conquest by the Caledonian, and that the combination of increased traffic and savings on the ferries made it most attractive economically,[68] shareholders remained unmoved. Certain that the Board was not playing straight with them, opponents had come to the meeting equipped with manifold proxy votes in their favour, and waved them furiously like parliamentary Order Papers. Underlying the shareholders' distrust was the lack of the promised return on their capital. To 'cries of disapprobation' Kippendavie responded mildly that he was seeking authority only to continue negotiations with the Bridge Company – if adding, incautiously, that he had sufficient proxy votes to allow him to do so anyway. Maurice Mocatta, a shareholder from Liverpool, spoke for many:

The Forth Bridge Scheme involved a very serious imposition upon the resources of the Company . . . So strong was the opinion in England and amongst large masses of the shareholders of the Company, that whatever future steps were taken, so long as the North British Railway ordinary shareholders received no dividend, he should be here most determinedly to oppose it . . . It was really distressing to think that the North British Company was now the only railway in Scotland that did not pay a dividend, notwithstanding that their traffic had increased from one and a quarter millions to two millions, in the last six years . . . They should ask the Board to abstain from any further expenditure in capital; that they would have pity upon the shareholders; for it really came to that.[69]

Mocatta had the right of it. When shares were below par (as so often they were) and no dividends were forthcoming, shareholders were trapped and helpless – lacking an income and able to realise their capital only at a loss. Poverty-struck 'small capitalists' – clergymen, widows and orphans who had no dividends upon which to live – were always brandished by railway politicians as the shibboleth with which to beat Railway Company Boards. Yet clergy, widows and orphans appeared at shareholders' meetings to speak for themselves so rarely as to imply that they were less numerous or less penurious than supposed. Nonetheless, since the objectors were divided amongst themselves, Kippendavie's proxies won where, in an earlier generation, Hodgson's had not. In any case, the malcontents had mistaken their target. Current running problems – particularly the costs of under-utilisation of railway carriages and engines, and the rapidly increasing staff and wages bill – were every bit as damaging to the company's prosperity as capital expenditure.[70]

Back in the relative calm of the new Wormit foundry on its cliff overlooking the Tay, protected from shareholders' gales, newly appointed foundrymen were now casting the iron columns for the Tay Bridge piers; but conditions in their state-of-the-art foundry could be unappetising. The problem was a shortage of fresh water needed to dampen the sand before tamping into the casting-moulds again when it dried out following the previous casting. An indifferent well had been sunk but, frequently dry, its water was required for the men's coffee.[71] Since the nearest burn was a mile away in Wormit Bay, water for wetting the moulds had to be pumped up from the estuary directly into the foundry; and whenever the tide was more than halfway in, the water became saline.[72] Beattie, responsible for the foundry, preferred the saltier water anyway because the iron (which he considered very inferior)[73] had too high a sulphur content, and when the molten metal was poured onto sand wet with salt water, the salt helped to extract that sulphur.

The foundrymen observed that salt water steam was corroding their clothes and irritating their hands,[74] and when molten iron was poured onto sand dampened with particularly saline water, the entire workforce had to flee the foundry to escape 'very disagreeable smells'. Since the construction programme had to be met, they could not stay outside for long and went back in with their mouths and noses tied up with napkins.[75] It must have been horrible. The gas being released was hydrogen sulphide, and what was rotting their clothes and irritating their hands was the sulphuric acid that formed in the air when hydrogen sulphide precipitated against the moisture in the foundry atmosphere. The workmen also observed that when their hands hurt and their clothes dissolved, there was a much higher incidence of scabs appearing on the surface of the iron columns. When Camphuis took over responsibility for the foundry on Beattie's departure, his unconcerned attitude to the inadequate supply of fresh water to the foundry says much about the relationship between him and the foundrymen. 'I never made it a point to enquire into it.'[76] This evidence gave the lie to his claim that he had always been present 'when the metal was running'.[77] If he had, he would have understood about the hydrogen sulphide.

The foundry may have been well equipped, but it was not always correctly equipped, as in the saga of the 18-foot-diameter columns. The foundrymen's drilling machine was too small to bore the fixing holes in the flanges of the 18-inch-diameter columns so that the upper one might be bolted to the lower.[78] These holes had to be cast rather than being bored and were therefore at the mercy of the skills and attention of the foundry men. The columns were tied to each other by 'straps' (horizontal or diagonal bracing bars), which were fixed to the columns by 'lugs' ('ears' in Scots) – twin parallel projections with a hole through them that stuck out from the column. The strap would be inserted between them, and a bolt run through the holes to fix it in place. Each lug had to be at the correct angle, correct thickness, and of a structural unity with the column itself. The boltholes had to be of an exact and consistent diameter to take the bolts that fixed the straps to the columns. Upon the competence of these lugs of the columns depended some of the strength of the bridge; and that depended, in turn, upon the casting being carried out precisely, requiring accuracy, attention and care from both foundrymen and erectors.

The foundry's first foreman, Hercules Strachan,[79] appointed as 'a man of good experience and well recommended',[80] was sacked by Beattie only a year later for his attitude toward accuracy in casting,[81] although it later transpired to be drunkenness.[82] Strachan was succeeded by Fergus Ferguson. A moulder since the age of thirteen with twenty-two years' experience, Ferguson was well skilled in workers' practices. He won Beattie's 'every confidence' and impressed Camphuis as a 'very attentive and accurate man'. Moulders were among the élite of Dundee artisans (such a high percentage of the town worked in cheap textiles) and Ferguson's men were being paid on a day rate rather than by the more normal piecework, and at rates higher than the Dundee norm. They had no motive to skimp on quality.[83]

As Supervising Manager, Grothe had far too many other responsibilities to supervise the foundry. In any case, he admitted to ignorance: 'I am a man who lacks practical foundry experience to a very great extent.'[84] So instead Strachan and Ferguson were responsible to Frank Beattie,[85] but Beattie does not appear to have been very close to the foundrymen. Alexander Milne, for example, a dresser in the foundry for 2 years, had never once talked to him.[86] Moreover, for all his practical experience, Beattie appears to have been rather naïve about those working under him. Whereas he saw a partnership of mutual trust between him and the foundrymen, Ferguson thought differently.

Fergus Ferguson was a typical time-served old lag very well aware of all the tricks with which to circumvent the bosses. The notion was to get the work done to a standard sufficient to satisfy them, rather than to get the work done correctly. He was astute enough to realise that he had to give the engineer the appearance of being in control, and devised a simple and seemingly transparent stratagem. Clearly flawed castings – over 200 columns – were smashed up very obviously and recast.[87] Doubtful ones were ostentatiously placed before Beattie for his judgement. For the remainder, it was concealment and fudge. Whenever Beattie was spotted coming toward the foundry, which he did three times daily, Ferguson would shout to the moulders to 'throw a cloth over the bad part': so that any columns with holes in them were hidden with cloths and sacks.[88] Even at the Inquiry, Beattie could scarcely bring himself to believe that he had been so deliberately and consistently deceived.

Camphuis, the erection engineer, took over the foundry in 1875, and resented it. Since his real interest was the sinking of the caissons and erection of the piers, he regarded the foundry as an irritating sideshow. He admitted to lack of experience of bridge construction, superintending castings, and even of passing work as satisfactory. Although he breezily informed the Inquiry that he was perfectly capable of judging foundry work, he still did not know how to test the integrity of a column, or gauge whether it was of even thickness by tapping it with a hammer in the customary way, and the workmen were aware of it. He raised no objection when moulders cast their columns horizontally rather than vertically, even though experience indicated that to cast columns vertically was the best way of securing an even thickness of metal wall all round. The core could shift when casting horizontally, resulting in unequal widths; and when the molten iron came round to join at the top, it had cooled too much to form a continuous whole – leaving an imperfect ridged joint known as a 'cold shut'. A column with a cold shut was fundamentally weaker than a homogeneous one. Inquiry investigators found several 'cold shuts', and columns where one side was under half the thickness of the other.[89]

The foundrymen saw themselves as working independently. Jack Tasker (who worked in the foundry for twenty months before being dismissed for drunkenness) was later to claim 'the contractors never looked at the castings at all . . . Beattie never looked at them . . . Camphuis knowed nothing about the castings.'[90] If Paterson, the resident engineer, and Wemyss – Bouch's assistant on site – were in the foundry several times a week, and Bouch himself made a point of visiting on his occasional visits to Wormit, it is noticeable that not a single workman mentioned their presence when under examination. Brunel might have supervised his castings, but Bouch did not. The quality controller of the iron columns that made up the bridge's piers was effectively the foreman Fergus Ferguson.

Under Ferguson, imperfections were masked rather than prevented. Ridges, scabs and other blemishes were first concealed from Beattie and Camphuis and then chiselled and polished off. Holes in the castings were filled with 'beaumontage' (literally 'good-looking appearance'), which the foundrymen called Beaumont's Egg. Made from beeswax, fiddler's resin, melted finest iron borings and lamp black,[91] Egg could be melted into blowholes with a red hot iron bar, and then rubbed with a stone to look like metal. Holes up to half an inch in diameter, and three-quarters of an inch deep were treated in this manner. Given that the original column specification was for column walls of one to one-and-a-quarter inches thick,[92] the foundrymen were filling in holes that penetrated well over halfway through. Egg was kept in a box in Ferguson's office – 'in a wee box that lay between the turning shop and the moulding shop, on a brick wall' or 'the gaffer's buckie'.[93] Tasker's job was to make it up, and Ferguson provided the cash to buy the ingredients at Dundee's West Port. There was such a demand, 'we could never get enough'.[94]

Although Beattie claimed to have sacked some workmen whom he found using Egg, Grothe was to deny any knowledge of it being used.[95] When he had challenged Ferguson about it, the latter had protested innocence. Grothe was being disingenuous, for the only reason that he then increased the thickness of the iron column wall by one-eighth could have been that he feared that bad workmanship might lead to potential structural weakness.[96] A design weakness would have been referred to Bouch to be solved at the engineer's or the client's expense rather than the contractor's. Grothe presented it to the inquiry as a safety measure introduced by the contractor *pro bono publico*, but one Inquiry Commissioner pointed out that since he was paid by weight and rates, the contractor would have recouped the additional cost at the railway company's expense anyway.[97] Moreover, even though Grothe had added 8% to the weight of the piers, he does not appear to have informed Bouch of it. Presumably, with his high margin of safety, Grothe assumed that there would be no need.

All this implies that Grothe accepted that the contractor might be liable for the consequences of poor foundry practice and had taken remedial action. But when it comes to the question of how Ferguson had been supplied with Beaumont's Egg, direct liability was getting close to Grothe himself. Who had provided the cash to give to Tasker to buy the ingredients? An old lag like Ferguson would never have had sufficient money of his own and, even if he had, would never have willingly subsidised his employers. Cash in hand was most likely to have come from the company itself. Bridge construction and turning in the foundry were both running alarmingly behind schedule and 'there was a considerable push to complete'[98] during the last eight months. Foundrymen were turning columns day and night, and decisions were being made purely on speed. The covering up of seemingly minor blemishes was probably one of them and, as he had become used to these curious British ways, Grothe himself had probably authorised the money.

Lugs presented another casting problem. If the core moved during casting, the lug's adherence to its column was either weakened or prevented from being formed at all.[99] The moulders thought that this problem was exacerbated by the sluggish nature of the poor iron.[100] When this was the case, good practice required the remoulding of the entire column and its lugs, but it was much speedier to 'burn' the lugs back onto the column. Both lug and column had to be heated to the same temperature until they fused together, and each burning required three barrowloads of coal.[101] Since the only section of the column to be heated up was the portion where the lug was to be attached, extreme temperature differentials were created in the remainder of the column, risking cracking – which one moulder recalled seeing.[102] Burning on was supported by both engineers and by Edgar Gilkes himself,[103] and provided it was done carefully, Camphuis was quite content.[104] The inquiry heard that it was daily procedure on other sites.[105] It was still bad practice.

Much was later to be made of poor casting and the use of Beaumont's Egg. The reality was that blemishes and blowholes were to be expected in cast-iron, and evidence at the Inquiry suggested that Egg was widely used within the industry.[106] The foundrymen told the Inquiry that they were well aware that it was not recommended, but did not see – whatever Beattie might have believed – that it was their job to express any concern to the management. They did what they were paid to do as well or as badly as they were allowed to do it.[107]

The quality of the wrought iron used for the girders was excellent (so good that they were saved and re-used in the replacement bridge), but the cast-iron for the piers and iron for the bolts was not. Hopkins Gilkes supplied the iron to the Cleveland Bolt and Nut Company (more or less across the street from their own works in Middlesbrough) to manufacture the bolts for the Tay Bridge. The Bolt Company had such a good reputation that it had received a two-year commission to supply bolts to the Indian State Railways. Cleveland worked with different categories and qualities of iron. In a very British grading of quality, they worked with ordinary Cleveland iron, best iron, then best, best iron, then best, best, best iron; and beyond best, best, best iron there was Low Moor iron – which nothing else surpassed and which had been specified for the Tay Bridge.[108] Cleveland rejected the first delivery of bolt iron from Gilkes as 'the reverse of satisfactory'. Later supplies were found too short and one was 'totally unfit for purpose'.[109] Unlike those being dispatched to India, none of the bolts supplied to the Tay Bridge ever reached even the lowest 'best' quality. Despite the specification, profoundly ordinary Cleveland would do for Scotland.

Two foot-six-inch-long iron bolts of the unusual dimension of one and an eighth inches in diameter were required to bolt together the cast-iron parts of each column. For these, Cleveland needed a different supplier, and bought the iron from Jaques & Co. next door. But as they were making the bolts, Jaques's iron was discovered to be worse than that supplied by Gilkes. Instead of rejecting it, they used it because, as the Bolt Company's Head Clerk testified, its manager had been bribed by Jaques to do so.[110] The Bolt Company's work-force took much greater care when 'under inspection' by the client – like, for example, the inspectors from the Indian State Railways. They virtually lived on site, and were on the premises sometimes every day, testing bolt quality by hammering sample bolts to destruction on the anvil.[111] Nobody ever crossed the street from Hopkins Gilkes to do likewise. So the bolts being dispatched to India were 'decidedly better' than those going north.[112]

What emerged at the Inquiry, therefore, was that Allan Stewart's calculations and the enormous factor of safety that had been built into the design were challenged by design modifications that made the bridge top heavy and insufficiently braced, and by sometimes poor materials and shoddy workmanship. Although they may have contributed to the bridge's collapse once it had been hit by the train, none were likely to be the sole cause. Bouch's view was that 'imperfections of material and workmanship exist in all large struc-tures, and so far as they are known to exist here, they do not materially affect the strength'. This view was widely shared.[113]

Pressure from the railway company to open the line was enor-mous. The bridge was late, the tunnel through Dundee was also running late as a result of some Tom Harrison modifications, as was the connection running south to Leuchars Junction. By 1876, moreover, the entire contract sum had long been spent.[114] Even had the foundations not failed, the repeated extensions of time blamed on the weather implies that the original timescale had made insufficient allowance for inclement weather. Unluckily for the NBR, the weather in the 1870s had been unusually severe – gales in August, storms in autumn, howling winds in winter and ice floes. Irritated and anxious shareholders were desperate that the North British complete the Tay Bridge as soon as it could, rather than stretch its resources any further. So any suspicion that it was colluding with the Forth Bridge Company was anathema. The Directors did not quite appreciate their mood. When the Forth Bridge Company next met in the North British Offices, chaired (like the Tay Bridge Undertaking) by Provost James Cox himself,[115] it minuted 'it only requires time to remove every prejudice'.[116] He was doing the shareholders an injustice. They were not inflamed by mere prejudice. The North British's commitment of £134,000 capital toward the Forth Bridge was contained in the newly published North British Railway (Fife Railways) Act; and the Tay Bridge was already over two years behind its original schedule with no end in sight.

On 21 July 1876, Gilkes appealed to Bouch for more money. He was probably already suffering from the grave cash flow problems that would lead to receivership and restructuring in 1880. Despite overtime running at 38%, it had taken him five weeks for the most recent 245-foot girder to be 'got together', floated out and raised up – 'even after cutting down every operation to the narrowest limits of time'. The weather had been so rough that the barges carrying concrete out to fill the caissons had spent most of their time storm bound. If the last girder was really to be floated by the end of June 1877, Gilkes had to deliver, erect, float and lift one girder per month with certainty, *regardless of weather* and other obstacles. Eighteen hundred tons of girder work remained to be done on which they had to pay 15 shillings more wages per ton. It was impossible unless he could buy steam-powered machinery (principally cranes) at a cost of £1000. He added: 'Necessary additions have forced themselves into notice, providing artificial light, extra lifting girders etc. I know you *do* give us credit for doing our best to forward the work.'[117] Gilkes's idea was that if Paterson, as resident engineer, certified the cost of the new machinery for payment under the contract as though it were work completed, he would then buy it. Even if the new plant were agreed, it would still take six weeks to get it ready for use on site. 'Every day lost now', he warned, would represent two lost when winter fell.

Bouch was in a quandary. As the Company's engineer, he would be liable for any costs or delay attributable to the design. His hasty redesign had introduced so many complications in fittings, with so few standard elements, that slower work had been a necessary consequence, and at the point when Gilkes's tender had been accepted, this had not been foreseen. Moreover, he was now a major shareholder in Hopkins Gilkes, having recently inherited his brother William's £40,000 shareholding.[118] After an emergency meeting in the site engineer's office, Paterson, as resident engineer, wrote to Kippendavie that same night, explaining that exceptionally inclement weather had retarded the heaviest part of the work considerably, by disarranging the apparatus for filling the larger caissons with concrete. Only steam machinery would retrieve the situation, and the engineers recommended that the Company should contribute 50% of the cost of it. Bouch later demurred privately. Since the contractor was at least partly to blame for the delay, he wrote to suggest that the Company would be better to offer a bonus for speedy completion of the bridge. After all, it had worked with Gilkes in Deepdale. Gilkes himself wanted to be remunerated at time-and-a-quarter, full stop.[119]

There was something distinctly odd about this correspondence. The Tay Bridge Undertaking was meant to be a separate entity chaired by James Cox, Kippendavie being, theoretically, only one of a number of shareholder representatives on it. These negotiations removed that fig leaf. The Tay Bridge Company was but a financial arrangement, and all operational decisions were in fact being taken by the North British Railway. On 27 July 1876, the NBR Board decided to accept none of the options, but to offer the contractor a bonus of £2000 if a mineral train could cross the bridge on 1 September 1877.[120] That was all. Kippendavie wrote to Bouch: 'It is not quite what Gilkes was asking for, but it is rather better for him as we get no part of the cost of the plant returned to us.'[121]

Part of Bouch's duty was to ensure efficient delivery of materials – particularly rails, chairs and sleepers, but he was not as proficient at this as he should have been. John Waddell, the contractor for the connection to Leuchars Junction, became testy and warned Bouch in May that the station at St Fort could not be ready until the end of the year through lack of materials. He was quite content to go to arbitration about it.[122] In July, he wrote that he had been delayed by a further month 'for want of a wagon load of spikes', and again in September. Therefore, because the company had failed to supply him with fish bolts, chairs and other permanent way material, the railway, he wrote, 'cannot open'.[123]

Although he got to keep the new plant provided that he stayed in business, Gilkes did not regard the North British's offer as 'proportioned to the extra risk and cost';[124] but he now increased the pressure on the site team to deliver on time. The yard, the foundry and the bridge worked day and night. It may be no coincidence that about this time, Henry Noble was asked to provide furtive progress reports directly to John Stirling of Kippendavie, presumably behind Bouch's back.[125] A miserable litany of adverse weather – severe gales in February, stormy weather in May (leading to a loss of three-and-a-half days' work) and even worse in the first week of June – alternated with notes on construction targets and employment. The construction gang had been increased to 446 people, although it varied up and down week on week.[126] Grothe illuminated night work in the girder assembly yard by two Serrins lamps powered by the foundry fixed to two sentry boxes. Fitted with parabolic reflectors, they produced the light of 1000 candles, allowing work to proceed 'with nearly the same ease as in the day time, and on a dark night, you can read the time on a watch at nearly two miles distant'.[127] What could be accelerated was accelerated, erection practices were scrutinised, and corners were cut.

Frank Beattie had had enough. He obtained the post of Manager at the Moorhouse Bridge Works in Birmingham, leaving the Tay Bridge 'on the worst possible terms' with Grothe. Much of it was personal. Beattie had been outraged by Grothe's article on the Tay Bridge in *Good Words*, in which he had attributed the invention of the sand pump solely to Frederick Reeves (repaying a friendship forged in Russia). Even when Beattie presented him with the evidence of his joint patent, Grothe had refused to retract. But Beattie had deeper concerns about construction safety being compromised in the haste to erect girders. The hydraulic machine Beattie had invented for lifting the girders presupposed that all six columns of the piers were in place before the girder was placed on top of them. It was quicker, however, to erect the girder before the two outer raking columns and bracing were in place, and Grothe had decided that it was perfectly safe to do so. Alarmed about what could happen in a heavy gale, Beattie travelled down to Middlesbrough to ask Gilkes to intervene, but Gilkes had no option but to support his chief engineer. Beattie then sought out Bouch, who was ill and recuperating in Italy, and then Cox who had no locus in site operations. When later asked to present evidence to the Inquiry, Beattie replied that what he knew about site practices was far too painful and unprofessional to put in writing,[128] and that he would only reveal it if the source of the information was kept confidential.[129]

A storm was to decide whether Grothe or Beattie was right. The contractors had done 'all that would quicken the work, and we were sanguine – so good had been the rate of progress – that we should complete the bridge by September 1'[130] when Nature struck on the night of 2 February 1877. Fifty-four men were working on the dark, lamp-illuminated girders a mile out to sea when a storm burst so savagely that Gilkes's steamer was unable to reach the men in time. When William Delpratt requisitioned the much larger steam ferry *Excelsior* out from Dundee Harbour, the gale tossed it about 'in the most alarming fashion', and its paddles were fouled by the quantities of planking and other debris blown off the bridge works. Despite its engines being on 'full ahead', the steamer was blown astern, and the men on the bridge remained marooned. Seeing the ship's lights receding, and faced with perhaps hours of being buffeted by a winter's storm on what was effectively a metal scaffold, they desperately sought shelter in the timber bothy they had constructed on one of the recently erected girders. 'It was their impression that if they got into the bothy and kindled a fire, they would be more safe and comfortable than on a girder.' Their fore-man, Charles McKinney, feared that the gale could blow the bothy off its girder and forbade them to shelter inside it. Moments later, the two most recently erected girders crashed into the sea with bothy attached. Most of the workmen were unscathed, but a piece of column came down on McKinney's foot, nearly severing it. By the time they were all rescued by *Excelsior* – at 5am, eight hours later – McKinney 'did not know whether my foot was off or not, as I had scarcely feeling in it, being so benumbed with cold'.[131]

Grothe and Gilkes claimed that when the gale suddenly sprung up, it caused the half-erected, suspended girders 'to vibrate con-siderably . . . hanging on the raising apparatus . . . and it would appear from the position in which the fallen girders are found lying, they must have wrought themselves out of position and canted eastwards, smashing in their fall the columns of the piers on which they were hanging'. The story of the girders still hanging from the lifting apparatus before the storm blew them away was accepted by the Inquiry. Beattie differed. The girders had been fully erected and fixed in their final position, which was why the men's bothy had been attached to their top, but the piers lacked their sup-porting east and west raking columns. If the girders had just been blown off the erection apparatus, they would have fallen vertically into the sea. Instead, both girders and columns had fallen some way downstream – at roughly the same distance from the bridge as the High Girders after the disaster, demonstrating the extent to which the entire pier had toppled in the absence of its bracing columns.[132] Beattie's version is the more credible. He left for Birmingham, writing that 'had I chosen to submit to a system of ruthlessness and irregularity, I should probably have remained to the close'.[133] Corner-cutting had proved as counter-productive to the erection process as it would be to the bridge's stability.

The firm of Hopkins Gilkes had been working on a 24-hour cycle to make the bonus it needed, and the collapse of the two southern High Girders was a desperate blow. One girder was dam-

aged beyond repair and, left by Gilkes, was eventually blown up by
Noble who had to make a surreptitious trip to Dundee to obtain
dynamite from quarries and transport it covertly back to the bridge
works, for there was a heavy penalty 'if it is known you are carrying it [dynamite] through a town'.[134] The other girder was
eventually lifted aboard the freighter *Olanna* and shipped down to
Gilkes's Middlesbrough works for examination. After it arrived in
early May, Gilkes informed Kippendavie that the 1 September
deadline was no longer possible. However, if he would agree to one
entirely new girder, and the straightening out of the rescued one,
infilled where necessary by new iron, a date somewhere in
September remained possible. It was a costly way of proceeding and
Gilkes sought an increase of bonus to £4000, together with a contribution to absolute loss of £3000.

From their Edinburgh vantage, the Forth Bridge directors were
naturally concerned at the events on the Tay, and concluded that it
would be prudent to delay on the Forth until the Tay Bridge was
open and successful, and then raise capital for their own venture.[135]
At a secret negotiation with Gilkes in Edinburgh, Kippendavie
agreed to a bonus of 4000 guineas if the bridge were open for a
train of forty loaded coal wagons on 15 September: nothing else.
After a fortnight's deliberation and, presumably, with heavy sighs,
Gilkes agreed, with the caveat 'trusting to your usual consideration
should we be a day or two out in our calculations'.[136] So, after
much Procrustes-like work, the first High Girder was suitably
straightened out, patched up, bits replaced, and shipped back up
again to form the southernmost of the High Girders. The progressive distortion noticeable during this girder's short life implies that
it had been fundamentally weakened by its February fall.

A fortnight before the contractual train was due to pass over the
bridge, the former USA President, General Ulysses S. Grant, paid
a visit. American presidents were supporters of nation building
achieved through railways, and Grant had been a particular supporter of both the United Pacific Railway, built by one of his
former officers, and of the Brooklyn Bridge.[137] He had made a
detour to see the Tay Bridge which was over four times longer than

The completed Tay Bridge viewed from the north. You can just make out, in the foreground, the esplanade on the left, not yet entirely filled in, and the sad remnant of Dundee's fine beaches marooned by the railway on the right.

Brooklyn, although less complicated in its structure. After sailing around it to the strains of the Canadian Boat Song from 'the juvenile crew' of the naval training ship *Mars*, Grant was taken by Cox to the contractor's offices in Wormit, where Grothe gave one of his speeches supported by little models, followed by lunch and toasts. Bouch was absent, giving the rather feeble excuse that there was insufficient room for him. Grant was polite but typically taciturn. The party was ferried back to Dundee where they clambered onto the viaduct and walked across as far as they could (the ladies going by rail), then back to Dundee to catch the ferry from Broughty Ferry to Tayport and on to Burntisland.[138] Apart from proposing a toast to Cox and his wife, Grant's only recorded comments on the structure were: 'It's a very big bridge.'

Public interest in the bridge, fostered by Grothe, had always been high – it was already viewed as a potential tourist attraction – and sometimes took the form of people jaywalking along the top. About a week before completion, Grothe was alerted by his men that two strangers were picking their way over the bridge. It turned out to be two of his directors, Peter Macintyre and James Yeaman

MP, sauntering across the viaduct and threading a path over single planks in the as yet unfloored High Girders. Grothe chided his paymasters for setting a bad example; but invited members of the Dundee Working Men's Club to do likewise once the flooring was complete the following week.[139] The escapade emphasised, however, how symbolic of progress and modernity the bridge was. Yeaman and Macintyre had felt perfectly safe since this man-made structure had conquered the fearsome Tay basin.

A special train left Edinburgh at 9.40am on Tuesday 25 September, carrying the Directors of both the North British and the Tay Bridge Undertaking. At noon, with an engine fore and aft, it steamed out to the middle of the bridge for a photocall by the antiquarian Alexander Lamb. It then completed the crossing, stopping at Dundee's new Esplanade on the north side to be greeted by thousands of spectators. The journey had taken twelve minutes. The Directors expressed great satisfaction and welcomed ninety-six guests to lunch in the neo-classical splendour of the Thistle Hall of Dundee's Royal Hotel. The previous Friday, Grothe had organised a ball for all the engineers and their wives in Dundee's Blyth Hall.[140] There were fireworks on the bridge that night.[141] Typically, Bouch was at neither.

The North British's railway bridge was adopted as a symbol of Dundee itself, and a blessedly anonymous poet submitted another effusion to the *Dundee Courier and Argus*:

> *Firm, firm, firm,*
> *The bridge o'er the Tay now stands;*
> *Firm, firm, firm,*
> *With its caissons sunk deep in the sands.*
> *And fast, fast, fast,*
> *O'er its whole length, two miles and more,*
> *The trains fly along, while their thundering song*
> *Re-echoes from shore to shore.*[142]

How had the engineering profession taken to the bridge? The Cleveland Institute of Engineers, whose first President had been

William Bouch, had made 'the finest and most successful [excursion] in the annals of the Institution' to see it the previous August, which had been followed by a paper on the bridge to the Institution delivered by Gilkes. The President introduced him like this: 'I have rarely visited works where there was such an amount of original method bestowed upon the various operations performed. Nature appears to have offered the minimum of advantages, but Mr Gilkes and his staff, left to their own resources, have attacked and vanquished these difficulties in a way which is most creditable to them.'[143]

CHAPTER FIVE

The Abbreviated Life of the First Tay Bridge

'Vain, vain are all works of mankind!'

THEODOR FONTANE

The crossing of the North British's contractual train may have secured Gilkes's bonus[1] and given the shareholders a sense of achievement and relief; but the bridge was not yet ready to open for passengers, and Gilkes was still to lodge a claim for additional payment.[2] The bridge also had to be transformed from a makeshift structure carrying goods trains into a fully bolted-up structure allowed to carry passengers. So it had to satisfy the Government Inspector. 'There was no higher authority,' as the *Scotsman* put it loftily, 'no more scientific or practical authority' than General Charles Hutchinson.[3]

Since there were no precedents for a bridge of this scale, Hutchinson studied the contract drawings in minute detail[4] and between 25 and 27 February 1878 he set about testing foundations, settlement, deflection and oscillation, and workmanship. Six 73-ton linked goods engines, combined into a moving object 291 feet long weighing 438 tons, were instructed to parade across the bridge – either stopping and starting like chunky iron horses at a dressage, or galloping at speeds up to 40mph. A similar performance took place on each girder *in seriatim* whilst Hutchinson's team recorded any movement at the top of each column by using a theodolite. On the third day, Bouch, Gilkes and Grothe joined Hutchinson upon one of the piers (presumably in their overcoats, it being February). They clambered up, each to embrace an iron column to see if they could feel any vibration as the trains pounded overhead. Hutchinson was then put in a harness and hoisted up inside the piers to the very top, so that he could observe both workmanship and movement. The structure proved 'much stiffer than I thought it would be'.[5]

Later, doubtless informed by hindsight since his judgement was under question, General Hutchinson revealed that he had been uneasy about the narrowness of the base of the bridge, and worried lest a racking motion at the top might loosen the structure. He appreciated that Bouch had allowed for such loosening by providing triangular cast-iron iron wedges (called gibs and cotters) that needed to be hammered in to tighten the structure up (although he did not comment on cast-iron's propensity to fracture when hammered sharply). He also felt disadvantaged that the unnaturally clement February weather had prevented him witnessing how the bridge might perform in a storm or high wind. Hutchinson's hardly ringing endorsement was that the bridge was 'not insufficient if everything was thoroughly good and made as solid and substantial as possible'.[6] It depended upon sound construction. Moreover, the bridge required constant maintenance to keep it appropriately tensioned.

He reported to the Board of Trade that the bridge had passed his inspection with only a few minor repairs and some tightening up; the painting of the bridge white to minimise the effect of expansion and contraction, and the insertion of iron crossbars to prevent the rails from moving closer to each other. He also imposed a maximum speed limit of 24 miles per hour to prevent any racking motion from developing. The speed restriction was irrelevant. Had he enquired, he would have found out that North British trains did not have speedometers at that period, and speed was generally gauged by distance and stopwatches.[7]

Tempted by the glitter of a royal opening, the North British Railway Company took soundings from Sir Robert Anstruther MP and the Earl of Strathmore who had the royal ear. Strathmore duly wrote to the Prince of Wales enclosing an enticing photograph of the bridge, with the suggestion that 'so great a monument to the engineering skill of the age' deserved regal recognition.[8] However, because the finished bridge stood isolated between unfinished railway lines, a royal opening was thought inappropriate. But the achievement was palpable. Frank Beattie wrote to congratulate Thomas Bouch on 'the success of building the cheapest bridge in the world'.[9]

The Tay Bridge remained marooned between the incomplete tunnel through Dundee and the unfinished connecting railway to Leuchars Junction.[10] There had been delays in the latter contract in deciding whether turnpike roads should be crossed by level crossings or by bridges (a matter of cost weighed against just how steeply horse-and-carriages could travel down and up in short distances); and frequent complaints from proprietors who, of course, had expected a quality job but found the contrary. Lord Dundee complained irritably that his roads were in a very bad state with the metalling incomplete, and the work was imperfect. His neighbour was barely able to use her road, and in the last nine months nothing had been done to remedy the problem.[11] The overwhelming impression is of indifferent contract management by Bouch. Weiland, the North British secretary, had the habit of writing to chase him, waiting for six weeks before writing again.

Waddell was encountering comparable dilatoriness and procrastination on the Arbroath–Montrose line, where he was building the track and Gilkes the bridges. In October 1879, he complained to Bouch that the work 'was being very much kept back for want of plans and instructions' particularly for the approaches to the shore at the north end of the iron viaduct at Montrose, under Bouch's son William's responsibility.[12] Waddell regarded the Bouch office inefficient, and repudiated any blame for late completion.[13] A measure of his deteriorating relationship with the company is that instead of attending the formal opening of the Tay Bridge in May

1878, Waddell went to Paris instead, and that week his solicitors submitted a claim for an additional £2500.[14]

Hutchinson's report on the Tay Bridge was delivered to the Board of Trade just in time to influence a Parliamentary hearing called to examine a new petition from the Caledonian Railway against the Forth Bridge. The Forth Bridge had been budgeted to cost £1.25 million, and its statute required it to return 6% minimum or £75,000 per annum.[15] The North British and the Midland had finally persuaded the other two great English railways who fed into the north-east – the Great Northern and the North Eastern – to join in a guarantee of a minimum amount of traffic over the Forth Bridge. They would, between them, pay a commuted annual toll sufficient to provide the Bridge Company with its required return. Since any traffic going north of Edinburgh that avoided the ferries currently had to use the Caledonian's rails, this new agreement would take the English traffic away from the Caledonian which, feeling under threat, represented this proposal to Parliament as anti-competitive. 'The North Eastern Company at present sends its traffic by the route which gives the best terms, but as soon as the Bill is passed, the North Eastern Company will become a partner in the Forth Bridge Company, and therefore will send the whole traffic now going over the Caledonian line, or which might hereafter be sent over that line, over the Forth Bridge.'[16] The Caledonian claimed that it would still have to run its connecting services for such traffic even if it were all diverted over the Forth Bridge. The North British passed off the Caledonian's fears as exaggerated, and the bill was duly passed.

When the Tay Bridge and connecting lines opened, all manner of adjustments followed. Some administrative personnel and goods traffic transferred from the old East Station (the original 1842 Dundee/Arbroath station) to the new Dundee Tay Bridge station, leading to some redundancies including twenty-two porters,[17] and to changes in ticketing arrangements. The NBR chief engineer, James Bell, was anxious to assimilate the management and maintenance for the new track and bridge within the broader NBR network, and needed an accurate set of Bouch's plans of the Tay

Bridge to do so.[18] It was 'absolutely necessary', he told General Manager John Walker, that he be provided with plans showing the depth of each pier, and the extent of rubble protecting it. From the emphasis, Bell evidently shared Bouch's perception that if the bridge was vulnerable at all, it would be in the adequacy of the foundations resisting the scour of the river. Walker's response was unexpected. He decided to keep the bridge's maintenance out of Bell's portfolio and contract it out to Bouch for the next nine or twelve months at least, for which the latter would be paid a fee of 100 guineas per annum (which Weiland, most atypically, paid in advance).[19] His maintenance staff were also all paid directly by the NBR, and even the painting of the bridge would come under Bouch's direction. Walker's concluding instruction that Bell should not 'trouble to communicate' with Bouch[20] implies either ill-feeling or anxiety on Bouch's part about his foundations. Hearing that Bouch had retained the maintenance contract for the Tay Bridge, Frank Beattie down in Birmingham wondered whether he might be offered a post in Bouch's office combining the mainte-nance of the Tay Bridge with the construction of the Forth. His prior experience on the Tay, and his last two years' experience in large spans and lifting machinery appropriate to the 'economical building of the large spans of the Forth' made him the ideal candi-date. He was dreadfully hurt when Bouch replied suggesting that he remain in his current 'respectable post' in Birmingham.[21]

At the head of Bouch's maintenance staff was Noble, appointed Inspector of the Tay Bridge. With his previous experience on the Thames Embankment, he would be perfectly capable of assessing the foundations. Under him there were fireman Neish, boatman Bell and lamplighter McKinney. When Walker sought to retrench on maintenance staff costs, he was rebuffed by Bouch. 'Two of the men are fully employed every day in tightening and renewing nuts and washers of the bolts which secure the way beams on which the permanent rails are laid. Another is employed tightening fish-plates, bolts and keys. The whole number of men employed is five. This number for two miles of railway is only about the average.'[22] Only once the bridge had settled down, did he agree to retrench. But

there was a flaw in this plan. Chief Engineer Bell remained responsible for the track itself, whereas Bouch was responsible for the
structure that held it up, and the two regimes neither overlapped
nor communicated. Bouch never appears to have been made aware
when the rails in the first girder – the one that had collapsed in the
sea and was then patched up – began to twist as the girder itself
began to deform.

The bridge was finally opened to public traffic on 31 May 1878
with ceremonial trains and ceremonial ferries, a mighty procession
and a feast. To the ringing of St Mary's church bells, and preceded
by halberds and Cox's Camperdown Works Band, 600 gentlemen
paraded through Dundee to the Albert Institute, and up the great
staircase into the Free Library hall where an afternoon banquet and
lengthy speeches awaited. The Provost announced that that very
morning, the Town Council had conferred the freedom of the
burgh (virtually an honorary burgess-ship) upon both Kippendavie
and Bouch. Kippendavie was delighted, but Bouch was absent.
George Weiland informed the throng that he was in the south of
England 'with a view to recruiting his health which stood in much
need of it'.[23] Bouch's diary just says that he took a day's holiday.
Communal joviality impelled the Chairman of the Caledonian,
probably well in his cups, to pledge perpetual friendship and an end
to all injurious competition. Although the Earl of Elgin, speaking
for many, was relieved to see 'very frequently bitter opponents
shaking hands', he was deluding himself if he thought it would last.

The celebratory speeches revealed much about the Zeitgeist;
about modernity, trade, railways, and the position that Dundee
could now carve for itself in the new Scotland. With all of its
unparalleled improvements, Cox said, it had virtually become a
new town. Amidst all the congratulation, Kippendavie admitted:
'There is no doubt that the North British Directors had a very anxious time of it for the last twelve years. When I had the honour of
being appointed Chairman . . . the Company was almost in a state
of bankruptcy . . . made up of five or six different Companies none
of which were eminently prosperous. The plant of every company
was different. Even the rails on each section were different.' Success

had come at the expense of a very large amount of work. To Cox, Kippendavie had this to say. 'As for the Tay Bridge, it is a special pet child of his own. I believe he has thought of it, and dreamt of it and nothing else for these last ten years and I am very glad to congratulate him on the birth of his pet child today.'

In his reply, Cox reiterated the point made so strongly by John Leng back in 1863. 'Instead of being shunted into a siding, Dundee will find itself in the direct line of through communication.'[24] He had never deviated from that goal. As a way of public celebration, Kippendavie promised to illuminate the High Girders during the Dundee Fair. Picking up Bouch's confident statement that the Forth Bridge would be ready in three years' time (1881),[25] he added however: 'I do trust . . . that many of the gentlemen I see here today will be at the opening ceremony of the Forth Bridge.'[26] The Forth Bridge, however, did not open until 1890, and Bouch, Kippendavie and Cox were all dead.

When the Queen was eventually tempted to cross the bridge on the way home from Balmoral the following year, the Council decided to make an event of it, and invited the engineer.[27] He, typically, declined (his diary says, tersely, 'holiday') – although he was happy to travel to Buckingham Palace at the end of the June to receive his knighthood. The *Scotsman*, an ardent supporter of the North British, reported that the flags which Dundee hung out, the crowds of her citizens who gathered, and their hearty cheers, were all 'intentionally or unintentionally tributes to the skill, the intelligence, the indomitable perseverance and unwearied industry of those who built the bridge'.[28] But it cautioned that without the Forth Bridge, the Tay Bridge remained incomplete, and 'upon the Tay Bridge there have been engaged men whose invaluable services must not be lost . . .'

They were lost. The construction team disbanded. A number went to work on the Arbroath–Montrose line, the last link in the East/West Coast route joining the main line into Aberdeen at a junction called Kinnaber, not far north of Montrose. Two railway bridges were needed across the mouth of Montrose's tidal basin and the river South Esk, supervised by Bouch's son William, and built by Gilkes. The Tay Bridge iron inspector McBeath now oversaw the casting of the columns for the viaduct at Lunan Bay. Underlining the internationalism of Victorian engineering, most engineers spread further afield: De Breugn left for India, Wemyss for South Australia, and Camphuis went to work with the exotic Aqueous Works and Rock Diamond Boring Company. Reeves found a post with the Royal Portuguese Railways in Lisbon and Grothe was offered the post of General Manager of the Great Tharsis Sulphur and Copper Co in southern Spain in November 1878. He took the Delpratts with him. Grothe's departure was mourned in Dundee. John Leng wrote, 'Thousands who have enjoyed the privilege of Mr Grothe's delightful lectures on the Tay Bridge, spectrum analysis, and other scientific subjects will join with us in congratulating Mr Grothe',[29] and chaired a farewell dinner for him in the British Hotel.[30] Gilkes himself finally quit the site and Dundee on 15 January 1879.[31]

From his tenement flat on a steep cobbled street leading down to Magdalen Green, a native self-declared genius seized upon the new bridge as both his inspiration and his opportunity. William McGonagall was an Edinburgh-born hand-loom weaver who had moved to Dundee (for that was where the work was to be had in mid-Victorian Scotland) and he and his family stayed at No. 19 Paton's Lane. The Tay Bridge was being constructed virtually at its foot. There was nothing particularly unusual in a Scottish industrial poet. The weavers of Paisley were celebrated for their poets, best known of whom had been the tragically suicidal Robert Tannahill. Poetry (or at least rhyme) flourished in mid-nineteenth-century Dundee as the full boxes in the local history library testify. The poet Hugh MacDiarmid thought this unsurprising. 'Dundee was then and has since been the great home and fostering centre of the cheapest popular literature in Scotland, and huge fortunes have been built up there precisely on the chief ingredients of McGonagall's art.'[32] McGonagall, however, had an uncharacteristic myopic arrogance. This gaunt, stringy and obsessive man regarded himself as a born-again full-blown bard, with need neither for apprenticeship nor practice to refine or evolve his eccentric craft.

An autodidact, writing in language derived from Shakespeare and the Bible that was striking for both its breadth and its unsuitability, the quiddities of his first poems are those of his last. MacDiarmid, a genuinely great poet, judged McGonagall not a great bad poet, but not a poet at all. He concluded that where McGonagall differed from other working-class poets 'was that he knew nothing of poetry – not even of the execrable models they copied, nothing of the whole debased tradition'. Instead, he characterised McGonagall's output thus:

> Having once performed the miraculous feat of knocking a bit of journalese into rough rhyming verses, he naturally conceived an inordinate admiration for his own powers – and so far as any question of comparative worth arose it naturally seemed to his type of mind, with its almost inconceivably complete absence of intellectual background, that this was only a question of one man's opinion against another.[33]

What made McGonagall unique was that he willingly adopted the role of jester in Dundee, with its necessary consequence of periodic humiliation, in order to satisfy his craving to be a poet, for he had learnt early that his greatest success was a butt for the mirth of others. Even when humiliated, if he thought there was money in it, he always returned for more, like a dog to its vomit. Worse, convinced of his place in history, he commissioned a ghosted autobiography. *The Book of Lamentations* was written by a thirty-five-year-old commercial traveller and Robert Burns aficionado, John Willocks,[34] and he turned it into an elaborate parody of McGonagall's life and his style of writing – which McGonagall then denounced and threatened to sue.[35] Yet it was so close to McGonagall's own admitted autobiography in content and style[36] that Willocks's only crime must have been the temptation to embellish cruelly, adding aspects of his unsatisfactory personal life to which the poet objected. It was dedicated to 'himself – knowing none greater,' and opened, with true McGonagallian modesty, 'Like most great men, I was born at a very early period of my

William McGonagall, portrayed on the cover of his *Lamentations* in full theatrical fig.

existence.' The cover was adorned with a drawing of McGonagall in spurious Highland garb – targe (shield), underscaled sword, feathered bonnet and dancing pumps – above a far from friendly verse scribed by the anonymous 'Lochee Lubricator' in a parody of the 'Burial of Sir John Moore at Corunna' blended with Carroll's 'Hunting of the Snark':

> *No useless trouser encircled his groin*
> *But in bonnet and tights we found him*
> *And he stood like a modest tobacconist sign*
> *With his tartan curtain around him.*

The Book of Lamentations contains a meticulous record of every slur and snub endured by McGonagall once he had adopted the tragic role of a bard.

In the saga of the Tay Bridge, McGonagall had the part of the chorus. On the Monday of the June 1877 Dundee Fair, he had been left on his own, 'hungry, penniless, and altogether unutterably miserable',[37] by his family; in which state of despondency, he was visited by the Muse of Poesy:

> I felt a delightful sensation of heat all around the soles of my feet, which increased so much in intensity that I started up, wide awake, amazed at the peculiar feeling. Bye and bye, in circling sinuosities, like the twining of a warm snake, the strange like caloric percolated upwards, and encircled my loins as with a girdle. Pausing there for a brief space, and filling my wondering soul with never-to-be-forgotten-awe, it speedily monopolised my entire frame, which anon glowed like a furnace.

A voice then thundered 'Write! Write! Write!' so he indited a poem to the celebrated Dundee evangelical minister, the Rev. George Gilfillan. Perhaps incautiously, it was published in the *Weekly News*.

So sure was he of his future as a bard that, to the consternation of his wife, he quit his trade as a hand-loom weaver to give public recitals, enactments and displays in cheap theatres and pubs in the manner of a working man's Henry Irving – largely to audiences of working men like him. The rhythm of his poetry, after all, is far less ghastly when recited and enacted rather than read. The author William Power dubbed him 'the Ossian of the ineffably absurd' after seeing him perform in Glasgow. Armed

> with the most dangerous-looking broadsword, [he] strode up and down the platform declaiming 'Clarence's Dream' and 'Give me another horse – Bind up my wounds'. His voice rose to a howl. He thrust and slashed at imaginary foes. A shower of apples and oranges fell on the platform. Almost before they touched it, they were met by the fell edge of McGonagall's claymore and cut to pieces. The Bard was beaded with perspiration and orange juice. The audience yelled with delight.[38]

Willocks recorded that his spouse was sceptical. When pointing out the skyline of the Old Town of Edinburgh to his practical wife as 'the fairest spot on earth', she replied: 'It's guid enough, Willie, but naething to mak' a song about. We canna live on scenery, an' up till noo we hivna lived michty fat on poetry.'[39] She then recommended, to his fury, that he got a job as a railway porter or a sandwich man.

Encouraged, and seized 'by divine afflatus', McGonagall set about what he thought was his best poem 'The Bridge over the Silvery Tay' – inspired by the structure dominant at the foot of his street. Chased from his house in Paton's Lane one day for using the fire bellows to write a poem on, McGonagall dashed off an *Address to the Railway Bridge over the Silvery Tay*, and submitted it to the *Dundee Weekly News*. The editor, finding it too long to publish in full, published three stanzas of a seven-stanza poem, beginning with what was to become the most celebrated:

> *Beautiful railway bridge of the silvery Tay*
> *With your numerous arches and pillars, in so grand array,*
> *And your centre girders which seems, to the eye*

To be almost towering to the sky.
The greatest wonder of the day
And a great beautification to the river Tay;
Most beautiful to be seen
Near by Dundee and the Magdalen Green.

The Rev. George Gilfillan (who was a considerable poetry buff, having published so popular an edition of Burns's poems that it was known as the *Gilfillan Burns*) observed of McGonagall's outburst: 'Shakespeare never wrote anything like this.' The poet took that as a compliment.

McGonagall then wrote to ex-Provost James Cox. 'I beg to be excused for writing to you to inform you that I am the author of the Tay Bridge poetical address. dear [*sic*] Sir, my first attempt at writing poetry was the Gilfillan Address and both of these were published in the *Dundee Weekly News* and highly appreciated by the Editor.' McGonagall was seeking patronage – both to subsidise the publication of the full poem, and to be allowed to walk across the bridge. The language of his poems seeped into his letter: 'I am only a poor handloom Weaver, and has [*sic*] suffered very much for a long time, and I have never had the opportunity yet of taking a walk along the beautiful railway Bridge of the silvery Tay – because I am rather seedy in bodily array.' Since a rejection would never have been omitted from the *Lamentations* and later poems praise ex-Provost Cox, he must have received some satisfaction.

The bridge was about to be painted. General Hutchinson had been concerned about the effects of heat expansion on an iron bridge two miles long,[40] and had required it to be painted white to counteract it. Bouch now returned to the Board of Trade seeking to paint it black for reasons of expediency, and they compromised on brown as an interim temporary measure. Instead of local people, Bouch then appointed Robert Bamlett of Sunderland as painting contractor, presumably because Bamlett was cheapest. Indeed he was. Rather than selecting experienced painters, Bamlett employed unemployed welders, divers, mechanics, moulders and even mill overseers: the only criteria being agility – the ability to scramble up the diagonal bracing bars as ladders – and no fear of heights.[41] Two squads of fifteen painters, each with an overseer (neither skilled) began painting on 24 June 1879, and continued until early November. Edward Simpson, the ex-soldier gaffer for the southern section, was expected to tell Noble if his men found anything wrong, but of the individual painters, only one – Neilson – later agreed with the Inquiry that he had had any duty to report anything unusual. The painters informed the Inquiry they had seen empty rivet holes, loose tie-bars, cracked columns and a great deal of debris but 'we see it was better to hold our tongues'.[42] Noble had also spotted a few cracked columns and, having notified Bouch, duly bound them with hoops of iron.

Trains, in the meantime, were flying over the bridge. Travelling northbound, the bridge's summit was part way through the High Girders, and the drivers clearly relished that it was downhill all the way thereafter. Observers noted how express passenger trains, particularly when running late, used the bridge to make up time. Whenever the painters, high on their girders, spotted the Newport to Dundee Ferry steaming ahead before the morning commuter train entered the bridge, they knew very well that they would have to hang on for dear life as the train raced the steamer to Dundee. It was two years since the bridge had opened for heavy coal wagon traffic, and the bridge would now *prance* and move in waves as the train left each span of the High Girders – but particularly the first one. The painters would lash all their paint pots to the structure, and make ready to cling on, for the movement was sufficient to shift a full, heavy paint pot several inches. John Neilsen judged that the prancing of the bridge got progressively worse, reaching 'an up and down motion of nine inches in my judgement' for which he blamed passenger trains travelling far faster than 25mph.[43] A commission agent, T.D. Baxter, became progressively so uneasy as he crossed the bridge each day to work that one day he was so relieved to reach the north shore safely 'that he never travelled that way again'.[44] Because he was similarly experiencing increasing 'discomfort and concern' whilst travelling northwards, Provost William Robertson, engineer and partner of the art patron James Guthrie

Orchar in the Calendering Works[45] of Robertson and Orchar, had taken to timing the engines as they crossed. The 'bounding motion' reminded him of walking along a suspension bridge, and was worst in the High Girders where he calculated that the train had travelled faster than 42mph.[46] It was so disconcerting that he forfeited the remainder of his season rail ticket in favour of using the Newport ferry.

Several complaints were lodged with the Station Master, James Smith. Although the drivers denied the allegations, a circular was issued to all engine drivers in early August. 'Complaints have been made that engine drivers do not pay sufficient attention to speed restraints. Cases of offence will be severely dealt with.'[47] As they passed through, train drivers would be sternly reminded by Smith that breaking the speed limit merited dismissal. But when he took some time checks of his own, Smith found the drivers so well behaved that he could not substantiate the complaints, and therefore did not bother to refer the matter up the hierarchy.[48] So the bridge continued to be pounded by heavy coal trains and speeding passenger trains.

On 4 July 1878, the Tay Bridge Undertaking held its final Board meeting before being absorbed into the North British Railway, its shareholders being offered a very favourable exchange of shares. The final cost of bridge, tunnel and connecting lines totalled £626,547, marginally under double the original contract price of £325,000.[49] The construction period was near treble the original estimate.

Just about then, a Board of Trade Inquiry into changes to the Forth Bridge design was opening in Edinburgh, chaired by General Hutchinson. Bouch's original design had spans of 1500 feet between the towers, with the bridge at a level of 150 feet above the Forth. He now proposed to lower the height to 135 feet above high water and widen the span to 1600 feet solely because it would save £30,000 in material costs, and provide an easier gradient on the approach from the south. Since the proposal would prevent tall sailing vessels from carrying on upstream, it was opposed by the considerable shipping interests upstream – particularly by the thriv-

LARGE GIRDERS, TAY BRIDGE. 1266.

A train running across the narrow, first Tay Bridge. Note the triangular angle irons tying the side to the base at each end of each girder. In the catastrophe, three of these were flattened by the off-track doomed carriage, which was stopped short by the fourth.

ing ports of Alloa and Grangemouth; and behind the latter was the Caledonian Railway. The Caledonian had acquired the Grangemouth Harbour when it bought the Forth and Clyde Canal in 1867, and had spent £1,200,000 on its enhancement so far, resulting in a tonnage increase of 350%. It could already accommodate timber shipped directly from America,[50] and its authorised expansion to 20 acres of dock (three times its prior size) at a cost of £350,000 would be complete in less than two years.[51] This new Forth Bridge proposition seemed designed to prevent the growing international shipping from reaching it. George Cunninghame, the Caledonian's engineer, maintained that 'their canal from Grangemouth was the means of transit between the east and west coasts of Scotland, and any interference with the proper trade of Grangemouth would be an interference with the trade of the country'.[52] Proprietors of the harbour at Alloa were likewise alarmed. Alloa Distillers imported 7000 tons of grain in large ships, annually, usually from the Black Sea. They had calculated that any impediment could add as much as three shillings per ton.[53]

It was partly a battle between old and new, between wind and steam. Whereas foreign trade was still mostly carried in sailing ships, home traffic was carried in ever larger steamers, and John Calder, a timber merchant from Alloa, observed that 'steamers were pushing out sailing vessels' already. The foreign importers claimed that if the bridge height was reduced, sailing ships over 1000 tons would have to lower their top gallants and sky-sails to get beneath. Alarming witnesses who claimed that taking down these sails could take two or three hours[54] were put to shame by one of the Tribunal, Admiral Bedford, who asked innocently: 'Do you not think that it is not very complimentary to the ingenuity of the present day that so much time is taken for lowering masts?'[55] Indeed, the NBR's witnesses testified that it was customary in Sunderland to lower top gallants in no more than an hour.[56] The North British even brought down Captain Scott of the Dundee Training ship *Mars* to claim that no wise mariner, anyway, would take a large sailing vessel up the Forth beyond Queensferry without being towed. It simply was not safe.

The Caledonian's engineer Cunninghame questioned the underlying motive for Bouch's change of heart. He scorned the proposed savings of £30,000 since it represented barely 2.5% of the total cost of the bridge; and as for the disputed gradient, it was no greater than that on the northern section of the Tay Bridge. He discerned a covert agenda to damage its rival's business at Grangemouth. Even given the customary asininities of the Caledonian/North British rivalry, that was a bit far-fetched. The motive was, more likely, vanity. Now slung between Brooklyn and New York, the Brooklyn

Bridge was gradually moving to completion 135 feet above the East River with a span of 1600 feet. In the 1850s, Bouch had the ambition to build the world's two biggest railway bridges, and it is quite probable that, hiding behind grounds of minor utility, he had persuaded the North British to go to this expense to prevent his Forth Bridge design from being outclassed by Roebling's Brooklyn.

Bouch's performance at the hearing, however, was not up to the task. Unprepared and hesitant under examination, he was either unwell or hiding something. He was unable to be precise in his estimates – 'I have not made any estimate of what the reduction would be' – and replied several times along the lines of 'Oh. I have forgot all about it.' He was duly mocked by John Trayner, counsel for the Board of Trade, who claimed that Bouch's intelligence and activity had been 'totally exhausted on this scheme'.[57] Was it really worth, Trayner asked, blocking the free navigation of the Forth for a saving of £30,000? The Inquiry concluded that the height of the Forth Bridge had to remain at the original 150 feet above high tide, but the widened spans were authorised. Bouch's Forth Railway Bridge would still be the largest in the world.

Bouch completed his plans and specifications by August, and the two lowest tenders opened on 1 September were from John Waddell, contractor of the approach lines to the Tay Bridge and director of the Forth Bridge Company, and from William Arrol of Glasgow. Arrol was fresh from completing a bridge for the Caledonian across the Clyde leading to Glasgow's Central Station. When it had been opened in July, the Caledonian Railway chairman had hoped that Arrol might establish his reputation with the success of this 'great engineering undertaking'. The consulting engineer, Benjamin Blyth, drew particular attention to Arrol's inventive bent. 'Greater ingenuity could not be brought to bear upon it; the cylinders were made of the largest castings of the kind, and Mr Arrol's drilling and riveting machines were most successful.' Blyth wished him well in his tender for the Forth Bridge.[58] Arrol was not just to be the contractor for Bouch's Forth Bridge, but also for both the successor bridges on Forth and Tay.

Anxious to minimise any risk raised by being reliant upon a

single contractor for such an unprecedented project, the Forth Bridge Company wondered whether the two lowest tenderers might set up a contracting consortium to built the bridge jointly. Waddell and Arrol preferred, instead, to divide the Forth Bridge project up into several contracts which they shared. Preliminary works – railway cutting, machinery, piers, levelling off for foundations – were awarded to Waddell, to allow Bouch to complete the contract information for the bridge structure. Bridge foundations and superstructure were awarded to Arrol for £830,529,[59] the supply of steel cables to Messrs Vickers of Sheffield for £205,000,[60] and the approach lines from the south and north, and the line from Inverkeithing to Burntisland to Waddell. The company then purchased the isle of Inchgarvie with Garvie Castle, sitting at the centre of the Queensferry narrows, where Waddell established an azimuth and other measuring apparatus, and constructed a pier there to take delivery of materials. At 11 o'clock of the forenoon on Monday 30 September 1879, the Forth Bridge foundation stone was laid on Inchgarvie. A special train brought guests from Waverley to Port Edgar, and then out to Inchgarvie by boat. Waddell invited them back afterwards to the Hawes Inn at South Queensferry (well known from R.L. Stevenson's *Kidnapped*) for luncheon.[61] The estimate for completion of the bridge had now

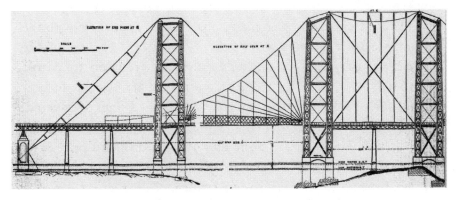

Elevations of Bouch's Forth Suspension Bridge, from the *Engineer*.

risen to four years (autumn 1882), but experience had taught the *Scotsman* to be wary. 'Allow six [years], and nothing in the Arabian Nights Tales will be more wonderful than will have then been achieved.'[62] Shareholders looked forward to an opened bridge some time between 1882 and 1884.

Bouch's design remained largely that of five years' earlier. An infinitely more complex structure than the horizontal iron snake that crossed the Tay, it depended upon the use of steel which only recently had been accepted by the Government as safe. Each span now matched Brooklyn's length of 1600 feet, suspended 15 feet higher above the sea. The novel use of steel, the *Scotsman* reported, 'was exciting very keen interest amongst metallurgists . . . If everything goes well with the Forth Bridge, and the structure comes up to the expectations of the engineer, it will give an immense impetus to the steel trade, because it will break down those prejudices.'[63] Bouch's office had collected second-hand information on other steel bridges like J.B. Eads's in St Louis, and Roebling's Brooklyn,[64] and he was in intense consultation with steelmakers and ironmasters throughout Britain, getting a number of them to undertake tests for him. Dr William Siemens in Wales, and Daniel Adamson near Manchester, who were competing for the chains of the bridge as sub-contractors to Vickers,[65] were both very excited about Bouch's 'wonderful bridge'. Monthly, they sent up results of various component and metal tests.[66] Bouch's perpetual weakness, however, was that he was learning about other bridges at second-hand, sometimes from newspaper reports or articles, whereas other engineers had direct experience gained from international work and travel.

Bridge optimism, moreover, was yet to percolate to North British shareholders. The 1870s had been generally poor for railway companies,[67] and when Kippendavie addressed their half-yearly meeting in Edinburgh that same September, both cheers and hissing greeted his report. Gloom and a rotten dividend prediction were relieved only by his promise that 'the Tay Bridge would be [the Company's] saviour'. Passenger traffic had fallen by 400,000 and receipts by £31,000, although these results were not unique to the North British since there had been a 'general falling off' over the entire Scottish railway system. Yet NBR's passenger train receipts per mile were 5% better than the Caledonian's and it earned 60% more per wagon. Now the Tay Bridge was open, the target was to win over 50% of the entire east coast traffic, and the 100% increase in the bridge's traffic over its first year led Kippendavie to expect that it would be easily achieved. He cautioned shareholders against allowing themselves to be overly influenced by the media, which he accused of having a vendetta against railway companies – particularly over the vexed matter of the railway companies' accident record. If the newspapers subjected the accident record of other industries to the scrutiny to which they subjected railways, the North British 'would not be held up to such odium'.

Unfortunately, the Board was unable to pay preference dividends in full and, presumably, the Ordinary voting shareholders anything at all. If it could not be paid back to them, shareholders were keen to discover where their money was going.[68] William Ainslie, who had travelled over from Fort William, could be heard through the heckling pointing out that the NBR's Directors' salaries, for example, were £12,000 more than the Caledonian's, whereas the latter's Directors were 'he was sorry to say, superior in every way'. He alleged that contracts let by the Board were awarded not according to their intrinsic value, 'but according to the influence [a contractor] could command at the Board'. Those who were getting nothing for their money, thundered Ainslie, had a right to speak – and many did. Some proposed generating more profit by cutting back on maintenance, whereas others attacked the Board for secrecy. Trust between Company and shareholders had sunk to such a low ebb that Ainslie accused the Directors – particularly the Secretary George Weiland – of speculating in Company shares.

Angrily defending his own integrity Kippendavie attacked the suggestion as 'most disgraceful'. He had 'devoted his time and sacrificed every other engagement' to the Company, and when he was not ill, the North British had always had first claim on his time. He had never speculated in the Company's stock, and in every case, had acted for the best. So far as performance was concerned, mile-for-mile maintenance costs in the NBR were generally lower than those of the Caledonian.[69] Nonetheless, for all the rhetoric, the shareholders had no option, with one bridge opened and another under construction, but to stick with the chairman and his strategy.

Railway competition between the NBR and the Caledonian had not changed. Only a North British engine would be permitted to pull the royal family across its Tay Bridge and when, on 12 October 1879, the Prince and Princess of Wales arrived at Camperdown Junction, just north of Dundee, to do that, their Caledonian Railway Company engine had to be unhitched and replaced by an NBR one. The delay provided 4000 'respectable' spectators with the opportunity to greet them, cheer and wave flags galore.

Just a few months later, competition brought the two Companies before Parliament yet again on a matter of monopoly. Now it had built the Tay Bridge, was busy constructing a line between Arbroath and Montrose, putting it within half an hour of Aberdeen, *and* had begun on the Forth Bridge, the North British could no longer tolerate being held to ransom by the Caledonian on the seventeen miles of rail between Dundee and Arbroath. It was inequitable that the Caledonian should control both the West Coast route to Aberdeen (the line from Perth through Strathmore to Brechin and Stonehaven, which they had absorbed when they took over the Scottish North–Eastern Railway) and continue to exert a stranglehold on the East/West Coast route. The North British petitioned Parliament for the disputed stretch to be put under joint ownership.

Evidence paraded by the North British left Parliament in no doubt about just how uncaring and how unaccountable was the Caledonian's record once it had obtained a monopoly on the West Coast route. Since the Caledonian had bought the railway to Aberdeen in 1866, lamented a former Provost of Arbroath, it had lost independence and efficiency, and now offered a slipshod and deteriorating service.[70] It operated such high carriage charges that the Aberdonian Commercial Company, for example, had simply been refusing to pay them. Slow trains were regularly 'put in front of the North British fast trains' to delay them.[71] Henry Oakley, General Manager of the London-based Great Northern, told a sorry tale of how his trade had withered in the face of price hikes, ineptitude and casualness. In the six years following the takeover, his trade with Arbroath had slumped by 89%, Dundee by 90% and Forfar by 60%. Passenger traffic, which had been increasing exponentially throughout the rest of the United Kingdom, had been reduced by 16%. The Caledonian cared so little for its customers that it had lost an enormous trade: the 50,000 tons of goods that they had carried between Aberdeen and London in 1866 had shrunk to only 615 tons in 1877. All three of the East Coast English Railway Companies that were pledged to the Forth Bridge supported the North British in this application.[72] Parliament was persuaded, and the line from Dundee to Arbroath was henceforth managed jointly. Once the North British's line from Arbroath north to Montrose was open, the East Coast route from London to Aberdeen waited only upon the bridges to become fully operational.

Not long afterwards, the Caledonian constructed a bombastic new station in Dundee. A towered baronial confection by the Edinburgh architects Peddie and Kinnear, the West Station made a magnificent *point de vue* west along Dundee's Dock Street, and totally overshadowed the North British's semi-underground Tay Bridge station alongside. But it was all rhetoric. Dundee had broken the Caledonian's monopoly on rail traffic between Aberdeen and London.

Unexpected volumes of freight now trundled north and south across the Tay Bridge, whilst the iron inspector McBeath examined every part of the bridge between December 1878 and May 1879, checking every cotter and, where necessary, hammering it tight. His pernickety attention to detail irritated the contractors who regarded him as over-careful and over-strict,[73] but he left the structure 'tight as a fiddlestring'.[74] The only audible chattering was vibration from the wind, as though the bridge were a gigantic Aeolian harp. Once McBeath had left for the Arbroath railway, ironwork checks fell to Inspector Noble, whose responsibility to date had been ensuring that the foundations were not being scoured away. He had been dumping boatload after boatload of rock around each pier to counter the effect of the swirling tides.

In early autumn 1879, Noble heard what he called a chattering and a clattering; and upon clambering up the tie-bars from his inspection boat (Bouch had, unfortunately, designed no access ladders for the bridge), he discovered that some of the tie-bars – the metal straps that formed the tension bracing between the columns of the bridge's structure – had worked loose, the natural consequence, maybe, of vibration from the pounding railway traffic. It was later suggested that, as a brick man, Noble had no responsibility for the superstructure, but that was not entirely correct. His prized title was that of the Inspector of the Tay Bridge, and he reported to Bouch on the ironwork as well as on the foundations.[75] For example, on 18 December 1878 Noble reported to Bouch that 'the superstructure stands the traffic first class. There is not the slightest defect in the whole.'[76] He failed to mentioned the ice floes then covering the Tay and creaking against the bridge.

Noble cannot have been given an adequate briefing for these additional duties, since he was unaware that what he had to do was to hammer in the cotters to tighten them again. Rattled by the clattering of the bracing straps, he thought he knew what had to be done by having earlier watched McBeath at work. He began buying iron in Dundee, which he cut into 150 thin wedge-shaped 'packing pieces' and hammered into any loose joint that he could find.[77] Being a very minor thing, and able to pay for the iron through petty cash, Noble saw no reason to inform Bouch about what he was doing. He was satisfied with his work. Once his wedge had been hammered in, the tie-bar appeared rigid, and that worrisome rattling stopped. Unfortunately, what Noble was doing was fixing the tie-bars in their distorted position in a way that could have weakened them.[78] General Hutchinson later stated that had he known that so many of those tie-bars required packing pieces, 'it would have made me very sceptical about the ultimate stability of the bridge'. When Bouch visited in October 1879 to inspect four columns with vertical cracks which he agreed should be bound with iron hoops, Noble made no mention of the chattering or how he had stopped it.

December 1879 was harsh. It was harsh for the Perthshire farmers whose harvest had been so poor that 'many will relinquish holdings and emigrate . . . if enough capital remains'.[79] It was harsh for the creditors of Hopkins Gilkes and the Teesside Iron Works, down on Teesside, where they discussed the reconstruction of the company and the works, and the appointment of a creditors' and shareholders' committee.[80] Fortunately for Gilkes, Bouch was a loyal man, and Gilkes was retained as contractor for the Montrose iron bridge. One of the problems that had brought down his firm had been the provision of sub-standard iron to the Australian Government, which then sued.[81] He cannot, however, have made much profit from the Tay Bridge despite the generous terms of its contract. It had been far too prolonged and labour intensive. That December was very difficult, also, for Thomas Bouch. He had inherited many shares in Gilkes, and two substantial liabilities from his brother.[82] His shares brought a liability of £13,000 on their own. His brother, however, had also been one of four people who had taken out a bond with the bank for a £100,000 loan to the company; and when the loan had been called, the other three bondholders were unable to meet their obligations. Bouch had to stand for the entire loan himself.[83]

The weather, also, was unusually harsh. The month opened with Dundee streets covered in snow and its trams iced up. Such 'large shoals of ice' blocked the Tay between Dundee and Perth by mid December that skippers with cargos for Perth had to unload them in Dundee and transport by train. Ships lay icebound in Broughty harbour.[84] However, there was something of a thaw toward Christmas. There was a thaw, also, in the North British's fortunes, for at long last, on December 22, the prospectus for the Forth Bridge was published. The strategic vision underlying the two bridges was to 'win a fair share of the through traffic between England and the north of Scotland, hitherto practically monopolised by the West Coast route'.[85] Once the two railway bridges were complete, the East/West Coast route would provide savings in both time and mileage in the run between London and Aberdeen, whereas, at present, their earnings per mile were 30% less than the Caledonian's simply due to 'the interjection into the centre of one system of a five-mile sea ferry as compared with the unimpeded land route of the other'.

This announcement – with the striking endorsement of the Forth Bridge from the engineering profession – was the high point of Bouch's career. His Tay Bridge – the longest railway bridge in the world – had enjoyed over a year's success. Construction had now begun on his innovative Forth Railway Bridge – the largest in the world – lauded by leading members of the engineering profession. *The Times* called it 'the most remarkable application of the suspension principle in the world'. No one, it concluded, 'can compare the engineer's plans with the physical aspect of the scene of his projected operations without being impressed by the combined boldness and ingenuity of his design'.[86] Bouch's place in the pantheon of heroic engineers looked confirmed.

But the very day after *The Times*'s accolade, Sunday travellers on the 5.50pm local train from Newport to Dundee felt their carriages lift up and tilt in the wind as they crossed the Tay Bridge, and observed sparks from the guardrail. The storm was gathering – practising almost – for its climax. The 4.15 from Edinburgh left Burntisland at 5.27, and was almost on time when it arrived at the halt at St Fort. The ticket collector and his assistant took fifty-seven tickets (the five or six passengers continuing to Broughty Ferry kept theirs), and including staff and children (one third-class passenger had three or four children with him), there may have been seventy-two people on board.[87] It arrived at Wormit at 7.08. Here it slowed down to 3mph whilst Barclay, the signalman in the bridge hut, handed the engine's coal stoker the trainstaff needed for the train to proceed. The storm was loud, and Barclay recalled: 'We heard nothing but the wind.'[88] Joining him in the bridge hut was a colleague, John Watt, who kept an eye on the train as it moved, as Barclay stoked his stove. When the train was some 900 yards out on the bridge, Watt noticed what looked like 'fire from the wheels' on the downstream side lasting for about three minutes, and then lost sight of the Guard's Van lights. He attributed it to poor visibility in the storm. But what he had seen were the sparks from carriage wheels pulled against the rails by the Second-Class carriage that had jumped off them after bouncing on the kinked rail in the first High Girder. As the engine entered the fifth High Girder, the Second-Class carriage at the rear smote the side of the fourth High Girder, halted, and was rammed and mounted by the weighty Guard's Van. The girders began to topple eastwards, falling eighty-eight feet down into the breakers, the train and its carriages trapped within them. Once the moon provided sufficient intermittent light to see, those on the shore could see that the approach viaducts had stood firm. But there was a void where the 13 High Girders had crossed the navigation channel at the centre.

At 7.16, the stoker was due to hand back the trainstaff to signal-man Sommerville at the hut on the northern side of the Tay Bridge, for Barclay had signalled at 7.09 that the train had gone through. When it did not arrive, Sommerville waited for a short while, then tried unsuccessfully to signal Barclay, but the telegraph to the south side was out. He left his cabin, and walked down to the Engine Shed to inform the Locomotive Manager.

The bridge's collapse was far more shocking than the grim death toll of customary crashes and derailments, for it struck at the nineteenth-century belief in the efficacy of the new technologies, at the credo that risks were required in order to progress. The trapped, drowned passengers were neither ciphers nor numbers: they were each identified and their names became public currency. Nor was the Tay Bridge any bridge. Although other railway bridges had collapsed – the bridge over the Dee at Chester and numberless examples abroad – the Tay Bridge collapse was conceptually different. In the popular imagination, the longest railway bridge in the world had become symbolic of man's ingenuity and technical progress. *The Times* lamented, 'It was strong and erected by cunning hands. No pains were spared to make the bridge as durable as it was wonderful . . . But strong though it was, it was graceful and seemed to any uneducated eye light and fragile . . . If [travellers] passed it while vibrating in a gale over the rough water far below,

Frantic passengers trying to escape from their carriages as they sunk under water – as portrayed in the *Christian Herald* – is exactly what did not happen. The carriages remained within their girders, and the impact of the fall, which broke so many bones, probably knocked passengers unconscious.

they may recall it as one of the most audacious of man's attempts to grapple with his natural enemies.'[89] James Cox, who had been so eager to promote the bridge for the benefit of Dundee, and had invested so much in it, never regained his sunny disposition. William McGonagall withdrew from circulation all copies of his *Address to the Tay Bridge* – even buying them back where necessary. Bouch and Kippendavie buckled down to getting the bridge repaired and in use again.

The horrible fate of the train suggested unnatural if not super-natural intervention. Was nature fighting back against presumptuous mankind? Theodor Fontane, an elderly German author and critic, was certain of it. In August 1858, he had made

the statutory trip to Scotland so popular with Continental roman-
tics with his friend Bernhard von Lepel. Scotland existed
principally in the Continental imagination through Walter Scott's
novels, and Fontane had based their itinerary upon *Tales of a
Grandfather.* They had visited the soul-stirring sites of Abbotsford,
Dunsinane, Loch Leven, Culloden, Melrose Abbey and Iona,[90] and
his imagination surmounted 'this starched, expensive and self-tor-
turing Britain'[91] to take flight in a series of vignettes about
Scotland. Two decades later, as inspired by the collapse of the Tay
Bridge as Goethe had been by Ossian, he summoned the spirit of
Macbeth's three witches up from the vasty deep in *Die Brueck' am
Tay:*

> *'When shall we three meet again?'*
>   *'At the seventh hour, at the bridge's dam.'*
>   *'At the middle pier'*
>   *'I'll extinguish the flames.'*
> *'So will I . . .'*
>   *'I'll come from the North.'*
>   *And I from the South'*
>   *'And I from the sea.'*
> *'Hey, what a ring-o'-roses we are going to have*
> *And the bridge must go down into the ground.'*
> *'And what about the train which enters the bridge*
> *At the seventh hour?'*
> *'Hey, it must go as well.'*
>   *'It must go.'*
>   *'Vain, vain*
>   *Are all works of mankind!'*[92]

The bridge's collapse would be ascribed to the witches, the Storm
Fiend, the Norns, the Fates, to God and to Nature; but over the
coming weeks, the British public would be presented with an altogether more accessible sacrifice.

CHAPTER SIX

A CHOREOGRAPHED INQUIRY

The bridge seemed to be amongst the things that last forever: it was unthinkable that it should break. The moment a Peruvian heard of the accident, he signed himself and made a mental calculation as to how recently he had crossed it and how soon he had intended crossing it again. People wandered around in a trance-like state muttering; they had hallucinations of seeing themselves falling into a gulf.

THORNTON WILDER, *THE BRIDGE OF SAN LUIS REY*[1]

By daylight on Monday 29 December 1879, survivors of the disaster were no longer likely. A call for divers went out through Dundee and Fife, but since only two diving suits had been provided,[2] the four divers were going below in shifts. They were under the scrutiny of a boat occupied by twenty-five British journalists. There was no visibility in the thick swirling estuarial silt, and divers, seeking to locate carriages and corpses, had to guide themselves in and out of girders and wreckage by touch, risking the snagging of their lifelines. At dusk on Tuesday, they found the train and its carriages trapped within their girders as in a metal cage. The divers were squeamish at the prospect of unexpectedly fingering corpses or body parts, and Harley was convinced that he had 'touched some of the dead whilst groping with his hook in the third-class carriage'.[3] He 'felt them floating about . . . He had hold of what he believed to be part of a lady's dress and some portion of a gentle-man's clothing.'[4] Harley probably need not have worried. The river was to suck everything moveable from within train and carriages.

Initially, 300 were believed to have gone down with the train.[5] That figure gradually diminished as people discovered that their relatives or colleagues who should have been on the train had missed it, and by the time William McGonagall produced his deathless elegy upon the Tay Bridge Disaster, the number of dead had reduced to ninety, and was eventually to settle somewhere between sixty and seventy-five. Countless tales were recounted of those who, either through good fortune, anxiety about the weather or sheer indolence, had saved their lives by failing to catch the doomed train. Patrols paced along the shores watching for bodies and passenger luggage, and a newspaper commissioned the aid of a medium to locate the bodies for relatives of the bereaved; to no avail. Such was the continuing morbid fascination in the missing that even nine days later, 'the dock walls were lined with hundreds of people watching with renewed excitement the movements of the whaling boats in the river' who were continuing the search.[6]

It was altogether gruesome. Bodies, or their coats or cravats, might be gripped by the grapnels, and then break free to sink again. A child's sock, a gentleman's hat, a lady's umbrella were among the jetsam, the umbrella being the only way of confirming that farmer's daughter Jessie Bain had indeed perished. The watch on James Leslie's body had stopped at 7.22pm, approximately six minutes after the bridge had begun to topple. Debris and luggage from the train were assembled on the wide curving stony beach of Broughty Ferry, downstream on the northern bank where, typically, fisher boats (some of which had been assisting in the search) would be drawn up. In April, the body of a compositor, Joseph Anderson, was washed up in Wick, far to the north,[7] and a side of a North British railway carriage which people thought came from the doomed train was washed up in Stavanger, Norway.[8]

Some of the flotsam thrown up on the beach at Broughty was seized for recycling by its poor fishing community. Before the authorities were fully aware of its significance to the Inquiry, timber

Although hopes of finding people alive quickly faded, divers searched for bodies and personal items, and investigated the location of the train and its condition.

from the bridge's floor had been carried off for firewood. However, the *Dundee Evening Telegraph* reported that on their upper face, those timbers bore 'deep transverse cuts, such as would be made by the wheels of the train tearing across them after leaving the metals'.[9] By the time that the Council despatched the bellman to proclaim in Broughty that anybody taking the wood would be prosecuted, the wood was gone. It had provided crucial evidence that one or more carriages had indeed left the tracks whilst still travelling upright, but was never presented to the Inquiry, and it was corroborated by the later discovery that the wheels of David Jobson's Second-Class carriage had burn marks consistent with friction against wood.

On behalf of the Dundee Harbour Trustees, Thomas Thornton took charge of corpse retrieval. Bodies were placed in a temporary dead house in Broughty Ferry pending identification; and it was there that the conscientious pathologist Dr Greig[10] undertook sample post-mortems. The corpses took a long time in coming and – judging by the number of tickets collected at St Fort – some never surfaced at all. Greig concluded that although they had all died of drowning, a substantial proportion had broken limbs – principally broken legs,[11] fractured by the impact either when the carriages smashed into the water, or when the sea slammed the carriages against the western girder. Corpses were still being recovered daily in mid-February, but any bodies that had been in the water for more than a fortnight were 'much eaten by birds and fish'. Cadavers of the rich were more easily identified since they were usually carrying more papers. One of the first was Jobson, the man who had so cogently argued for the nationalisation of railways on the grounds of their ineffectiveness. He left a wife and five children, and his widow was to sue for £1600. Such was the Company's procrastination, and the effectiveness of Thornton as her solicitor, that settlement was reached a year later for £5,000.[12]

Recycling salvage at Broughty Ferry. This drawing from the *Illustrated London News* shows people picking up timbers for firewood, before they could be used for evidence.

A fund 'for the relief of the bereaved left destitute' was proposed by Thornton to a packed and supportive public meeting, and the two largest initial contributors were the North British Railway and Thomas Bouch.[13] Claims against the fund were lodged on behalf of dependent relatives, usually by their church ministers. A land steward from Inverness, William Peebles, who had been hurrying to the funeral of his father-in-law at Broughty Ferry, was buried alongside him in the same grave. Peebles had left eight children between eighteen months and fifteen 'utterly bereft'.[14] Compensation payments were usually small. The Dundee Working Man's Coffee and Reading Room was awarded £90; as, curiously, were the relatives of the suspicious sounding 'John Doe'.[15] Allegations of damage to the Tay salmon fishery was rejected by a terse 'salmon are not terrified by a stationery object'.[16] It may have proved a different matter once the huge operations to raise the girders, engine and carriages began, followed by cutting up the enormous girders by controlled blasts of dynamite.

Beleaguered shareholders made ready to repel any claims regarding the fall of the bridge on the grounds that God alone was responsible. Since the train running within the High Girders had coincided with the strongest gust of a gale that had 'tirred roofs, blown over chimneys and shattered gravestones',[17] divine intervention in the form of wind pressure must have been the culprit. Kippendavie himself had lost thirteen acres of fir trees 'prostrate by the gale' and 40,000 trees had been blown down in the forest of Atholl. McGonagall, who replaced his withdrawn Tay Bridge panygeric with a thundering effusion on the fall, concurred:

> But when the train came near to Wormit Bay
> Boreas he did loud and angry bray,
> And shook the central girders of the bridge of Tay.

And the demotic local newspaper, *Wizard of the North*, illustrated it appropriately. Since the accident had occurred on a Sunday evening, some Sabbatarians believed that their campaign against Sunday travel had finally been vindicated. 'A Covenanter' informed the *Dundee*

Advertiser that the disaster was God's judgement upon the North British Railway for 'being heedless of God's Law', and the following Sunday, the Minister of the Free Kirk in Dudhope picked up on the theme. 'At the risk of sounding puritanical, I would say that if there was a voice louder than another in this terrible event, it was that God was guarding his Sabbath with jealous care.'[18] Once published in the newspapers, as sermons were, his view caused outrage – characterised by the magazine *Punch* as 'Sabbatarian Savages at their customs'.[19] Somewhat cowed by the reaction, the Presbytery retracted the following Sunday, passing a motion simply regretting the increased railway traffic on Sundays, sweetened by an exhortation to the populace to keep God's day holy, and an encouragement to its members to show generosity to the bereaved. The Dudhope sermon had been an exception. Most ministers in pragmatic Dundee had taken a rational view, brooding upon the uncertainty of life, and two had preached against the presumption of the Sabbatarians. 'We cannot affirm', thundered the United Presbyterian Rev. C. Jerdan in Tay Square, 'that God sent this as a direct punishment for Sabbath breaking. The ways of God are mysterious.' The Rev. D. McRae, in the Gilfillan Memorial Church, concurred: 'The cause of the disaster more likely was man's fallibility.'[20]

As was the predominant view in the press correspondence columns. They overflowed with disaster theories of a practical nature, blaming the old scapegoats of railway cost-cutting and contractor 'scamping'. The claim that 'no one doubted but that the bridge was "a cheap job"' resurfaced, but cheapness meant different things to different people and no longer just meant lightweight. To Leng of the *Dundee Advertiser* it meant, not that the bridge was cheap, but that the railway company had been cheapskate in building only a single track bridge, since twin tracks would not only have been more efficient but inherently more stable. *Herapath's Railway Journal* regarded the bridge as absolutely cheap, in that it had allegedly cost only £350,000 as compared to the £600,000 cost of Stephenson's Britannia Tubular Bridge over the Menai Straits.[21] The real cost lay hidden in the Tay Bridge Undertaking's minute book.

Engineers were concerned that the bridge's collapse would be taken as 'a reproach to engineering science in Great Britain', and poured north to inspect the gaunt remains for themselves. They then clogged newspaper letters pages with theories that the bridge had been too light, top heavy, built of doubtful ironwork, or even to a flawed design. In other words, it would be wrong for the public to damn nineteenth-century engineering by the failure of a maverick. That the *Engineer* magazine, the profession's mouthpiece, should urge Gilkes and Grothe to reassure the public by making their calculations public,[22] implies not just a deep professional unease, but also uncertainty as to who was responsible for the bridge. Structural calculations were not normally the responsibility of the contractor: they had been provided by the consultant engineer's consultant Allan Stewart.

A number of the professional elite wrote directly to the President of the Board of Trade lamenting that 'such a catastrophe should have taken place in England where we pride ourselves on our engineering achievements'. They suggested, with a dreadful irony, because it was to have the opposite effect, that a Public Inquiry would restore the reputation of the engineering profession. The iron master E. Talbot recommended that the iron be tested, since Middlesbrough iron had a tendency to 'what we in the iron trade call a "cold shut". J.P. Walker questioned whether the top-heavy nature of the High Girders had set the accepted principles of engineering at defiance; and Robert Brown, former engineer for the Great Eastern Railway, whilst questioning whether the cast-iron columns were of sufficient thickness, concluded that something 'must have lurched the train off the track'.[23] Thomas Morris, acting like an 'ambulance chaser' in seeking to benefit from a disaster, sent in a design for a replacement bridge in timber.

The engineer Dr Peter Barlow FRS, father of William Barlow, President of the Institution of Civil Engineers and about to be appointed as a Commissioner to the Inquiry, recommended that any inquiry should focus upon the correct method of bridge construction. He favoured arched structures as the most stable, but observed that the structures of the Britannia (tubular), St Louis (arched–cantilever), Niagara (suspension), Cincinatti (lattice–girder) and Saltash (girder) bridges were all so different that they could not all be correct. 'All engineers like to have a plan of their own which they fondle with as much care as a mother does her baby, and are equally blind to its defects.' Future bridge designs should be vetted by the Board of Trade before erection, since it was so important that England should maintain the lead in this as well as other engineering points. 'Allowing a French Engineer to execute the Suez Canal', he wrote, 'damaged not only the prestige of English engineering but the political influence of the nation'.[24] It was perhaps a sign of the self-absorption of Victorian engineers that they believed that the political influence of Britain, normally enforced by armies and gun-boat diplomacy, would be materially affected by its engineering achievements. Nevertheless, the structure of the Inquiry's own investigations followed such speculations so very closely, it is likely that the President of the Board of Trade passed all such letters to the Commissioners.

The Tay Bridge Inquiry would become a public demonstration of the internationalism of British engineering. Examples from Japan, Brazil, Afghanistan, Russia and even Henry Law's three bridge towers in Pernambuco 'with identical properties' were to be paraded before the Commissioners. From a world perspective, engineers argued how society had to take risks to advance. Yet ironically the structure of the Tay Bridge was exceptional only in its length, location and foundations, and the least travelled engineer of all was probably Bouch himself.

One letter drew the President's attention to the matter of conflict of interest. Seaton Carew, magistrate for Durham and Northumberland, and shareholder in Hopkins Gilkes, very bitter at the loss of his investment, suggested fraud. The liquidation and restructuring had been a swindle to allow Gilkes to carry on trading whilst avoiding the £100,000 lawsuit by the South Australian government for supplying defective material. Bouch was not only one of Hopkins Gilkes's largest shareholders, owning 2408 of the old £15 and 520 of the new £15 shares, but also one of its liquidators. Carew wondered whether there was any evidence that the collapse had been attributable to the work being scamped or shoddy iron being used.[25] So far as can be told, the President did not reply.

The populace, in the meantime, had discovered a new hero. Newspapers encouraged comparisons between the noble railway-man and the noble soldier both of whom might die doing their duty. 'The mails must get through.' The storm, they said, had already been apparent as the doomed train approached the signal-man's cabin but, driven to ensure that the mails arrived on time, the railwaymen had pressed on regardless to their doom. Although not quite in the same league as the countless 'runaway train' ballads, Anonymous obliged with this in the *Wizard of the North*:

> *All praise to the men who the signal obeyed*
> *When it flashed its 'All Right' down the line;*
> *And wherever they lie, let their epitaph be –*
> *'They were heroes, and up to their time.'*[26]

Heroism implied that the train crew were aware that they were steaming into danger, and pressed on regardless. In reality, the engine drivers were so accustomed to racing across the bridge in all weathers, that they had probably not the slightest qualm about its stability.

The newspapers immediately sought Bouch's explanation for the disaster, and he replied without hesitation that the train, or part of it, must have jumped track and collided with the girders. He was proud of his economical structures and was certain that the cause lay neither in under-design nor under-investment. Significantly, most of those who had witnessed the bridge in operation – like Benjamin Baker – or had worked on the bridge – all the contractor's men – or who helped to lift the wreckage, agreed with Bouch's assessment: a carriage hitting the girder must have taken the bridge over. But Bouch needed evidence for his claim and, sadly, his evidence was too little, too late. The authorities, anxious to free up navigation to Newburgh and Perth, gave priority to clearing the channel rather than to recovery for forensic reasons.

The contractor Waddell was instructed to begin salvaging the bridge forthwith, and it took him the following seven months to do so.[27]

The North British and the Dundee mercantile community were both desperate to get the bridge reopened and neither wanted the delays associated with having to submit for a new parliamentary approval. If no significant change were made to height or alignment, they were free to go ahead with repair and reopening. Popular opinion, however, held that the bridge had been too tall and spindly, and campaigned for its height to be lowered; and if agreed to, that would necessitate a return to Parliament. The North British hierarchy appeared paralysed by events passing out of their control. The emergency Board Meeting called to approve the repair and reopening of the bridge met only after the first session of the Inquiry had closed;[28] and it appeared unable to respond to the Inquiry's requests for evidence. It was Bouch who took the initiative. To reassure himself of the stability of the surviving bridge, he commissioned a structural report at his own expense from Allan Stewart and Dr William Pole, the engineer who had advised on his Forth River Bridge eight years earlier.

Railway business could not wait. So the General Superintendent of the North British, James McLaren, reopened the passenger ferry service from Broughty to Tayport, and negotiated NBR freight carriage over the Caledonian Railway's lines to Perth and Stirling. The Caledonian was neither sentimental nor forgiving. Its co-operation came at the heavy price of two-thirds of the North British's goods revenue that passed over their rails.

The President of the Board of Trade appointed as Commisioners to inquire into the collapse, Henry Cadogan Rothery, Wreck Commissioner, William Barlow, President of the Institution of Civil Engineers, and Lt Col. William Yolland, Chief Inspector of Railways. Five days after the train went down, their Inquiry into the disaster opened in the imposing, porticoed Assize Court in Dundee.[29] That they could report under six months later – *and* apologise for the length of time it had taken – compares very favourably indeed with the time taken for inquiries of comparable depth 130 years later. The Commissioners sat for twenty-five days, spread over three hearings and five months, and asked just under 20,000 questions with a record extending to over 500 pages of close print. The primary purpose of the Inquiry was to establish the cause of the bridge's collapse, to see what lessons might be learnt for the future. The secondary purpose was to establish whether the surviving portions of the bridge were sufficiently 'safe and proper' to be repaired.[30] The North British's game plan was to begin repairs so quickly as to pre-empt the second objective.

The first hearing of the Inquiry collected evidence on local circumstances – the storm, the fall and the victims – from witnesses who need not be invited to the principal hearing in London, and it was over in only three days. As is normal in inquiries, the leading figures were well known to each other. Counsel for the Board of Trade, John Trayner,[31] was the counsel for the Caledonian Railway who had so mangled Bouch about the revised designs for the Forth Bridge only months before. J.B. Balfour, instructed by Thornton and Adam Johnston (the North British solicitor), was again counsel for the North British. In the final hearing, G. Bidder, son of the eminent engineer George Parker Bidder with whom Bouch had worked, appeared as counsel for him. Bidder specialised in railway work as parliamentary counsel for the North British. During the Inquiry, legal counsel were paid fifty guineas a day,[32] ten times the remuneration of the engineering witness appointed by the Court. In just five months of the Inquiry, a counsel would earn a twelfth of what Bouch's engineering practice had earned over eight years in supervising the bridge. Priorities did not differ so very much between the nineteenth and the twenty-first centuries.

Two of the Commissioners were known to Bouch and were familiar with the Tay Bridge project. Barlow, the Civil Engineers' President and Vice President of the Royal Society, had examined Bouch's Forth Bridge back in 1873, and had written of his Tay design: 'Mr Bouch's great Tay Bridge is a success which will familiarise the minds of capitalists with large engineering works capable of earning their money's worth.'[33] Barlow's bent was structures and the properties of metal, and Bouch had been down to consult him on steelwork for the Forth Bridge just a few months earlier. The elderly Col. William Yolland, likewise a Fellow of the Royal Society, was a serial crash investigator. After serving with the Royal Engineers and the Ordnance Survey, he had spent twenty-six long years as Principal Inspector of Railways,[34] and had advised Bouch several times on both the Tay and Forth bridges. The Wreck Commissioner Henry Rothery lay outside that engineering circuit. A barrister from a legal dynasty, Rothery had previously been adviser to the Treasury on matters relating to the slave trade, and then registrar to the Admiralty Court.[35] His conduct at the Inquiry implies that he had been briefed privately by the Board of Trade against the engineering profession's propensity to look after its own. Although all three Commissioners had been appointed as equals, Rothery swiftly assumed the post of chairman, and the two modest engineers permitted him to get away with it. The result was that the Inquiry moved from being a typical Board of Trade Inquiry set up to seek the causes of the accident so as to prevent repetition, to being a virtual inquisition seeking a scapegoat. That was what Rothery, as Commissioner for Wrecks, was good at; and having usurped the chairman's role, he behaved like a prosecutor, asking around 70% of all the questions.[36]

In *The Hunting of the Snark,* Lewis Carroll had written, 'What I tell you three times is true,' as though simple repetition makes it so. Many more than three times did the players at the Inquiry – chairman Rothery, Trayner for the Board of Trade, Webster for Hopkins Gilkes, Bidder for Bouch, and Balfour for the North British Railway – protest that their only purpose was to uncover the truth behind the bridge's collapse. However, the hunt for the truth was quickly overtaken by Rothery's pursuit of the designer and, to a much lesser extent, of the contractor. During the final hearing in London, Bouch's counsel Bidder quizzed Rothery several times as to whether there was an underlying Board of Trade agenda. Strenuously denied, naturally. Yet Rothery structured the sequence and selection of witnesses so as to prejudice the proceedings to the extent that long before Bouch appeared as a witness, his credibility had been shot by the choreography of others.

Fallen girders disrupted seaborne traffic up the Tay and there was great pressure to cut them into pieces with gunpowder and remove them from the seaway.

Seven painters had spotted bolts lying around and empty rivet sockets, without knowing whether they were intentional or not, and conveyed the impression of sloppy construction. Eight bourgeoisie who had timed trains tanking far faster than Hutchinson's limit of 25mph implied that rail operations had been out of control. Nine angst-ridden moulders who provided evidence of shocking deceit in the foundry were much more credible than the professionals who claimed that these practices had been neither unusual nor significant. Ten railway users who had experienced progressive leaps and oscillations on the bridge indicated a bridge lacking even the most rudimentary supervision and attention. So whereas the Inquiry may not have been structured as a case for the prosecution, it had the same result.

The three Commissioners had begun by boarding a steamship to inspect the ruins. Only two stages of the southernmost pier, and a collapsed jumble of ironwork remained of the High Girders. The rest of the railway viaduct stood complete, tall and inert in its marble sea, stretching north and south toward the distant shores, tendrils of twisted and snapped iron rail reaching out forlornly for their missing siblings. Contemporary photographs show a slick-like sea gently heaving about the surface of the girders that lay on their side on the seabed.

Taking down of precognitions (statements of potential witnesses) for the Inquiry began as a neutral exercise, with interviews being held jointly by lawyers for both the Board of Trade and for the NBR. Divers were examined each evening once they had come up from their dip, and Thornton busied himself late into the night precognosing all those who wanted to unburden themselves: seadogs who studied the barometer as it plummeted; sailors who experienced the storm on the estuary; onlookers who chanced to be gazing at the bridge at the critical time to see it topple quite slowly downstream into the river. Never in all his fifteen years' experience had Charles Wright, captain of the Tay Ferries, seen such a gale as on Sunday night, or anything nearly so strong – and that included sailing round Cape Horn. The wind had come 'in such heavy gusts', that after he had landed his passengers from Fife in Dundee at 6pm, he had not dared risk making the scheduled return journey at 8pm. By the time he finally arrived back at Newport, the train had been down for two hours.[37]

The first hearing proceeded at a spanking pace. On the second day alone, Commissioners and counsel asked 1360 questions of twenty-two witnesses, and that was by no means unusual. One result was that the answers were frequently misheard or misunderstood, and the court stenographer frequently made mistakes that remained uncorrected.[38] By the end of the third day, it had been established that the bridge had been blown down in an unusually explosive gale, that the train's last few minutes had been accounted for, and its wreckage had been found. All relevant local knowledge now exhausted, the Inquiry adjourned awaiting the technical report from an expert witness yet to be appointed, and for an explanation from the North British Railway Company as to what actions it had taken to ensure the bridge's safety, and what conclusions it had come to as to its fall. The Inquiry to date had been studiously neutral, and if anybody was in the dock, it was God – that is to say, the unforeseeably terrible tempest. Just before adjournment, however, Barlow (a man who knew his metals) raised a niggling doubt. The divers had reported so much fractured metal that it would be wise to have some of it tested by David Kirkaldy. That agreed, the hearing closed, fully expecting to meet next in London a few months hence; yet they found themselves back in Dundee again a few weeks later.

On 22 January, Rothery's office announced that the engineer Henry Law had been appointed as the Inquiry's expert witness, paid at five guineas per day inclusive of his hotel costs.[39] Law, who arrived in Dundee four days later, had been one of Brunel's pupils on the Thames Tunnel, and his firm Law and Chatterton had worked with the Metropolitan Board and Works on many of its projects. Regarded as astute, a thinker from first principles, possessed of 'mathematical powers of a high order', Law was also an inventor;[40] but in that one of his bridge designs had already been constructed successfully by Edgar Gilkes, he was not entirely independent. It was quickly apparent, however, that the fussy Law was particularly 'desireous that it be known that he is an independent engineer'.[41] Some time before he presented his report, Law was murmuring questions into Rothery's ear on what might be asked of witnesses, and likewise briefing Trayner.[42] It is difficult to be sure that Law had conceived a prejudice against Bouch at this juncture, but he had certainly concluded that the bridge's structure had been insufficient. Balfour, counsel for the railway, warned his colleagues, 'Mr Law has entirely made up his mind to go for the Bridge.'[43] Under Law's influence, the Inquiry itself was to turn against the bridge and its builders, metamorphosing from an investigation into a trial. Law provided sufficient ammunition for Rothery to become Bouch's nemesis.

Many of those involved with the bridge construction felt disenfranchised that the first hearing had ended so abruptly. It had been 'insufficiently searching' and all relevant local knowledge was far from having been tapped.[44] Those who had worked on or had used the bridge wanted to give evidence. On 10 January 'one who crossed the bridge daily' wrote to the *Scotsman* expressing astonishment that the Inquiry had not seen fit to interview people like him.[45] As rumours about the bridge's construction grew, John Leng wrote in the *Advertiser* that all allegations of flaws in bridge construction had to be investigated. The possibility of human error was gradually creeping into the frame.

Methods of assembling evidence began to move away from those of an Inquiry purposed to arrive at the truth, as to one in which much of the truth would be concealed. Thornton sought to obtain advance warning of any evidence potentially damaging to the railway company. Whereas you would expect a good business manager to filter out the clearly irrelevant, the mad, the bad, and the merely deluded from clogging up an Inquiry, the potential witnesses he precognosed but did not call to give evidence implies something more systematic was going on. He had ceased taking precognitions jointly with the Board of Trade as soon as he had appreciated the prejudicial nature of much of the new evidence, taking them on his own, in private, instead. He was also against encouraging witnesses to come forward. 'I hear that the Board of Trade are so anxious to keep themselves right with the public that they will be likely to spin out the Inquiry by hearing everybody who has anything to say, however foolish or incompetent it may be.' He filtered witnesses in what he regarded as the railway company's best interests. One consequence of his actions was that crucial evidence from painters relating to distortion in the railway track in the High Girders was never put before the Commissioners.

Thornton despatched a daily evaluation of the evidence to the solicitor Adam Johnston, who ultimately controlled North British participation in the Inquiry. As each principal tranche of adverse evidence was precognosed or presented, Thornton advised Johnston whether any witnesses were needed in rebuttal. Take the matter of speeding trains. Thornton urged Johnston to hunt down 'two good and experienced engine drivers who were in the practice of driving over the bridge who would be able to say that they never exceeded speed and never observed anything really calling for remark – e.g. tremor or oscillation'.[46] The Locomotive Engineer duly supplied four stout, long-serving and faithful drivers who claimed not only to have obeyed the speed limit, but who maintained that the locomotives could simply not achieve the alleged speeds in the distances involved. Thornton's approach was mistaken on several counts. By protecting the NBR's drivers, he was necessarily forcing the Commissioners to look elsewhere for the cause of collapse. Indeed, had he concentrated on speeding trains, more evidence might have been forthcoming about the deformation of the track. Worst, however, was that by feeding largely incredible witnesses to defend the indefensible, the credibility of North British witnesses as a whole was undermined. Trayner selected Driver Coutts as the first sacrifice, and swiftly demolished him. Coutts's alleged times were literally impossible if trains were to be kept to time. Something similar happened to other rebuttal witnesses. Their loyalty to the North British over the facts of the matter was made perfectly transparent, and the Commissioners became irritated. The North British was behaving as though there was something to hide, but what it was, was not yet apparent.

The evidence of Bridge Inspector Henry Able Noble was crucial to a consideration of the effectiveness of the bridge's maintenance. He structured it defensively around a detail-by-detail rebuttal of the rattling, clattering and sighting of debris mentioned by earlier witnesses.[47] To the claim by several painters that they had seen empty rivet sockets, implying that the structure had already sprung, Noble responded that they had not understood the bridge construction sequence. 'The diagonal bracings, or straps as we call them, slackened once the girders were lowered into place. The plates were then taken off, the straps shortened, and plates put on anew. That required cutting out the original rivets, and that is what people saw lying around.'[48] Not only had he carried out his duties conscientiously, he had gone far beyond them in maintaining an overview of the iron work as well once McBeath, the iron inspector, had left for the Arbroath–Montrose Railway. Nevertheless, it remained unclear whom Bouch intended to keep the cotters (wedges) hammered in once McBeath left, since he does not appear to have mentioned it to Noble.

When the foundry workmen themselves volunteered evidence about casting the columns, Gilkes (who had been forewarned) responded smartly: 'I am not afraid of any challenge of the materials or workmanship of the Tay Bridge. I do not mean that I think that, in a work where there was such an infinite duplication of parts, none should be found *indifferently* done, but I am certain that the general scope of evidence of it will be that it was truly and honestly erected. Believe me.'[49] Surprisingly, given the context, he did not bring forward qualified witnesses of his own to defend his construction practices – other than those members of the construction team that the Inquiry itself had summoned – Camphuis, Beattie, McBeath and Grothe – who were tainted by association. Even more astonishing, it appears from Gilkes's own cross-examination being so genially superficial, that the Commissioners were indeed minded to believe him.

The Board of the Forth Bridge Company, meanwhile, received a deputation anxious about the nature of the Forth Bridge design. In view of the questions being asked in the media about the Tay Bridge, which was only eighty-eight feet high, the much greater height of 550 feet of Bouch's Forth Suspension Bridge was causing disquiet. The Board decided to continue work on preparation and the foundations, but to cap expenditure at £25,000 whilst the structural principles of the bridge were to be reviewed. At the half-yearly shareholders' meeting, there was both good news and bad. The shareholding for the Forth Bridge had been completely subscribed, and the secretary had rediscovered the enthusiastic report on the Forth Bridge design from G.P. Bidder, Hawkshaw, Barlow and Harrison, produced in April 1873. The bad news was that the Board had decided to resubmit the Forth Bridge plans to Sir John

Hawkshaw, Thomas Harrison, and to William Barlow (then sitting as a Commissioner into the Tay Bridge Inquiry) to revise in the light of whatever the Tay Bridge Commissioners might conclude.[50]

The Inquiry Commissioners, meantime, had returned to Dundee on 26 February for an unscheduled five-day session – because, as Rothery informed the throng, the Provost and Council of Dundee 'had knowledge of certain witnesses who would be able to throw some light upon the Inquiry'. It was at this second hearing that responsibility for the bridge's collapse shifted from the presumption of an act of God. Thornton busily prepared briefs for Balfour. 'Please examine frequent travelling witnesses early. Nothing but their desire to oblige Mr Thornton has hitherto kept some of them from attending. They are now grumbling sadly.'[51] New witnesses would testify to speeding trains and to the bridge shaking, oscillating and bounding as trains passed over it. Three addressed metal fabrication, and nine described how the columns were cast – culminating in the appearance of Strachan, Ferguson and Tasker at the end. It must have made brilliant theatre. Gilkes listened to his moulders with astonishment. 'Of course I have been watching the evidence of which I have daily reports . . . I have no doubt but that the evidence today will fully rebut and cancel the lying statements of the moulders. Their allegations are too gross to attain any credence from the Commissioners.'[52] He was deluding himself. Although the North British fielded nine rebuttal witnesses, the Commissioners moved to a position of profound distrust of the bridge's construction, but whether that was the fault of its design or construction remained unclear. Their judgment was probably correct. At the time of its collapse, the bridge seems to have been held up primarily by gravity.

In mid-February, the NBR's Superintendent James McLaren had warned Johnston that it was time for the railway company to make up its mind whether it wished to defend any action for damages, or preferred to compromise as best it might. In March, things looked much worse. 'I think it right to let you know that at the proper time evidence will be produced which will clearly shew the bridge was badly constructed, that the castings were of insufficient or

rather bad materials, that there was a want of supervision . . .
Evidence will amount to this: that though the bridge may have
been well enough designed, the construction was rotten, bad workmanship, bad materials and no supervision. In this state of matters,
Mr Balfour strongly advises that the friends of the killed should be
settled with at once. He thinks that the question of liability is
beyond doubt.' Every claim should be settled within three weeks,
since the company's position could only get worse.

It was a gross miscalculation of the slippery George Weiland,
Secretary of the NBR, therefore, to antagonise Henry Rothery, the
Inquiry Chairman, quite as thoughtlessly as he now did. The
North British had still failed to reply to the Inquiry's request for its
assessment as to why the bridge had fallen, and Rothery considered
that the NBR was stalling the investigation. But when he wrote a
reminder, Weiland's response was not a report but a blunt abbreviated single-page bureaucratic memorandum: 1. The North British
had exercised proper responsibility by having the bridge designed
and constructed under the direction of an engineer of experience.
2. Since the bridge had been subjected to the 'severe tests' of the
Inspecting Officer of the Board of Trade (Hutchinson) they had
never entertained any doubt about its safety. 3. As for why it had
come down, 'apart from the overwhelming force of the wind, they
are not yet aware of any circumstances which in themselves would
satisfactorily explain the disaster'. Weiland could assist no further
since he was not himself an engineer.[53] Rothery exploded: 'I
would beg to observe that it is not your individual opinion that the
Court was desirous of hearing . . . What we wanted was the deliberate opinion of the Company with the full knowledge they now
have of all the facts more than two months having elapsed, and after
full consultation with its Engineers and Officers.'[54]

On the same day that Rothery so magisterially rebuked George
Weiland and the North British, Frank Beattie took the stand at the
Inquiry. Thornton later reported to Johnston that although he
'made a remarkably good appearance . . . it is plain that the Board
of Trade Commissioners have a bad opinion of materials and workmanship'.[55] Beattie had been cross-examined over the matter of

inspection of the castings. In his evidence, Beattie had denied that he had had responsibility for supervising casting in the foundry. He had said, 'As regards the inspection of the wrought and cast iron-work . . . there was simply none at all (up to the time when I left). The practical men among my colleagues together with myself always insisted in expressing our astonishment at such a state of things, and I believe I particularly felt that the burden and respon-sibility for passing or rejecting material for the Bridges should never have been thrown on the shoulders of the already overworked members of the staff.'[56] Thornton reported that as a result, the Commissioners had also begun to suspect 'a total want of supervi-sion and inspection'.[57]

The North British had undertaken no post-mortem into the collapse, no internal enquiry nor any consultation with its employ-ees or its consultants, and now stood exposed as irresponsible if not incompetent. It had so little premonition of threat that the Company had not even considered calling its own expert witnesses. It implies that Weiland and Johnston had been discounting Thornton's increasingly anxious bulletins as alarmist. Luckily, Bouch was able to present the Company with Stewart and Pole's supportive report on the strength of the bridge that he had com-missioned back in January and of which the NBR had been wholly unaware.[58] He had also approached the Institution of Civil Engineers for names of a potential expert witness. Amongst the ICE's recommendations was the contractor, John Cochrane of Cochrane and Co. Cochrane had worked with Paxton on the Great Exhibition in 1851, on Brunel's Clifton Suspension Bridge in Bristol, on Charing Cross, Cannon Street and Westminster bridges and upon a bridge crossing the Mersey.

Kippendavie, Deputy Chairman Falshaw, and Bouch met in the Company's headquarters to discuss what to do next. Falshaw, as an engineering contractor (formerly one of Brassey's men), proved particularly useful. Agreeing that Cochrane would make a splendid witness, he added, 'Why not use Brunlees as well?' James Brunlees, later to be knighted for his design of the Mersey Tunnel (built by Waddell), had been consultant engineer for railways in Ireland and the north of England prior to appointment to the São Paulo railway in Brazil in 1856. His particular forte was the design of iron structures across estuaries, including one 1.5 miles long across the Solway.[59] By selecting formidable contractors and consultants such as these, nobody could accuse either Bouch or the NBR of trying to hide behind favourable witnesses. Equally, the engineers' agreement to attend suggests that there was no shortage of prominent engineers prepared to assist Bouch.

Bouch had unwavering confidence in his bridge. Like a good general, he had delegated all aspects of its design to reliable consultants, colleagues, subordinates and contractors on whom he could depend. Additionally, he had spent a vast sum on employing engineers and inspectors to supervise its construction.[60] The cause of the disaster had to lie elsewhere, and the train coming off line was the only answer he could think of. Yet the bridge's cerebral if not experimental slimline structure, carefully calculated by Stewart in reaction to the evident over-design of earlier structures, had been unusually dependent upon careful and precise construction. Whereas both Bouch's expert witnesses had found that the cast and wrought iron was very good, the casting was poor and the workmanship – save the bolts – very variable. They questioned the adequacy of the piers. Yet, since no credible evidence had been presented to justify the speculation that a carriage had jumped the rails, they concluded that the bridge's failure had been caused by wind pressure, and that therefore the piers must have been too narrow, inadequately tied at the top, and framed by 'altogether insufficient'[61] diagonal bracing. When Henry Law's expert report was delivered on 9 April, between the hearings, Bouch's peril was further enhanced, for Law had concluded that insufficient design and bad workmanship had damaged the bridge's capacity to resist a storm of such ferocity. The base of the piers was too narrow, the struts and ties were imperfectly connected, and their yielding was the immediate cause of the disaster. As with so many of the theories as to why the bridge fell, Law's did not explain the entire evidence. He largely ignored the evidence of the railway carriages themselves.

The sombre March shareholders' meeting in Edinburgh's Queen's Hall was held against a backdrop of lurid publicity generated by the second hearing of the Inquiry. The Board had already voted £125,000 for claims and related costs, but had decided to finance the Tay Bridge repair through an appeal to shareholders. Certain that such an appeal would be successful, Weiland had drafted a circular for Johnston to 'gild and refine and elevate in taste and sentiment'.[62] Shareholders were moved neither by gilt nor by refinement, and gave the circular an 'indifferent response', leaving the preference shareholders' half-yearly dividend as the only accessible source of finance for the repair. The Board proposed to retain half of it for rebuilding the bridge.[63] The only problem was that the dividend had been guaranteed to Preference shareholders.

Kippendavie admitted that just when the Company had been on track to make a profit sufficient to meet all the Preference shares with even 'a small surplus for the Ordinary shareholders', the bridge's fall had thrown 'the Company a long way back'. Over the pre-lapsarian eighteen months, traffic to Dundee had doubled, and the North British's share of the entire passenger traffic between Dundee and Edinburgh had reached 80%. It had dropped by 50% since. Yet the forecast repair costs were dismissed as inconsequential by *Herapath's Journal* (which boasted of its independence – 'neither the property of an engineer nor under the CONTROL OF A COMPANY' [*sic*]): 'What is £200,000 by the side of the North British total capital of £30,000,000, and whose gross revenue exceeds £2,250,000 per annum?'[64] The trouble was that the NBR's margins were thin. It was still spending so close to its income that there was nothing left for Ordinary shareholders, much less the capital required to rebuild the bridge.

Shareholders, however, had gone to the meeting believing that the Board was not telling them the truth. The Company's liability for compensation had dominated the correspondence columns of railway magazines since January. The extent to which shareholders should be liable for compensation to relatives 'is a point for lawyers to determine', thought *Herapath*. Since compensation did not arise from what the law called 'the act of God',[65] it was vital to demonstrate that a storm had been responsible for toppling the bridge. Shareholders, however, suspected that Kippendavie and his fellow directors planned to raid the guaranteed dividend to provide not against the rebuilding but the compensation liabilities, and erupted. 'Is it to the "public interest" that tradesmen all over the country should have payment of their bills suddenly delayed because thousands of shareholders have had their dividends suddenly stopped by reason of heavy compensations for some working man's folly or negligence on a railway? SURELY NOT!'[66] The debate spread. 'Mr Editor, in 1866, when the North British Directors had incurred debts to the amount of £1,800,000, some "stock" was raised to pay the sum. And yet, when the winds of heaven have destroyed the Tay Bridge, the preference shareholders are suddenly expected to surrender half their dividend.'[67]

Thomas Chester, leading a contingent of preference shareholders from Liverpool, lamented that he was 'an unfortunate shareholder compelled to spend his Easter holidays in hunting up this truant dividend'. He argued that whereas Ordinary stock was speculative, in which Ordinary investors could invest and then realise their gains, Preference shares were investment mediums 'for all good ladies and other people who had no ideas of speculation and thought if they got preference shares, these would never be touched'.[68] It was unjust to penalise those who had invested for a guaranteed income and never had, nor ever would, benefit from any increasing prosperity in the company. Furthermore, the costs of replacement should surely be charged against the original Tay Bridge shareholders. Directors were darkly accused of protecting their own pockets.

Inevitably, the debate turned to the Forth Bridge. Earlier that month, a small ceremony had taken place in North Queensferry. A shareholder had cut the first barrowload of turf, after which a hundred guests had retired to the Newhall Inn for refreshment. It appears that the contractor William Arrol had had his own foundation ceremony following Waddell's two years earlier. Publicity for a railway jamboree at such a sensitive stage in the Tay Bridge Inquiry was particularly unwelcome, so Arrol wrote to the *Scotsman* to deny it had taken place.[69] Once the *Scotsman* stuck to its guns, the event earned an unlooked-for notoriety, reminding shareholders that the Forth Bridge project was proceeding to schedule. Arroll had leased Inverkeithing's clayfields to make his bricks, contracted for 20,000 tons of cement from Leith and, because of the rise in British steel prices, was contemplating transferring the contract for the steel chains from Vickers to Krupps of Essen (as indeed had Roebling for the Brooklyn Bridge).[70] He had not long since commissioned an eighty-ton lighter from Port Glasgow shipbuilders Blackwood and Gordon which, on its delivery in July, he would name 'Inchgarvie' after the island at the centre of the Queensferry narrows.

The aggrieved Liverpool shareholder Thomas Chester had duly visited the site, and found just a 'shed and about half-a-dozen of what contractors call "horses" and a siding'. He very much doubted that it had been wise to contract for the steel before the foundations were in. The Board's defence was predictably that the Forth Bridge was being built by a separate undertaking – although Kippendavie admitted unrepentantly that he had shares in it and advised other shareholders to do so as well. The Preference shareholders lost the motion to shift the liability for the Tay Bridge costs from the Preference to the Ordinary shareholders, or to stagger the repayment over several years. Having won his vote, Kippendavie anticipated beginning repair work in May. However, once the Inquiry reconvened in mid-April, that prospect became remoter.

The North British had amassed its rebuttal witnesses ready for the final hearing in London, but a chance conversation reminded it that nobody had considered bringing Grothe back from Spain. Johnston, realising that the plan to repair the bridge as soon as possible was in clear and present danger, wrote to him: 'We very much require your advice and assistance in defending the Tay Bridge against the proceedings of the Board of Trade.'[71] The Scottish industrialist Charles Tennant, who owned the Great Tharsis works which Grothe managed, agreed that he might return to attend the Inquiry, and he arrived in London unannounced a week before the final hearing began. Thornton had also been corresponding with Beattie and Camphuis. Beattie was happy to appear, but warned that he considered that Bouch had been badly treated by the contractors. 'None of the Directors thoroughly realise all that has taken place from first to last. Mr Cox will remember I disapproved strongly of many things, and I left the operation prematurely to avoid further association with the management.'[72] Thornton would perfectly understand why he could only write in a confidential manner on such matters for not only did he consider Grothe to be personally responsible for the collapse, but that Bouch had been kept deliberately ignorant of what had happened on site.[73]

Bouch was obsessed by his theory that a train carriage had come off the rail to hit the fourth girder in which the Second-Class carriage had been found.[74] Three of the triangular metal 'ties' bolted to the side and the base of each girder to strengthen the 'box' had been flattened from a southerly direction, and glass from the carriage had been found in the open trough at the bottom of the girder. It could only have been there if it had fallen vertically from the carriage before it toppled over.[75] He had been waiting increasingly anxiously for at least three months for the chance to inspect it to see if the girder showed signs of impact with a carriage which would prove that it had jumped track. It would be catastrophic if crucial evidence from the bridge was salvaged too late to be used in evidence. But when the Inquiry reconvened in London on 19 April, he had to be there. He was furious that Dugald Drummond, the Locomotive Engineer, had so perversely insisted on lifting the engine first (and then had dropped it *twice* back into the river on its way to be beached.[76] No wonder, when it was later reconditioned for further use, that engine was nicknamed 'The Diver'.) Salvage was accelerated throughout April, the material being laid either on the beach at Broughty Ferry or the shore by Tayport, where it could be photographed by John Valentine, who had obtained permission from the Board of Trade to sell prints of any of the photographs he took for the Inquiry.[77] But Bouch's assistant Thomas Peddie warned him that although they were working day and night from the wooden pontoons, the fourth girder was so intertwined with columns and lattice bracings that it could take up to a further week to disentangle and lift.[78]

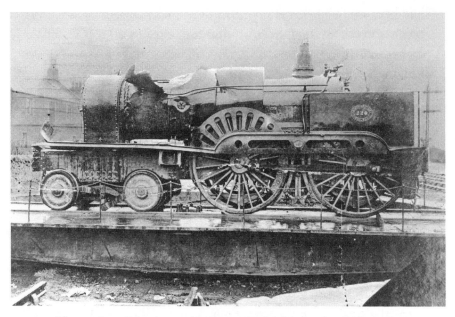

The engine of the doomed train, on dry land at last, having been in the sea three times (twice as a consequence of inept salvage attempts). It went back into many more years of service with the mordant nickname 'The Diver'.

It was only on 27 April, after the final session in London had begun, that Waddell and his assistant Armit managed to land the girder containing the remains of the Second-Class carriage. Their examination provided the evidence that Bouch had surmised. 'There is strong evidence that the Second-Class Carriage and van must have been overthrown against the east side of the girder *before* [my italics] the bridge went down. Number 4 girder is much more damaged . . . all broken up, chairs torn from the timbers, rails twisted in all directions.' Since the Guard's Van was no longer coupled to the Second-Class carriage in front of it, they concluded that the Second-Class carriage had been pulled to the right, and the Guard's Van had crashed broadside into it. Armit wrote to Peddie, 'I am convinced that the rear of the train must have been dragged along this girder for a considerable distance',[79] partly because the inside of the carriage's wheels had rubbings 'like charred timbers';[80]

and because the girders themselves had long scratch marks in black paint, and the rivets had been compressed inwards.[81] This evidence had emerged too late to influence Law, Cochrane or Brunlees and, judging from their questions, the Commissioners treated it on a par with the evidence of the loyal engine drivers who had driven to time, or the loyal passengers who had never noticed any oscillation. Brunlees, Cochrane and Law all ruminated upon whether the carriage might have been blown against the girder by the gale, but concluded against. The angle of tilt would have meant that the carriage roof would have been too low to have made those marks on the girder, and the iron girder would have shredded the carriage's light timber superstructure like a knife through cheese.[82] Without any reason to believe why or how part of the train might have jumped track, the new evidence of marks on the girder and of the wheel marks scouring the timber, was treated as inexplicable.

As the final hearing approached, the North British was becoming anxious about Bouch. He had gone through a particularly uncommunicative phase in early March, and they were uncertain whether they dare risk him on the witness stand. On 4 March James McLaren had urged Johnston: 'No time should be lost in getting Sir Thomas Bouch's proof prepared, and I can see that it will be no easy matter. I scarcely feel able to cope with him though . . . I will not shirk it . . . I cannot get a satisfactory assurance from him that he will do anything at all.'[83] Thornton wrote two days later: 'I will do my best . . . but it will be uphill work', adding three days later, 'Mr Bouch looked much brighter than I have seen him for some time.' Thornton prepared an excellent and confident proof of evidence for Bouch, which addressed equally the structure, construction and supervision; but their counsel warned that he was 'afraid that Sir Thomas Bouch was not able to stand an examination – his head had gone'.[84] Luckily there had been a sufficient number of aggrieved moulders to keep the second hearing fully occupied, so that Bouch had time to recover equipoise before the final hearing opened in London.

In April 1880, Gilkes's fight to keep his engineering firm afloat finally failed. Whether in an attempt to forestall any liability for the bridge disaster is not known, he restructured and retitled his firm the Teesside Iron and Engine Works Company: no mention of bridges and no mention of Gilkes.[85] When he wrote to Johnston to inform him that, henceforth, he would be instructing his own counsel, he warned 'as to *design* I shall say nothing. But if I am unfairly attacked, I shall speak . . .'[86] Bouch likewise appointed G.P. Bidder as his own counsel. In a note of oozing sanctimony, Johnston informed the NBR counsel, Balfour, that since both contractor and engineer had their own legal representation, the North British interest in the Inquiry was now solely confined to seeing that it came to 'a just and accurate conclusion'.[87]

The third hearing coincided with a change of government and the appointment by Gladstone, the new Prime Minister, of Joseph Chamberlain as President of the Board of Trade. Chamberlain was to reveal himself as somebody wanting to make his name quickly, and the Tay Bridge Inquiry might have seemed to him a good opportunity, and Rothery a most suitable agent. Whatever his civil servants might urge, he would shift the Board's focus of trying to learn from mistakes towards applying blame.[88]

In the hearing itself, tempers rose. Perhaps, like experimental rats, too many counsel in a confined space are compelled to bite each other, for the counsel-packed final session of the Inquiry was marked by particular ill temper by comparison with the earlier ones. Bidder had immediately appreciated that it was less an Inquiry than a trial of his client, and was probably over-swift and aggressive with a pre-emptive defence. He dispensed legal condescension and impertinence not just to Bouch's own witnesses Cochrane and Brunlees, but to his fellow counsel and to Rothery himself. He so identified with his brief that, at one point, he referred to Brunlees's evidence as 'against *me* [my italics]'.[89] Engineers are not easily intimidated, and the transcript is ripe with exchanges where witnesses were accused of not listening to or answering the question, or volunteering unasked-for information, and remaining happily unrepentant. Henry Law was Bidder's principal target, so powerful and damaging had been the thoroughness and conclusions of his report questioning the design and construction of the bridge.

Bidder sought to shift Law from his position with statements like 'You must not put nonsense in my mouth for the purposes of contradicting it'.[90] Protected by invincible rectitude and total certainty, Law remained steadfast. When he was asked by Webster, for the contractor, whether the cotters (wedges) meant to tension the strap bars would work loose, Law replied: 'Yes, that is why I should have fitted them so carefully.' Webster: 'There was no necessity to add that after the question.' Law: 'Excuse me, I think it was necessary and proper to add it.'[91] He judged the strap bars had been fitted very casually.

Trayner was a particular Bidder target. A spat had arisen over whether evidence from Grothe was permissable. After all, it had been his bridge. Trayner objected to his being called because he had had no opportunity of examining his evidence first. Bidder put his finger on it. 'Mr Trayner should remember that he is not counsel for a plaintiff struggling for a verdict, but that he represents a great public body whose object is simply to ascertain the truth.'[92] Even the Wrecks Commissioner was puzzled. 'You do not yet know what he is going to say,' and Webster rubbed in some salt: 'It is hardly consistent with the usual practice of the Board of Trade to decline to call a gentleman because they do not know which way his evidence is going to tell.' Trayner's reaction to Grothe's sudden appearance demonstrates just how stage-managed the Inquiry was. Aware of the potential damage to the Inquiry's reputation were Grothe excluded (such was his local reputation), Rothery agreed to admit him. Grothe, unfortunately, did not prove to be the saviour the North British had looked for. Henry Law was scathing about the lack of quality control during the erection of the bridge, commenting of the supervision of the fixing of the bolts of each pier: 'I can hardly believe that such carelessness is credible.' Doubt was cast on the value of Grothe's evidence as a whole.[93]

The repeated clashes of advocates endeared neither Bidder, nor Bouch, nor the North British to the Commissioners. However, far from preventing such interchanges, Rothery almost encouraged them, content to allow aggression, harassment and downright rudeness to prevail, when not asking technically inadmissible leading questions of his own. Even more curious is that the Inquiry never sought any expert independent evidence on matters such as the foundry and the castings, allowing the moulders to present their evidence largely unchallenged. It was a very curious chairmanship.

During Law's cross-examination, Commissioner Barlow and Law mutually agreed that Bouch's redesign using iron columns filled with cement had not been the lighter, cheaper and faster engineering solution that Bouch had believed. His iron columns were heavier, more time-consuming to fashion, less stable and – worst of all – more expensive than hollow brick columns would have been, albeit the latter carried other technical difficulties.[94] Nonetheless, David Kirkaldy's tests on the pieces of iron selected by Law showed that they were adequate and sometimes very good indeed – to everybody's astonishment, given the evidence from both moulders and the Cleveland Bolt Company. Perhaps that explains why, when Gilkes came to give evidence, he was not examined on the palpable problems of management and quality control during construction. The proven quality of the iron, per se, damaged the credibility of those who had described bad casting practices and, by extension, those who had claimed poor quality construction. That shifted the blame to the design. When Sir Thomas Bouch first appeared on 30 April, Bidder compelled Rothery to deny that there a charge was being laid against him. Rothery responded: 'We must keep ourselves perfectly distinct from anything like charges.' Although it looked good on the record, it influenced the increasingly poisoned atmosphere of the Inquiry not one jot.

Despite his opening declamation that 'I do not suppose anybody has built more [bridges and viaducts]', Bouch gave a desperately sad performance[95] by comparison with the other engineering witnesses. Where they had been unable to provide the information immediately, they had promised to return with it the following day; and were regularly consulting work diaries and drawings to show what had been done and when. In enormous contrast to the powerfully argued written proof of evidence which Thornton had lodged on his behalf, Bouch appeared hesitant, rather deaf,[96] hazy of memory and extraordinarily ill-prepared – very much as he had been at the Forth Suspension Bridge Inquiry the previous year. He returned imprecise answers, repeatedly qualified by 'It is seven years since I made the designs and I can hardly bear them in my recollection';[97] which onlookers took to mean that he had not bothered to prepare himself or refresh his memory. Even allowing for the fact that he was simultaneously working hard on the Forth Bridge, the Tay Bridge reconstruction and the Edinburgh suburban railways, his attitude was almost surreally withdrawn. He does not appear to have bothered to read the report that he himself had commissioned on his own bridge from Pole and Stewart,[98] confessing to being unaware that Stewart had allowed for 20lbs of wind pressure (i.e. double the recommended pressure) in the original design. He only came alive when discussing supervision, and whether the train had left the rails. There is simply no information to explain Bouch's performance, but the QC's view that 'his mind has gone' implies a recurrent mental problem.

Bouch intended to confront the allegations of insufficient supervision. He had spent £9000 on site staff[99] – an investment far higher than customary – and had absolute faith in the skills and experience of Paterson, his resident engineer,[100] in his assistants and in his two inspectors Noble and McBeath. Trayner suggested that this was avoiding the issue. How adequate was the supervision and inspection when Bouch wasn't there? Why had his people not noticed the problems in the foundry? Then there was the evidence of David Young, a salmon fisher who had become personal boatman to Grothe, who observed that 'Mr Bouch's examination was very cursory, and when he appeared, there was always a desire on the part of the men to put the best possible face on things'. That was not unusual. From time immemorial, contractors have covered up or concealed unpalatable construction when faced by a visiting consultant engineer or architect. It is part of the system. The clever consultant, of course, makes rapid and unplanned visits to site to prevent just this kind of cover-up. Bouch, it seems, did not. Young told Thornton that the management of the 'affairs at building the bridge' was very loose, and he had returned home confiding to his wife that 'he would not be grey before the bridge required to be rebuilt'.[101]

For eleven years, Col. Washington Roebling, Chief Engineer of the Brooklyn Bridge, had been prevented from visiting his bridge by a disabling illness, and exercised control through a telescope from his sick room in Brooklyn Heights,[102] issuing daily written instructions to his highly skilled, fully delegated subordinates. The Tay Bridge was too far from Bouch's new offices in Edinburgh's George Street to watch by telescope, but he also had a team in place. Daily responsibility lay not with Bouch but with the resident engineer Paterson and the younger site engineers. Young's observation implies that Bouch's subordinates were either not of the same calibre as Roebling's or not given sufficient authority. Paterson not only appears to have postponed decisions pending authorisation by Bouch, but was referred to by so few witnesses as to imply that his impact upon the construction team was minimal. Perhaps that was one consequence of appointing a middle-aged station engineer, who still lived in Perth and retained the nominal duties of the Station Engineer there, as site engineer of the longest bridge in the world.

The Inquiry began on a Saturday, and closed on a Saturday, twenty-five days of evidence later. The longest summing up was Bidder's. 'The impression made upon the minds of the public generally owing to the reports in the public prints [was] that this bridge in its execution and construction was one of the most disgracefully scamped, slipshod and inferior pieces of workmanship that ever was put together.'[103] He demonstrated, in painstaking detail, the extent to which Bouch had sought the correct advice from the correct people, had met that advice, and had allowed a much greater margin of safety than had been recommended. He concluded that Bouch had done 'everything that a man could do to ensure efficient supervision and construction of his work', and that the design was 'amply sufficient'.[104] The contractor's counsel, Webster, suggested that since the iron tests had shown the moulders' evidence to be wrong, they could not be trusted about anything else. The bridge had been well-built and well-supervised, and had been brought down by a collision – a shock – caused by a train. Balfour, counsel for the North British, did a competent impression of Pontius Pilate. The Railway Company had no view, but would be interested in the result.

That left the Board of Trade. Trayner's conclusion was a personal attack on Bouch. 'Sir Thomas Bouch gave his evidence in a way which showed that he was, to use a common phrase, rather fidgety [*sic*]; he is a little deaf; he did not follow the questions; he did not show the same aptitude for business, if I may so speak, as one was wont to find him show. It may be that ill health and other things have contributed.'[105] Trayner was not prepared to challenge the technicalities presented by Bidder: 'No one has suggested that the design,' he stated, 'if well carried out, would not have been sufficient for the work it had to do.' Given the evidence of Law, Cochrane and Brunlees, that was blatantly untrue, but it set the scene for Trayner's charge – namely that absence of professional supervision had permitted the contractor's men to deviate from design and specification. 'It points with other things to this fact, that Sir Thomas Bouch was trusting a great deal too much to his subordinates and, unfortunately, we have seen by how much he has been deceived.'[106] The Commissioners then agreed which documents should be printed in the final report, closed the Inquiry, and went into six weeks of purdah to contemplate guilt.

It is noticeable that not a single one of the summings up placed before the Commissioners reached the conclusion that Bouch's design had been flawed. The Board of Trade had suggested that the cause had been poor construction – Gilkes's responsibility – which he had been permitted to get away with by insufficient supervision by Bouch's team. The others had maintained that everything had been professionally carried out, and that a storm of that severity had never been contemplated. The outcome of the Inquiry, however, would be manipulated by Rothery to place the entire blame on Bouch irrespective of the evidence.

CHAPTER SEVEN

THE TUMBLING OF
BOUCH'S BRIDGES

Of what use is a bridge if it is liable to be blown down? It is better to be without it.

HERAPATH'S RAILWAY JOURNAL 10.7.80

The North British increased the pressure on its professionals during May 1880 to get the repair to the Tay Bridge approved by Parliament before the Commissioners published their findings. The shareholders demanded their bridge, Dundee needed it, and the expensive infrastructure in place would be largely meaningless without it. The Inquiry had not yet determined whether the Tay Bridge collapse had been occasioned by McGonagall's imaginary Storm Fiend playing upon a weak bridge, or by human miscalculation, incompetence or by wilful human error. In public, at least, there was no question but that Bouch would repair his own bridge. However, his lamentable performance in those closing days of the Inquiry implied that the engineer upon whom the North British depended for its two largest capital projects – the pioneering Forth Bridge, and the rebuilding of the Tay Bridge – upon which its entire strategy for the East Coast trunk route depended, was losing the plot either from illness or madness.

Publicly, Kippendavie's position remained that the North British had done all that could possibly be expected of it 'by especially engaging Sir Thomas Bouch'. Privately, the Board was deeply concerned and divided on whether to continue to do so.[1] Its problems were exacerbated by the fact that Kippendavie had promised his shareholders to keep the rebuilding costs to the £120,000 sliced from the Preference dividend (hiding other costs in capital), but a secret note calculated costs for rebuilding and compensation reaching £350,000, just about the same as the budget for the original bridge, depending upon how much of the old bridge they could re-use.

Badly shaken by Trayner's cross-examination of Bouch at the Inquiry, the North British Board reiterated that Bouch had to be 'associated with the Parliamentary plan for the reconstruction of the bridge';[2] but its weaselly phraseology – 'associated with' rather than 'designer' – left open exactly what role it intended. It had begun hunting for someone else 'who might be taken on as engineer with Bouch in the reconstruction of the bridge'.[3] After disagreement about Bouch's role on 14 May ('a considerable divergence of opinion', according to a telegram sent to London[4]), the NBR finally authorised the reconstruction of a single track bridge modified by new piers in the centre of all or some of the wide spans, solely 'under the name of Sir Thomas Bouch'.[5]

Since the bridge was to be rebuilt lower,[6] the upstream shipping interests – particularly those of Perth – had to be squared once again. The city of Perth already received an annual pension of £463, technically as compensation for interruption to shipping caused by the original bridge,[7] but really as a recompense for withdrawing its opposition. If it was to agree to a lower bridge, Perth was seeking an increased settlement which it planned to use to revive its harbour. The little port of Newburgh on the south side of the estuary, however, which principally imported timber and barley from Aarhus, planned to use its own compensation to improve its streets and drains.[8] A survey, however, revealed that upstream shipping had not contracted after the construction of the Tay Bridge as forecast, but had in fact marginally increased. Dirty Runcorn coasters with salt-caked smokestacks were butting up the Tay with slates from Wales. There were cargoes of peats, of slates and of manure from Berwick and from Kirkwall and from Caernarfon.[9] Sailing ships from St Petersburg, from Memel, and from Cronstadt brought cargoes of oilseed, of barley, and of long-span wood. They were all towed prosaically upriver by steam tugs.[10]

Thornton's initial meeting with Perth's Town Clerk William McLeish went satisfactorily. 'He will aid me in any way he reasonably can. A sixty-foot bridge is ample for all requirements';[11] but he needed leeway to close a deal. 'We shall have no great difficulty with them. The best policy – go on strongly and promptly with your Bill without showing you want a settlement or fear them in any way. Give me much more power in negotiation. All Perth wants is money. I have hinted at a reduction to 60 feet . . . I shall offer to recommend the lowest figure provided they agree to your terms. This, I think, is the way to work them.'[12] He then took the Town Clerk and Magistrates out to dinner,[13] and reported back 'they wish to get as much money as possible'.[14] Thornton had, in fact, talked them down to a bridge of only a fifty-six-foot clearance above the high tide mark which, in one way, was an excellent result. Unfortunately, that meant that the surviving piers of the north and south viaducts would have to be cut down substantially, which was going to be considerably more expensive than rebuilding at the original height. The North British had appreciated neither the engineering consequences of Thornton's negotiations, nor that Bouch would be unable to effect such a significant modification within either his budget or timescale.[15]

The Deputy Chairman, Sir James Falshaw, misunderstood the real purpose of Perth's pension, believing that the money was being paid genuinely in compensation for navigation interruption. Since navigation had been proved not to have been interrupted, Falshaw demanded that it should be discontinued.[16] Persuading him of the continued utility of buying friends and oiling the bill through Parliament took all of Thornton's skills. But back in Perth, the magistrates had now lost the support of their own constituency, for there was a growing belief that Perth was selling its birthright.

From its position of railway power twenty years earlier, when it aspired to being the York of Scotland, modernisation was now bypassing it. There was obvious resentment at the inevitable decline of its small tidal harbour in comparison to the enormous growth of Dundee's docks. When Thornton went to take precognitions from Perth supporters of the proposed bill, he reported that 'the vast number were hostile, but I found three pretty fair men'.[17] Once the Bill was published, merchants of Perth organised a protest meeting, but to little avail.[18]

Thornton also arranged that once the Bill was ready, a flurry of new petitions would be lodged before Parliament – not just by the Dundee Town Council, the Guildry, Harbour Trustees, the Water Commissioners and the Police Board, but also by neighbouring burghs to whom he sent a pro forma.[19] The Provosts and Town Councils of Cupar, Fife, Brechin and Forfar – effectively the entire region – duly obliged by petitioning Parliament to support the rebuilding of the Tay Bridge at a lower level, emphasising that it was 'essential for the public interest that the restoration of the Bridge be effected with all dispatch'.[20] They desired that Parliament ensure that the new bridge be double track – even though that was still not the North British intention.

On 25 May, the completed plans for the repair of the bridge with a clearance of only fifty-seven feet were dispatched to London. The surviving north and south viaducts – i.e. the majority of the bridge – were left intact but lowered in height. The height of the proposed reconstructed centre would be fifty-four to fifty-seven feet above high water (compared to the eighty-eight-foot height of the original bridge), but its design was left blank as though still undetermined. In the place of the thirteen doomed 245-foot-long High Girders, there would be twenty-two girders half the length, 109 feet long at the centre, and two of 100 feet on each end. The steep 1:74 gradient as the bridge leaned toward the northern shore was maintained.[21] The bridge would be reopened in three years. By contrast with Bouch's earlier parliamentary bills, his name as the leading civil engineer was ominously omitted, not just from the bill's cover page, but from the entire document.

The *Wizard of the North* offered its own advice on safety checks for the new Tay Bridge.

Whatever they stated publicly, North British Directors and senior officials were now allocating Bouch only a token role in the rebuilding of the Tay Bridge. They had decided to drop the pilot, and the only question was how. They first approached Cochrane to tender as contractor; and he, honest man, went to talk to Bouch first. Meanwhile, chairman, vice-chairman and solicitor were each approaching other engineers, unaware that their colleagues were doing likewise, to ask whether they might be interested in assisting in the bridge's reconstruction. Kippendavie favoured Commissioner Barlow, whereas Falshaw was a Brunlees man. The solicitor Adam Johnston considered Henry Law safest. Naïvely, they were not seeking new designs for their bridge, but simply engineers who would be prepared to work with Bouch's submitted redesign – although given how Law had pilloried the bridge at the Inquiry, it is difficult to imagine how that pair might have made effective collaborators.

Henry Law was summoned to a private meeting with Johnston a few days after the Bill was submitted. 'You then informed me,' Law wrote later, 'that the Directors of the North British Railway wished me to undertake the reconstruction of the Tay Bridge in conjunction with Sir Thomas Bouch, and you further informed me that Sir Thomas had been consulted on this matter.'[22] He had recorded the meeting in his careful engineer's diary. Law was writing, livid, after learning on the grapevine that Brunlees had been appointed whereas he had thought that the commission was his. Johnston denied everything, but Law's diary has the greater credibility. Johnston had clearly been overruled from above.

Innocuously subtitled 'A Bill for the Alteration of Levels', the North British (Tay Bridge) Bill[23] was deposited before Parliament and published in the newspapers. Judging by the sheaves of telegrams exchanged each day throughout June the North British, deeply apprehensive at what the Commissioners might conclude, was determined to get the Reconstruction Bill approved before the report's publication.[24] The publicity also alerted unhappy shareholders, one of whom wrote to the company in shaky, elderly handwriting: 'The Tay Bridge will be an obvious risk to preference shareholders and no good! And I hope that opposition will soon be made *unless* clauses be inserted to protect us. The 4.5% stock of 1875 that I took at 102 has not been at 97 since the accident . . . However will the North British raise more capital? Whoever will take it up if protection is not granted in the bill?'[25] Somebody must also have sent a copy of 'the New Tay Bridge Viaduct' to Albert Grothe in Spain, because, under a week later, he wrote to Johnston scornfully: 'The current proposal is a patchwork. It reduces the waterway and increases the risk of scour. I have designed a very handsome one, enclosed.'[26] This further attempt by Grothe to be recognised as a design engineer was fruitless since Johnston, busy preparing for the parliamentary hearing, failed to take the bait. Grothe remained in Spain.

As the Commissioners had been preparing their report, in the meantime, a division emerged between Rothery and the two engineers. Rothery's usurpation of the role of chairman, treating Barlow and Yolland as though they had been merely his expert assessors, had gone to his head. When he had had transcripts of the earlier hearings privately printed and circulated only to Trayner, civil service eyebrows had been raised.[27] He had then concluded that Yolland and Barlow were too pro-Bouch, and accused Barlow, in particular, of colluding with Bouch. He then attempted to persuade the Board of Trade to refuse to pay Barlow on those grounds.[28] The divisions between them were to appear in their conclusions.

On 30 June 1880, rather earlier than the North British had hoped, the Commissioners reported to Joseph Chamberlain, the new President of the Board of Trade, on the fall of the Tay Bridge.[29] Two separate reports were delivered to him. In a striking departure from convention, Henry Rothery declined to join himself to the majority report of his fellow Commissioners, and issued a minority report. It was, and remains, Rothery's minority report that is remembered.

Yolland and Barlow concluded that the foundations had not moved, the iron was satisfactory if workmanship poor, but that quality control during construction had been grossly insufficient. Bouch's arrangements for maintenance had been inadequate, putting too much responsibility on Henry Noble for which he was not qualified. Nonetheless, the only cause that they could identify for the collapse was wind pressure: 'the insufficiency of the cross bracings and its fastenings to sustain the force of the gale' upon a bridge that had already been strained by earlier storms. The extent of the collapse was attributable to the use of 'long continuous girders'.[30] They endorsed Law's recommendation that a minute examination of the surviving piers should be made prior to any re-use. Since their brief had only been to discover the causes of the collapse, and to identify what lessons might be learnt, rather than attribute blame, they studiously avoided pinning responsibility upon any individual. The principal lesson to be learnt was that there should be an Inquiry into standards for wind pressure. Because Bouch had obtained his guidelines for wind pressure from Yolland himself, Barlow and Yolland's report largely exonerated Bouch, blaming instead a combination of Gilkes for bad workmanship, and God for unprecedented wind pressure.

Rothery had not felt so constrained either in the interpretation of the evidence of the collapse, which differed markedly from the interpretation of both the engineers and the expert witnesses,[31] or in relation to Bouch. Smugly, he wrote, 'We ought not to shrink from the duty, however painful it may be, of saying where the responsibility for this casualty rests': namely Thomas Bouch. In his view, the bridge's general structural weakness – narrow columns, missing joints and poor construction – exemplified Bouch's inadequate attention to construction, instancing the latter's approach to the bridge's foundation problem and Ower's inaccurate survey. 'I should have thought that, if engineers are liable to be deceived by borers, it is all the more important that, before designing a bridge, they should satisfy themselves, beyond a doubt, of the accuracy of the borings, which there would have been no difficulty in doing in the present case.' He was equally scathing about Bouch's apparently casual approach to the matter of wind pressure, observing that France allowed for a wind pressure of 58lbs per square foot, America 50lbs, Brunlees 30lbs and Baker 28lbs. Bouch, on the other hand, had relied upon Airy and Yolland's recommendation of

10lbs – which had been provided for an entirely different bridge in a different location. Rothery's conclusion as to the immediate cause of the bridge's collapse was a gust of wind. He was precise as to where the responsibility lay:

> The conclusion then to which I have come is that this bridge was badly designed, badly constructed, and badly maintained, and that its downfall was due to inherent defects in its structure . . . For these defects in the design, the execution and the maintenance, Sir Thomas Bouch is, in my opinion, mainly to blame. For the faults of design he is entirely responsible. For those of construction he is principally to blame in not having exercised that supervision over the work which would have enabled him to detect and apply a remedy to them. And for the faults of maintenance, he is also principally, if not entirely, to blame in having neglected to maintain such an inspection over the structure as its character demanded.

Rothery was on a personal crusade. The conclusion that there had been faults in design was tendentious, at odds with most of the evidence and the Board of Trade's own counsel's summing up. It was contractually inaccurate to blame the engineer for all the faults of construction, and strange that the contractor, Gilkes, escaped with only a minor censure. During the Inquiry, no hint had emerged that Rothery had judged Bouch's supervisory staff to be less competent by comparison with, for example, Roebling's on the Brooklyn Bridge, and he did not say so now. Instead, as though he was wholly unaware of how a construction site works, he discounted any supervision other than by Bouch as largely irrelevant, placing on him the personal charge to be present at all times. Roebling had just the single project whereas throughout the Tay Bridge contract, Bouch had been working on several large projects simultaneously. Perhaps engineering working practices were Rothery's target. The railway industry had a high accident record, it was time to bring it to heel, and the President of the Board of Trade was keen to win a famous victory.

The Times, probably embarrassed by its extravagant lament upon the bridge's collapse ('crafted by cunning hands'), now took its revenge. 'The competition of railway companies, of engineers, and of contractors has now become so keen that the margin of safety has gradually been ground down until it has, at last, become evanescent.'[32] *The Times* was right that railway competition had indeed been appallingly wasteful, but wrong about the margin of safety on the Tay Bridge, which had varied from 500 to 900%. *The Times* also alleged that bridges were built for cheapness rather than durability; yet the North British had been prepared to pay what was needed, and had ended up paying double. *The Times*, however, was getting into its stride. The moral was that 'railway construction is now approaching recklessness and that inspection in certain circumstances affords no adequate security . . . Inspection is worse than useless if it is merely formal or perfunctory.' The paper concluded with a warning: 'It would certainly be profitable and instructive to ascertain, if it were possible, how far the vicious system of construction and maintenance disclosed in the disastrous history of the Tay Bridge has extended throughout our railway system.'[33]

Was the rhetoric merited? The Inquiry's conclusion that the Tay Bridge had collapsed because of a sudden gust of wind was speculative, and had failed to take much contradictory evidence into account. Thereafter, theories to account for why the bridge fell have multiplied, sometimes blaming individuals, sometimes systems, and sometimes the level of knowledge then available – in other words, the bridge had stretched contemporary technology too far. Then as now, the theories fall into three principal groups: poor construction and inadequate supervision; second, exceptional wind pressure leading to structural failure; and – most recently – metal fatigue. Poor construction with insufficient supervision by the engineer had been Trayner's conclusion: imperfectly cast columns[34] and/or poor workmanship brought down an otherwise satisfactory (if risky) design. Cochrane had concurred. 'If properly constructed, the bridge was amply strong.'[35] And that was the view popularised by John Prebble in *The High Girders*. Exceptional wind pressure upon a bridge insufficiently strong to withstand it, was Barlow and Yolland's conclusion. Their view was shared by Law and Brunlees,[36] and by most twentieth-century commentators. The poet McGonagall managed, with poetic concision, to précis thousands of technical questions on the narrowness of the foundations into a few lines of doggerel:

> . . . *Your central girders would not have given way,*
> *At least many sensible men do say,*
> *Had they been supported on each side by buttresses . . .*
> *For the stronger we our houses do build,*
> *The less chance we have of being killed.*[37]

The Inquiry had also concluded that if the lightweight timber superstructure of the Second-Class carriage had been blown sideways against the girders, it would have been sliced by the iron girders, leaving the bridge fundamentally unscathed. So that explanation was insufficient. Moreover, had the gale been that severe? Baker had cast doubt on the severity of the storm at the Inquiry, Barlow and Yolland concurred in their report,[38] and twentieth-century computer modelling has shown them to be correct.[39] The gale had not been exceptional. Pole and Stewart, both of whose reputations emerged from the Inquiry well intact, had demonstrated how the bridge could have withstood gusts substantially stronger than even the most outrageous calculation for that Sunday evening. The possibility that the cast-iron might have failed through progressive metal fatigue is a recent arrival. Strained by its heavy goods trains and battered by repeated gales, and then frozen in distorted shapes by Noble's packing pieces, the iron was weakened and finally gave way.[40]

The problem with each theory – wind pressure, poor construction or metal fatigue – is that while it might explain some of the evidence, it does not explain all of it. Whereas each of those factors may well have played a part once the bridge had been wounded, the Inquiry's overall conclusion that the trigger for the collapse had been an exceptional gust of wind which had coincided with the

The last pier on the north side. If the overall construction of the bridge had been so poor, as was alleged by the Inquiry chairman, why did the enormous pressure of the falling High Girders fail to pull over the piers on either side?

train rattling at 24mph at least across the bridge's most vulnerable point, namely the High Girders, contradicted Pole and Stewart's undisputed calculations that the bridge's safety margins should have been easily sufficient to have withstood such a gust. They had written: 'The stresses resulting from the wind alone, however fiercely it may blow, are so insignificant as not to merit notice.'[41] Any explanation founded upon the gale remained speculation.

Something had to have acted upon the bridge's structure to take it over. Whatever that was, it had to explain why both girders and carriages suffered significantly different damage. Carriages at the front of the train had remained remarkably intact whereas the carriages within Girder 4 – the Second-Class carriage and the Guard's Van – were mangled utterly. Only Girder 4 had black-painted strike marks at carriage-roof height and smashed rails and chairs. Significantly, three of the Girder 4's triangular plates that strengthened the girder box by tying the side girder to the base had been mown down from a southerly direction. Comparable damage occurred nowhere else. Any explanation of the tragedy would have to explain away such evidence. Bouch's unwavering intuition, supported by Gilkes and his team, was that a carriage had hit that girder.[42] The only candidate was the light Second-Class carriage with its three passengers, one of Dugald Drummond's three-axle, high-sprung and notoriously rough and bouncy carriages[43] which, as everybody accepted, had been brought to a sudden halt, turning slightly to the right,[44] making the Guard's Van smash into its rear left, mounting up over its chassis to destroy its superstructure.

Henry Law had testified that if the bridge's side had been hit by carriage and van, weighing 16 tons (35,000 lbs) together travelling at forty feet per second, they would have acted like a battering ram sufficient to take the bridge over.[45] The impact would also explain why the cast-iron lugs of the columns below had fractured. But nobody could provide a credible cause for why that might have occurred, or why the carriage and van might have jumped track, as Law put it, 'in the sense they would run upon their wheels against the girder'. Yet the wheels of the Second-Class carriage had indeed been burnt in a manner characteristic of being forced across wood, supported by the evidence of the timbers washed ashore in Broughty gouged by metal wheels running over them – as they had also run over the iron bars that had been inserted to keep the rails apart after Hutchinson's inspection.[46] Moreover, the locomotive engineers themselves had spotted that the axle-box from the Second-Class carriage had detached and was lying in the 'eastward book of the bottom girders' providing 'important evidence towards proving the carriage had left the rails'.[47] The Inquiry had been unable to explain how parts of the wreckage could have ended up in locations that would have been impossible if the carriage had suffered damage *only after* it had been blown over. Window glass from the Second-Class carriage had fallen vertically into the trough at the bottom of the girder beside the axle box. Gravity indicated they could only have done so if both carriage and girder were still upright when the two collided. If that collision had occurred *after* the bridge began to topple sideways, the broken glass and the axle box would surely have tumbled out vertically into the sea. Law, Brunlees, Cochrane and the two engineer Commissioners were all aware that they had not managed to explain evidence like that. But they had not been provided with any adequate evidence as to why or how the Second-Class carriage might have jumped the guard rail and left track, and so did not believe that it did so. An exceptional gust of wind was, therefore, the default conclusion.

The Second-Class carriage, with its curved roof and bouncy springs, was the lightest on the train, and therefore most susceptible to any upward wind pressure. Upward pressure – wind like a whirlwind – had been observed by onlookers,[48] and any upward movement would have been increased by Bernoulli's Effect – whereby the action of wind streaming over its convex roof would have produced an uplift force. What, therefore, could have made the Second-Class carriage lift up sufficiently for Bernoulli's Effect to make it jump track? The crucial evidence remains hidden in the unheard precognitions censored by Thornton, and never presented at the Inquiry. At least three observers had noticed something wrong with the rail track in the southernmost high girder. This girder was the one that had blown down in February 1877, had been shipped to Middlesbrough, lashed up, beaten back into shape, and then re-erected. 'Evans [the painter]', Thornton had written to Johnston back in February, 'particularly says: at the junction of the High Girders on the south, there was a slight twist on the rails. It looked as though the pier had gone to the side a little and pulled the rail off the straight.'[49] The painter Neilsen had corroborated. 'There was an inequality in the Rails at the south entrance to the High Girders. I could see it, and hear the Engine and carriage wheels strike and jerk over it.'[50] That jerking might also explain the increasingly noticeable bounding motion observed by painters and frightened passengers. If the girder had been weakened fundamentally by its fall and subsequent reshaping, the passage of the heavy freight cars might have begun to distort it. Since the track was firmly fixed to the girder, any distortion in the one would necessarily lead to distortion in the other. The kink in the rail had evidently become sufficiently obvious to be visible to the naked, non-expert eye. So who was responsible for it? Maintenance of the track had not been Bouch's responsibility, but that of James Bell, the NBR Chief Engineer. Split responsibility for the bridge and a lack of collaboration led to no action being taken.

The North British had been running a train over a bridge which it itself had not built, using carriages rented from others, over a track for which it retained only partial responsibility, the bulk of the responsibility for maintenance having been contracted out. Resonances with the twenty-first century are inescapable.

Previous analyses of the disaster paid insufficient attention to the twisted rail, the condition of Girder 4, and to the unusual damage to the Second-Class carriage. Taking all the evidence into account, therefore, the bridge's collapse might have occurred like this. At around 7.16pm on Sunday evening, 28 December 1879, the twisted rail in the first High Girder caused the light Second-Class carriage to bounce upwards sufficiently for a heavy gust of storm wind to carry it off-rail, although remaining coupled to the carriage in front and the heavy Guard's Van behind, and continuing to run forward. The wheels of the carriages front and back were pulled laterally against the downwind rail causing that stream of sparks. Then, whether blown further to the east by another gust of wind or not, the Second-Class carriage's wheels were brought to a dead stop when they hit the fourth triangular tie-bar. The Guard's Van immediately behind crashed into its rear, mounting up over its chassis and smashing its superstructure to smithereens. The bridge was not designed to withstand the force of an impact like that. The cast-iron lugs in the columns below fractured, and could not prevent the smashed Girder 4 which, by then, was mostly held in place largely by gravity through the failure of the bracing, from toppling lazily eastwards, its legs crumpling beneath it. If the track had not been continuous, perhaps parts of the High Girders containing the front sections of the train might have withstood the fall. But as one girder collapsed, the continuous track, devised originally as a safety measure, pulled down its neighbour; and Girder 4 took all other High Girders with it.

It was normal for the engine driver to shut off steam at the top of the bridge's summit,[51] and throttle down significantly as the train tanked downhill toward the northern curve round into Dundee. Maybe he felt the train dragging backwards as the Second-Class carriage was pulled over the softer timbers, or maybe he felt the train being sucked back as it began to fall, but the driver had opened the throttle valve to full.[52] His bid to escape was futile, as the train was pulled back like a shrimp from its shell. But the sturdy north and south viaducts, although tied to the High Girders by four sets of continuous steel rails, resisted the pressure to fall, and the steel rails snapped. If Rothery's conclusion that the viaduct's structure was faulty in its entirety had been justified, all the piers, given the forces involved, would have gone over. Because his agenda was other than unearthing the real cause of the accident, because significant evidence had been withheld, and because Bouch had performed so poorly as an advocate for his solution to the conundrum of the disaster, the Inquiry never did discover the truth it set out to find. With the acknowledged problems in both foundations and quality of construction, Bouch made a convenient scapegoat.

Down at Tharsis Mining in the south of Spain Grothe, realising that his reputation could also be at stake, wrote to Johnston on

1 July requesting a copy of the report as soon as it was available; and again the next day to offer help with constructing Bouch's new bridge – although he was unenthusiastic about the stodginess of its redesign. 'Everything is made ultra strong, and must reassure the timid.' His most serious objection was the plan to lower the height of the existing viaduct piers girders. 'It is so nasty a work that I, for one, would not like to undertake in contract.'[53] Rothery's report, however, so much worse than the worst North British fears, put any question of re-assembling the old team out of the question. The *Scotsman* had accused the railway of culpable 'and even scandalous' carelessness in the supervision of the bridge's construction, stating that it should have kept a closer eye on Bouch;[54] and the public reaction followed suit.

Adam Johnston, the North British solicitor, was at the eye of the storm. Bouch's solicitor wrote pre-emptively to him, 'What an unmerciful report this is . . . It seems too severe in every sense to be just. The public mind, after the proceedings in London, has evidently been made up . . . This report magnifies and rides to death every fault that can be picked out.' Whether the Inquiry had indeed identified the cause of the collapse was, he wrote, something 'which must, in essential facts, probably remain a mystery until the end of all things'.[55] Thornton also telegrammed Johnston: 'The Tay Bridge Reports are most distressing. What are you to do? Are you still to go on with the Bill this session?' Johnson then received a letter from Bouch, stating that he had read the report, but remained in London to complete his Proof of Evidence for the forthcoming Parliamentary hearing according to the deposited plans.[56] The Bill, however, was the thing, and the North British would sacrifice what it had to, to achieve it. Fully aware that the Tay Bridge Reconstruction Bill was doomed if it still had Bouch's name on it, the North British privately decided to cut Bouch loose.

The North British Board had now risen for the summer, and at this critical juncture, the Chairman was away and the General Manager escaped for a month's leave. In their place, the Secretary George Weiland informed Johnston that Deputy Chairman Falshaw was now content 'to leave the employment of engineers entirely to your discretion. While we cannot entirely overlook Bouch, it is clear that independent engineers must be appointed . . . I think it would be a good thing to see Barlow.'[57] Thus the NBR Board washed its hands of an engineer with whom it had worked in one guise or another for at least thirty-five years: too pusillanimous to do it in person. It was left to Johnston to give Bouch the bad news that the reconstruction of the bridge would be transferred to Cochrane and Brunlees, retaining Bouch only on some form of consultancy package. It would probably have been a complete break had not Weiland reminded Johnston not to 'forget the importance of Bouch's position in relation to the Forth Bridge'. For that was the NBR's other problem. Construction on the Forth Bridge project had been proceeding rapidly, with Arrol on the bridge and Waddell on the approach line between Burntisland and Inverkeithing.[58] The Forth Bridge Company, which had not yet received its report from Hawkshaw, Harrison and Barlow, was still working on the assumption that bridge construction could proceed.

Back in Dundee, Thornton made ready to dispatch another letter for burghs, towns and counties in north-eastern Scotland to send to Parliament to support the bill,[59] and set about lobbying Members of Parliament and key businessmen. The mood had changed. A typical response was received from W.E. Baxter, MP of the London-based merchant banking arm of Baxter Brothers' linen works at Dens Works, Dundee. 'The fall of the Tay Bridge, even apart from the loss of life, is a great public calamity, and its speedy restoration is of the utmost importance to us all. My constituents are specially interested.' He added, 'The revelations connected with it structure and maintenance are, however, so startling that I feel sure the House and the Country will insist on nothing being done in a hurry. I cannot but fear that mischief may arise from pressing on the Bill this session.'[60] It was much the same locally. Although Thornton reassured Johnston that he would 'make all other business subordinate to that of promoting the bridge . . . [yet] I cannot disguise from you that the feeling here is very strong that you should delay presenting the Bill for the present session'.[61]

The North British rinsed Bouch out of its affairs with a signal lack of graciousness. It was all over in barely a week. On 8 July, the Reconstruction Bill finally reached Parliament eight days after the reports' publication, to be greeted with an acrimonious debate, 'in which censure was freely cast'. Weiland had meanwhile met Barlow and Hawkshaw, who appear to have suggested that Bouch's soaring Forth Suspension Bridge might be too slender to meet any increase in wind-loading requirements following the Tay Bridge Inquiry. He immediately wrote to Bouch on behalf of the Forth Bridge Company suggesting that 'in view of the present adverse state of public opinion, he [Bouch] would probably prefer to be relieved of his position as engineer', and instructed him to request Arrol to discontinue work immediately (which he did not).[62] A few days later, Bouch rejected a placebo consultancy for the Tay Bridge reconstruction, writing to Johnson, 'I must consider my position as Engineer for the Tay Bridge to be terminated', although he sought the opportunity of explaining his plans personally. 'The very adverse feeling manifested in the House of Commons', Bouch wrote, was 'as you are aware, entirely due to the very strong statements in Mr Rothery's report with reference to myself in which he states that his colleagues concur. You will see in tomorrow's papers correspondence that contradicts that.' There is no response in Johnston's papers, and no mention of Bouch's departure in the North British Minute Book.[63]

As soon as Rothery's minority report on the Tay Bridge became public, Bouch's solicitors wrote to Barlow and to Yolland enquiring whether they had endorsed Rothery's judgment. Displeased at having been outflanked, the latter disassociated themselves from everything in Rothery's report not explicitly included in their own report. Their letter was circulated to MPs and to the newspapers, but its lack of effect became apparent the following day. Joseph Chamberlain, sensing appropriate political mileage in overriding his chief civil servant, Thomas Farrer, Permanent Secretary of the Board of Trade, decided to support Rothery and cast the entire blame on Bouch.[64] When he referred the Tay Bridge Reconstruction Bill to a Select Committee three weeks later, instructing it to examine any interruption to the navigation, the economic needs of the region, and the safety of the travelling public, Chamberlain mentioned only Rothery's minority report.[65] When two MPs asked the Home Secretary 'whether any instructions [had] been given to the public prosecutors to take any action in respect of the great loss of life occasioned by [the Tay-bridge disaster]',[66] the Home Secretary referred the Tay Bridge Report to the Scottish Lord Advocate for just such an opinion, in view of the disaster's location in Scotland. Bouch's solicitors wrote that 'we are disappointed to see . . . that not a word was said by any of [the MPs] as to the repudiation by Yolland and Barlow',[67] but they should not have been surprised. A scapegoat was just the ticket. Four days later, far too late to have any effect, the Yolland–Barlow correspondence was published in *The Times*.

The NBR's General Manager John Walker wrote to Johnston from his vacation, alarmed at the effect Weiland's letter had had on Bouch. He was 'in a sad way as to the terms of your letter . . . After what he has done in connection with the Company, I do hope that some arrangement may be devised . . . that may yet admit of his name being associated with it when permanently put right. He has run great risks from first to last and I don't believe he has ever made a single penny of profit himself.'[68] Kippendavie also appears to have had doubts, writing to Johnston: 'I should be sorry to throw Bouch over altogether, but if it comes to be a question of losing our Bill [to reconstruct] we cannot keep ourselves.' He added: 'I was quite satisfied all along that altho' we might employ him to get our Bill through Parliament, yet to secure public confidence, the plans, whatever they are, we must have the sanction of a first class engineer and I consider that Barlow . . . was the best man we could get.'[69] Kippendavie and his General Manager were less ruthless about ditching Sir Thomas Bouch than the Deputy Chairman and the Secretary, and felt ambivalent about the way they had done it. His choice of engineer for the replacement bridge was Barlow 'and no plan for the new work [should be] carried out without his full sanction and inspection. I am prepared to do as they wish regarding Bouch.'[70] It is not evident to whose wishes the chairman was acceding in this egregious Pontius Pilatism: probably the clamorous public.

In accordance with practice, the Board of Trade sent a copy of the Inquiry Report to all railway companies in the United Kingdom on 14 July, and sought formal reassurance from each that they took adequate responsibility for the safety of their structures, particularly for bridges with a similar construction to the Tay Bridge. It announced the establishment of a committee to study wind pressure on bridges.

When the Select Committee met to consider the Tay Bridge reconstruction, the North British placed before it, with greater clarity than ever before, just how essential were these two bridges in the Scottish trunk railway war. Only once the Forth and Tay Bridges were complete could the North British be on an equal footing with the Caledonian in the competition for traffic with London and the other parts of England.[71] So it did not take the Committee long to agree that the bridge had to be rebuilt, that the present site was the most suitable in view of the infrastructure and – considering that all seven original petitions against the bill had been bought off with appropriate sweeteners – that the proposed height was satisfactory. The design itself, however, had been done in haste. Cochrane and Brunlees had had barely a fortnight to prepare this eleventh design for crossing the Tay estuary, and were still not quite ready when the Select Committee met.

The disaster had created unease about engineering, which Rothery had compounded in his report, and the Committee was dismayed that the two engineers before them were still undecided about whether to move from iron to entirely brick columns even when they were giving evidence.[72] Cochrane and Brunlees intended to capitalise as far as possible upon the existing bridge structure, and planned to sink caissons of identical size just down-stream of the original ones, and tie the two together as they rose. Each re-used pier from the old bridge would be supported by a new raking column. The spans would be slightly shorter and lower, and for the four high seventy-seven-foot spans above the fairway (the options for tall-masted vessels to sail upstream narrowing),

Brunlees preferred using 245-foot-long bow-string girders (round-headed tops looking and acting like a bow).[73] The committee heard from Henry Noble, who vouchsafed the strength of the existing brickwork, and Henry Law who did the opposite. Law doubted that the original foundations could stand the proposed design and reiterated that the ironwork and piers had to be tested before anybody could agree to their re-use.[74]

Since neither Brunlees nor Cochrane had yet been able to inspect the existing structure in the detail required, the Board of Trade took apocalyptic fright at the suggestion that any of it should be re-used in the replacement bridge. The Board's counsel dismissed their designs as 'entirely tentative, seeing that its fulfilment depended entirely upon the result of the experiments of Mr Brunlees after he had tested the existing work'.[75] Counsel condemned any proposal 'to join together in . . . an unholy union, the old work and the new – a "marriage entered in haste to be repented of at leisure" – and he was there on the part of the Board of Trade most solemnly to forbid the banns'.[76] The Committee had little option but to reject Brunlees's redesign. Although it could hardly have been unexpected, it was 'a staggering blow' according to the *Dundee Advertiser*.[77] Any new design would have to be scrutinised by Tom Harrison, appointed by the Board of Trade,[78] and the bridge had to be double track. So the North British had won everything it needed save for the design itself. It had no option but to begin again.

On Friday 6 August, just as the works at Queensferry were suspended and the Forth Bridge workmen dismissed,[79] Bouch was back in London before the House of Lords to ensure that his Edinburgh Suburban Railway Bill passed satisfactorily. He was far from written off. But on his return to Edinburgh the following day he became very unwell – so unwell, indeed, that he and his wife rented a house in the fashionable spa town of Moffat to help him recuperate by taking the waters. His performance during the Forth Bridge hearing and the Tay Bridge Inquiry had been extraordinarily unfocused. Since he had sold his guns (for he was a keen shooter) in the previous year, it has been suggested that he might

have had a heart condition.[80] Overwork was quite likely to have
contributed since he had certainly kept to a 'punishing schedule' in
preparing for the resubmission of the Tay Bridge plans, whilst
working simultaneously on the Forth Bridge, and the Edinburgh
Suburban and various other tramway projects. Alternatively, perhaps, he had a recurrence of the unknown disease of 1877 that had
driven him to spend months recuperating in Europe. Moffat's recu-
perative powers failed, and Bouch died at 1.30am on 29 October.
His office diary noted: 'Aged 58 only!'[81] His death was recorded in
the minutes of neither the North British Railway nor the Forth
Bridge companies. Having embarrassed a major company in public,
Bouch was erased from the record.

At his funeral on 3 November, only James Falshaw represented
the hierarchy of the railway companies, although there was a faithful attendance by his own engineers, and those with whom he had
worked – John Walker, Weiland, Adam Johnston, contractors like
Waddell and William Arrol, and his 'stressman' or structural theoretician Allan Stewart. James Cox came up from Dundee in a
personal capacity. Poor Edgar Gilkes had slipped so far from public
memory that the *Scotsman* recorded him as 'Ginks'.[82]

How good a designer had Thomas Bouch been? The majority of
his commissions had come his way not by thorough inspection and
publication, as had been the case when John Roebling had been
selected for the Brooklyn Bridge, but through personal and family
contact. His slimline bridges like the Deepdale and Belah and his
cheap railways had both been admired as pioneering even if there
was a persistent undertone of impatience with the ineffectiveness of
the Bouch office. If his original Tay Bridge design had been based
on an accurate survey of the Tay riverbed and given appropriate
foundations, it would almost certainly have survived, and the 500-
foot-high silver towers of his Forth Suspension Bridge might still
have been glittering above the Queensferry narrows. Attempts then
and later to ridicule both Bouch's bridges were frequent, but his
designs were far from risible. Bouch had depended entirely upon
Allan Stewart for his structural calculations, and when Arrol later
came to receive plaudits for the Forth Bridge, he selected Stewart

for particular praise. With Stewart's imprimatur, the Tay Bridge had probably been strong enough however slender it had been, but it had been brought down by inadequate construction and a faulty girder. In 1873, William Barlow had praised his Forth Bridge design 'as a monument of commercial enterprise and constructive skill . . . an honour to the British Nation',[83] qualified only by the caution that 'it will require much care in execution'. Bouch, however, tended to leave care in execution to others, and his choice of contractor was based more upon personal networks than upon professionalism.

His campaign to simplify and cheapen railway construction had led to generic problems both with foundations on several bridges[84] and with contractors. His managerial efficiency was frequently challenged and in 1873, during the critical period in the Tay Bridge saga, he was stretched very thinly between projects in many parts of Britain. He spent far more time appearing before Parliament and other politicians than upon design. Perhaps he was less of a practical site man than what Arrol called an 'armchair engineer',[85] leaving most of it to his assistant, Thomas Peddie.[86] Although Thomas Bouch was little different in this from other great Victorian engineers or architects, there was a sense of detachment about him that one would never come across in, for example, the architect George Gilbert Scott. Nonetheless, in his pursuit of commissions, he had done very well indeed. His estate at his death (had he not had to pay out £100,000 for his brother's bond when Hopkins Gilkes went bankrupt), would have equalled that of James Cox, Dundee's largest industrialist, and was more than three times that of Sir William Arrol, the contractor for the Tay, Forth and Tower bridges when the latter died in 1913.[87] Even given the fact that he had inherited from his brother, Bouch was probably more of an engineering businessman than an engineer.

Following his condemnation by Rothery, Bouch's death was widely believed to have been the consequence of remorse for the Tay Bridge disaster, as recorded in typical Dundonian fashion in this poem by the otherwise unknown acronymous M.T.W.:

O fearful shock! O awful stroke of fate
That sent thee withered, sorrowing to thy tomb!
Though thou dist not behold that horror great –
Its first dread crash toll'd forth thine earthly doom . . .[88]

At the end of that grim July of 1880, Thornton had written to Johnston trying to accelerate action on the Tay Bridge, reporting keen speculation about who should replace Bouch as the North British's engineer. 'Pardon me for urging that you should now put the company in the hands of some high class engineers in whom both the Board of Trade and the public would have confidence. How would Fowler and Hawkshaw or Barlow do?'[89] With Bouch gone, other ambitious engineers pestered the North British for the appointment. Some, like John Douglas, threw bread upon the water by writing to Walker seeking the appointment, prefaced by the customary 'sorry for poor Sir Thomas Bouch now it is all over'. He enclosed drawings and a description of a high bridge in America with wider spans (presumably either the St Louis or the Brooklyn). The engineer W.R. Galbraith wrote to Kippendavie that he had held back so long as Bouch held his position, but now that he had gone, 'I venture to ask whether the Directors might not to some extent trust me.'[90] Gerrit Camphuis, writing from Morasesti in Romania, also volunteered, 'In not removing blame from myself with regard to this unfortunate Tay Bridge foundry (which would have been very easy) I am afraid that I have done serious harm to my reputation as a professional man . . . even although the ability of managing a foundry is not a necessary requisite for a civil engineer.' The only way he could redeem himself would be to have some responsibility for the reconstruction and, having read that the new engineers were to be Brunlees and Cochrane, thought that with his intimate knowledge of the bridge, he would be their ideal resident engineer.[91] What he failed to appreciate is that a former association with the old Tay Bridge was more a black mark than an opportunity for redemption. It was even more so at the level of the skilled workman, particularly anybody related to the unfortunate foundry who were held to have damaged the town's high reputation for mechanical quality. One foundry-man, Gowans, found it impossible to get further work in Dundee, as indeed did his son.[92]

The polymathic Dundonian engineer, artist and patron James Orchar, partner of Provost William Robertson in a firm manufacturing and selling internationally acclaimed calendaring machines, then devised a scheme of his own for bridging the Tay, and forwarded it to his friend Thornton. The drawings were accompanied by a letter from Robertson judging them 'the best thing he had ever seen'. Commending Orchar as 'a man of great talent and experience' whose scheme ingeniously re-used the existing piers, Thornton duly passed his drawings to Johnston.[93] The Board of Trade, however, had made it clear that any new bridge across the Tay would have to be designed from first principles, and any saving to be made from using the existing structure would be incidental. In view of their exceptional efforts before the parliamentary Committee, the NBR was much more likely to appoint either Cochrane or Brunlees. Kippendavie remained steadfastly a Barlow man.

The annual report from the US consul in Edinburgh on the Scottish railway system during 1879 made gloomy reading for all railway shareholders. The average railway dividend had been only 1.92%. Only 2.9% of ordinary shareholders received a dividend over 5%, whereas 35% had received nothing at all. The consul concluded that a significant part of the reason behind such a low rate of return was the high cost of land and the expense incurred in promoting bills in Parliament.[94] It was in this poor climate that the North British had to begin again, and the chairman had prevailed in the selection of engineer. For in early September 1880, the NBR had appointed Messrs Barlow, Son and Baker of Old Palace Yard, Westminster, to design a new Tay Bridge. Kippendavie presented a surprisingly bullish report to his shareholders at the end of the month. Barlow 'stood at the head of his profession in England' and would give the North British 'the best advice possible'. The damage the company had suffered from the bridge collapse was great. Passenger traffic between Dundee and Edinburgh was down

William Barlow, painted by John Collier. First an advisor to Bouch
then a Commissioner in the Inquiry and subsequently Bouch's
successor; Barlow was one of the great theoretical engineers of his
day.

75%, and between Dundee and Glasgow over 90%. Yet, leaving
aside the Tay Bridge, their capital expenditure was down, and their
income substantially up. Kippendavie concluded: 'He did not like
to be a prophet, but he could not help thinking that the prospects
for the coming winter were far better than they had been this time
last year' as a result of a good harvest and a large potato traffic.[95]

The coming winter dashed those hopes. The week after the
shareholders' meeting, the Arbroath to Montrose railway – the last
link to Aberdeen constructed by Gilkes under the supervision of
Bouch's son William – opened for goods traffic like coal, lime and

manure. Once it opened to passengers, thought the *Advertiser*, Lunan Bay could become a watering hole for tourists to rival Scarborough.[96] It now awaited its passenger certificate, and Col. Yolland arrived in November to undertake the necessary inspection for the Board of Trade. But there proved to be something seriously adrift with the iron viaduct over the South Esk, one of two bridges into Montrose. The bridge deviated from the approved plans to such a degree that it had to be taken down and rebuilt.[97] Yolland might have been overly strict, following his early involvement in the Tay Bridge design, and then his position as Commissioner in the Inquiry into its demise. A report commissioned from Benjamin Baker identified the fault as lying squarely with the Bouch office and outlined what needed to be done.

The previous June, Bouch had offered to supervise the Tay Bridge rebuilding for nothing,[98] and his fee for supervision of his Forth Suspension Bridge be £35,000 in deferred debentures. Once he had been so summarily dismissed, he had sued NBR directors for fees and expenses in the relation to the replacement Tay Bridge, and for £31,156 in relation to the Forth.[99] Steel thereupon entered the North British directors' hearts, and they decided to consult counsel about the possibility of taking legal proceedings 'against any parties for the Tay bridge accident',[100] with only Falshaw demurring. Since all mention of proceedings ceased at Bouch's death (and they would have had a far stronger claim against Gilkes, unless he had been protected by his bankruptcy and restructuring), it seems obvious that Bouch had been the only target. After his death, the North British directors faced a suit from his Trustees, who rejected a settlement offer of £15,000.[101] So although the North British had a claim against the Bouch estate over the South Esk viaduct, and a further potential claim over the Tay Bridge, they had to be set against the claims of Bouch's Trustees which now mounted to £47,000. Ironically, Bouch's Trustees appointed as their counsel John Trayner QC, Bouch's destroyer at the Inquiry. Trayner recommended settlement.

Matters at the Forth Bridge, meanwhile, had reached crisis point. Bouch's bridge needed to be assessed for its conformity to new government requirements that it had to withstand 56lbs wind pressure, and the contractors were entitled to compensation since building work had been stopped. Allan Stewart had been asked to revisit his calculations for the bridge, and had concluded that necessary modifications to make the bridge withstand the new wind pressure level would cost an additional £700,000. The Board doubted that a contractor could be found who would take on a Bouch design and then be prepared to guarantee its stability.[102] In any case, the Board had insufficient capital to proceed.

William Arrol's firm had been placed in a financial catastrophe as soon as the Board had instructed him to stop work, for his sub-contractors required payment for supplying or fabricating parts for him. If construction were merely postponed, they might have been prepared to accept payment to account or to hold on. Once the bridge was cancelled, however, substantial sums were required to pay those who had undertaken work in good faith – the largest being the steel chain fabricator Vickers, in Sheffield. Cement and steel sub-contractors pressed Arrol for payment at the end of July but, lacking an engineer to certify the necessary payments (Bouch having been dismissed), Arrol had written to George Weiland, the Forth Bridge and North British's secretary, seeking urgent funds. Weiland now revealed himself at his most slippery. Shamelessly alternating friendship with flattery, procrastination and inducement, Weiland played for time. There was necessity, he preached, for great forbearance and consideration since 'the present feeling about bridges will not disappear quickly'.[103] Forbearance pays few bills. Almost by return, Weiland received a claim for Arrol's loss of profit and other expenses from the redoubtable Glasgow lawyers Maclay, Murray and Spens.[104]

Weiland's continuing inactivity forced Arrol to propose a settlement. The Bridge company would offer him relief from all sub-contractors, pay for all materials on site, and award him £27,500 in compensation for breach of contract,[105] 40% of which would be treated as payment to account if he was awarded the Tay Bridge contract, and a further 35% if he was awarded the Forth Bridge contract within five years. Although the Forth Bridge

Board promptly agreed, Weiland then strung out the settlement with blandishments like, 'Although you have proved that you do not think the company worthy of credit, they see no reason to entertain a similar opinion on you.'[106] He was, typically, not playing straight. Stewart's report on Bouch's Forth Suspension Bridge design had forced the company to consider its abandonment, and on 22 November 1880, the Forth Bridge Directors gave up the struggle. The expenditure necessary to amend Bouch's design for the Forth Suspension Bridge was more than they could afford, and it announced its intention to abandon the bridge project, and distribute the company's assets.[107] Weiland obviously had intended to use unfulfilled promises to postpone settlement with Arrol until it would be too late for him to petition against the Forth Bridge Abandonment Bill. Thereafter, he would just have become another creditor in a bankruptcy case. Arrol smelt a rat, and petitioned against the bill anyway, which Weiland characterised as 'was an act of most unnecessary hostility'.[108]

So, within a twelvemonth, the North British Railway Company had moved from the optimistic position of having a highly profitable new bridge over the Tay, a major share in the pioneering bridge being constructed across the Forth, with the East Coast line to Aberdeen on the verge of completion, to a business with a broken bridge on the Tay, and unusable bridge blocking the line to Aberdeen, and its share in the bridge over the Forth now valueless.

CHAPTER EIGHT

PHOENIX IN THE TAY

The failures of the past prepare the triumphs of the future

MAX MULLER

The East Coast trunk route was rescued by England. Just as English investors had provided the bulk of the original investment in Scottish railways, and English railway companies had helped prise the Caledonian's grip off the east coast railway route from London to Aberdeen, English railway companies now stepped in to prevent the Forth Bridge Abandonment Bill from proceeding through Parliament.

The three railway companies from England that had originally guaranteed an income to the Forth Bridge approached the fourth – the North British – to see what new deal might be offered and to haggle over the proportion each should have to bear.[1] At a meeting in York in July 1881, the four agreed to guarantee traffic across the Forth Bridge to provide a sufficient income to cover the Bridge Company's interest repayments on the new construction cost, and to provide a dividend of 4%.[2] The Forth Bridge Company would limit its risk to the construction and future maintenance of a single bridge (just like Brooklyn), its function becoming that of a construction agent to the four great railway companies. Its Board then dismissed its directors and reconstituted itself with nominees for the four companies solely, a solitary director representing the Forth Bridge shareholders themselves.[3]

In closing off the past, the messy claim and counter-claim with the Bouch Trustees came to settlement early in 1881. The North British suit for damages over the South Esk and Tay Bridge viaducts, and the Bouch estate's for outstanding fees and expenses were mutually abandoned to William Bouch's great dissatisfaction. The estate was repaid only £625 in outstanding expenses,[4] and William Bouch retired from engineering to settle in southern England as a landed gent.[5] The reconstruction of the South Esk bridge was put out to tender, and although Gilkes was one of the tenderers under his new company, the contract was won by William Arrol.[6] In the strong currents of the South Esk, he was to pioneer construction using a four-legged pontoon or construction platform which he had designed, the prototype for the 'quadruped' which was to become such a prominent feature of Tay Bridge construction.[7]

The replacement for the longest railway bridge in the world over the River Tay, in the meantime, was under new direction. William Barlow, as consultant engineer, had taken charge opening an office in Broughty Ferry in autumn 1880. Thornton therefore had to reply to J.G. Orchar, the Dundonian businessman and aesthete, about the much-praised bridge design he had volunteered. Irrespective of its merits, it was too late. 'Seeing as the engineering is entrusted to Mr Barlow [it would be rather irregular] for either Johnston or myself to entertain plans.'[8] Perhaps this letter marked another break with the past: a shift from the amateur enthusiasms that had been unleashed by the bridge collapse – where every man had his own theory about the causes of the collapse, and every man felt able to propose designs for its replacement – to the profound professionalism that now governed bridge construction on the east coast route.

Kippendavie's championing of Barlow – one of the Inquiry Commissioners and President of the Institution of Civil Engineers – could have been regarded as pure cynicism; but Barlow was a noted structural theoretician who, in 1859, had put his ideas into practice by taking out a patent for a girder design.[9] Like Bouch, Barlow's responsibilities were broad and extended to many projects throughout the United Kingdom; and, like Bouch, he was to introduce his son into the project with him. There the comparison ended. Crawford Barlow proved a worthy partner of his father on the Tay Bridge and – together with his engineer assistants – exercised a close grip on its construction. In design terms, Barlow had been constrained by three imperatives. First, there was always pressure on time. Second, he was expressly prohibited from using innovative design by a frightened Parliament. Third, the North British desired that he should re-use as much of the old bridge as he could for reasons of economy. Contradictorily, the Board of Trade had taken a 'scunner' (extreme dislike) to the original structure, and regarded it as both damned and doomed. Barlow's first task was to check the extent to which the Board of Trade's assumptions were correct, for that would govern the extent to which he could save money by re-using what he could, as the NBR desired.

He began by testing the foundations of the old bridge and quickly discovered an unexpected degree of ad hoc construction which reinforced the Inquiry's perception that Gilkes, Grothe, Bouch and Paterson had not been nearly as rigorous as they had claimed. For the foundations had been 'made with single cylinders, others with double cylinders, some elliptical, some partly square and partly round, while some were placed on piles'.[10] He then tested three different ways in which he could re-use them and compared the results to the benefits of designing an entirely new bridge.[11] He found that Bouch's bridge had indeed caused a deepening of the riverbed in its vicinity (as Bouch had feared), with the result that the original caissons were no longer deep enough to be safe from the scour of the tide. Furthermore, they showed differential settlement when loaded and tested, which cast doubt on whether they could bear the additional weight of Barlow's design. Finally, the Board of Trade had banned a structure of cast-iron columns strapped with wrought-iron ties that characterised Bouch's bridge, which precluded the recycling of any of the superstructure of the old bridge with the exception of the well-made wrought-iron girders.[12]

Faced with unreliability in the foundations and the forbidden nature of the superstructure, the inescapable conclusion was that an entirely new bridge structure was required, albeit supplemented by some re-used girders. Barlow concluded that the principal cost advantage to the new bridge in using any of Bouch's structure at all was as an aid to its construction. If the new one were placed sufficiently close to the old, the latter's north and south viaducts would provide a very convenient carrier for the transportation of the components of the new one right out into the centre of the estuary. Crawford Barlow lamented however that the decision to re-use the girders constrained the design significantly, because the spans of the old bridge therefore determined the spans of the new.

Barlow's professional enthusiasm for the potential of steel encouraged him to consider its use for the Tay, and he had been carefully observing how steel girders had performed elsewhere. But in their fright, the Select Committee had specifically excluded 'novel design',[13] and the Board of Trade persisted in regarding steel as insufficiently tested, requiring him to 'adopt no new or untried principles of engineering' by sticking to established methods of construction. The forces of conservatism, therefore, curbed any Barlow tendency toward building without precedent, and his Tay Bridge design was considerably less adventurous than might otherwise have been the case.[14] It was a waste to use a man with his reputation and knowledge like this. Nonetheless, using established methods of construction probably explains why he was able to complete the plans so very quickly: they were deposited before Parliament barely two months after his appointment. The new Tay Bridge, 10,527 feet long and sixty feet upstream of the old one, took no risks. It was to cross the water in seventy-four spans, eleven of which were 245 feet wide over the fairway at the centre, eleven feet lower than Bouch's, and massively broader – 59% wider at the waterline. It was reassuringly visually monolithic. Its stocky almost Wagnerian appearance expressed its ability easily to withstand wind pressure of 56lbs per square foot, and the more it emerged from the sea, the more it made the relics of the old bridge alongside appear far more fragile than they had been.

The bridge was supported on twin cylindrical piers thirty-two feet apart, with foundations sunk twenty to thirty feet below the bed of the river, safe from the scouring tides. Twin thick columns of impervious blue Staffordshire bricks, lining a concrete core, rose up to just above high-tide mark, where they were bound together by an eight-foot cast-iron, wrought-iron, brick and concrete 'connecting piece' looking like enormous iron underpants. The solid-looking superstructure that arose above comprised twin octagonal metal legs. But far from being solid, they were hollow, and the structure inside was of strong metal posts or uprights sufficiently robust to carry the weight of both lifting apparatus and the girders.[15] The structure was made to appear solid, being clad in three-quarter-inch thick wrought-iron plates which 'combined great lateral stiffness and rigidity with lightness'.[16] At the top, the piers curved inward to form the massive arch that carried the girders above. Barlow's design remedied the faults of Bouch's and won the support of the Board of Trade.

The tolls that the North British were now paying the Caledonian amounted to some £28,500 per annum[17] – virtually what it would have to pay to a bank to borrow the money to build the new bridge. It was unsupportable. But despite the Commons Select Committee's strong support for replacing the Tay Bridge, the British political approach to railways required yet another tedious and expensive parliamentary battle – this time with the Caledonian's supporters in the Lords. Lord Redesdale tried to scupper the project by claiming that since the North British was already at – if not beyond – the extent of its legal borrowing powers, it should not be permitted to take the project any further. Johnston, ensconced as usual in the Tavistock Hotel, sent a scoffing note back to Walker in Edinburgh dismissing the objection as nonsense. 'In this respect, we are a vast deal better than when we got the power [to build the first bridge] in 1869.'[18]

The height of the bridge had again become a political issue in the Tay valley. The previous autumn, Thomas Thornton and Perth's

Town Clerk William McLeish agreed mutually to sell a height of seventy-seven feet above high tide to their principals in each town. McLeish, as Town Clerk, had undertaken to deliver Perth, and Thornton, as manipulator extraordinary, Dundee. In January, the Board of Trade – in the normal manner of a government department over-reacting to a safety matter without fully understanding the technicalities – now pressed the North British to reduce the bridge's height yet further. Thornton was concerned that the city of Perth might take the opportunity to exaggerate the extent of its harbour trade and thereby increase its claim for compensation, and dispatched his assistant to find out the truth from Perth's Customs' Records.[19] Contrary to legislation (as Thornton peremptorily pointed out), McLeish had refused the fellow access to the records. Thornton's formidable fury forced a change of heart, and McLeish promised to provide access to his records – with the condition, probably futile given Thornton's nature, that what the assistant discovered would not be used against Perth's interests. This incident illuminated the depth of the entirely understandable mutual distrust, competition and dispute between the two towns.

Thornton had to come clean, explaining, 'It is quite evident that the Bridge we agreed upon last year is too high. Would your people not consent to a lower bridge? It is quite plain that all traffic to and from Perth must sooner or later be done by steam vessels.'[20] When McLeish forecast the 'most determined opposition', Thornton pointed out that the diminishing maritime figures that his assistant had discovered would not support his case. These McLeish contested. 'Either I must be stupid or you must be incomprehensive,' to which Thornton returned smoothly, 'There is really no necessity for giving yourself a bad character.' The following month, a 'magnificent meeting' held to defend the rights of Perth citizens on the Tay deplored as craven the policy of the North British Directors in submitting so meekly to Board of Trade requirements. 'The annals of railway promotion, which are not by any means manifestations of the Beautiful, do not contain so dastardly a page as this same Tay Bridge Controversy.'[21] Although they were later to blame the railways for the decline of Perth harbour, they were only using them as a scapegoat. Perth harbour was being beached by progress. Vessels had become larger. A harbour reached by an estuary which, at low tide, offered a landscape of sandbanks and varying channels, and which itself was only really accessible during the short high tide, was doomed. Railway freight was fundamentally more reliable. In any case, after all the negotiations and fuss, the height of the new Tay Bridge remained at seventy-seven feet.

The Board of Trade had attached two particular conditions to their assent to the Tay Bridge reconstruction. In his evidence, Barlow had offered to test each cylindrical foundation to 33% above the maximum weight to which it might be subjected, and this the Board had happily accepted but had made it mandatory. The second was that the North British was responsible for removing the debris of the old bridge, as Patrick Matthew had foreseen over a decade earlier. The Board of Trade insisted that it had meant removal of the ruins *before* construction of the new bridge could begin.[22] Not only had Barlow assumed that the old bridge would be available to facilitate the construction of the new one, but he judged that the complete removal of the old piers right down to the bottom could destabilise a seabed already hugely cluttered by Noble's thousands of tons of scattered rock.

However much people wanted the bridge rebuilt, nobody trusted the North British Railway Company to do a proper job, given its track record. Dundee and Perth Harbour Boards, their town councils and other organisations all believed that the railway company would seek to dodge its obligations if it could, and leave the navigation cluttered up and dangerous. But although they lobbied hard over the next year, the functional argument of the old structure assisting in the construction of the new one won, and the Board of Trade eventually relented to permit construction of the new bridge whilst most of the old one was still up.

This, however, was only a temporary reprieve. The Board expected the old bridge to be removed by the North British once it ceased being a construction aid, and the matter remained a running sore over the following seven years. In 1885, the North British proved everyone's lowest expectations of it by seeking permission to leave the original cutwaters in place. Its inspectors, it claimed, considered that their removal might be dangerous.[23] Unsuccessful, it then introduced a bill to the same effect in Parliament in 1887, just as the second bridge was reaching completion. If its intention was to alienate its local constituency, then it succeeded beyond measure. Local opinion was outraged, and the regional establishment duly petitioned Parliament against it. Appearing on behalf of Dundee Harbour Trustees, David Cunninghame, eighteen years Harbour Engineer, rehearsed the extent to which the Trustees had bent over backward to assist the North British and the Tay Bridge, seeing 'great benefit in it'.[24] They had permitted a portion of 'their most valuable dock' to be sliced off to accommodate the 1000-yard tunnel between east and west Dundee, charging only a nominal rent of £5 p.a. for it. Yet the North British, far from reciprocating, was thoughtlessly endangering their shipping interests.

There was far more shipping travelling upstream than the NBR had expected. Charles Yule, Dundee's Harbour Master, logged 4,128 vessel movements beneath the bridge during the previous year, with cargoes of manure, coal, potatoes, slate, salt and foreign timber mainly for Newburgh, with several additional passenger steamers in summer. The powerful tides of the Tay Estuary rendered obstructions to navigation extremely dangerous in the dark, and Yule suggested that the danger could be lessened outside the Navigation Channel by aligning the old piers exactly with the piers of the new bridge. If the old piers could not be demolished, they should be made much more visible above high-water level, and a light or beacon placed on top.[25] The compromise reached is visible today. Where the old piers remain, they are parallel with the piers of the new bridge, and none block the navigation channels.

At the point that Arrol's tender to construct the bridge was accepted in October 1881, agreement with the Board of Trade over the matter of the old bridge had yet to be reached, and that remained the case when the contract was signed in the following March (although if the North British was prepared to commit itself to a contract, it must have been fairly certain that an agreement was imminent).[26] Arrol used the intervening time to plan, to organise, to calculate the components, and to identify whether any new machines might need inventing. Since little of this was evident on the site, rumours began to swirl round Dundee in June 1882, to the effect that the bridge had been cancelled. A councillor, dispatched to the construction site to check, reported that 'nothing whatever was being done'. The Provost contacted Thornton, who contacted Walker at the North British, who contacted Arrol. Arrol replied sternly that 'his men were working day and night in preparing the appliances necessary to carry on the work . . . About ten or a dozen steam cranes were being made so that when the works were commenced at Dundee, they will be carried on with all possible speed.'[27] Completion date for the bridge was now agreed for the end of 1885.[28]

No fanfare greeted the beginning of the construction on the new Tay Bridge. This 'herculanean task [began] in the quietest possible manner. There was no display of any kind; there was no fuss, and from first to last there never has been any.' Quietest, that is, metaphorically, for its construction began with a blast of rock for the foundations on 30 June 1882.[29] A few weeks afterwards, John Stirling of Kippendavie and Kippenross, the chairman of the North British since December 1866, died.[30] He had been the ideal chairman for the North British following the stormy years of Richard Hodgson. In his calm and patrician manner, he had provided continuity and steadfastness when faced with continuing war with the Caledonian, and had been reassuring in the face of unexpected adversity – such as the Tay Bridge running so much over time, over cost and then collapsing, or when the Forth Bridge was brought to the brink of cancellation. Kippendavie was replaced by Falshaw.

William Arrol was to say later that the proudest moment of his life was when he entered into the contract for the Tay Bridge.[31] Remembered as the greatest engineering contractor of nineteenth-century Scotland, Arrol exemplified the heroic engineer, the self-made Victorian technocrat. He took pride in his humble origins.[32] Although from the age of nine he had combined working as a piecer in a bobbin-mill factory in Renfrewshire with his schooling, his family had not been not quite so poor as he pretended.[33] His grandfather had been the manufacturer and supplier of gas to the town of Johnstone, and his father and uncle had been partners in a cotton spinning mill before it disastrously burnt down. His father then became manager of J. & P. Coats thread works of Paisley, so Arrol was hardly starting at the very bottom.[34] Nonetheless, he believed that he represented those who had, and was worried that increasing class ambition was forcing 'our better young men' to become socially superior clerks. When granted the Freedom of the town of Ayr in 1890, he said:

> My character is representative of the working classes of Scotland, as one of those who has been able to raise themselves by their own energy and industry . . . I hold it altogether wrong that so many young men are not learning trades. Give them, certainly, the best education you can, but at the same time, give them a trade along with their education. Our trade has got into the hands of a few, and you cannot get so many decent tradesmen. If you advertise for a tradesman you will perhaps get a single application. Whereas if you advertise for a clerk you will get 400 or 500.[35]

William Arrol undertook four years' apprenticeship in a blacksmith and general engineering works whilst attending night school, before travelling as a journeyman blacksmith for a further six. He returned to Glasgow aged twenty-four, to become foreman in the bridge and boiler departments in the Bridgeton works of Laidlaw & Sons. In 1866, whilst still foreman at Laidlaw's, Arrol was entrusted with the construction of the West Pier at Brighton.[36] Two years later, with capital of £84, he established a partnership undertaking general blacksmithing, repairing machinery and boilermaking on a small site off London Road on the eastern fringe of Glasgow. Initially, work was episodic, and he had to buy out his partner. Yet soon the demand was such that he needed larger premises, and began constructing the nearby wide-span, steel and glass workshops of the Dalmarnock Iron Works for himself in 1871.

William Arrol before his knighthood, extracted from a group photograph taken to celebrate the completion of the second Tay Bridge. His force of personality is patent, and he looks as though he is chafing in his suit and bowler, resenting wasting time.

These workshops had the height and strength he needed to take the machines he was inventing. Without ever having tackled a bridge before, as the *Engineer* noted wryly, he then won a contract to construct a railway bridge over the Clyde at Bothwell.

Three Arrol characteristics stand out: his talent for improving or inventing machinery, his talent for organisation, and his personality. Machinery was his bent. His knowledge and training had been practical, and he exemplified the engineer James Nasmyth's belief in how machines could transform engineering construction. In his *Autobiography*, Nasmyth had written:

The irregularity and carelessness of the workmen naturally proved very annoying to the employers. But it gave an increased stimulus to the demand for self-acting machine tools, by which the untrustworthy efforts of hand labour might be avoided. The machines never got drunk; their hands never shook from excess; they were never absent from work; they did not strike for wages; they were unfailing in their accuracy and regularity, while producing the most delicate or ponderous portions of mechanical structures.[37]

That was the nub of the opposition between engineering and the rising Arts and Crafts philosophy. John Ruskin argued that it was wrong in principle to expect technical perfection from humankind:

Men were not intended to work with the accuracy of tools, to be precise and perfect in all their actions. If you will have that precision out of them, and make their fingers measure degrees like cog-wheels, and their arms strike curves like compasses, you must unhumanize them. All the energy of their spirits must be given to make cogs and compasses of themselves. All their attention and strength must go to the accomplishment of the mean act.[38]

Arrol implicitly agreed with Ruskin as to what was the domain of man and what of the machine; for it was in the invention of self-acting machine tools that he excelled. His obituary recorded how he 'hailed with delight any new difficulty met with', for that presented him with the opportunity of solving it with some new invention. Contriving tools was something he appears to have found enormously satisfying. He invented multiple drilling machines and a hydraulic riveter, for example, when working on the Caledonian Railway's bridge in Glasgow. When General Hutchinson came to prepare his quarterly reports on the progress of the Forth Bridge he was mesmerised in the early years more by the variety and quantity of Arrol's machinery than by his construction. Crawford Barlow wrote approvingly of Arrol's approach to the Tay Bridge: 'Wherever possible machinery took the place of hand labour, which ensured greater accuracy'[39] – and of course greater speed. A number of Arrol's lesser known inventions – moveable working platforms, for example, riveters' cages and mobile furnaces to heat the rivets – had been devised to make working conditions more convenient and less dangerous for his workmen.

Even if it is impossible to penetrate entirely beyond the panegyrics, Arrol appears to have been a strong, paternalistic employer. He was unassuming but very clear-eyed, decisive and unsentimental, and careful of his workforce. Risks were inevitable in constructing two bridges of this scale over water, but Arrol sought to minimise them. Lighters were on hand to rescue workers from the water, and the company had its own doctors and ambulances to deliver the injured to the relevant infirmary, where, it appears, the company paid the charges.[40] He established the Dalmarnock Accident Fund in 1876, to which the company contributed 11/3d for each £100 of wages. Its purpose was to cover the doctors' fees, compensation and other costs, and accident insurance. There would be, additionally, a Forth Bridge Sickness and Accident Fund to which all the workforce contributed one hour's pay per week.[41] His interest extended to the morale of his men, and in 1884 he established an annual 'Festival and Assembly of the Employees of Wm Arrol & Co (Tay Bridge Works)' which met in the Thistle Hall, Dundee, to enjoy a musical soirée of singers, instrumentalists and a comic.[42] He also organised, or at least encouraged, twice-yearly regattas. Crews were made up either by discipline – riveters versus bricklayers and painters, or by their work station – the pontoon men versus the girder men. Judging from reports, these events were exercises in team building.[43] By the standards of contemporary construction, this was remarkable. During the five years' construction of the Tay Bridge, involving up to 900 briggers at a time, there were only fourteen deaths, mostly from drowning, which contemporaries attributed to the care Arrol took in devising his construction method.[44]

When Arrol received the Freedom of Dundee in 1889, he had this to say about his men:

When a skirmish takes place with a few half-starved Arabs, and the report of the engagement – I think they always call it a

Tay Bridge workers in one of the bothies on the bridge, heating their cans on the stove. This photograph was taken by Alexander Wilson, a jute mill supervisor.

brilliant engagement (laughter) – comes home, a great deal is said about the commanders, and their conspicuous gallantry is painfully elaborated; but very little is said of poor Tommy Atkins except the list at the end of the story which gives the number of privates who have been killed or wounded. (Hear, hear and applause.) Now our working privates, like the other fighting privates, were the men upon whom it fell to do the business. They carried their lives in their hands for the better part of eight or nine years,[45] and I think they are not to be passed over at the end of the battle as so many unimportant items in the camp of the commander.[46]

Arrol's work philosophy was strenuous but simple: 'I look for work because I want it to do; I stick to it because I like it; and I always do it as well and as quickly as I can.'[47] His organisation and forward planning was exemplary. In the months between the Tay Bridge contract being signed, and the Board of Trade permitting work to begin (because of the dispute about removing the old bridge), he had been making careful arrangements for the layout of the four acres of ground he had obtained on the north bank, between the rising brick arches of the railway viaduct as it approached the bridge, and the sea (now occupied by Riverside Drive, supermarkets and other indifferent twenty-first-century constructions). On this foreshore he invested in a mile of railway and siding, to bring materials as close to the construction site as possible; he erected a large workshop, and cannily converted the brick arches of the railway viaduct into others. On the south bank, he piled into the river an enormous jetty of 6000 square yards, and installed cement stores and − more or less − a form of funicular railway connecting the shore to the stores on the top of Wormit cliff. When it came to the Forth Bridge, Arrol would follow an identical pattern of planning, laying out the site, constructing the necessary workshops and inventing and manufacturing the machinery required to construct its superstructure. For both bridges, he requested and received special cash advances to help finance the high initial capital cost.[48]

We do not know whether the tensions that swirled around the first Tay Bridge infected the second; but then there was no Inquiry to expose its working practices. Local demotic newspapers like the *Wizard of the North* or the *Piper o' Dundee*, which were most likely to pick up any discontents, scarcely mention it, although the *Wizard* editorialised the deaths and injuries on the Forth Bridge. The sense, however, is one of calm resolution in addressing the three aspects of the Tay Bridge project: the northern viaduct with its spans across Dundee's Esplanade, the southern viaduct with a new junction to the Newport railway, and the structure carrying the railway across the sea. No new principle of design, as Barlow had admitted, was involved in its superstructure.[49] As with Bouch's bridge, the caisson foundations would absorb most time, greatest effort and the largest share of the available finance. Since Arrol planned to sink pairs of caissons simultaneously, at three separate spots, he required appropriate machinery, and the solution he came up with was a form of floating cradle or construction platform – a larger version of the pontoon he had developed for the South Esk viaduct.

Each of the four pontoons was made up of five waterproof flotation tanks, with four wrought-iron tubular legs sixty-five feet long and six feet in diameter.[50] Their dimensions otherwise differed according to the dimensions of the caissons, whose size was governed by the differing weight each had to carry. When in position, the legs of the pontoon were extended hydraulically down to the seabed to maintain it firmly in place even when considerable seas were running. It was a forerunner of the 'jack-up platform' used in the oil industry.[51] Locals nicknamed this massive metallic arachnid the 'Quadruped'.

The quadruped was much more than just a platform; it was a mobile construction site manned by a squad of twenty men. They were divided into day and night shifts, operating three steam cranes, a concrete-mixing machine, the steam engines that powered the excavating apparatus, and a welcome bothy in which the men could take shelter and rest. The two large holes twenty-five feet square at the centre of each quadruped were designed to carry a pair of caissons at the correct width apart. Each pair of caissons was made up on the shore, lifted into the holes in the quadruped and suspended there whilst it was towed to site. Once in location, the interiors of the caissons were lined with brickwork for both strength and weight; and as each stage was completed, they would be lowered hydraulically through the base of the quadruped into the sea so that another stage of iron and brick could be added on top; and the process would then be repeated until the caissons touched the bottom, with their top remaining above low-water mark. They were kept vertical by the rigidity of the pontoon.[52] Initially, there were two quadrupeds, but eighteen months later the programme had fallen behind because of poor weather, and Arrol doubled the number.

The rhythm of the construction work was governed by the sinking of eighty-six pairs of those caissons. Whereas the battle between

One of the smaller quadrupeds invented by William Arrol for constructing the second Tay Bridge. When in the middle of the sea, the legs would be lowered to the riverbed to provide a firm working base for lowering the caissons.

Bouch, Grothe and the River Tay had at times appeared to be a close-run thing, there was something remorseless in the undramatic way that Barlow and Arrol steadily colonised the Tay estuary by the calm deposit of pairs of caissons upon the seabed. It was as though the quadrupeds were laying eggs. Once deposited on the seabed, the silt would be extracted through the caisson's bottom at the rate of forty cubic yards of sand and silt per hour by the mechanical grab, sufficient for it to sink two feet. Most caissons should have been able to reach their correct level in ten to fifteen hours. Unfortunately, the weather was no kinder to Barlow and Arrol than it had been to Bouch and Grothe, and work was always being 'a good deal interrupted especially in winter by the storms which are frequent in the Tay valley'.[53] Moreover, the 1000 tons odd of the rubble dumped by Henry Noble around the old bridge's foundations had in fact been scattered so wide of it that it was obstructing the founding of the new one sixty feet upstream.[54]

In the first six months, Arrol's men managed to lay seven caissons, accelerating to an exceptional twenty-eight in the following half-year. The rate slipped back to fourteen and then down to seven in a half-year, by which time the Directors accepted that, for the second time, their programme had taken insufficient account of the Tay valley weather. Completion was first estimated to be delayed for a year,[55] but foundations were not completely laid until autumn 1886, which delayed the bridge's completion until mid-1887 – eighteen months later than originally programmed.

Once each pair of caissons was settled in place, concrete was poured into their core to make them sufficiently solid for the brick columns to be built upon them.[56] Before the brick columns were begun, temporary girders were laid across them and loaded with 30,000 cast-iron blocks to test their stability, under close scrutiny by Major Marindin of the Board of Trade. No chances were being taken. Nor were chances being taken with the superstructure. Each section was temporarily erected at Arrol's Dalmarnock Iron Works, partially riveted together, then marked for ease of re-erection, and then disassembled, and shipped by train to Dundee.[57] The legs of the superstructure were bolted to their brick and concrete base by eight 2.5-inch bolts, twenty feet in length, and the wrought-iron thighs and torso of the piers gradually rose to their full height, ready to carry their girders. The final sections were lifted from barges into place on the piers by a five-ton steam derrick with a sixty-four-foot-long jib fitted onto the quadrupeds. When weather permitted, an entire pier could be bolted together in six working days or, if closer to the shore, within three tides.[58]

Despite basing his bridge design upon the dimensions of Bouch's girders, Barlow soon concluded that the latter were insufficiently strong to be used on their own. So the decision to re-use them at all looks more and more like tokenism. If their inherent weakness had been discerned earlier, not only would much time and effort have been saved but Barlow might have taken the opportunity to design a more innovative structure. Used, however, they were, over two-thirds of the length of the new bridge. Initially, they were placed side by side on top of the new bridge so that Arrol could run carriages over them bringing new girders to the site.[59] Thereafter they were placed parallel to new girders on the new bridge. Closer to the shore, the levels of old and new bridges were about the same, so carrying girders were laid from the old bridge across to the new, over which girders from the old bridge were lifted up and slid over. Toward the centre of the river, levels between the two bridges differed by up to eleven feet. Arrol provided steeply sloping rope companionways for his intrepid workmen to pass across the sixty feet of racing tide from one bridge to the other, but shifting the bridge girders required a new technique. At low tide, Arrol would fix a pontoon beneath each girder, and jam a hydraulic ram up against it. As the tide rose, the rim lifted the girder up from the old bridge, and the pontoon would be towed upstream to the new site, where the rams would retract to lower the girder to its new site.

The Dalmarnock Iron Works was extremely busy supplying materials for projects other than the Tay Bridge, so Arrol left it in the hands of his brother James, assisted by his large staff of carefully picked foremen.[60] It had become absolutely necessary to do so since Arrol's availability had been compressed again. When the Tay Bridge was barely 20% complete, he was awarded the contract for the Forth Bridge, in a consortium with other contractors; and when the Tay Bridge was about two-thirds complete, he was awarded the contract for London's Tower Bridge and for a viaduct over the Hawksbury River in New South Wales. Given Rothery's inexpert emphasis upon the need for intense contract supervision, Arrol's increasing absence from Dundee could have created the potential for the slipshod work of the previous bridge. He therefore

Raising the girders on the new Tay Bridge, from within. The photographer is standing on a girder being jacked up from below to reach the height of those in the distance. Metal panelling was removed from the piers just ahead and replaced once the girder had moved up.

restructured his site staff according to what he later described as his
'one main principle' – namely 'devolving on particular men the
responsibility for the success of certain parts of the work placed
under their control. But for the presence of these men in their
positions, I need hardly tell you than I should not be here today to
receive your congratulations.'[61] His chief site engineer in Dundee
was William Inglis, whom he had poached from the North British.
Inglis appears to have been a natural machines man, for his best-
known publication is a paper that lovingly describes the machines
and the processes of erection of the Tay Bridge.[62] Crawford
Barlow, in turn, relied upon Fletcher Kelsey as his resident engineer
with Francis Caffin as deputy.

    This structure of site staff did not differ fundamentally from
Bouch and Grothe's. There were professionals working on the
bridge who made it their life, whereas both contractor and consultant had other projects. The principal differences were that
Barlow's Tay Bridge was a traditional rather than an innovative
structure, Crawford Barlow was much on site, and the teams of site
engineers appear to have worked collaboratively and trusted each
other. Responsibility was delegated appropriately and decisions
were made on time by those with practical experience. It demonstrated that a project such as this would succeed or fail according to
the nature and quality of the people involved, rather than Rothery's
theoretical idea about the necessity for constant supervision by the
design engineer.

    With his team in place, Arrol developed an extraordinary work
schedule. On a Monday, he would rise at 5am in Glasgow to be in
the Dalmarnock Iron Works by six. Thereafter, he snatched breakfast at one of Kate Cranston's fashionable tea rooms before catching
the 8.45am to Edinburgh to visit the Forth Bridge. There he
remained until he took the 6pm train on Tuesday evening to
Dundee. The Tay Bridge team met at dawn on the Wednesday followed by an inspection of the construction. Arrol returned to
Glasgow that evening. On Thursday the cycle began again – 6am
at Dalmarnock, breakfast at Cranston's, then Edinburgh and on to
Dundee on Friday. On Friday evening, however, he took a North

British sleeper to London for a site meeting on the Tower Bridge on Saturday.[63] Such a regime would have been almost impossible to sustain if he had had a family life, but his wife had become deranged after only a short period of marriage, and there were no children.[64] Compulsive bridge construction was the substitute.

After hanging on waiting for the bridge's completion, the North British finally decided to renew the engines on the roll-on, roll-off railway ferry – the weatherbeaten thirty-five-year old *Leviathan* – in May 1886. Although Arrol had 700 men working day and night,[65] it was obvious that the ferry would still be required for some time.[66] The high-point of the construction – the floating-off of the thirteen 500-ton large girders – was only reached six months later. Using the rising levels of high tide, a pontoon would lift a girder from its jetty and float it out to its destination where it was chained to the superstructure, and left resting on beech blocks on top of the brick piers as the pontoon floated away on the ebbing tide. Hydraulic jacks – one in each of the four piers – would then be inserted underneath the girder, and they would raise it in bursts of fifteen inches. The ends of the girder rose within the completed pier at each side; and the most complicated part of the process was the opening up of the pier's wrought-iron plated skin to allow the girder's extremities to rise within it, only to be closed again beneath it. Each girder took eight working days to raise.[67]

The process of raising the large girders was virtually finished when, in March 1887, Sir James Falshaw retired as chairman of the North British. A former Lord Provost of Edinburgh with excellent connections, he had brought a no-nonsense engineering background combined with rough and sometimes ruthless commonsense to the company, an excellent foil to Kippendavie. He was replaced by the Marquis of Tweeddale. The bridge, painted the dull red oxide colour that we now associate with the Forth Bridge,[68] opened three months later.

On a gorgeous Friday, 10 June 1887, the North British Directors, accompanied by engineers, officials and a few friends, travelled up in a special train of two saloons first to inspect the partially complete Forth Bridge and then up through Fife to cross the

Tay Bridge. They paused at the midpoint of the bridge for a photocall for the Dundee antiquarian and chronicler Andrew Lamb,
before being offered luncheon in the Board Room at Tay Bridge
station. The Marquess of Tweeddale paid particular tribute to
Barlow's 'energy, skill and care', and then dropped a big hint. 'He
was expressing the sentiments of those present when he hoped that
some other mark of approbation would be bestowed upon him by
those whose business it was to recognise such work as had been
achieved by him.'[69] Such a broad hint that the Prime Minister
might invite the queen to knight Barlow went unheeded. Arrol,
whom Tweeddale described in the same speech as 'one of the most
remarkable men of his time', was only forty-eight.

The bridge opened for goods traffic the following Monday,[70]
and was tested for passenger traffic by General Hutchinson on
Thursday, Friday and Saturday. Trains tanked across at 40mph, the
piers were inspected for scouring, and Arrol, Hutchinson and
Kelsey had paced slowly along 'minutely inspecting' the track.
They were entirely satisfied. One of the Inspectors confided to
Arrol, 'I like your bridge.'[71] Hutchinson telegrammed his approval
to the Board of Trade and a 200-strong party of councillors, ladies
and friends crossed very slowly the same evening, to enter Newport
station to cheers, counter-cheers, and the waving of hats. To coincide with the fiftieth anniversary of Queen Victoria's accession,[72]
the Tay Bridge formally opened for passengers on Monday 20 June
1887. That seventy-four passenger trains and fifty-two goods trains
passed over it on that Monday indicates a substantial pent-up
demand.[73] Walking across the bridge was promptly advertised as a
new Dundee tourist attraction.[74]

The completion of the bridge naturally spawned comparisons
with Bouch's earlier bridge, usually to the disparagement of the
latter. The *Dundee Advertiser*'s conclusion that the new bridge had
'not been built as an experiment, but to last for all time'[75] implied
that Bouch's bridge had been experimental. This retrospective perception – the principal legacy of Rothery's report – was incorrect.
The *Advertiser* then explained that the disaster had not been Bouch's
fault since 'the first bridge was starved of money'[76] thus setting off

The opening party for the Tay Bridge, photographed on the north shore at Roseangle, with William Arrol in the front row; probably Thornton seated extreme right, and the balding John Leng standing in the centre back.

a new myth. Bouch's bridge had fallen, so it became thought, because the North British had been unwilling to invest sufficient in its construction,[77] and Barlow's stands today partly because the company had invested more capital in it. The minutes of the second last meeting of the Tay Bridge Undertaking revealed otherwise. The total cost for Bouch's single-track single-caisson bridge had been £626,547 (including tunnel and link lines),[78] whereas Barlow's double-track double-caisson bridge began with a budget of only £670,000, albeit excluding tunnel and link lines, and its outturn cost was 25% greater.[79] The principal difference between the two projects is that Barlow's bridge's final cost fell much closer to his original estimate than had Bouch's.[80]

The significant differences between the two bridges lie, rather, in the timescale, the complexity of design and construction, and in the contractor. In both Bouch's original Tay Bridge contract of 1870, and redesigned bridge contract of 1874, he had set a timescale of three years for construction. Retrospectively, we can see that he had made a grossly inadequate allowance for the climate and likely weather of the Tay basin. Despite continuous and serious weather interruptions, tremendous pressure had been put on the construction team to keep to the programme, and some of the construction problems were the consequence of the disastrous short cuts introduced as a result. Moreover, when Bouch redesigned the structure after the foundations had failed, he had introduced a superstructure that was complex to erect and to maintain in tension. Although Barlow's Tay Bridge was more straightforward, and its superstructure, as Arrol observed, very simple, it was programmed to take five years and, thanks again to the weather, took even longer. Yet this time, the pressure to complete to an unrealistic deadline was absent. The fate of Bouch's bridge had demonstrated the consequences of doing otherwise.

In both bridges, getting the foundations right had absorbed most time and money, and that was the stage when the construction was most at the mercy of the sea. Under Arrol, construction was undertaken by a relatively small number of people, carefully and methodically repeating the same tasks and refining how they did it, avoiding inconsistencies whilst always dodging the disruptive tendencies of the weather. Comparable information is not available for Bouch's bridge, but the disposition of the engineers revealed at the Inquiry implies that construction gangs had been organised more around location (i.e. which section of the bridge) rather than function (i.e what particular task was being undertaken). Perhaps that had been necessary in the light of Grothe's decision to build simultaneously at the two ends and in the middle. One way of assessing the relative simplicity of the Tay Bridge lies in the small number of workers involved, judged against its length of almost two miles. In January 1887, the Tay Bridge workforce was about 700 men[81] working on a bridge 10,527 feet long, whereas the workforce on the Forth Bridge was 3280[82] working on a bridge 5349 feet long. That works out as a ratio of 0.07 worker per foot on the Tay Bridge as compared to a ratio 0.6 – almost nine times more – on the Forth. There lies evidence of the relative complexity of the two structures.

The final point of comparison between Barlow's and Bouch's

Tay bridges lay in the nature of the contractor. It was a difference between generations of contractors. Gilkes, the 1870s' contractor, was pragmatic, improvisory, and his staff responded to unforecast crises by ad hoc decisions. The 1880s' contractor, Arrol, was a master of organisation and delegation, and based his work on exceptionally thorough pre-planning and the use of machines. Muddle-through construction was ceding to new contracting.

Barlow's Tay Bridge did not lack controversy within the engineering profession. Colleagues questioned whether the frequency of piers had not been an unnecessarily expensive method of construction; why girders from the old bridge had been re-used if they were insufficiently strong and limited the dimensions of the new spans; and why the superstructure was wrought iron rather than brick. One, in particular, had this to say:

> He might be wrong: but he fancied that the appearance of the piers above the water-line rather resembled masonry than wrought-iron work. He thought the panic, which undoubtedly existed at the time of the failure of the old bridge must have led the designers to consider not only the strength necessary for the piers, *but also their appearance* [my italics] so that everyone might be impressed with their solidity. Otherwise it might be open to question whether the form of the upper part of the piers was that which would produce the required strength with the maximum of economy.[83]

He was right. These great arched piers, entirely concealing the hollow light structure within, were designed deliberately to look so solidly clamped to the seabed that nothing could ever shift them. So beyond being an engineering achievement, it was an exercise in psychological reassurance.

The new bridge's apparent power inspired the Muse sheltering up Paton's Lane, leading to McGonagall's third and final effusion on the subject. His poem on the disaster had attributed the bridge's collapse to a lack of buttresses, and he happily perceived buttresses in the new one where there were none.

The king is dead: long live the king. Arrol's bridge is virtually complete, and the structures joining Bouch's (on the right) to his have been removed.

Beautiful new railway bridge of the Silvery Tay
With your strong brick piers and buttresses in so grand array . . .

He took the opportunity of the Tay's new triumph to wreak his revenge on New York for his brief, unwelcoming and unsuccessful visit he had made there in March 1887.

The New Yorkers boast about their Brooklyn Bridge,
But in comparison to thee it seems like a midge,
Because thou spannest the silvery Tay
A mile or more longer I venture to say;
Besides the railway carriages are pulled across by a rope
Therefore Brooklyn Bridge cannot with thee cope . . .

The completion of the Tay Bridge more or less ended Dundee's intervention in the development of a national railway strategy. It had been conceived when Dundee was the fastest growing town in Scotland; jute was its principal import, and jute manufacturers like James Cox were reaching their zenith. Dundee in 1887 was a different place. About half of its medieval fabric had been replaced by the Parisian 'new town' of which Cox was so proud – modern commercial streets built in the manner of Baron Haussmann's recent boulevards. However, jute had entered what would become its irreversible decline – although it would not become apparent for a number of years yet.

Of the Dundee railway triad of James Cox, John Leng and Thomas Thornton who had plotted together to bridge the Tay in 1863, Cox was no longer alive to witness its completion. The directors, as Barlow observed wryly, had shown a 'lively interest in the undertaking' of the bridge's construction, far more than in Bouch's time, and had made numerous visits to the construction site. This habit killed Cox. The 78-year-old caught a chill when taking some guests on a seaborne directors' inspection in the autumn, and he died on 1 December 1885. Without his energy, as his obituarist put it, 'the North British Railway could never have entered Dundee, [and] the town itself would have continued to be subjected to great disadvantages so far as trade and travelling were concerned'.[84] In 1893, Thornton was finally appointed Town Clerk, the new post comprising, in a single appointment, an amalgamation of all the duties that Thornton had previously undertaken for his Boards and his Trusts. Since he had devoted most of his career to the management of Dundee through non-governmental agencies, the poacher had rather curiously turned gamekeeper. Such was his dominance over his city's affairs that the Council permitted him to act as Town Clerk, simultaneously running his private legal practice – which, hardly coincidentally, had grown into one of the largest in Scotland.[85] He purchased the decayed Thornton Castle by Laurencekirk, since he shared its name, modernised it and established it as the family seat. John Leng entered Parliament as a Liberal in 1889, campaigning particularly for

Bouch's bridge had performed its final task and the next step, as required by Parliament, was to remove it.

shorter hours for railway servants.[86] He was knighted four years later, but did not retire as editor of the *Dundee Advertiser* for another nine years. 'His belief in progress remained firm to the last.'[87]

And what of the chorus? William McGonagall, poet and tragedian, was to give up on the town that had become identified with him (and whose curse he remains). Although used to being tormented, he had been duped by a student jape in Perth in 1884. He had received hoax notification that he had been offered a knighthood from the court of King Thebaw in the Andamnan Islands in 1884. It was only an undergraduate jest, but he styled himself thereafter Sir William Topaz McGonagall knight of the White Elephant of Burma. On his return to Dundee from an unsuccessful trip to America in 1887, he was 'very well treated by the more civilised community', but his reception 'by a few ignorant boys and the Magistrates of the city' had been very unkind,[88] and the mockery eventually turned physical. He wrote to a colleague. 'My Dear Friend, I write to inform you that I am resolved to leave Dundee, owing to the shameful treatment I meet with daily while walking the streets . . . because I can get no protection in Dundee.'[89] He lingered, however, and was still there two years later when he penned:

> *Welcome! Thrice Welcome! To the year 1893*
> *For it is the year I intend to leave Dundee,*
> *Owing to the treatment I receive*
> *Which does my heart sadly grieve.*
> *Every morning when I go out*
> *The ignorant rabble they do shout*
> *'There goes Mad McGonagall.'* [90]

And in 1895 he left.

CHAPTER NINE

CONQUERING THE FORTH

We feel ourselves elevated because we identify ourselves with the powers of nature, ascribing their vast impact to ourselves, because our fantasy rests on the wings of the storm as we soar into the heights and wander into the depths of infinity . . .'

THEODOR VISCHER[1]

The construction of the Forth Bridge would complete the East Coast line running from London to Aberdeen and Inverness. It was the last to be built not because it presented the greatest engineering challenge (although it did), but because the Tay Bridge had enjoyed the more forceful lobby, and the Caledonian's strategy to crush the North British had finally been repulsed at Dundee. The Forth Bridge Company and its supporting railway companies were simply looking for a railway bridge across the river to fulfil their strategy of defeating the Caledonian; yet, of all the bridges on the east coast, the Forth Bridge stood out with its unprecedented design and manufacture, and its pioneering mode of erection.

The principal consequence of the new financial structure of the Forth Bridge Company was that Bouch's Forth Suspension Bridge design was abandoned. The guaranteeing companies – the North Eastern, Great Northern and the Midland, imperiously and imperially, intended to bring their own engineers with them – Thomas

Harrison for the North Eastern, John (later Sir John) Fowler for the
Midland, and William Barlow for the Great Northern. The North
British had not replaced the sacked and deceased Bouch. These
engineers were given only seven weeks to design a bridge in probably the most difficult location in Britain without interrupting its
substantial naval and commercial sea traffic: a bridge over a mile of
the River Forth, comprising two, fast-running deep-water navigable channels 200 feet deep, with a tide rise of eighteen feet at spring
tide (sometimes rising to twenty-two feet). The railway companies,
moreover, required that a contractor build it for a guaranteed
price.[2]

To satisfy the Board of Trade's new structural regulations, the
bridge would have to be able to withstand a minimum wind pressure of 56lbs, and its location at Queensferry precluded using any
form of arched structure or one that required erection from scaffolding, since that would block the seaway. Fowler and Baker
collaborated on a design for a fixed girder bridge, whereas Barlow
worked on a suspension one, and Harrison does not seem to have
entered the contest. Although 'free from most of the defects of
[Bouch's] design' and £200,000 cheaper than it, Barlow's design
was nonetheless £300,000 more expensive than Fowler and
Baker's, and it was the latter that was selected for further refinement. Whilst it is pleasant to surmise that our forefathers chose the
Forth Bridge design at least partly upon its ingenuity, innovation
and striking appearance, the truth was otherwise. It was the cheapest. Fowler and Baker's design was for a level and straight fixed steel
girder bridge,[3] with two principal spans of 1700 feet with 150
clearance, leaving a navigable channel of 500 feet wide at the centre
of each span.[4] The railway viaduct would run through the middle
of an enormous framed structure resembling three lattice lozenges.
The Board of Trade had agreed that the clearance of 150 feet above
sea level could be restricted to central 500 feet of each span allowing the structure to curve downwards at the sides. It also approved
the use of steel provided that it was of adequate tenacity and sufficiently tested.[5]

Seven weeks later, the engineers duly returned to the railway

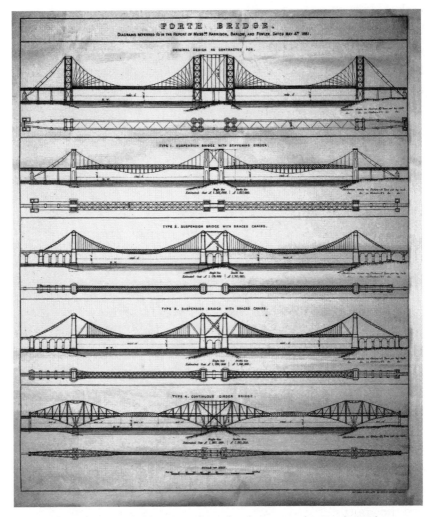

The suspension bridges tested as alternatives to the Forth Bridge design by Fowler and Baker. Bouch's original design is at the top, and the three alternative designs below were presumably by William Barlow.

companies with a bridge design that met their conditions, and which could be built to a maximum cost of £1,550,000 at the current cost of steel (though Fowler thought it could probably be built for around £100,000 less).[6] To emphasise the degree of attention that it intended to devote to the project, the Board travelled to London to pore over Baker's specification for the bridge, which included the requirement that one out of every 50 items – rivets, bars, plates etc – should be tested for their strength. After taking in some significant alterations suggested by Harrison and Barlow, Fowler and Baker's design for the Forth Bridge was adopted,[7] and they agreed to a fixed fee of £75,000 all in.[8] Unusually, the specification stated that the engineers' hands should not be tied if they changed their mind and adopted other forms of superstructure during construction, which must have made it supernaturally difficult to price.[9]

When the Forth Bridge Company finally submitted its plans to Parliament in February 1882, the Caledonian Railway promptly opposed it, despite earlier legislation which had explicitly prohibited it from opposing a railway bridge over the Forth.[10] In a flagrant disregard for its own ruling, the Select Committee duly heard the Caledonian's argument that its investment in Grangemouth harbour would be damaged by the bridge, supported by various shipowners and the Alloa Harbour Trustees. There was nothing new in these arguments that Parliament had not already heard and dismissed, so assent was granted in June 1882.[11] A flanking attack on the new design erupted in *Nature* contributed by the Astronomer Royal, Sir George Airy. Airy condemned the fundamental stability of Fowler and Baker's design in comparison with Bouch's abandoned one. Sir George urged the withdrawal of the scheme in the interests of public safety. As *Engineering* pointed out, Airy was scarcely objective in view of his partisan enthusiasm for Bouch's original design, and the controversy soon withered. The design for the largest railway bridge in the world, with a promised completion date of 12 December 1887,[12] went out to tender that autumn.

The head of the engineering team was John Fowler, knighted in 1885 for work in Egypt and assistance to the government in its attempt to relieve Khartoum from the Mahdi's army. He signed all the reports, undertook the principal negotiations with William Arrol, and remained solely responsible for negotiating the engineers' remuneration. He had had a broad engineering experience, advising on schemes in New South Wales, Algeria, Belgium, France, the United States and Germany. When only fifty-eight, he had been elected the youngest President of the Institution of Civil Engineers.[13] In the 1850s, he had designed a tubular bridge over the Trent which, amidst great controversy, had been rejected by the Board of Trade. In the 1860s, when Baker joined Fowler's office, he persuaded Baker against emigrating,[14] appointed him chief assistant on the Metropolitan Line, and then partner in 1875. During the 1860s and 1870s, their office was busy inserting the Metropolitan Railway, the Waterloo to City line, and the Central tube line through inner London. It had been Baker who had conceived the notion that tube lines should dip between stations to reduce the amount of pulling power required. Even though there was a twenty-seven-year age gap between them, Fowler and Baker got on extremely well. Fowler referred to Baker as his friend, whereas Baker once stated 'during the many years that he and Sir John Fowler had been associated, they had come to the conclusion that whenever they agreed, their opinions must be right'.[15] Fowler was responsible for the Forth Bridge approach viaducts: Baker for the bridge itself.[16] Fowler, who had a country house in north-west Scotland, found it easy to make frequent visits to the Forth Bridge site; Baker was to remain there almost continuously during construction.[17]

Baker, a vivid, brisk and dapper man, was an excellent communicator (not unlike like an engineering Sir Basil Spence before his time), who enjoyed giving public lectures, and produced enormous multi-coloured drawings of the bridge's construction to exhibit during them. He combined an early reputation for theory with immense practicality, and must have enjoyed a particular affinity with Arrol. They were virtually the same age, and both had undertaken a four-year metalwork apprenticeship in the Celtic fringe – Arrol in east Glasgow and Baker in an ironworks in Neath Abbey, south Wales. A sense of mutual respect between engineer and contractor on the Forth Bridge project is palpable from the records. While Arrol was building up his fabrication business, Baker was building up an international reputation for his research into the properties of materials – on long span bridges (James Eads had consulted him on the design of the St Louis Bridge in 1868), and on the strength of beams, of columns and arches, and of brickwork –

Sir John Fowler

Sir Benjamin Baker

which were first published in *Engineering* and then in book form.[18] He was anxious neither to play down the risks of bridge design, nor to demonise Thomas Bouch. He pitched his and Fowler's achievement modestly: 'Where no precedent exists, the successful engineer is he who makes the fewest mistakes.'[19]

Baker was excellent at communicating his engineering concepts in the simplest terms. 'A cantilever', he told the Royal Institution, 'is simply another name for a bracket,' and an unsatisfactory one at that.[20] He invited his audience to imagine the Forth Bridge structure in terms of a bracket extending out from each bank of the River Forth to support a girder in the middle. He then demonstrated how the stresses worked by showing a lantern slide of a demonstration that he had staged at South Queensferry. An elevated platform in the middle, as though it were the girder[21] was supported in the air by two people sitting on chairs on each side, acting like human brackets or cantilevers. When a load came on to that platform or central girder, the Japanese engineer Kaichi Watanebe was asked to represent a train in the experiment by sitting on the central platform, the upper structure (the men's arms and shoulders) was pulled into tension (representing huge upper steel lattice members of the bridge – known as ties) whereas the lower sticks the men were holding against their chairs (representing the bridge's lower twelve-foot-diameter tubes of 1.25 inches thick steel – known as struts), were compressed. Looking at the bridge today, you can tell which parts are in tension since they take the form of open lattice girder ties, and those which are in compression, since they take the form of solid steel tubular struts.

The core of the design lay in three 343-foot-high 'great steel towers'[22] – one at South Queensferry, one on the island of Inchgarvie, and one at North Queensferry – of two pairs of splayed tubular columns, that narrowed inwards from 120 feet at ground level to thirty-three-feet wide at the top, like straddled legs.[23]

Baker enjoyed public lectures, and staged this demonstration at Queensferry to illustrate the cantilever principal of the Forth Bridge. Although the British Railways Archives refer to this as a 'boy on a swing', it is the Japanese engineer Kaichi Watanebe being supported on his chair by two of his engineering colleagues.

Imagine two enormous *slimline* sumo wrestlers leaning against each other. The brackets, or cantilevers, that stretched 680 feet out over the sea, were anchored to the shore by these towers; and supported two 350-foot-long connecting girders in the middle above the navigation channels.[24] The size of the bridge was entirely governed by the necessity to construct the cantilevers sufficiently high as to support the girders at the right height above those channels. Yet Baker liked to emphasise just how unoriginal his structure was in essence by referring to native Canadian rope bridges from the Kicking Horse Trail or delicate timber cantilevered bridges in Nepal. 'I protested against its being stigmatised as a new and untried type of construction, and claimed that it had probably a longer and more respectable ancestry even than the arch.'[25] *Engineering* added, 'Skeleton bridges on the same principle have for ages been thrown by savages across rivers', illustrating one discovered on the route of the Canadian Pacific Railway. It was, however, a rather more sophisticated version of the same principle, built at Wandipore and published in 1800, that was taken to be the intellectual ancestor of the Forth Bridge.[26]

The Bridge Company needed fixed timescales and fixed estimates from their consultants as much as from their contractors in order to plan its capital expenditure. Since neither engineer nor contractors had ever tackled anything quite like this before, estimating time and cost was tricky; and although both provided the required quotations at the outset, both found that they had to return to the company periodically to seek a revision of their contracts caused by, as Arrol put it, the 'novelty and character of the Undertaking',[27] and of the additional duties consequently required.[28] Long used to special pleading by railway contractors, railway companies were no longer prepared to be exploited by them as they believed that they had been a few decades earlier. So the Forth Bridge Company stuck regardless to the original contracts – as their clones in the North British had done on the Tay Bridge in similar circumstances, but offered to advance capital to the contractor to manufacture or purchase machinery required for the construction. Immense sums of capital were made available –

£200,000 over four years – equivalent to a quarter of the total cost of Barlow's Tay Bridge. But as the extraordinary nature of the undertaking unfolded, becoming more and more rather than less and less complex as the structure emerged, the Company realised that its utter dependence upon its engineers and contractor required something more. So it issued virtual promissory notes – promises of adequate recompense – to both contractor and engineers – contingent upon satisfactory completion by the due date.

In December 1881, just after tenders had been issued, Fowler warned the Boards of the guaranteeing companies to expect rather higher quotations from the contractors than his original estimate – probably nearer to £1,705,000 – 'the railway works being somewhat heavier than we had assumed'.[29] Arrol was always going to be one of the tenderers since that had been a key clause in the earlier agreement terminating the contract for Bouch's bridge. His firm was already being paid for the watching over and the upkeep of £10,000 worth of portable drilling machinery and plant that had remained from Bouch's bridge on the construction site at Queensferry (implying that the Forth Bridge Company had always anticipated that the project would be revived).[30] Fowler's warning had been unnecessary: the tenders received were generally lower than expected, and Arrol's was the lowest.

The directors now needed reassurance that their cheapest contractor had sufficient resources to undertake such a scale of project.[31] So they invited the three lowest tenderers – William Arrol & Co, Falkiner and Sir Thomas Tancred, and Thomas Phillips – to consider whether they might be prepared to combine to build the Forth Bridge.[32] Previously, that had meant either dividing the approach lines and viaducts between separate contractors (as in Bouch's Forth Bridge) or that different contractors would tackle particular elements of the project – implying separate contracts for viaducts, foundations, columns and piers, and the superstructure. In this instance, the contractors decided to form themselves into a single-project consortium called Tancred Arrol – Phillips on foundations, Tancred on the large deployment of labour, and Arrol on superstructure and machinery – who offered to build the bridge in a single contract at a cost of £1,600,000. The Board accepted, and Sir Thomas Tancred and William Arrol attended its meeting on 21 December 1882 to seal the agreement. The Forth Bridge would be built by Tancred Arrol according to the design under the name of John Fowler, as contracted chief engineer, although it was largely the work of his junior partner Benjamin Baker, and completed for trains to run across it exactly five years hence – on 21 December 1887.

Before construction began, Dr William Siemens asked Baker to prepare a pamphlet on the bridge for the British Association. Baker was tentative since the design was all still in his mind and only construction would demonstrate its feasibility. So he focused instead upon its scale. He had 'often experienced no little difficulty in realising the scale upon which he was working . . . Hence to enable anyone to appreciate the size of the Forth Bridge, we have merely to suggest the following simple rule-of-three sum: As a Grenadier Guardsman is to a new-born infant, so is the Forth Bridge to the largest railway bridge [the Britannia Bridge] yet built in this country.'[33] The trains, he informed one of his audiences, would be steaming across the Forth at a height higher than the top of the dome of the Albert Hall.[34]

The Board of Trade planned much more intensive supervision than had been the case on either of the Tay Bridges. It took the form of inspections by General Charles Hutchinson and his colleague Major Marindin who reported quarterly. When weather permitted, they observed construction progress, the men employed, machinery, safety, and quality of workmanship. Their reports were printed and duly entered into the Bridge Company's minute book. Arrol deployed the same methodology, planning, attention to detail, and care for his workforce as he had upon the Tay Bridge, and during the seven years' construction of the Forth Bridge, not once did the Inspectors have cause to comment adversely on the quality of materials or of workmanship. They did not find it necessary to reject a single steel plate of the Forth's – emphasising the extent to which the high failure rate in casting Bouch's Tay Bridge's columns only a decade earlier was a different world. The twenty–eight quarterly inspection reports redound with admiration for just how well the bridge was being put together.[35]

Arrol spent the first six months on preparatory work, temporary construction and inventing machinery, whilst Baker developed the design and devised certificates to be used when authorising monthly payments to the contractors (they strongly resemble those still in use). 'Temporary works', however, is an inadequate term for what Arrol had to construct to make his site operational. At North Queensferry, on the north bank, he had to demolish and relocate the coastguard station to construct an enormous pier. He built timber huts for workmen and their families, a canteen, stores, dining and reading rooms. On Inchgarvie Island, he adapted the ruins of the Dundas family's fortress of Garvie Castle by re-roofing and reoccupying its tower and converting some of the structures in its inner court for shops, offices and stores. Accommodation was limited initially by the discovery that the castle did not have a well, but merely a cistern to collect rainwater. Nonetheless, when they required an isolated spot to corral the ninety Continental workmen imported by M.L. Coiseau (who had won the subcontract for sinking the caissons), there was space to add a kitchen and sufficient sleeping accommodation. Additional drinking water was taken from the Dunfermline mains and supplied in iron boxes.[36]

Before the structure of the giant cantilever towers began to penetrate the clouds in late 1886, it was the sixty-acre construction site – the bustling open-air manufactory on the South Queensferry shore – that caught visitors' imagination. Bouch's original workshops had to be adapted, modified and enlarged to cope with an entirely different construction method. To them were likewise added a canteen, dining and reading rooms, forty wooden huts, stores selling food and appropriate clothing, and sixteen brick houses for foremen and other staff (with sixty tenement flats in nearby Queensferry for gangers or foremen). Further accommodation was added later as the workforce doubled. As well as an enormous drawing loft where full-size drawings and templates were made, there were offices, workshops, sawmill, and furnaces, gas furnaces, engines, an accumulator for providing hydraulic power, cement stores, testing house, and endless huts, general stores and storage and the assembly plant.

By 1884, the site had accumulated twenty-two vessels, thirty-two boilers, ninety-seven cranes and winches, sixty-four drilling machines, thirty-three engines and 220 drilling, punching, bending, planning, riveting and other miscellaneous machines on site including emery grinders, lathes and goliath cranes.[37] The Bridge Company advanced 85% of the £140,000 cost of all this and, under the revised agreement, Arrol kept 15% of the machinery for himself once it was all over.[38]

South Queensferry's sloping shore and raised beach were terraced to provide land for what was collectively known as the Drilling Yards or Drilling Road. The steel plates for the superstructure were sixteen feet long, six feet wide and 1.25 inches thick and, if laid end to end, would have extended forty-two miles.[39] They were delivered by train onto the sidings at Queensferry where cranes would stack them beside the appropriate workshop, ready for heating and pressing. Once lifted red-hot from the furnaces, they were placed onto hydraulic presses and compressed into the correct shape. Lifted out, stacked, cooled down, curvature re-checked, the plates were then moved onto the drill road for assembly. The drill road was a flat platform like a railway marshalling yard with parallel railway lines 400 feet long. Here the bridge plates were fitted around a frame of the size and scale of the large steel tubular strut. When complete, the tube was wheeled into an Arrol-devised drilling machine to have all the necessary rivet holes drilled into it like a multiple metallic dental operation. The end of each tube was then planed to a perfect edge for butting against its neighbour. Once ready, each plate was marked and numbered, and the tube then disassembled ready for transport to site and re-assembly upon the superstructure. The works looked, to *The Times,* like 'beehives of industry ... with the varied din of hammers beating, engines puffing, wheels whirring, and drills booming so that the "air is filled with noises". Everything is done with mathematical precision, yet with a speed that is marvellous.'[40]

The yards also provided space to undertake the temporary erec-

tion of bridge components, such as the skewback. The twelve crucially important skewbacks (named because of their lack of right
angles) were acknowledged to be the most difficult single component of the structure. A skewback is a multiple joint where ten
separate structural members of the bridge were buckled together in
a form that resembled an outsized metallic insect: two at the foot
and two at the apex of each of the three great steel towers. Five
tubular struts projected at different angles from its tubular torso, like
monstrous legs, and five rectangular ties projected like antennae. It
was so enormously complicated that it was essential to erect it on
a dummy run, to ensure that everything was labelled for the correct
location and set at the correct angle. Erection for testing, which has
since become commonplace in the oil industry, was probably pio-
neered on the Forth.

To service each of the three principal workstations, new jetties
were built for loading and unloading cranes and other material, and
for mooring barges for landing briggers from the firm's paddle-
steamer which plied back and forth. The steep-sided and relatively
inaccessible rock of Inchgarvie in the middle was served by the
construction of a large iron pier extending upstream, whereas at
South Queensferry, a 2100-foot-long jetty was built as the principal transhipment point for the steel work, and a 1900-foot-long
wooden stage for the erection of the viaduct girders.[41]

In the meantime, Fowler was proceeding with the 2946-foot-
long north and south approach viaducts, which were carried on
granite columns 130.5 feet high above sea-level. That was a mighty
enough task in itself. Their foundations had to be prepared either
by excavating the unexpectedly hard boulder clay or by levelling off
the even harder freestone. The piers were then built upwards, their
girders hoisted by hydraulic jacks so that the two could rise in
tandem. Arrol was meanwhile commissioning the metal caissons
from another organisation, Arrol Brothers,[42] and steel plates for the
superstructure from Siemens, near Swansea.[43] Fowler claimed that
those plates would 'surpass in strength and toughness any material
hitherto used in the construction of railway bridges'. The
Inspectors' first report found everything entirely satisfactory.[44]

The three distinct phases in the construction of the Forth Bridge can be tracked by the rising number of briggers (bridge erectors) employed, and by the increasing risks to which they were exposed. The first phase, employing under 2000 men, comprised temporary works, staging and operational structures, the construction of the north and south approach viaducts, and the preparation for the foundations and the piers of the cantilever towers. The second phase, altogether more dangerous, included the sinking of the caissons for the tower foundations into the sea, and the beginning of the great steel towers above. The third phase – finishing the towers and constructing the cantilevers – began in 1887. It was by far the most dangerous phase of the work, undertaken at up to 340 feet above water level, with the workforce rising upwards of 4000.[45]

Baker's admiration for the briggers' 'great coolness, courage and hardiness . . . in crawling along narrow planks or angle bars three or four hundred feet up',[46] was moderated by his mordant view of their capacity for alcohol. He would refer to the Hawes Inn at South Queensferry, internationally celebrated for its bit part in Robert Louis Stevenson's *Kidnapped*, to locate where the bridge was being built. Yet, the inn

> flourishes too well, for being in the middle of our works, its attractions prove irresistible to a large proportion of our 3500 workforce. The accident ward adjoins the pretty garden with hawthorns, and many dead and injured men have been carried there who would have escaped had it not been for the whisky of the Hawes Inn.[47]

William Westhofen, the engineer in charge of the central tower rising from Inchgarvie and chronicler of the bridge, evidently thought that Baker had exaggerated the problem of drink. He wrote later that 'black sheep are found everywhere', and many of those working on the bridge were birds of passage – including the occasional tramp who had arrived on site simply because he had hitched a ride on the free paddle-steamer across the river which the contractor provided for his men –

it is no exaggeration to say that no one need desire to have to do with a more civil or well-behaved lot of men, always ready to oblige, always ready to go where they were told to go, cheerfully obeying orders to change from one place to another, and, above all things, ready to help others in misfortune, not with advice, but with hands and purses.[48]

Most briggers lived locally, but as their numbers increased sharply, Arrol added accommodation on site, and laid on special trains from Edinburgh and a commuter steamer from the Port of Leith.[49] He provided his workmen with foundation boots and waterproofs, and made available woollen jackets, overalls and waterproof suits at 'nominal' cost.[50] However nominal the cost had been, photographs of the workers taken during construction shows such a great variety of dress that it suggests that little of Arrol's clothing offers were taken up.

Although it appears retrospectively that the contract was managed throughout by Arrol, and the purpose of Tancred and Phillips' firms and resources was to give the project *bottom*, it was not always quite like that. In late 1884, the contractors appealed to the Bridge Company for additional capital with which to buy more machinery, since its expenditure had been 'considerably in excess of that originally contemplated'. They acknowledged that the programme had been slipping, but had devised a new operational plan to improve management and increase economy which depended upon a further substantial investment in machinery if they were to achieve the necessary 'vigorous prosecution of the works'. They could not afford it without assistance from the Bridge Company.[51] Fowler and Baker were dispatched to investigate, and discovered that the three contracting firms had not coalesced into a single firm as had been anticipated. There were divided loyalties and muddled lines of responsibility, and Arrol's boasted pattern of delegation to trusted subordinates had not worked evenly across the three firms.

Fowler and Baker laid down stringent conditions if they were to support the contractor's request for more capital. Since divided responsibility had to cease, William Arrol – perhaps because he was the only local contractor, or perhaps for his personal qualities – was to have control over the entire project. He had to appoint 'a first rate man experienced in bridge work' to be his agent or general superintendent of works who would oversee named subordinates with particular responsibility for the components of the construction – the staging, caissons, airlocks, the skewbacks, the lower workshops, the upper workshops, surveys, measurement and the drawing office. The intention was to make a single, efficient contracting firm emerge from the three separate contracting companies. Fortnightly meetings would monitor its progress.[52] What the other contractors thought of this new arrangement is unknown; but whereas all of the key figures in both consulting and contracting during the erection of the bridge – including Joseph Phillips – were to be photographed for the souvenir edition of *Industries* in 1890,[53] Tancred and Falkiner (whose partnership had been dissolved in 1886) are notably missing – which implies that they were unhappy at the arrangement.

Out of this new arrangement emerged the monocled William Westhofen, named responsible for the erection of the steelwork jointly with Andrew Biggart. Westhofen, a mechanical engineer from Mainz, was initially responsible for foundations and the piers, before being promoted to overall manager of the Inchgarvie cantilever in 1887. He was also the biographer of the bridge project, and his monograph *The Forth Bridge*, published by *Engineering* in 1890, remains the primary source of information on the project. It is intriguing to compare this exhaustive and superbly well-illustrated volume with his compatriot Grothe's summary chap-book on the first Tay Bridge most of which was given over to the opening banquet speeches; or perhaps even with Crawford Barlow's smooth and rather detached record of the second. It more resembles John Leng's sixteen-page memorial booklet, with its technical drawings, on the new Tay Bridge – but is five times the length, five times more dense, and illustrated by incomparable drawings of the bridge's structure, of its machinery and of its erection process. No joint was too complicated and no rivet too small to escape Westhofen.

On Fowler's recommendation, the Bridge Company agreed to provide a further £80,000 for purchase of a plant to Tancred Arrol, subject to audit of the contractor's books and accounts and, at the end of the project, the plant becoming property of the railway company.[54] Baker had to approve its purchase, and was given authority to vary the price for the steel cantilevers beyond the scheduled rate if he thought necessary. The Forth Bridge Company then offered a maximum bonus of £50,000 if the bridge opened to general passenger traffic by 1 October 1889. By placing the responsibility uniquely upon Arrol, the guaranteeing railway companies were placing the future of the entire British east coast line – through the simultaneous construction of the longest and the largest railway bridges in the world – into the hands of a single individual – and his workmen.

'I speak of men', said Benjamin Baker to the Royal Institution, 'working with precarious foothold at dizzy heights in stormy weather.'[55] The contract expected the contractor to take every care of his men since it contained the proviso that compensation for any accidents had to be deducted from the contractor's promised terminal bonus. A financial imperative had been put on Arrol, if ever one had been needed, to ensure the highest possible safety standards; and it was to this end that he devised many of his inventions.

The first wave of injuries, however, was not to occur on high (for the towers were not yet up), but below, under water – and sometimes extraordinarily deep under water, caused by the sinking of the caissons as foundations for the great cantilever towers in 1885. The Forth Bridge cantilevers required twelve enormous circular foundations – four for each tower – of which half were on dry land, and half had to be floated out to the correct position and placed on the seabed. Once there, diggers had to excavate the seabed beneath them until the caisson sunk to the correct level – and occasionally that meant very deep: deeper indeed than the Brooklyn. The first caisson, ceremonially launched on 26 May 1884,[56] was of a very different order from those sitting on the bed of the Tay. At seventy feet in diameter, it was close to half the size of the Brooklyn-side caisson of the Brooklyn Bridge, but at a

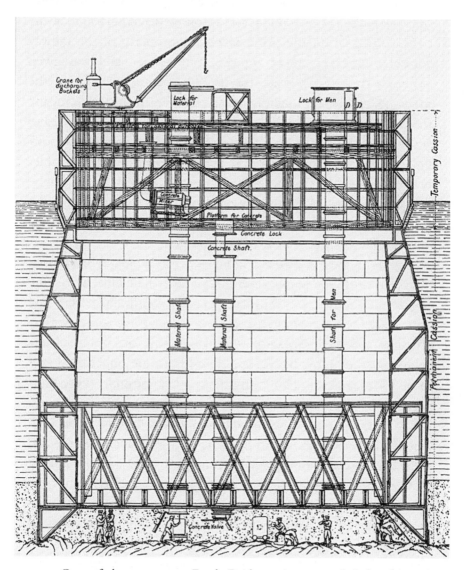

One of the enormous Forth Bridge caissons needed for the
Inchgarvie cantilever, showing the cramped 7-foot-high excavation
chamber at the base, its outer rim blocked by sandbags, although
occasionally permeated by salmon.

weight of 2877 tons was barely 10% less heavy. The caissons also had to be sunk twice as deep, varying from seventy-two to eighty-nine feet below high water, as compared to Brooklyn's forty-four. This giant metal cylinder was lined with Arrol's blue Staffordshire brick and filled by concrete. A seven-foot-high space, bounded by the outer skin, was left void for the excavation chamber at the bottom. Shafts were cast through the concrete to allow the diggers access to it, and for extracting the excavated spoil. About the width of a door, the access shaft was entered through an airlock and contained a metal ladder down which men clambered to reach the excavation chamber. They found themselves in a large, brilliantly lit, low – almost claustrophobic – space seventy-feet wide and seven-feet high compressed between hundreds of tons of concrete above and the clay or rock seabed below. The water was prevented from entering this chamber by compressed air which, at full depth, was three times the pressure on the ground; and when the compressed air escaped out into the sea, as periodically it did, the excavation chamber would fill with a fine mist. The constant fear, of course, was that the weight of the concrete above their heads might suddenly force the caisson down into the mud and squash them. One came very close when it dropped just under seven feet, burying the diggers up to their chins.[57]

The sinking of the caissons had been awarded to M. Coiseau, a subcontractor from Paris and Antwerp, whose polyglot workforce of Italians, French, Belgians, Austrians and Germans was largely ghettoised on Inchgarvie Island. His diggers needed, according to Westhofen, 'good health, freedom from pulmonary or gastric weakness, and abstemiousness, or at any rate, moderation in taking strong spirituous liquors'.[58] If they had been making too free with the whisky overnight, they suffered down below the following day. Men worked in shifts, and the deeper the caisson, the shorter the shift. The actual experience, as the *Industries'* compiler put it, varied from person to person, but almost everybody suffered acute earache. It was impossible to whistle while they worked, and the effervescent drinks that they had taken down for refreshment became flat and horrid. The deeper the caisson was sunk (and some

The cantilevers emerge, entirely transforming the scale of Queensferry, rendering substantial buildings minute. Photographed by keen
photographer, Prof. John Steggal of Dundee University.

'Death often supervenes.'[62] So Baker was proud that, whereas sixteen of the 119 workers on the St Louis Bridge affected by the
bends had died and two had been permanently crippled, no deaths
occurred on the Forth Bridge directly attributable to air pressure.[63]
Westhofen, however, recorded two dead and one insane, although
he excused it by claiming the men had been consumptive already
and the Scottish winter was more likely the culprit. The man who
was driven insane, however, could not so readily be blamed upon
the Scottish weather, for there would surely have been more of
them.

The shifts of the twenty-seven men working in the South
Queensferry caissons were limited to six hours and to four hours in
the highest-pressure caisson off Inchgarvie, followed by eight hours

off.[64] These conditions were considerably more generous than the terms enjoyed by the workers on the Brooklyn Bridge. When Arrol finally visited America, he was taken aback by its working conditions, writing to his friend Andrew Biggart (head of the Forth Bridge Drawing Office), 'There is a great amount of misery, and there are poor people here as well as at home . . . The ordinary working class seem to work very hard, and are a care-worn-out looking people. They work long hours – ten hours every day except nine on Saturday. I was in two large factories and they were working like slaves. If our men at home had to work like them they would have something to complain of.'[65]

Short visits below were also attractive to the thousands of tourists who visited the construction site. One had taken a spirit flask with him as he went down and, doubtless taken aback by the conditions, drained it. As he returned back up through the airlock, the compressed air in his flask exploded.[66] Occasionally compressed air would burst out from the bottom rim of the caissons and bubble up to the surface. Nearby salmon were persuaded by the bubbles that they must be at the bottom of a waterfall that must be climbed. Attracted by the bubbly light, they swam down deep into the sea to emerge gasping into the caisson chamber, providing a useful dietary supplement to diggers with the 'bends'.[67] Arrol's biographer claimed that one of the divers who was attempting to seal a leak at the base of a caisson by placing sandbags of concrete around the outer rim suddenly found himself sucked inside the chamber, emerging like an alien to affright the diggers; but that seems hardly credible.

Since the boulder clay was much harder than anticipated, Arrol invented a hydraulic spade operated by three men, which sliced through it easily. He later presented one as a souvenir to Tom Harrison in Newcastle.[68] It was such an innovation that one of the engineers, the amateur photographer Evelyn Carey (who produced a superb photographic record of the bridge's erection), attempted to take a photograph of the men with this mammoth puffing spade at work down below. He had the entire chamber whitewashed, and increased the lighting to 6000 candle power. During a variety of exposures – of five, ten and twenty-five minutes – the diggers were expected to remain motionless, posing with their weapon.[69]

Compressed air also escaped sometimes under the edge of the caisson during the photographic session, creating a fog inside. Baker noted that the results were not as he had wished, for the workmen's eyes came out 'in glaring spectral fashion'. But the consequences of the fog were rather more serious. The mist must have reacted with something, for it caused intense irritation to the eyes of everyone in the chamber, which only passed away if the eyes were bathed in weak tea and milk, and it took a few days.[70]

On 31 December 1884, one of the 400-ton caissons for the South Queensferry Tower was placed on site, ready for excavation to begin after the New Year holiday. It was sufficiently light that it should have risen and fallen with the tide, but should that not happen and the sea pour over its rim, it was fitted with valves to let the sea pour out again so that the caisson stayed level. On 1 January, the caisson failed to float up with the New Year tide.[71] Since an unsupervised foreman had forgotten to leave the valve open, it became top-heavy and tilted sharply downhill to settle deep in the mud.[72] Arrol lined and braced it with timber and pumped the water out – but too hastily. The internal bracing proved insufficient (for at its upper levels the metal was not lined with brickwork) and the force of the sea outside caused the thin metal plates of the upper part of the caisson to rip apart, killing the two carpenters inside.[73] It took until the following October – over nine months after it slipped – for the caisson to be restored to use. False rumours claiming that the caisson had failed a second time led to sharp selling of Forth Bridge shares, indicating the high level of nervousness that investors felt about the bridge's construction.[74]

For each of the three towers, four columns of whinstone concrete lined with Aberdeen granite rose up to be capped by the enormous sanded and oiled baseplates of the superstructure. Skewbacks were then fixed on top of these baseplates, and bolted through them deep into the columns below. The next step was to erect the three great steel towers above. Inside each twelve-foot-diameter tube there was a hydraulic lifting press, and its function

Engraving of conditions in the caissons, published in *Industries*. Two men are holding one of the Arrol-invented two-man hydraulic spades. The engraving derived from photographs taken by Evelyn Carey, but there was insufficient light, and the workers' eyes were strained and staring, so the photographs did not come out well.

was to raise the erection platforms, staging and decks that would be constructed around the tube, like rectangular bangles around an arm. The main deck of an erection platform supported gantries, cranes, and oil-heated rivet furnaces, with a lower deck, reached by a ladder, with shelters for the briggers. Material would be hoisted up by cranes. Everything was fixed methodically at each stage, since it was essential that the structure could withstand a hurricane even when only partially assembled. The first team would assemble the marked components into a tube or girder, using temporary fixings. Their platform or stage would be raised up to the next location whilst a riveting gang followed behind to rivet everything rigid. Photographs taken during erection show the tubular struts and girder ties decorated with clusters of parallel spidery platforms. Once cranes were operating 343 feet up at tower-top, the erection of the cantilevers and the girders could begin.

New teams of workmen arrived with the superstructure: those who assembled the structure, and those who riveted it tight. Each riveting gang, comprising two riveters and a rivet boy, was paid by piece-work. The boy would heat the rivets in his Arrol-designed portable furnace and lob them red hot to his two riveters who would catch them in a tool adapted for that purpose. The habit, as now, was probably to throw rivets at the riveter's face, making the latter that much more anxious to catch them.[75] It was inevitable that some would be missed and go over, so netting was introduced to protect workmen and tourists below. A steady throwing-boy could make a substantial difference to the rivet gang's income and vice versa. However, as Westhofen noted, riveters were 'not generally very steady' people, and if they did not turn up after an unsteady night, the rivet-heating boys lost their income. But having a captive market, these rivet-heating boys set out to exploit it for what they could. They successfully 'stood out' (effectively went on strike) for a guaranteed weekly income whether or not their riveters proved unsteady. Westhofen concluded, 'It is said the boy is father to the man; here the boy was master of several men.'[76] Their wages were paid weekly thereafter.

By autumn 1886, it was evident that the programme had slipped back farther. The girders on the north and south viaducts had only just been jacked up to the correct level, and only the central towers of each cantilever were complete.[77] Fowler asked Baker to review the entire project and, having received his report, wrote Arrol a stern letter. The arrangements for the erection and completion of the Forth Bridge were inadequate. Although he and Baker had brought 'continuous, and sometimes painful pressure' regarding Arrol's 'defective arrangements and organisation', assisting him in every way, the latter had always failed to comply with their remonstrances.

> The work is unusual in magnitude and character and therefore it is that the assistance of ourselves and staff, and the many suggestions founded on my own large experience, have been freely at your service. . . From the investigation just concluded, you cannot now fail to see that the completion of the work will be delayed by several years beyond the contract time, and a most serious loss be thrown upon the Company of interest alone. I gather from Baker's letter that at last you admit and thoroughly realise the insufficiency of your organisation . . . I cannot permit the present system to be continued . . . Its disastrous results are certain.[78]

Acknowledging 'the excellent quality of the work you have executed', Fowler warned Arrol that unless the latter could satisfy him that he had put in place adequate managerial changes, he would advise the directors to terminate the contract.[79]

It seems that management in the shops had got lax and faulty equipment was reaching the superstructure. Untried machinery could not possibly be risked 300 feet above the River Forth. In a distant echo of Bouch's problems with his foundrymen (the significant difference being that Bouch had never realised that there *were* problems with the foundrymen), Fowler observed that the cost of the same work under the same circumstances varied to an unacceptable degree. The machines themselves were not being used effectively.

> The large special advance on tools which the company have made to you imposes upon me the duty of seeing that the greatest amount of work in drilling and otherwise is obtained from these tools, and you are, of course, deeply interested in the economy which results from all tools being employed in the best manner. Beside vigilant superintendence, I am of the opinion that accounts should be kept in such a manner as to show every

week the actual cost of drilling and the processes connected therewith by the different tools and men.

Worst, Baker appears to have discovered that Arrol had been spreading himself far too thinly and, being only human, was spending a disproportionate amount of time on those elements that gave him most pleasure – namely the manufacture of machinery.

A week later, Fowler transmitted his decision. 'The experience of the past and the result of the recent special investigation have so clearly disclosed the disastrous consequences of the "hand to mouth" method of proceeding with the work of erection (as the present matters may be fairly characterised) that it is unnecessary further to refer to them. The present business is to provide remedies.' Arrol was to be released from other responsibilities so that he could 'give his attention to the general arrangements and supervision of the work, and by constant reference with [his principal subordinates][80] he could watch the progress, provide for the future, and remove all obstacles'. That required a new command structure. A mechanical engineer of great experience and authority, responsible to Arrol, must be given express charge for all machinery outside the shops, with full power to do whatever may be necessary to prevent delay with the work. This new chief mechanical engineer should have a subordinate 'capable mechanical engineer . . . attached to each of the three great groups of work – viz. at Queensferry, Garvie and Fife' (hence Westhofen's appointment) and they, in turn, should have 'a superior mechanical foreman . . . attached to each skewback'. A week later, Fowler was able to reassure the directors that his meeting with Arrol had proved satisfactory, and that he had promised 'to carry out all my suggestions'.[81]

1887 was the key year in the Forth Bridge's fortunes. By February, 80% of the entire contract sum had been spent, and the three great steel towers were barely complete, the cantilevers not begun[82] and three-fifths of the superstructure remained to be erected. Arrol's finances were also running short, and Fowler's dramatic intervention into his organisation, with his requirement to staff up at middle management level, increased his costs. One of

Arrol's principal steel suppliers, the Steel Company of Scotland, began to let him down (Arrol would win his case against them in the High Court three years later). To make up time, the workforce was increased by over 1000, and whereas there had always been an element of night-working, it now became customary. 'When the sun goes down,' reported the *Bradford Observer*, 'hundreds of electric lamps light up the great cantilevers and in all but very stormy weather, the work may be said to be continuous save on Sundays.'[83]

Staffing up too quickly can present its own problems. The 27% increase in the workforce brought a 300% increase in accidents,[84] implying that the influx of rookies had something to do with it. Accidents were almost impossible to prevent if you consider the nature of the erection. Height lay at the core of Arrol's construction method since staging and materials were suspended from above,[85] with the result, as Baker wrote later, that workmen lost all sense of the height at which they were working.[86] In late 1887, the great steel towers finally reached their 343 feet, and large workers' shelters and dining rooms were fixed to the top of each,[87] so high as to avoid the danger of any falling rivets plunging into the soup. If things of greater weight than a rivet went over the side, the consequences were grave. Baker recorded how 'a dropped spanner entered a man's waistcoat below and came out at his ankle, tearing open the whole of his clothes, but not injuring the man himself in any way'. He was extraordinarily fortunate. A spanner falling 300 feet punched a hole one inch in diameter through a four-inch block of wood.[88]

Whereas only twenty workers had been killed on the Brooklyn Bridge,[89] sixty-three lost their lives on the Forth, and over 500 required some form of medical treatment.[90] Almost half had been killed by falling from a height, and nine by being hit by a falling object. Only four had drowned.[91] Arrol would pay full wages of any worker injured *not through his own fault* until he recovered, but the engineers' view was that much of the danger had been caused by the briggers themselves as Westhofen described:

Elevation of a Forth Bridge cantilever, showing its high structure and how the erection platforms clustered on to it. The two, multi-strut joints at the base and at the top, like metal arachnids, are called skewbacks. Lattice work is in tension, and the steel tubes in compression.

In every-day work — with that fatal familiarity that is said to breed contempt — while working on stages which could hardly be made large enough or strong enough to hold the litter of tools and rubbish which they constantly gathered, they were throwing about hammers and drifts and chisels, and pieces of wood, which in a moment were over the side, and tumbled down upon maybe three or four other tiers of staging, where men were engaged upon their work . . . It needed the sight of a wounded and mangled fellow-creature, or his bloody corpse, to bring home to them the seriousness of the situation.[92]

The Board of Trade Inspectors had kept a eye upon the casualties, growing particularly concerned in mid-1887 when, with the highest work taking place, fifteen men were killed in six months.

Although some accidents had been caused by foolhardiness, others were attributable to inadequate supervision by the foreman or by the leading hand. 'We ourselves noticed one due entirely to the carelessness or ignorance of a foreman. No expense should be spared in order to provide a sufficiently numerous and experienced staff of overseers.'[93] Gangways running along the top of the North Queensferry tower 343 feet above water level lacked a guardrail, and they recommended that one be installed.[94] The other principal cause was mechanical failure – either in the plant itself, or in the staging upon which all workers on the superstructure depended. In a number of cases, gangways or staging supports snapped, toppling machines or men out and down onto others or into the sea far below.

Two particularly gruesome accidents occurred in mid-1887. Six men on a painting stage 130 feet above the sea level were thrown off when the beam supporting the stage snapped. Three men hung on and were rescued by intrepid colleagues; one fell into the sea and was rescued, his system shocked, whereas the pair who fell onto other parts of the bridge, or the jetty, were killed outright.[95] A similar accident six weeks earlier had caused the men to down tools. As a riveting stage suspended on steel cables was being raised from one position to the next, one of its timbers snagged a girder. Sensing an obstruction, but not discovering the reason, they continued to winch it up. Something was going to give and the winching wheel snapped. 'The whole stage rattled down, throwing off and killing two men and the rivet-heating boy.' The men struck for an increase of a penny an hour danger money. After holding out for a week, reported Westhofen rather smugly, 'most of the strikers were glad to be allowed to come back'.[96]

Arrol was as sensitive to the accident figures as the media was alive to them. During the carnage of 1887, the *Scotsman* and the *Glasgow Herald* were replete with stories of serious and fatal accidents, drawing an angry response from Arrol who accused them of falsehood, gross exaggeration, and giving 'a sensational character to many insignificant mishaps'. There were, he wrote, 4200 people working on site, including the night shifts, and it was improper to be spreading reports of deaths and severe accidents that were untruthful. Rather than the 100 deaths reported in the media, there had been only twenty-nine to date, of which only ten were of a character particular to that contract. The annual report of the Forth Bridge Working Men's Accident and Sickness Club, newly published, showed that sixty-seven men had been hospitalised since the works began, there had been 357 minor accidents, and 22,699 doctor's visits.[97] Safety precautions on the bridge were extraordinary for that period. 'All that good appliances, safeguards and supervision can do, we do try, but we cannot successfully contend against recklessness or thoughtlessness of the men themselves.'[98] A number of workmen, or their dependents, sued the Company for damages, but judging by the fact that the judge usually ruled in Arrol's favour, his claim to be following best practice was probably correct. Speaking on behalf of the engineers, Baker told the Royal Institution that 'we never ask a workman to do a thing which we are not prepared to do ourselves, but of course men will, on their own initiative, occasionally do rash things'.[99] Nothing could prevent a macho brigger from perching in the most precarious places – as Carey's photographs show – or making a short-cut where jumping was speedier than following the gangways and ladders all the way round. The Board of Trade inspectors agreed that no reasonable precautions for the men's safety had been omitted.[100]

That same June there had been unwelcome news for Fowler and Baker. Tancred Arrol decided that the revised contractual arrangements were no longer sufficient to keep the project afloat, and informed them that they could not complete the bridge on the basis of the original contract. 'The cost of erecting and riveting the great cantilevers, including the necessary plant and elaborate appliances required for the work, will be such that payment at the scheduled rate for steelwork will not even cover cost price.' They were unable to estimate the total cost with any reasonable certainty, and proposed that either the Bridge Company should take over the contract, and simply relieve contractors for all existing liabilities, or it should provide funds to allow them to discharge them themselves.

With so much capital already expended and so much of this particular design already built, the Board really had no choice but to continue. It decided to return to Parliament for a further extension of time, and to seek powers to raise additional capital. It then agreed that Tancred Arrol must continue with the bridge, leave its 'expedition and economy', and the overall management of the project, in the hands of William Arrol, and delegated the question of additional remuneration to Fowler, Baker and Harrison. It also agreed to pay for all necessary new plant and equipment, subject to the Bridge Company's auditor checking the accounts.[101] By the time of the shareholders' meeting in March, things were back on track. By comparison, with their predecessors, the shareholders in the Forth Bridge project – and in the railways companies supporting them – were a remarkably quiescent bunch. Perhaps now that the Company was delivering 4.5% to ordinary shareholders, at long last a reasonable and reliably delivered dividend, there was no need for histrionics. There was an occasional glitch – such as an unsuccessful shareholders' revolt against demolishing their Edinburgh hotel and building a new one, but the minutes of the March meeting, like the meeting itself, were unusually brief.

So long as weather permitted and tourists did not get too much in the way, the bridge would be finished in 1889. The number of tourists and other visitors appears to have been approaching plague proportions, and those of a certain rank signed Fowler's leatherbound Visitors' Book.[102] Westhofen commented, 'Their name is simply legion, for from beginning to end there has been an extraordinary amount of interest by all classes of society.'[103] Naturally monarchs like the Shah of Persia (whose Grand Vizier left an inscrutable message in Arabic in the Visitors' Book), aristocrats and other dignitaries required special arrangements, but there was a constant stream of artistic, literary, scientific and engineering societies. The Amalgamated Railway Servants expressed their thanks with a whip-round for the Sickness and Accident Fund. The Edinburgh Association for Science and Arts' annual visit, almost always greeted graciously by Arrol, attracted 500 of its members along for the trip. Precautions were taken, and the *Manchester Guardian* noted how they walked 'beneath a horizontal screen of wire netting designed to protect our heads from falling rivets'.[104] Arrol was sufficiently sure of his safety precautions to let them go as high as they wished. 'Hundreds of visitors, men of science of all nationals, turbaned Indian princes, and even venturesome young ladies' made the trip right to the top, 343 feet above sea level.[105] The steel shavings, observed Baker who was very proud of his Siemens steel, when planed off, 'form such long, true and flexible spirals that they are largely used for ladies' bracelets when fitted with clasps and electroplated.[106] They also became tourist souvenirs. On a visit by the Lord High Commissioner in 1886, 'the young ladies especially seemed much interested, many of them carrying away iron filings of fantastic shape as souvenirs of the visit'.[107]

The weather remained adverse. Possibly as another lesson learnt from the Tay Bridge, the original Forth Bridge contract had provided £70,000 against compensation for men being laid off in exceptionally inclement weather. It was unlikely to have been adequate. In these warmer days, it is almost impossible to conceive of the Tay jammed with creaking ice-floes, or the Forth Bridge resembling a Christmas tree with icicles over a foot long.[108] March was always the cruellest month. No work was done in March 1886, a Scotland-wide snowstorm brought the country to a standstill in 1887, and March and April 1888 were, according to Hutchinson's report, 'exceptionally severe'.[109] It must have been somebody blind to this history that organised the royal opening in March 1890. Between February and April, hundreds of briggers were normally idle. The temperature also affected the steel since it was easier to work when warmer, and judging from the erection of the cantilevers in 1887–8, the work rate was exponentially greater between April and October than over the winter months.[110]

By July 1889, only 100 feet of the Queensferry south cantilever remained unriveted, and the other cantilevers had only twenty-five feet left unconstructed,[111] and the central girder on the southern span was ready to complete by early autumn when the briggers began its construction. Minute and spidery against the mammoth scale of the cantilevers, it was built out from the end of each cantilever, half a bay by half a bay, until the two ends closed in the middle.[112] As the steelwork from each side got closer, new opportunities for playing 'chicken' were seized eagerly. Late one September evening, Fitch, a top cranesman, took his chance and placed a forty-foot ladder over the jib of the crane on his side and manoeuvred the other end of the ladder over the jib of the crane at the end of the girder on the far side. Without waiting for his colleagues to lash it fast, he promptly crossed the ladder and achieved a short-lived immortality.[113]

Soon afterwards, the southern girder finally joined the Inchgarvie cantilever to the South Queensferry cantilever. It had been delayed by both storms and cold, for the steel had not expanded uniformly as intended. The side of the girder facing west had expanded with the intermittent afternoon sun allowing it to be fixed to its counterpart under pressure from hydraulic jacks. No matter the pressure from jacks and rams, however, the east side, cooler in the shade, left a gap of inches. Arrol's men – with what the *Scotsman* described as their typical fertility of resource – piled waste material into the trough at the bottom of the girder, poured on naptha, and set it alight. Within fifteen minutes, burning waste had warmed up the east girder sufficiently to expand so that its ends could be rapidly fixed together before it cooled down again. Where cranesmen lead, directors soon follow, and the Forth Bridge company directors and their friends mounted a train at Forth Bridge station a few days afterwards and travelled to the directors' meeting in the engineers' office in the Yards. They then walked slowly along the structure until they reached the sixty-foot gap that remained in the north span, and waited for cranes, perched on top of each end of the central girder, to lift a gangway from a barge struggling in an exceptionally strong current 160 feet below. After fifteen minutes manoeuvring, the gangway was up and, to cheers of workmen, a party of forty walked across it before proceeding to North Queensferry, a steamer trip and lunch.[114]

If the directors believed that they were creating a new wonder of the world, there was a shock awaiting. When the National Association for the Advancement of Art and its Application to Industry opened its second Art Congress in Edinburgh's Queen Street Hall on 28 October, attracting artists like J.H. Lorimer and William Hole, antiquarians, historians, architects like J.D. Sedding, John Honeyman and Robert Rowand Anderson, luminaries like Patrick Geddes, and the spiritual leaders of the Arts and Crafts movement from England, Walter Crane, and the wondrously barking William Morris, the bridge's aesthetics came under attack.[115] Given its lineage, the natural undertone of the Congress was the dehumanisation of man's creative powers by machinery and industrialisation, and what role Art could play in an industrialised world. Art Schools were not proving as successful as had been hoped, and there was still controversy over whether to admit women – particularly to life classes. The Congress debated public interference in architectural design and the ugliness of so much recent building – in a manner that eerily presaged identical discussions in the Commission for the Built Environment and Architecture and Design of Scotland over a century later.

The Congress was anxious rather than triumphant, and lectures were meagrely attended although Morris and Crane gave separate evening lectures for working men. The Glasgow architect John Honeyman had suggested that the only way to advance art was to promote art education, not among art students, but to 'the great mass of the population who had no proper conception of what art was',[116] but the great mass of the population stayed away. The *Scotsman* felt that the Congress could have achieved more. 'Through it all has run a rumbling and grumbling undertone of pessimism, almost of despair . . . We have been told that this is the Age of Ugliness, and it is almost hopeless of making things better. A nightmare of hideous utilitarian work and ideas weighs upon the world and upon the city.'[117]

It is arguable that the majesty of the Forth Bridge was what had depressed the fine artists. It had naturally been the destination of a Congress excursion leading, inevitably, to a discussion as to whether the bridge could be classified as architecture. William

Countless groups and societies visited the Forth Bridge under construction. This visit, almost certainly, was by members of the new Dundee University photographed by Prof. John Steggall, one of their number. The North Queensferry cantilever has almost reached its approach viaduct, which indicates a date probably in 1889.

Morris let fly. 'As for an iron architecture, there never was and never could be such. Every improvement in the art of engineering made the use of iron more ugly, until at last they had that supreme specimen of ugliness, the Forth Bridge.'[118] The engineers were shocked. They were not accustomed to defending their structures in aesthetic terms, and were less than fleet of foot when it came to defending them as art objects. The journal *Industries* thought it beside the point, although strived to defend the bridge from the accusation of ugliness:

What was required was not a piece of decoration over a mile long and a hundred and twenty yards high . . . but a manifestly strong bridge . . . One of the virtues of the design of the Forth Bridge is that there is no attempt at ornamentation of any kind whatever. The columns, top and bottom members, struts and ties, are left to tell their own tale; they are there for use and not for decoration . . . The Forth Bridge owes little of its impressiveness to mere magnitude . . . [It] has elements of beauty in its design, and these elements of beauty, consisting as they do in detail, in lines, and forms, carried out in material on a scale of immense size, must be observed from an appropriate distance.[119]

Later that month, Baker used a platform given by the Edinburgh Literary Institute to rebut Morris. From the very start, he and Fowler had considered the design of the bridge from an aesthetic perspective. They had agreed that an arched structure would have been the most beautiful, but it was impossible in that location. Instead, they had endeavoured to make the bridge as visually honest and as graceful as they could 'so that to any intelligent eye the nature of the stresses and the sufficiency of the members of the structure to resist them, were emphasised at all points'. Desiring to 'keep the whole work in harmony', they had designed it deliberately to emphasise how the leading lines of the structure were 'expressive of great strength and stability both in a lateral and vertical direction', to reassure the nervous traveller.[120] So another of Bouch's legacies was that both the new Tay and the Forth bridges had to appear massive and stable and safe for psychological reasons. The architect Alfred Waterhouse, one of the leading English architects of the epoch, wrote to Fowler:

One feature especially delights me – the absence of ornament. Any architectural detail borrowed from any style would have been out of place in such a work. As it is, the bridge is a style unto itself: the simple directness of purpose with which it does its work is splendid and invests your vast monument with a kind of beauty of its own, differing though it certainly does from all other beautiful things I have seen.[121]

In February 1890, General Hutchinson and Major Marindin made their twenty-eighth and concluding report to the Board of Trade. The severe tests to which they had subjected every part of the bridge had produced deflections much smaller than they had expected. The Forth Bridge was 'of exceptional strength and stability − a wonderful example of thoroughly good workmanship with excellent materials',[122] and could open for passenger traffic immediately. It had used 50,958 tons of steel, and at least six and a half million rivets.[123] The final cost of the bridge had risen to £2,549,200, 50% higher than the original tender, and the various railway companies had collectively spent £378,000 − 15% of the construction cost − on getting the relevant bills through Parliament.[124]

The bridge was formally opened on 3 March 1890. The equerry who set that date had failed to check the weather records, and the weather was consistent with the Marches of the previous four years. It was dreadful. The Prince of Wales and entourage had travelled from London in a special train at averages of fifty miles per hour in what was really a royal progress of national rejoicing 'to celebrate and officially complete the greatest feat of engineering the world has ever seen'.[125] But whereas the Tay Bridge had opened under the bluest of skies in the balmiest June weather,[126] the Prince of Wales found Scotland in March characterised by 'a grey sky with clouds scurrying across it; a grey sea with "white horses" rampant everywhere; now and then a shower of rain; and along with these a wind which roared and thundered upon the bridge and whistled among the cortege of craft on the sea below', drenching the passengers.[127] Although the wind was gusting at 15lbs per square foot − two-thirds of the strength of the gust when the Tay Bridge had come down − there was scarcely a tremor. Using an Arrol-invented hydraulic riveter, the princely hand was guided by Arrol to rivet the last rivet. The ceremonial rivet was only gilded, and remains in place, by comparison with the

Canadian Pacific's silver spike at Craigellachie, which was stolen.[128]

The howling gale reduced whatever speeches may have been intended to the simple regal pronouncement that the bridge was open, before they were all rushed off to the Engineers' Model Loft, brilliantly transformed into an enormous glittery banqueting suite. There, the speeches caught up with their audience, to an extensive programme devised by George Weiland, the North British secretary, and illustrated by artists of Weiland's particular selection. Each principal figure in the Forth Bridge was portrayed on the menu card in a form, and accompanied by a poetic effusion worse than anything McGonagall could have envisaged.

Queen Victoria had empowered the Prince of Wales to announce that she would make Sir John Fowler a baronet, and offer different degrees of knighthoods (in a most British way) to Benjamin Baker, engineer, and William Arrol, contractor. The Prince was not only much taken with the bridge, but proved his exceptionally good briefing by rehearsing to his audience an exhaustive tally of the quantities of materials used to build the bridge. Other speakers emphasised how the name 'North British' represented a unity between Scotland and England, and how the bridge was the finest expression of that idea. But even though the North British Railway had been the 'onlie begetter' of the idea, and the chairman of the Bridge Company was also knighted, the ceremony was not to do with the railway companies. It provided an unparalleled marketing opportunity to show that British engineering had relegated the disaster of the first Tay Bridge to history. Senior engineers from Saxony, Austria, Hungary, Prussia and France who had been invited to the opening and banquet duly eulogised the bridge in their speeches. There was a further banquet for them in London the following day, where Gustav Eiffel stated that the bridge was 'one of the finest works of mechanical science he had ever witnessed', but refused to say more since his English was not sufficient.[129] The media sniffed that each cantilever of the Forth Bridge was worth two Eiffel Towers,[130] and Baker himself muttered that the Eiffel Tower was 'ugly, ill-proportioned and of no

The Forth Bridge complete.

real use to anyone'.[131] That same night, 600 of the Forth Briggers were entertained to dinner in the drawing loft.[132]

In April 1890, the Bridge Company finally fulfilled its promises to its contractor and its engineers by paying out the agreed additional bonuses: £20,000 fees to the engineers, and £64,000 to the contractor.[133] The site had been reducing throughout the previous year and the workmen dismissed, so Arrol had recommended to the Company that it make an *ex gratia* payment to the remaining workforce, for which they put aside £2,265 – or not far from 0.1% of the construction cost. For those left working on the bridge it was about £1 – or two-thirds of a week's wages each. It was strange that the huge increase in construction cost had caused so little comment. Given that the cost was to be covered by the four guaranteeing railway companies, *The Times* trusted that they had a satisfactory plan for how they were going to manage it.

On 1 June 1890, the Forth Bridge opened to normal traffic. Two days later the new express from Edinburgh to Dundee, scheduled to take one hour fifty-five minutes, arrived in Dundee in one hour fifteen minutes – faster than is being achieved by the fastest train on that route today.[134] Traffic increased exponentially, and to such a degree that it quickly led to an embolism further down the line into Edinburgh.

In the Forth Bridge, the North British Railway had produced the outstanding icon of Scottish railway engineering, decisively trumping the Caledonian. It had provided a perfect international brand image, and the North British soon found itself marketed on shortbread tins. However much that Benjamin Baker might suggest to the Edinburgh Literary Institute that 'peace hath her victories not less renowned than war', the construction of the Forth Bridge had nonetheless been an act of economic warfare. With the East Coast trunk route now open, the North British at last equalled the Caledonian operationally, and the trunk railway war would now have to evolve in new ways.

Seen the bridge, got the T-shirt.

CHAPTER TEN

WARFARE SUBLIMATED

From London to Aberdeen within ten hours! To our grandfathers, who opened their eyes roundly at the prodigious speed attained by the stage coaches that spent days and nights on the same route, the statement would have been promptly placed in the same category as Puck's boast of putting a girdle round the earth in forty minutes.

SCOTSMAN 1 AUGUST 1895

An external threat often proves the best way to impel enemies toward reconciliation; and when they faced a strike of the Scottish Railway Servants in winter 1890, the Caledonian and the North British Railway companies discovered mutual interests of far greater significance than the rivalry of the previous half-century.

Their employees were demanding a maximum ten-hour day, payment of overtime after sixty hours' work a week, Sunday work at time and a half, and a maximum eight-hour day for drivers of shunting engines.[1] They backed their case by examples such as the North British engine-driver who had worked over seventy-seven hours in the four days before he smashed his engine into a goods train when dozing off.[2] Since the results of its ballot had been insufficiently overwhelming to guarantee national support, the Amalgamated Society of Railway Servants for Scotland had decided against a strike. Its radical Glasgow branch pressed on and struck just before Christmas 1890, at a time calculated – or so the news-papers surmised – to cause maximum disruption. Its branches in all three principal Scottish railways soon joined in. The North British refused to deal with the union, regarding it as an external organi-sation, but offered to meet representatives of its own employees – provided always that the men resumed work first.[3] The Caledonian likewise rejected the union's demands, but allowed anybody on strike to return to work without penalty provided it was by 8 January. The strike was over by 29 January.

The spectacle of 'the two great companies which have in their hands the central communications in Scotland [standing] shoulder to shoulder' was unusual, and the public wanted more of it. An unusually well-informed commentator in the *Scotsman* suggested that whereas they had 'hitherto conducted their business on the principles of fierce competition', an arrangement that produced 'more economical working and greater public convenience' would be in the interests of both the companies and of the nation.[4] It was also a matter of the Caledonian facing facts. With the Forth Bridge now open, and the east coast line underpinned by some of the most powerful railway companies in Britain, the Caledonian could no longer dream of annihilating its rival. Future competition would have to be on more rational lines – such as fares, quality of service or speed.

There had been sporadic collaboration for some time, and during the previous decade, a certain maturity had already begun to infect the two companies' relationship. Their respective General Managers had met periodically to discuss running powers, opera-tions, disputed accounts and operational difficulties,[5] and the very reasonableness of their minutes implies that common sense was pre-vailing at last. The new harmony, however, was shattered by an unexpectedly bitter takeover battle. The North British was looking for a new connection to Carlisle for its service to London via Settle with its Midland Railway partner. Its bleak upland line through Hawick and Langholm was laborious and the trains habitually arrived late. However, all other reasonable routes for railway lines between Glasgow and Carlisle were already occupied. The alternative was to obtain the route by buying the railway company that occupied it and, encouraged to believe that the Glasgow & South West Railway was willing, the North British set parliamentary procedures in hand.[6] Albeit a close-run thing, the North British was defeated in a battle that cost it almost £40,500 in parliamentary costs. Such contests had to be avoided in the future, particularly if railway companies were about to enter an era of uncertain labour relations.

That was the genesis of a new peace agreement between the Caledonian and the North British – the so-called 'New (or Joint) Lines' agreement. It promised to be more long-lasting than its two abortive predecessors of 1856 and 1867–8, given the new circumstances. Each company agreed to abstain from 'promoting or in any way aiding the promotion of lines into the districts of the other'; for a period of twenty-five years,[7] and neither could propose new lines to Parliament without giving due notice to the other. A 'Caledonian and North British (Peace Agreement) Committee' was established to police it. If its objective was to bring about 'a cessation of the costly expenditure on Parliamentary litigation which has constituted such an onerous burden upon the revenues of the Company', the peace agreement was dramatically successful. Between 1865 and 1867 the North British had annually been spending almost £100,000 on Parliamentary and legal expenses, and which had risen again to £40,500 in 1891. By 1896, annual parliamentary expenditure dropped to just £1,500;[8] and the New Lines Committee, unlike its predecessors, continued to meet.[9]

In the ranks, however, operational competition between the two companies remained fierce, and the Scottish railway trunk line war was to reach a climax of competing railway engines and passenger trains. A midsummer race between London and Edinburgh in summer 1888 had been suddenly sparked off by – or so it was said later – the fact that the west coast railway companies (the London & North Western Railway and the Caledonian Railway companies) feared losing all their Edinburgh traffic.[10] On 2 June 1888, an unheralded train had steamed out of Euston at 10am and arrived in Edinburgh at 6.53pm that same evening taking just under nine hours. It aroused considerable attention. The east coast railway companies (Great Northern, North Eastern and the North British) retaliated the following month, running a train leaving King's Cross at exactly the same time to arrive in Edinburgh twenty-three minutes sooner.

A special body of west coast directors met to plot a riposte, and by late July they had equalled the east coast's improved time of eight and a half hours – partly by curtailing the luncheon stop. Since the west coast route was seventeen miles longer, and their trains had had to steam at a higher average speed to achieve the same result, the west coasters regarded the result as a moral victory for their men and machines. Tit-for-tat of this kind continued throughout that month as seasonal traffic gradually increased.

'The tide of summer migration from the South to the North', as the *Scotsman* described the annual influx of huntsmen, began 'to rise in earnest towards the high flood of the 12th of August',[11]and the railway companies raced for their patronage. A joint railway conference on 14 August 1888, once the hunters were all safely deposited in Caledonia, finally brought the race to a halt. Journey times between London and Edinburgh were agreed at seven and three-quarters hours up the east coast, and eight hours up the west.[12] Barely weeks after some of the participating railway companies had been enforcing a maximum speed of only 40mph upon their trains, the expresses had achieved average speeds of over sixty-one miles over some stretches, and express time between London and Edinburgh had been permanently cut by over an hour.

Seeking to maximise the value it could extract from its decades of troubled bridge construction seven years later, North British contemplated a renewed race extending north to Aberdeen across its two expensively conquered river estuaries. It was not merely an exercise in vainglory. The commercial potential of the east coast line was significant, and the railway that offered greatest speed with greatest efficiency was likely to obtain most of lucrative Scottish/English goods and passenger trade. The chairman of the Great Northern put to his shareholders that 'Scottish traffic was of such importance to the Great Northern Company that he dared not, having accepted the responsibility of chairman, sanction any steps which would tend to diminish the traffic. (Cheers)'[13] Indeed, John Walker, the North British's General Manager, had already tried to capitalise on the Forth Bridge by drawing the attention of the Post Office to the fact that mails going up the east coast now arrived in Aberdeen almost half an hour earlier than those coming from Euston. He suggested that it might be a great advantage to the Post Office 'to forward the mails to Aberdeen by the Forth Bridge route'.[14] Implicit was the suggestion that the fastest journey would have greatest leverage in obtaining the mails contract.

Naturally, he said nothing about a little local difficulty that was still tarnishing the NBR's operations. As his trains entered Aberdeen, they encountered severe difficulties. As with so many peace agreements, the footsoldiers indoctrinated by almost fifty years of perpetual warfare and petty skirmishing were not entirely in harmony with their Company Directors. Thrawn Aberdeenshire Caledonian staff remained untouched by the peace agreement, and habitually harassed North British trains coming up the east coast over the Forth Bridge as they were approaching the city. Wagons were left blocking lines, trains were held up by over an hour by apparently deaf signalmen, and – in one case – an engine was prevented from joining its train for almost six hours.[15]

The west coast railway companies were well aware that they were in danger of being eclipsed by the opening of the Forth Bridge, and that the threat to its Scottish business had been heightened. They needed to demonstrate that 'it was possible for us to arrive in Aberdeen in the same time as the East Coast Railways'.[16] To his shareholders, Lord Stalbridge, chairman of the London & North Western, declared that the company 'had at last determined to show once and for all that they would not allow themselves to be kept in the background'. He was determined to maintain 'our fair share of the traffic to the north. The Scotch traffic grows year by year, and by competition, the public benefits.'[17]

John Walker, General Manager of the North British over the previous twenty-five years, died in 1891, and its secretary, George Weiland, resigned soon afterwards through ill health – to be

The completion of the bridge provided the opportunity for the 1895 railway race between London and Aberdeen. The bridge's simplicity belies just how enormous and sophisticated its structure is.

rewarded with a directorship of the company and, nine years later, its chairmanship.[18] Walker was replaced by the esteemed John Conachar, who came up to Edinburgh from managing the Cambrian Railways in Wales. Conachar is generally presented as not just a superlative railway manager, but a practical railwayman who, when the railway race flared up in the summer months of 1895, remained sceptical about the worth of any railway contest.[19] Although he was indeed practical, he joined the race unhesitatingly, and even sought to extend it long after it had exhausted everybody else. Early summer of 1895 had been particularly poor, all railway companies attributing their depressed income to 'the protracted depression in trade' which had led to a particular reduction in third-class travel since 'so many workpeople were working little more than half time'.[20] A railway race was just the ticket.

Dramatic cuts to travelling times would require cooperation between the different railway companies making up each route. Previously, a shared interest had not always been appreciated, and relations at operational level between the North British and the North Eastern up the east coast had sometimes been under great strain, alleviated only by their collaboration in agreeing to guarantee the Forth Bridge. The grouping of the west coast companies into an identifiable threat compelled the east coast ones to cooperate as a team. Both sides established a running conference where connections, carriages, goods and timetables would be hammered out (nothing of which would be permitted to appear in their Board minutes). The only hint of what was to come was a tiny note in the North British's Traffic Committee minutes in late April 1895 recording that the companies had met to discuss accelerating their trains.

The race forced the railways to modernise. It required decisions about limiting where express trains should stop, how far trains could travel without refuelling or watering, whether engines and carriages could cope with much higher average speeds, how many carriages should be carried, and how the crews were to be organised. Doubters warned that safety would be compromised, that travelling conditions would become insupportable, that greater 'oscillation' would cause vomiting, and that crashes were inevitable. John Burns MP had witnessed the mental and physical strain being put on train crews when travelling on the footplates of speeding trains in Britain and America. There was 'a terrible strain . . . on the mind of the driver, who had to be continually on the alert to see that the line was clear and the signals were all right'.[21] Some drivers relished the challenge. One wrote to the *Daily Telegraph* on 23 August, that 'there is a fascination in fast running that cannot be realised by an outsider, and given that steam can be maintained, there is nothing I enjoy more than trying to pull up a little lost time' – as indeed had been the custom tanking northwards over Bouch's Tay Bridge. The 1888 race had probably been the first time that faster journey times had been factored in as the principal passenger benefit, and in spring 1895 the railway superintendents for the east coast companies were charged to make ready.

The contest was ultimately about time and weight; but since the race broke out almost spontaneously rather than being run to agreed rules, multiple opportunities for not playing straight remained open to the unscrupulous. Consider timing. There was no agreement as to whether the time spent stationary in stations or at signals would be included in the time or not, nor any about whether the racing trains were scheduled services or specials. Naively, the NBR and its partners scheduled and advertised its racing services, which meant that they had to keep to scheduled stops, load and unload baggage, and lay on sufficient carriages for unforecast traffic. The west coast racers, as the *Scotsman* observed sourly, 'did not compete under the same conditions. [It] was practically a special, with no advertised times at intermediate stations. No delay was caused by loading or unloading luggage so that it could leave as soon as the necessary work was done.'[22] An unscheduled service could make it purely a contest of man, machine, stopwatch and weight.

For weight was the other principal factor. Who would ensure that competing trains had the same number of carriages and therefore a similar weight? An unscheduled train could carry fewer passengers, fewer carriages and thus be lighter. In their anxiety to retrieve their market, the west coasters ran light trains of only 'three or so carriages' which Sir Henry Oakley, General Manager of the Great Northern, condemned as a 'senseless practice' because it was so uneconomic.[23] Rumours circulated that carriage fittings were being ripped out and flung through the windows to allow lighter trains to travel even faster. Had it been so, the eager passengers who populated the racers – the young bucks travelling for the thrill, or the ubiquitous journalists chronicling the event – would surely have mentioned it.

There was something enormously artificial about the exercise. Bypassed cities like Glasgow got no benefit, and local railway services elsewhere were seriously disrupted. Lord Windermere complained bitterly to *The Times*. 'Meanwhile, between London and Windermere . . . no punctuality whatever can be relied on, though the advertised time is not much more than 40 miles an hour . . . Few through trains come in less than half-an-hour late, and all apparently for establishing "records" between London and an important but remote town in Scotland.'[24]

In June 1895, without informing its collaborators in the eastern conference – the North Eastern and the North British – the Great Northern decided to lay on a prestige Anglo-Scottish service which would leave King's Cross at 10pm to arrive in Aberdeen thirteen hours later.[25] Thus, 'in a fitful and hesitating way', as the *London Daily Chronicle* put it, 'a kind of race began, quickening by a few minutes' throughout the rest of the month. By 1 July, the trains running up the west coast had managed to reach Aberdeen in eleven hours forty minutes, and yet the east coast remained twenty minutes faster.[26] It had taken just a few weeks to lop 10%, one hour forty minutes, from the travelling time.

The Great Northern's 10pm evening service may not have attracted many passengers, but it alarmed the west coast companies sufficiently that, a fortnight later, they announced that their 8pm night from Euston would be a racer and would arrive in Aberdeen in eleven hours. The lineaments of the race to the north was thereby set, and throughout July 8pm night trains would speed out from Euston and King's Cross to Aberdeen. The east coast companies steadily reduced their early morning arrival times, whereas the west coast trains were customarily ten to twenty minutes behind them.[27]

At a time in late August 1895 when, with horse racing and the America Cup, racing dominated the national attention, the railway race reached its climax, and to their surprise, journalists found the railway race to Scotland every bit as thrilling as racing yachts or horses both to them and to their public. The racing railway companies had thereby bred themselves a monster. No train could depart without a hack and his stopwatch determinedly logging every motion, every deviation and, naturally, every departure from the timetable. The railway company programmers must have been greatly relieved when, in mid-September, the media focus shifted elsewhere.

On 29 July, the *Daily Chronicle*'s man had enjoyed a splendid trip up the east coast to Aberdeen; but was mortified to find that the west coasters had beaten him by eighteen minutes. The problem must have lain in that first leg just out of London: 'Officers of the eastern companies, but especially of the Great Northern, you must look to your laurels. Nothing short of ten hours will break the record.'[28] The honours for July, therefore, went to the west coast, which had sped over their 540 miles in a minute under ten hours[29] (i.e. already three hours faster than the short-lived 10pm train introduced by the Great Northern in June). The following fortnight there was a lull as railway companies busied themselves with their half-yearly shareholders' meetings. If raised at all, the race was blandly denied by the railway company boards. All they were doing was exploiting their assets to the full. The North Eastern, for example, 'did not see why they should give up a position which they had earned at the expense of a good deal of intelligence and capital'.[30]

The *Scotsman* suspected that behind their bland passivity, the east coast companies had something up their sleeves. Just so. They had met furtively on 13 August to plot revenge. Between 19 and 23 August 1895, they would run an accelerated service of sleeping carriages and no more than seven other vehicles leaving King's Cross at 8pm, to arrive at Kinnaber Junction, thirty-eight miles south of Aberdeen just eight and a half hours later. This timetable remained secret.

The west coast companies were given no warning. At 8pm on 19 August, the east coasters' retaliation train steamed out of King's Cross replete with journalists. They travelled 'in splendid style', arriving at Aberdeen in nine hours forty minutes. They could have been even faster, but because it had been treated as a scheduled (if unpublicised) service, it had not been able to leave Edinburgh prior to its advertised time, no matter how much earlier it had arrived there than scheduled. On cue (it was unlikely to be entirely coincidental), the citizens of Aberdeen petitioned the Post Office for earlier delivery of mail based upon the NBR's improved times.[31] The implication was that the postal contract should shift to the North British.

To accelerate the service even more the day afterwards, the NBR split its train into two portions – the one to arrive in Aberdeen at 4.40am (a reduction of a further forty-five minutes) – and the other to stroll in casually at 6.25am having picked up anyone or anything left behind by the earlier one. Drivers were instructed to arrive at each station at least a quarter of an hour before schedule.[32] The *Aberdeen Journal* forecast that 'there is no pretence now that it is not a race to the finish! Both routes are making a supreme effort today'.[33] The NBR thought that their sleight-of-hand would confirm their superiority.

They erred. On that Wednesday morning, the west coasters broke the record with a 'flying train' travelling at an average speed of 60.2mph which reached Aberdeen in only two minutes under nine hours. It had steamed the 300 miles from Euston to the Scottish Border in just 299 minutes, over two hours forty minutes faster than six weeks earlier. There had been 'intense excitement on the platform' as it panted into Carlisle at the dead of night, for Carlisle was symbolic as the chief northern depot of the London &

North-Western, the starting point of the Caledonian, and the point of convergence for five other railways.[34] The east coast train, heavier by an additional carriage, and cheered by 'a considerable number of people' as it thundered down into the tunnel at Dundee's Tay Bridge Station at 3.42am,[35] took thirteen minutes longer, achieving an average of 3mph less.[36] Not only did it have to slow down for the 'bad road' – the Kinghorn tunnel – but, crucially, it had lost the battle for Kinnaber, just north of Montrose. As the *Aberdeen Journal* observed, the train that reached Kinnaber first won the race to Aberdeen.[37]

Thirty-eight miles south of Aberdeen, the otherwise unremarkable junction signal box of Kinnaber governed the junction where the East Coast and the West Coast railway lines merged as they approached the city northbound. The Caledonian Railway, which operated the track between Kinnaber and Aberdeen, staffed its Kinnaber junction signal box and its points; and its loyal signalmen, whatever their instructions, gave precedence to Caledonian trains over the NBR's whenever they were running close together. One of the trains would have to stop, and by the time it had started up again, up to fifteen minutes might have elapsed. In the highly charged stop watched railway race – that was to be everything. Protests had little effect and Parliament had none. The Kinnaber Junction became the Khyber Pass of the railway race.

Long before any hint of a race, the North British had been claiming that west coast trains were being given preferential treatment at Kinnaber. Regulations stated that a signalman should award precedence to an approaching train when it was two minutes away,[38] but Kinnaber signalmen would always award Caledonian trains precedence when they were still four minutes distant, even if the east coast train was nearer. The latter would be delayed for between four to sixteen minutes as the signalmen waited for their own company's train to catch up and puff by. Stung into defending themselves, the Caledonian pointed out that whereas a Kinnaber signalman had a clear sight of the western train over four miles, he could not actually see the eastern train until it was only a few hundred yards away – by which time he had already signalled the other to come on.

Travellers in that August west coast train could discern their rival across the broad tidal basin as they both raced for Kinnaber past Montrose. The *Dundee Advertiser*'s man was on board. 'On the still morning air, the heavy rumble of the trains can be heard from afar, and in the grey light of dawn, travellers by the west coast train can see across the lagoon of Montrose Basin the lighted carriages of the rival train. Now fractions of minutes determine the result ... Excitement is at fever heat, a tension which is not released among the passengers until the tail light of the winner are seen whirled past the signal box.'[39] It was no longer down to trains and times, but to the objectivity of a signalman – who was employed by the Caledonian.

The race focused public attention on that remote signal box. The racers were full of observant journalists, and they not only shared the view that the Kinnaber signalmen were not playing straight, they broadcast it. They reported that the North British was being so obstructed in its attempts to create a satisfactory service into Aberdeen that it was being forced to contemplate construct-ing 'a new North British line right into Aberdeen unless an arrangement can be arrived at'.[40] To have done so would have breached the Peace Agreement; and for the Caledonian to have forced them to do so would likewise have breached the Peace Agreement. The spectre of ruinous competitive parliamentary expenses re-emerged. So the publicity created by the railway race did indeed help to create a better arrangement for access into Aberdeen even if it was too late to affect the race. Conversely, the race had been worth running just to achieve that outcome – and perhaps that had been its implicit agenda.

It was widely bruited that, the west coasters were going to go for bust on the night of 22/3 August. A large crowd again assembled on the Carlisle platform again to cheer their train past, 'it having become generally known that the west coast companies were making a supreme effort to attain superiority', and it arrived in Aberdeen eight hours thirty-two minutes after leaving London. It had won by eight clear minutes. Having proved their point, the west coast companies announced their intention to return to their ploughshares and scheduled timetable. The east coasters, however, denied that there ever had been a race and refused to concede that the west coast had won it. They had eschewed anything quite so silly as cutting back on their carriages, had been keeping to their published schedules, and had been doing no more than testing how to improve their normal service. As Oakley of the Great Northern wrote to Conachar, 'the speed at which we ran last night was not higher than we run daily with our expresses. I did not, and do not feel that there was any risk in the performance.'[41]

On 24 August, the *Glasgow Herald* concluded that now that all records had been broken by the west coast service, the railway race was over. The North Eastern's blood, however, was still up, demanding a further racer that very night, and Conachar was concerned about the impact of the west coast's win upon the commercial market. He agreed only reluctantly that it would be 'childish to begin to run again at the present . . . Let us wait and see the effect on the public'.[42] An immediate re-run was vetoed by the Great Northern, whose idea it had been originally; and when asked why, the east coast companies spinned casually: 'We can beat it if it is the public interest. We prefer to do good work quietly.' The Great Northern loftily added that it was 'really absurd to call it a race; there is no race at all'. It was running its trains no faster than it had ever done, and the enhanced times were the consequence of better organisation and 'not stopping so often *en route*'. Noting ironically that the Great Northern was reverting 'from racing speed to ordinary accelerated speed',[43] *The Times* observed that whereas the record had been achieved by the western companies, they had done so by running short trains and curtailing stops, whereas the east coast retained 'a slight lead in ordinary running.'[44] That, of course, was the entire point. If the underlying purpose was commercial competitiveness, customers were far more likely to be influenced by the speed and quality and reliability of regular timetabled services rather than flighty artificial ones.

For the North British, however, Conachar had not given up

altogether: rather it was *reculer pour mieux sauter* (only a tactical retreat). Having worked out what needed to be done next, he wrote to Oakley on 26 August:

> Although I share to the full your opinion regarding the child-ishness of the whole business, I think we must guard ourselves against an improper use being hereafter made the achievement of the night of the 22nd, and I am quite prepared to run another train as much like theirs as possible, when I have no doubt that we could again show our superiority. I have been comparing their run with ours, as detailed in the newspapers, with a view to seeing how they were able to run 17 miles more in eight min-utes . . . Their advantage, you will see, divides itself into three heads viz: lighter load, fewer stops and higher speed on certain stages of the journey. We could also have a lighter load at this season of the year, but I do not know whether we could also reduce our stops to three. Mr Holmes tells me he might possibly be able to run the 110 miles from Edinburgh to Aberdeen with-out a stop if the train consisted of these ordinary carriages only, but adds that it would be risky seeing such high speed has to be maintained.[45]

When it came to gamesmanship, Conachar was every bit a match for the west coasters. With his letter, he had enclosed a compara-tive analysis of running times between stations on the two routes which revealed that the west coast service stopped at only six sta-tions to the east's eleven, and had two stretches of much faster running.

He proposed that they should run a shorter and lighter train in early September, with two fewer stops. By foregoing the stop at Grantham, the driver would have 185 miles length of uninter-rupted steaming, thirty-five miles more than the west's longest run, where he was certain that trains could achieve the higher average speed of sixty-five miles an hour. The omission of two stops over the entire run would make the east coast run equal with the west coast's. 'It is for you to say whether your tenders could carry enough water for that length. If the two stops were abandoned, never mind the lightening of the load, we ought therefore to be able to make the run easily in 8 hours 25 minutes, or seven minutes less than our friends' record . . . I think we ought to do it unless some strong reason can be urged to the contrary, choosing a night when the traffic is likely to be light.'[46] The North Eastern agreed to the proposal. 'We seem to have proved that we can run a train of ordinary size to Aberdeen in 10 hr 25 minutes and the West Coast, in order to get in front of that, must run a special train with a few carriages, and I doubt if they will continue that somewhat useless proceeding.' Oakley of the Great Northern, who had always been something of a sceptic, was now hooked and agreed to place it before his chairman. The latter, however, was so 'strongly averse to any renewal of the racing', that the others chose not to press it. Thus the railway race ended.[47]

After it was all over, none of the august Victorians who chaired the railway companies would publicly admit to anything so child-ish as racing railway trains. The London & North West declared, 'We don't admit that we were racing at all.'[48] Its chairman, Lord Stalbridge, informed his shareholders, 'so far as their company was concerned there had been no race at all'. The North Eastern main-tained, 'They had not provoked the competition. They had simply entered into it',[49] whereas the Great Northern (probably the insti-gator with its 10pm Aberdeen express) claimed to have regretted it. 'It had not begun with the Great Northern . . . The Great Northern Board desired harmony.'[50] Neither Scottish railway com-pany said a word. They would never admit that if they had not actually started it (that had been the Great Northern) they had prosecuted it with all possible vigour. Although they could all point to their Board minutes, which lacked even the faintest whiff of a race, the files contain other material. During that limbering up period in July, Lord Tweeddale, chairman of the North British, had telegrammed Conachar: 'My opinion is to beat them at any cost and having done it, proceed to remonstrate'; i.e. beat them first, and then complain about having to race in the first place[51] – and that was exactly what Conachar had done.

The presentiments of death and disaster had not been realised. Fears of oscillation and nausea had been replaced by reports of trips 'so smooth and so comfortable that the occupants could hardly realise that they were travelling at higher rates of speed'.[52] There had, however, been considerable disruption. The *Standard* was relieved that there would be 'a reversion to the comparative jog-trot of the ordinary express. A terrible tension will be taken from the minds of those who were responsible for keeping the engines going and the lines clear . . . and many a passenger . . . will have ground . . . for rejoicing that his marriage is not shunted for a weary half hour to permit the comet to rush by.'[53] John Leng (now an MP and Sir John), who had praised the railway companies for their desire 'to test what could be done', had worried that the railway race would end 'in a tremendous smash and loss of life' and suggested that it was time for the Board of Trade to establish speed limits. The latter refused, preferring to leave it to the good sense of the railway companies[54] which returned with the arrival of early autumn. *The Times* lauded how, 'in the past three months, Scotland has come practically a full hour nearer London than it was . . .'[55] and concluded that the west coast had 'fully established its claim to a virtual equality'. The improved west coast winter service with its lighter trains, increasing frequency and fewer stoppages was attributed to 'the late railway race'. Even trains between Glasgow and Edinburgh had been accelerated to complete the journey in sixty-five minutes.[56] But although passengers had benefited enormously in terms of technical performance, and young bucks and journalists had relished their memorable rides, the east and the west coast routes had raced themselves only to a draw.

The railway race had been a continuation by other means of the trunk railway war for domination of the Scottish commercial railway business, and that war was not yet over. It now moved to image and to competitive architecture. As *Building News* was to put it, 'railway termini and hotels are to the nineteenth century what monasteries and cathedrals were to the thirteenth century. They are truly the only real representative building we possess.'[57] Both lack-

ing an adequate presence in Scotland's capital city, the North British and the Caledonian proceeded to one of their most expensive competitions – the construction of luxury railway hotels at opposing ends of Edinburgh's Princes Street. Railway companies built hotels to promote rail tourism particularly over the summer months and London had done very well by them. With their excellent and exotic food, fine wines, and integrated livery of monogrammed linen, crockery, glassware and cutlery, they offered their customers an opulent experience that many of them did not normally enjoy. If they could add an exotic or as stunning a location as the Canadian Pacific Railway's baronial Banff Springs Hotel in Canada, with its incomparable views, custom was assured. At both ends of Princes Street, railway customers would be offered unbeatable views of Edinburgh Castle. The Caledonian's flagship Central Hotel in Glasgow, designed by Rowand Anderson in 1879, had helped set new standards in British hotel provision,[58] whereas its presence in the capital of Scotland was signalled by an insignif-

The railway companies' contribution to Scottish architectural culture: blowsy baroque erupts into the calm classicism of Edinburgh's New Town as bookends to each end of Edinburgh's Princes Street.

icant single-storeyed interim terminal building intruding mouse-like into Princes Street.

Back in 1867, the Caledonian Railway had commissioned a flamboyant, six-storeyed, domed hotel for the western end of Princes Street from the Edinburgh architect John Dick Peddie, and was just about to build it when its finances crashed. Its interim terminal became a permanent one; but when it burnt down in 1890, the Caledonian commissioned the next generation of their original architects to design a terminal and hotel of a scale appropriate for Scotland's capital.[59] The ethos of the time was not subtle. 'Elephantiasis overtook every aspect of railroading, including the terminals, now built to dimensions never before approached. Aesthetically, the obviously striking effects of the previous more romantic decades were replaced by the equally obvious appeal of unprecedented size.'[60] The Caledonian's new hotel, built of machine-cut red sandstone shipped by train from Dumfries, arrived like an overblown baroque bookend to mark the western end of Princes Street. Wags claimed that it had actually been built in Glasgow and placed upon a train to burst out of the railway tunnel when it arrived in Edinburgh. Work on it began in 1894.

The North British was well aware of the new challenge to its status half a mile away, but its attention was in the meantime focused elsewhere. It had completely underestimated the effect that the opening of the Forth Bridge would have upon its antiquated terminus at Waverley Station, and had made no provision for the increase in traffic. In summer 1890, four months after the bridge opened, difficulties came to a head when a train could be at a standstill at every signal, and an express might take three hours to traverse the last three miles. After one express goods train was delayed for twenty-four hours,[61] there was a public outcry. The *Scotsman* was appalled that the directors could have so failed to exercise even ordinary foresight;[62] and a wonderfully ironic leader from *The Times* under the heading of ''Tis sixty minutes late', (parodying the sub-title to Sir Walter Scott's *Waverley* – 'Tis sixty years hence'), described how blockages in Edinburgh had a knock-on throughout the rest of the country. 'A block of half an hour at [Waverley] will be felt in the derangement of the service 10 to 15 hours afterwards as far west as Plymouth and as far north as Wick.'[63]

Total reconstruction of Waverley began two years later, providing eventually the largest railway accommodation in Britain other than Waterloo. Partly because it extended over the rails themselves, and partly because several storeys could be inserted between station and street level, the site was enormous; and it was to be rebuilt from the depth of the Waverley valley up to Princes Street and North Bridge. That very depth caused construction anxieties lest the adjoining roads collapse into this enormous hole once demolition was begun, but it also provided greater opportunities than merely adding to the platforms. Over the previous thirty years, the NBR had been concentrating its offices in the Waverley area, particularly after its amalgamation with the Edinburgh & Glasgow in 1864; and when reconstruction was being contemplated, the Board decided to concentrate its administration and legal services together onto the one site, splitting it with its proposed hotel.[64]

In 1895, the North British held an architectural competition for the design of its flagship hotel, seeking designs from the leading architect of Scotland, Robert Rowand Anderson, from William Leiper, and from W. Hamilton Beattie.[65] Anderson proposed a vast square pile in late seventeenth-century Scots, with an enormously overscaled, tiled pyramid roof, like a swollen version of his Conservative Club just west along Princes Street. Leiper's design was a spiky neo-Scots confection that looked as though an entire city block of the Old Town had been cut out and relocated in Princes Street. Beattie offered an echo of the baroque giganticism that had characterised the Chicago Fair two years earlier: a four-square pile with a three-stage tower rising from its Princes Street façade like a beacon.[66] Even had Anderson's and Leiper's designs been at all appropriate for the New Town, it was inevitable – with its name and its history – that the North British would eschew any-thing overtly Scots in favour of something more cosmopolitan. In particular, the challenge was to overwhelm the Caledonian's blowsy pink jelly-mould at the far end of the street. So Beattie's design was selected, and he was offered a 5% fee.[67]

Rowand Anderson was so pre-eminent in Scottish architecture that he appears to have believed that a site of that importance should be his by *droit de seigneur*, and he was mortified by the deci-sion to appoint Beattie and his unscholarly design. He wrote twice to the North British to remonstrate and, failing to receive satisfac-tion, he then persuaded the Royal Institute of British Architects to weigh in behind him. A remonstrative letter was dispatched to no noticeable effect. The North British remained obdurate,[68] and in March 1895 Beattie was formally appointed.[69]

The North British had established a Hotels &c. Committee which travelled through Belgium, Germany, Austria, Switzerland and Hungary in early 1896 to inspect their principal hotels, and on another the following year to eleven of 'the most recently erected hotels in Central Europe' accompanied by Weiland.[70] Four main points emerged from the tours: the importance of an imposing entrance hall, features that were 'rapidly becoming of the same type as those in American hotels'; the income to be derived from a wholesale and retain wine trade; the provision of grand Banqueting Halls and Ballrooms to provide income when the tourist income was slack; and the insufferably slow and very small elevators.[71]

The architectural competition brief required a building split between the hotel and the NBR's new headquarters, but the Hotel Committee encouraged Beattie to expand his hotel to 391 bedrooms, almost double the Caledonian's 205, assuming that headquarters staff would be moved off site into the Waterloo Hotel nearby, which was available to be bought for that purpose. The target was to fill every room in the hotel for three months of the year, to compensate for lack of occupants throughout the remaining nine months. Under pressure, Beattie reduced his design to 315 bedrooms, but Conachar still thought that this change from original agreed policy was daft. '315 rooms is so greatly in excess of the accommodation contained in any hotel now existing in Scotland, as well as in any other station in Great Britain excepting St Pancras, which it exceeds by only 15 rooms.' He calculated that it would need an average of at least 520 guests per night to fill the hotel during the peak months. If seventy of those bedrooms on the railway side of the building could be isolated vertically for use as the company's headquarters, that would avoid the expense of buying the Waterloo Hotel.[72] Miffed, Beattie responded that the hotel would be not nearly so high class an establishment, and it would be less easily worked. Since the season was so short, the logic was to pack in as many people as possible. The company was divided between the quality aspirations of the hotel committee and its architect, and the General Manager and his operations team, backed by the chairman. It went up to a Board decision. The directors, tempted by European sophistication, opted for opulence – a hotel only girdled by shops at street level.[73]

Long before completion, the Hotel &c. Committee was beset by hotel managers who wanted to run it, by suppliers seeking contracts, and by Weiland insisting on tasting, selecting and laying down appropriate wines. When the building was not far beyond its cellar floor at the end of 1898, its architect William Hamilton Beattie died. Although his office carried on the project under his brother George, the North British asked the London architect Alfred Waterhouse, who had been so supportive over the Forth Bridge, to review the hotel project – rather in the same way that the NBR had submitted their bridge plans for scrutiny by other engineers. Architects think differently to engineers. Waterhouse believed that he was being invited to take up a paid consultancy upon the commission, and geared his report accordingly. He praised the beauty and appropriateness of the details, and was very favourably impressed by the workmanship. But he disliked the unlit and unventilated corridors, and bedrooms without fireplaces or opening windows, and considered that the public spaces could be made rather more imposing.[74] When he then proposed to undertake completing the project for a fee of 1%, the correspondence ceased.

As the nineteenth century closed, both hotels were moving toward completion like two fairground souvenirs bracketing each end of Princes Street. Although the North British (now Balmoral) Hotel appeared to be only four storeys beneath its cornice, that was principally because so many other storeys had been hidden below street level. It seemed square rather than tall, a proportion emphasised by its soaring campanile or clock tower crested with its faint iron mimic of the crown of St Giles' cathedral. The Caledonian Hotel by contrast, with its huge flat red walls lining the streets, its splayed chamfered entrance and its multi-storeyed French roof, appeared the taller and the more alien. Although both hotels became renowned for their luxury, neither was great architecture. Entirely characteristic of the way in which railways had treated their host towns over the previous sixty years, these railway hotels had bulldozed their way into the very edge of Edinburgh's classical New Town with shameless bombast. They provided a most apt metaphor both of the trunk railway war and of the railway race for, more or less equal in size, they were distinguished only in colour, style and vulgarity. The result was an approximate draw and, as the final product of the Scottish trunk railway wars of the previous half-century, they symbolised the outcome perfectly.

ENVOI

---

*The English travelling public may congratulate itself on the possession
of a choice of railway systems whose efficiency and organisation are one
of the fairy tales of commerce*

DAILY CHRONICLE[1]

When the Forth Bridge opened in March 1890, the *Scotsman*
reviewed the blessings that railways had brought to the nation.

> Wealth is more evenly distributed in this country now than ever
> it was, and the process of more equal distribution goes steadily
> on. In no class has there been a greater growth of comfort than
> among working men. They have more steady employment and
> better wages. For all this, the country has to thank, in the first
> instance, our fiscal system, and next – one of the consequences
> of that system – the extension of the railways. They have
> increased manufactures; helped thousands of men to steady
> employment; equalised the conditions of different parts of the
> country; promoted friendly intercourse; and given a stimulus to
> profitable interchange of ideas. Every step they have made for-
> ward has been a step in the direction of greater national welfare.[2]

Scotland's railway network had been constructed at virtually no public expense, but was its efficiency really a fairytale of commerce?

When stumping the land proselytising for the Forth Bridge, Benjamin Baker enjoyed teasing his audiences about why there had been any need to build the Tay and Forth bridges at all. 'It is not the physical features of the country,' he said, 'but the habits of the population that render the construction of a 1,700-foot span expedient. If the British public can save a few minutes by going a particular route, by that route they will go . . .'[3] In fact, it was neither the geography nor the Scottish public. It was the trunk railway war that had made the bridges a commercial necessity; and the saga had been neither edifying nor cost-effective, nor the route the most efficient. The railway race highlighted the inefficiencies, the gradients, twistings, turnings, inadequate tunnels and sharp curves of each line, which, in a better organised world with more expert scrutiny, might have been avoided.

Inflated promises had tricked Ordinary shareholders into plunging far more into railways than had been their original desire, to fight battles of which they were often kept in ignorance and remained largely oblivious. Even if they deserved to forfeit their savings as penance for such cupidity, the unproductive wastage of that enormous quantity of capital was beyond reason – wasted on fourteen abortive railway bridge designs over the Forth and Tay; on duplicated lines and on stillborn lines and stillborn amalgamations. Above all, it had been wasted on the fruitless months and years attending ineffective Parliamentary and Board of Trade Committees, and paying for expert witnesses, lawyers and London hotels. Competition had frequently forced the companies into local ad hoc decisions with long term adverse consequences. The duplication of unproductive lines produced by the trunk war might have been one of the problems that underlay the savage line closures of the 1960s. Since high speed trains today still have to slow down through the Kinghorn tunnel, the journey between Edinburgh and Dundee remains slower by train than it is by car in the reverse of the norm, and it is little consolation that it was cheaply achieved for slow coal wagons.[4]

Not long after their two flagship hotels had opened, the rival companies were audited, and it revealed that the Caledonian Railway operated 1034 miles of track whereas the North British operated 30% more and carried 5% more passengers. So had the North British won? Not entirely. That same audit showed that the Caledonian's total income was greater by a small margin than the NBR's if goods traffic were taken into account. Either the Caledonian was making better use of its lines, or its dominance in industrial Glasgow had given them the edge.[5] Nonetheless, sixty years after the trunk railway war had begun, after all the posturing, the amalgamations, the contests, the peace agreements and the renewed warfare, the result remained roughly a draw. That may have been some satisfaction to the North British which had always regarded itself as the struggling underdog, whereas it must have been less pleasing to the Caledonian with its belief that it had been anointed the premier railway of Scotland. Parliament could always point to the balance between the two Scottish railway giants as proof that its role in balancing local interests worked over the long run. And the Ordinary shareholders could at last be sure of their 4.5%.

Had ideal railway routes been mapped out for Scotland as they were for France, the bridge over the Tay might never have been built, and the town of Dundee would have been the poorer for it. Had a more cooperative atmosphere imbued railway operations in Scotland, the Forth Bridge would not have been built. But in his bid to make the North British the equal if not the vanquisher of the Caledonian, Richard Hodgson had appreciated that to be free of any ransom, the company required its own track, and he was prepared to face up to the enormity of the consequence – having to bridge the two estuaries. His grandeur of vision transformed the North British Railway Company from a minor railway company to rival the Caledonian, and he had little interest in just seeking equality with it. In seeking domination, he overreached himself, and was forced to resign and return to his fields. In the aftermath of his departure, it was Dundee's triumvirate of industrialist (Cox), fixer (Thornton) and communicator (Leng) that kept Hodgson's vision alive and influenced national railway policy.

In his biography of Thomas Brassey, Sir Arthur Phelps concluded that politicians and railway companies had failed to show professionalism comparable to that shown by the engineers and contractors. He had a point. The engineers, the contractors, the briggers, the diggers and the railwaymen had indeed generally done very well. They had created railways over difficult terrain and fearsome seas, and one of their principal legacies was a railway structure – the Forth Bridge – that came to represent the nation. Although the dead and injured were numerous, they were not excessively so given the challenge and the epoch. More civilians were killed in the 4.15pm train from Edinburgh on 28 December 1879 than on all three bridge contracts combined, and a modern approach to safety, morale and welfare emerged from Arrol's innovations on his construction sites.

The construction of the bridges had not been just a parochial Scottish affair. The cream of British engineering had participated in the Scottish estuarial bridges over three decades, and their concepts were discussed as much in London as in Edinburgh. The bridges had attracted young men seeking experience from round the world. One young engineer, the earnest Albert Grothe, found himself in sole charge of the erection of the first Tay Bridge during the two years of de Bergue's madness and death. It was probably too early in his career, for he appears to have exercised insufficient authority on site, and did not enjoy a close working relationship with the consultant engineer Thomas Bouch. He had sufficiently impressed Benjamin Baker to be Baker's first choice for the nomination of a major engineering project overseas, but the Tay Bridge disaster overtook him, and he was to die in Mexico. Because his bridge is no longer there, he is largely forgotten.

Thomas Bouch had very nearly made it into the pantheon of world engineers with his two railway bridges – the largest, the longest, and possibly the tallest in the then world; and the causes of his nemesis remain disputed over 120 years later. He was not a typical Victorian engineer spending time down in London debating new structural concepts with his peers. His time in London was spent on parliamentary bills. He had won his major commissions through a combination of family influence in northern England, and being in the right place at the right time in Scotland. To the extent that he evinced a casual approach to foundations, and a disregard for or disinterest in the minutiae of erection, he may have been the cause of his own downfall; but he never merited Henry Rothery or his condemnation. At the last, his health betrayed him. Greater vigour, acumen, and conviction from him at the Inquiry might well have persuaded the two engineer Commissioners to a different conclusion about the causes of the collapse, that would have made far better sense of the evidence. John Trayner, the advocate who, as much as anyone, was responsible for Bouch's downfall, was elevated to the Bench the year following the Inquiry, became Sheriff of Forfar and rose to be Railway Commissioner for Scotland, well known for a book on Latin maxims.[6]

Fowler's reputation was already well made before the Forth Bridge; but rather than the Tay Bridge, Tower Bridge, the Aswan Dam or the many other projects that they designed or built, the ingenuity and sheer inventiveness with which Baker and Arrol tackled the construction of the Forth Bridge made theirs. Unadventurous by comparison, Barlow's thick-set Tay Bridge attracts less attention than it merits, although that could change if they reopened its tourist footpath and painted it red oxide as it once was. As they cross it, railway travellers can still enjoy a frisson as they peer through the windows down to the row of desolate stumps at tide level that the NBR had obdurately refused to dismantle. Few now remember William Barlow, whom contemporaries regarded as one of the greatest engineers of his time, probably because a timid government had refused to permit him any pyrotechnics in his new Tay Bridge. It remains, nonetheless, one of the world's longest railway bridges and straddles its temperamental estuary buffeted by periodic howling gales.

In the fifty years between the establishment of the rival railway companies and their great race in 1895, Scotland had modernised itself, and railways were at the heart of that process. Lands and estates had been severed, towns and cities divided up and transformed, streets blocked, rivers crossed, nature tamed and the landscape levelled. The result was that the great mass of people and goods could now travel to places and at speeds never previously imagined. Inland harbours and inland towns were of course losers, and the communities that were bypassed by the railways suffered even more than those which had been eviscerated by them. That was in the nature of progress.

The war of the Scottish trunk routes left Scotland adorned with the longest and the largest railway bridges built for a line that, in world traffic terms, seemed to be going almost from nowhere to nowhere. So *The Times* may well have been correct when it wrote:

> We shall have to regard the Forth Bridge as a splendid extrava-gance, to be justified on the principle of *Noblesse oblige*; on the principal that lines so illustrious as the Northern, the North Eastern and the North British must not allow themselves to be defeated by a natural obstacle like the Forth. If so, the idea may not be commerce, but it is magnificent.[7]

NOTES

PROLOGUE

1 GD/TD 21/17 Tay Bridge Disaster Petitions. Case of Margaret Pirnie, domestic servant, residing in Albert Court, Nethergate.
2 GD/TD 21/17.
3 *Dundee Courier and Argus* 15.12.79.
4 *Inquiry* 1693.
5 *Inquiry* 1764. Rev. George Grubb referred to its percussive effect.
6 *Inquiry* 1595.
7 *Inquiry* 1764. Rev. George Grubb.
8 A suggestion by Normile Baxter.
9 J. Simmons, *The Victorian Railway* (London, 1995), p. 283.
10 *The Times* 11.10.65.
11 *Inquiry* 3146. James Smith.
12 *Inquiry* 484.
13 *Inquiry* 3094. James Smith. When the train was late, it always ran faster.
14 The figure is still disputed. There were fifty-seven tickets for Dundee, six for Broughty Ferry, seven for Newport (who would not have crossed the bridge), three guards, a driver and a fireman. Children were not issued with tickets, and one traveller had at least three with him.
15 *Inquiry* 609.
16 *Inquiry* 654.
17 Minutes of Relief Committee, *Dundee City Archives*, TC/CC 15/29 p. 1, 15 Jan, case of 'Margaret Purvie' but Maggie Pirnie according to her Minister, engaged to Robert Culross 'boatbuilder' assigned number 17; £3 interim relief; p. 34, 14 June, previous payment of £10 reported.
18 I am very grateful to Jim Tomlinson for this perception.

CHAPTER 1 THE ENGINE OF MODERNISATION

1 Quoted in K.A. Doukas, *The French Railroads and the State* (New York, 1976), p. 19.
2 I am grateful to Barbara Czarniawska for this observation.
3 BR/NBR/1/396 Minutes of Meetings of Officers.
4 BR/CAL/1/11/4 Minute Book, 27.8.45.

5 DUA/MS 103/VI/1/3 Meeting before the House of Lords, 1.7.63.

6 DUA/MS 105/V/3 He said that the reason why the North British was not preparing to subscribe to the Forth Bridge undertaking itself was because it 'did not have the means'.

7 DUA/MS 105/VI/1/4.

8 NAS/GD/556/1–11.

9 S.E. Ambrose, *Nothing Quite Like It in the World: The Men Who Built the Transcontinental Railroad 1863–1869* (New York, 2001), p. 26.

10 Ambrose, *Transcontinental Railroad*, p. 94.

11 Berton, *Last Spike* (Canada, 2001), p. 11.

12 Ambrose, *Transcontinental Railroad*, p. 152.

13 *San Francisco Chronicle*, frequently in the 1880s.

14 Berton, *Last Spike*, pp. 412–16.

15 Quoted in Ambrose, *Transcontinental Railroad*, p. 102.

16 W. Vamplew, 'The North British Railway Inquiry of 1866', in *Scottish Industrial History Miscellany* (Edinburgh, 1978), p. 143.

17 Archibald Galloway to Archibald Reid, Scottish Central Railway Company, Perth, 28.1.47. PKCA/PE 19.

18 PKCA/PE 19 bundle 33. Copy of Answers for Central Scotland Railway Company 1849.

19 Diary of William Pease, quoted in H. Pollins, 'Railway Contractors and the Finance of Railway Development in Britain', in M.C. Reed (ed.), *Railways in the Victorian Economy* (Newton Abbot, 1969).

20 Berton, *Last Spike*, pp. 25–6.

21 M.C. Reed, 'Railways and the Growth of the Capital Market', in M.C. Reed (ed.), *Railways in the Victorian Economy* (Newton Abbot, 1969), p. 165.

22 Ambrose, *Transcontinental Railroad*, p. 206.

23 DUA/MS 105/V/3 Letter 21.4.75 to National Bank of Scotland from the Callander and Oban Railway Company.

24 See the advertising pages in *The Times* and the *Scotsman* in the 1860s.

25 The number of vessels going up the Tay beyond Dundee 1854–79 diminished from 669 to 112. NBR/27/4 and NBR/10/23.

26 See for example the agreement between the Scottish Central Railway Company and the Perth and Crieff Road Trustees, PKCA/PE 19, bundle 16.

27 North British engines set only one field on fire in 1869–71.

28 DUA/MS 105/V/2/16 CRC Letter Book, 31.3.70.

29 BR/NBR/1/17 Law and Claims Committee 1869.

30 Ibid., p. 351.

31 *Wigton Free Press* 9.12.76 Claim by Messrs Harcombe and Galloway.

32 Quoted in R.C. Michie, 'Investment and Railways in nineteenth-century Scotland', in *Scottish Industrial History*, vol. 5.1 (1982).

33 T.R. Gourvish, 'Railway Enterprise', in R. Church (ed.), *The Dynamics of Victorian Business* (London, 1980).

34 J. Reid, *Manual of the Scottish Stocks and British Funds* (Edinburgh, 1842), p. 36, cited in R.C. Michie, 'Investment and Railways in Nineteenth-century Scotland', in M.C. Reed (ed.), *Railways in the Victorian Economy* (Newton Abbot, 1969).

35 L. Miskell, 'Civic Leadership and the Manufacturing Elite', in L. Miskell,

C.A. Whatley and B. Harris (eds), *Victorian Dundee: Image and Realities* (East Linton, 2000).

36 P.F. Marshall, *The Railways of Dundee* (Headington, 1996), p. 11.

37 Alongside the city of Dundee, the Earl of Airlie, and a few lairds. The chairman was the radical MP George Kinloch. C. Tennant, *The Radical Laird* (Kineton, 1970), p. 224.

38 Charles Landale, *Report . . . whether it is practical and expedient to construct A RAILWAY between the Valley of Strathmore and Dundee* (Dundee, 1825).

39 Landale, *Report*, p. 3.

40 Simmons, *Victorian Railway* (London, 1995), p. 176.

41 Marshall, *Railways*, p. 14.

42 Marshall, *Railways*, pp. 16–18.

43 Tennant, *Radical Laird*, pp. 226–7.

44 Reed, 'Railways and the Growth of the Capital Market', p. 168.

45 PKCA/PE 19, bundle 2. Perth to Little Dunkeld, Perth to Crieff, Perth to Dundee, and Dundee to Arbroath.

46 *Personal Memoirs*, vol. 2, p. 31, quoted in Ambrose, *Transcontinental Railroad*, p. 85.

47 *Dundee Advertiser* 8.10.38.

48 As a sign of how uncoordinated railway initiatives remained, Dundee's three railways were all to different gauges – Newtyle four foot six inches, Arbroath five foot six inches, and Perth four foot eight and a half inches (Bill Dow).

49 J.R. Kellett, *The Impact of Railways on Victorian Cities* (London, 1969).

50 P. O'Brien, *The New Economic History of the Railways* (London, 1977).

51 PKCA/PE 19, bundle 39.

52 PKCA/PE 19, bundle 15. Report by Messrs Stevenson, 1847.

53 PKCA/PE 19, bundles 14, 15, 44, 45.

54 Information from Rob Duck.

55 In one case the minimum was 4%. Doukas, *French Railroads*, pp. 44–8.

56 Parliamentary Papers, 1836, (511) XX1, quoted in C.J.A. Robertson, *The Origins of the Scottish Railway System 1722–1844* (Edinburgh, 1983), p. 277.

57 *Railway News*, 9.6.38, quoted in Robertson, *Origins*, p. 278.

58 PKCA/PE 19, bundle 2.

59 I am grateful to Alaister Dury for this information.

60 H. Cockburn, *Memorials of His Time* (new edn Edinburgh, 1910), pp. 414–15.

61 P. Geddes, 'Beginnings of a Survey of Edinburgh', in *Scottish Geographical Magazine* (Edinburgh, 1919), p. 290.

62 *Scotsman* 5.1.48.

CHAPTER 2 THE BATTLE FOR SCOTLAND

1 Described by Berton as 'a unique mobile community that never stayed in place for more than a few hours at a time, comprising eight or nine Boarding Cars, three storeys tall, with offices, dining rooms, kitchens, and two storeys of dormitories above! *Last Spike*, pp. 105–8.

2 Ambrose, *Nothing Quite Like It*, pp. 349–51.

3 Simmons, *Victorian Railway*, pp. 261–2.

4 *The Times* 19.9.49. Letters.

5 Agreement Glasgow, Dumfries and Ayr Railway with the Caledonian; *The Times* 17.2.48.
6 J. Butt and J.T. Ward, 'The Promotion of the Caledonian Railway Company', in *Transport History*, vol. 3 (1970), part 1, p. 166.
7 ODNB, Joseph Locke, G.C. Boase, Rev. R. Harrington (Oxford, 2004).
8 J. Butt and J. T. Ward, 'The Promotion of the Caledonian Railway Company', in *Transport History*, vol. 3 (1970), p. 177.
9 *Scotsman* 17.11.38.
10 Ibid.
11 Quoted in Robertson, *Origins*, p. 267.
12 Table 1 in B.R. Mitchell, 'The Coming of the Railway and United Kingdom Economic Growth', in Reed, *Railways.*
13 R.C. Michie, 'Investment and Railways in Nineteenth-century Scotland', in *Scottish Industrial History*, vol. 5.1.(1982), pp. 45–53.
14 *Scotsman* 19.5.41.
15 Vamplew, 'Railway Inquiry', p. 144.
16 DUA/MS 105/VI/1/4.
17 Learmonth of Dean and Trotter of Mortonhall.
18 BR/NBR, Minute book 1, 8.1.42.
19 BR/NBR, Minute book 1.
20 Reed, *Railways*, p. 176.
21 PKCA/PE 19, bundle 22. William Small, merchant of Dundee.
22 Reed, *Railways*, p. 176.
23 BR/NBR, Minute book 1, 23.6.44.
24 Four guineas per day, when in Scotland, and five guineas when in London arguing the case. Usual fees would be paid to assistants.
25 BR/NBR, Minute book 1, 20.1.42.
26 BR/CAL/1/11/4.
27 BR/CAL/1/11/4 Minutes 27.8.45.
28 BR/CRC/11/4 Minutes 27.8.45.
29 BR/CRC/11/4 Minutes 27.8.45.
30 BR/CRC/11/4 Minutes 27.8.45.
31 Kellett, *Impact of Railways*, Appendix 1.
32 Sir Arthur Phelps, *Life and Labours of Mr Brassey* (London, 1876), p. 170.
33 National Archives of Scotland, BR/CRC/4/26, p. 25. (Caledonian Railway Company records)
34 National Archives of Scotland, BR/CRC/11/4 Minutes 25.2.46.
35 Chairman, Glasgow, Dumfries & Ayr Railway, quoted in *The Times* 19.3.47.
36 Joseph Locke, ODNB (Oxford, 2004).
37 A contemporary drawing shows Brassey, Locke and Errington as amongst the promoters of the railway. Nock, *Caledonian Railway*, facing p. 16.
38 Thomas Brassey, D. Brooke, ODNB (Oxford, 2004).
39 C.J.A. Robertson, 'The Cheap Railway Movement in Scotland', in *Transport History*, vol. 7, no. 1 (Spring, 1974), p. 4.
40 J. Thomas, *The North British Railway*, vol. 1 (1975), pp. 25–7.
41 BR/NBR/1/396. Meeting of Officers, 1874.
42 H. G. Lewin, *The Railway Mania and its Aftermath* (new edn, Newton Abbot, 1968), Appendices.
43 BR/CAL/11/4 Minutes 26.8.46.

44 BR/CAL/1/1/4 Minutes 27.8.45, p. 10.
45 D. Brooke, *The Railway Navvy* (Newton Abbot, 1983), table V, referring to the line at St Boswells.
46 R.S. Joby, *The Railway Builders* (Newton Abbot, 1983), p. 65.
47 Letter August 1846, quoted in Nock, *Caledonian Railway*, p. 17.
48 T. Coleman, *The Railway Navvies* (London, 1968), pp. 94–5.
49 Joby, *Railway Builders*, p. 66.
50 Coleman, *Railway Navvies*, pp. 99 ff.
51 National Archives of Scotland, BR/CRC/11/4 Minutes November 1845.
52 National Archives of Scotland, BR/CRC/11/4 Minutes November 1845.
53 National Archives of Scotland, BR/CRC/11/4 Minutes 25.2.46.
54 Brooke, *Railway Navvy*, p. 97.
55 *The Times* 18.7.48.
56 There is a good chance that shareholders were generally uneasy and distrusting of the railway companies after the three years of extraordinary railway mania.
57 BR/CRC/11/4 Minutes November 1848, February 1849, EGM September 1849.
58 BR/CRC/11/4 Minutes February 1850, p. 503.
59 BR/CRC/11/4 Minutes February 1850, pp. 376, 278.
60 Minerals had increased by only 21%, merchandise by 16% and revenue from the mails had been virtually static.
61 In January 1855, the *Building Chronicle* reported that 'the flood of operatives which the railway mania hatched, has been happily absorbed, to some extent, by the Australian emigration movement', p. 1250.
62 The reason why the tiny Yorkshire village of Easingwold, for example, was so anxious to support the Leeds, North Yorkshire & Durham Railway. *Easingwold Times and Thirsk Advertiser*, 4.3.65. I am grateful to Rob Duck for this.
63 N. Munro, 'Origins of the North British Railway', in *North British Railway Study Group Journal*, Issue 50, December 1992.
64 *The Times* 5.12.64.
65 *The Times* 5.7.56.
66 Chairman E & G Railway Company, EGM, 30 June 1864, *Scotsman* 1.7.64.
67 *The Times* 9.11.66.
68 *Daily Telegraph*, quoted in the *Scotsman* 5.11.66.
69 A.J. Arnold and S. McCartney, *Railway King* (London, 2004), chapter 7; R. Beaumont, *The Railway King* (London, 2002), chapter 10.
70 Arnold & McCartney, *Railway King*, p. 195.
71 H. Pollins, 'Aspects of Railway Accounting before 1868', in Reed, *Railways*, pp. 138–61.
72 W Bailey, 'Railway Accounts – Old and New', 1914, quoted in Pollins, 'Railway Accounting', p. 140.
73 Thomas, *North British*, p. 18.
74 BR/NBR/4/120/1 Letter 10.2.47.
75 Also 7% on branch line share capital and a share of profits if returns were higher.
76 BR/NBR/4/120/1 Statement 10.2.47 pp. 35–7.
77 BR/NBR/4/120/1.

78 *Scotsman* 29.9.66. Hodgson's strategy only became apparent when he was justifying himself retrospectively in 1866. See, for example, *The Times* and the *Scotsman* in August–October 1866.

79 *Scotsman* 23.3.60.

80 DUA/MS 105/VI/1/4 1864. Hearing into the NB and E & G proposal for a new Forth Crossing. 'The English traffic is very seriously affected by the existence of the Ferry and almost entirely uses the Larbert route.'

81 *The Times* 9.11.66.

82 *Scotsman*, Sir John Don Wauchope, 28.9.64.

83 *The Times* 15.9.45

84 St Andrews Museum, D 126. N.H. Fotheringham to Baxter and MacDougall.

85 Simmons, *Victorian Railway*, chapter 10.

86 *Scotsman* 20.4.44.

87 *Scotsman* 13.4.44.

88 *Scotsman* 20.4.44.

89 Amended prospectus 30.7.44, St Andrews Museum, D 116.

90 Ibid.

91 PKCA/PE 19. These were the first and second Tay Bridges.

92 *Scotsman* 28.9.69.

93 John Rapley, pers. com. 6.1.2005. I am very grateful to Mr Rapley for his assistance.

94 Institution of Civil Engineers, *Memoirs*, pp. 301ff.

95 I am very grateful to Kate Sampsell for this.

96 R.J. Morris, 'Samuel Smiles and the Genesis of Self Help', in *Historical Journal* 24 (1981).

97 C.A. Whatley (ed.), *The Diary of John Sturrock* (Tuckwell, East Linton, 1996).

98 S. Smiles, *Lives of the Engineers* (London, 1874), pp. 113–16.

99 Vaughan, *Brunel*, p. 27.

100 McCullough, *Great Bridge*, pp. 320–2.

101 Obituary, *Engineer* 28.2.1913.

102 Sir Arthur Phelps, *Life and Labours of Mr Brassey* (London, 1876), p. 14.

103 Vaughan, *Brunel*, p. 29. Entry for 19 October 1827.

104 R.A. Buchanan, *ODNB* (Oxford, 2004).

105 Shareholder, 29.8.48, quoted in A. Vaughan, *Isambard Kingdom Brunel* (London, 2003), p. 180.

106 NAS/GD 266/167 25.7.70.

107 DUA MS 105 VI/1/1 Evidence of Thomas Bouch to the House of Lords against the Edinburgh & Glasgow Railway Bill 1862.

108 NAS/GD 266/167 Letter Thomas Thornton – Bouch 10.3.70.

109 DUA 30/1/20 *Dundee Advertiser*.

110 ICE Obituary Sir Thomas Bouch, *Minutes of Proceedings Vol. 63*, Session 1880–1881, p. 303.

111 Ibid., p. 304.

112 His terms were £50 per mile for preparing the designs up to submitting them to Parliament, and £150 per mile thereafter for drawings, specification and supervision. If the scheme were abortive, he would charge expenses only, but would welcome a present. He pointed out that the

going rate was normally £80 per mile in preparation, and £300 per mile during construction. DUA/MS 30/1/20 letter to G. Brown 2.10.54. Occasionally he would offer a lump sum price of £1000 for engineering services up to the Act.

113 DUA/MS 30/1/8.

114 *North East Railway Magazine*, no date. DUA/MS 30/1/12.

115 Quoted in W.S. Bruce, *The Railways of Fife* (Edinburgh, 1980), p. 85.

116 National Archives of Scotland, GD/266/167 Bouch to Paterson re Newport railway, 14.12.70.

117 Robertson, 'The Cheap Railway Movement in Scotland', in *Transport History*, vol. 7, no. 1 (1974).

118 Bouch, quoted in Robertson, 'Cheap Railway Movement', p.17.

119 *The Opening o' St Andrews Railway*, printed by David Page (St Andrews, 1851), p.11.

120 J. Thomas, *Forgotten Railways: Scotland*, pp. 13–14.

121 *Dundee Courier*, quoted in Bruce, *Railways of Fife* (1980), p. 83.

122 Robertson, 'Cheap Railway Movement', p. 89.

123 Thomas, *Forgotten Railways*, pp. 16–18.

124 Thomas, *Forgotten Railways*, pp. 21–2.

125 *Scotsman* 24.3.65.

126 RHP 85311/2.

127 *Scotsman* September 1864.

128 *Scotsman* 7.3.64.

129 John Anderson to contractor to Bouch, 7.11.64. Quoted in Thomas, *North British*, p. 218.

130 *Scotsman* 20.3.65.

131 NAS/BR/FOR/4/2 Evidence of Thomas Bouch to Board of Trade Inquiry into the height of the Forth Bridge.

132 *Scotsman* 14.6.66.

CHAPTER 3 BOUCH'S BRIDGES

1 Quoted in E. de Maré, *The Bridges of Britain* (London, 1954), p. 21.

2 De Maré, *Bridges*, p. 15.

3 *Dundee Year Book*, 1903.

4 Edmund Robertson MP in Prof. Knight (ed.), *A Biographical Sketch with Reminiscences of Sir Thomas Thornton* (Dundee, 1905), p. 67.

5 *The Times* 22.4.1903.

6 Provost Moncur, in *Biographical Sketch*, p. 83.

7 GD/TD 1.

8 Knight, *Reminiscences*, p. 48.

9 Ibid., p. 45.

10 Ibid., p. 74.

11 Obituary, *Dundee Year Book*, 1903, p. 59.

12 Speech in Kinnaird Hall, 27.11.71 Lamb Collection 132 (15).

13 *Dundee Advertiser* 6.11.63.

14 DUA/MS 6/2/4 Cox autobiography.

15 This fourth scheme to cross the Tay was exhibited in October 1864. The third attempt had been from Newport to Stannergate at the east end of the

town; the second a chain bridge between Broughty and Ferryport on Tay, and the first crossing upstream at Mugdrum.

16 In Dundee University Archives MS 105/548.

17 *Dundee Advertiser* 18.10.64.

18 DUA/MS 30/12/1 Report of the Special Committee.

19 The Council tried to bargain for the embankment being permeable for its citizens, the railway gifting the town a new river embankment as a public esplanade all the way up to the bridge, and some of the streets to be blocked by this monstrous viaduct being given a drawbridge rather than an arch. *Scotsman* 23.2.65.

20 Knight, *Recollections*, pp. 18–19.

21 *Scotsman* 1.7.64.

22 *Scotsman* 17.8.65.

23 Vamplew, 'The North British Railway Enquiry of 1866'.

24 *Scotsman* 28.9.64.

25 *Scotsman* 14.6.66.

26 *Scotsman* 17.8.65.

27 The North British (Tay Bridge) Railway Bill, November 1865.

28 BR/NBR/PYB (S) 1/23.

29 Quoted in Thomas, *North British* 1, p. 127.

30 Vamplew, 'The North British Railway Inquiry of 1866'.

31 E.G. Carter, *A Historical Geography of the Railways of the British Isles* (London, 1959), p. 382.

32 Phelps, *Brassey*, pp. 143ff.

33 BR/NBR/4/189 Letter 4.6.66.

34 Neither company should, in future, propose any bill whatever, without notice and a full explanation of its objects to the other's board by 31 August each year; any objection should be referred to agreed referees, whose task would be to 'preserve the balance of power and profit between the companies in the relevant proportions which will have been established'.

35 BR/NBR/4/189 A. Johnston (NBR) to C. Johnstone (CRC) August 1866.

36 BR/NBR/4/189.

37 *Scotsman* 14.6.66.

38 *Scotsman* 14.6.66. The engineer was a Mr Anderson, accompanied by Mr Jilkes of the firm that had created the iron columns. Although there is no record, it is possible that it was a misspelling of Gilkes.

39 An excellent account of the downfall of Hodgson is contained in W. Vamplew, 'The North British Railway inquiry of 1866', in *Scottish Industrial History: A Miscellany* (Edinburgh, 1978).

40 *Scotsman* 29.9.66.

41 *Scotsman* 29.9.66.

42 Hodgson did not intend to go quietly. Four days before the meeting he issued a letter to all shareholders explaining his strategy, and appealed for proxies for the shareholders' meeting. White, on the other hand, refused to circulate the report in advance. It was circulated at the Directors' meeting in the morning. The meeting adjourned to read it. When it resumed, Hodgson made himself unavailable, and the Directors minuted that they had not been poodles, but had been deliberately deceived. At the shareholders'

meeting in the afternoon, White went through the report which they had not yet seen, minutely, taking two hours to do so. When he finished, he was accused of acting in a very un-English way in not just reporting, but in acting as though he were a counsel for the prosecution. Tempers got very high since a good number were unwilling to believe that Hodgson would have acted against their interests – even if he had bent the rules. Such people White called 'traitors' to the interests of the Company.

43 London, Leeds and Carlisle, for example.
44 Report quoted verbatim in Vamplew, 'Railway Inquiry', p. 164.
45 Vamplew, 'Railway Inquiry', p. 60.
46 Vamplew, 'Railway Inquiry', p. 178.
47 *Scotsman* 15.11.66.
48 Quoted in the *Scotsman* 12.11.66.
49 Ibid.
50 *Scotsman* 12.11.66.
51 *The Times* 18.3.67.
52 Scottish Midland, Scottish North-Eastern, and the Dunblane, Doune & Callander railways. Obituary, *Stirling Observer*, 3.8.82.
53 *The Times* 30.7.67.
54 *The Times* 29.7.67.
55 Phelps, *Brassey*, pp. 332–3.
56 Ibid., p. 330.
57 *Scotsman* 15.11.66.
58 Report of the Committee of Inquiry 4.1.68, BR/CAL/1/97.
59 *The Times* 24.1.68.
60 BR/CAL/1/97 Report to Shareholders 4.1.68.
61 Ibid., 13.4.71.
62 CAL 4/14.
63 CAL 4/26/21 January 1870. The most expensive was the Victoria Junction collision in 1876.
64 BR/NBR/Law and Claims Cttee. There were 52 separate claims alone for the single accident at Newmills.
65 BR/CAL/4/26 declared 3.10.72.
66 *Scotsman* 6.1.68.
67 *Scotsman* 29.4.68.
68 *Scotsman* 11.3.68.
69 *Scotsman* 5.5.68.
70 GD/266/240 Office Time Diaries.
71 Thomas, *North British*, p. 221.
72 McCullough, *Great Bridge*, Chapter 6.
73 McCullough, *Great Bridge*, Chapter 3.
74 McCullough, *Great Bridge*, Chapter 4.
75 NBR 10/9.
76 Thomas, *North British*, p. 221.
77 BR/NBR/10/23 TB to NBR 27.10.69.
78 NBR/10/23 Letter Bouch 27.10.69.
79 GD 266/259/1 Bouch Time Diary, 1.11.69.
80 BR/NBR/10/23 28.10.69. P. and W. MacLellan declined to tender directly 'but with Mr Brassey' and a tender was received from Brassey himself for

£289,000; but by the same post, Benton and Woodiness of Sheffield appear to have accepted the contract. It was awarded to Butler and Pitts, so the tendering process was not exemplary.

81 *Scotsman* 15.11.69 in Lamb, 303 (9).

82 *Scotsman* 13.11.69.

83 He was also the Vice-Consul of Haiti at Port au Prince, DUA/MS 6/2.

84 James Cox, *Autobiography*, written probably 1876, DUA/MS6/2/7/74.

85 Information from Claire Swan.

86 Local History Library, *Obituaries Book*, Wellgate Library, 1.12.85.

87 James Cox, *Autobiography*, written probably 1876, DUA/MS6/2/7/74.

88 Obituaries: *Evening Telegraph* 1.12.85, *Courier and Argus* 7.12.85.

89 BR/NBR/8/12/19.

90 *Scotsman* 29.9.69.

91 Ibid.

92 The toll had been £5000–£6000 when the railway had been run by the Scottish North Eastern. It had risen 50% in just over two years of Caledonian ownership.

93 BR/NBR/10/23.

94 Ibid., 17.12.69.

95 BR/NBR /1/17 24.6.70.

96 BR/NBR 8/12/19, *Scotsman* 13.11.69.

97 *Scotsman* 29.9.69.

98 Darwin to Matthew 13.6.62 quoted in W.J. Dempster, *Patrick Matthew and Natural Selection* (Edinburgh, 1983), Appendix 2.

99 Dempster, *Matthew*, p. 142.

100 Dempster, *Matthew*, p. 143.

101 *Dundee Advertiser* 11.2.70.

102 *Dundee Advertiser*, December 1869–March 1870.

103 Circular to Shareholders 29.12.69. BR/NBR/10/23.

104 ICE *Obituaries Book*, p. 311.

105 Circular to shareholders, 29.12.69. BR/NBR/10.23.

106 NBR Board Meeting 14.7.70. Also BR/NBR/1/275 Tay Bridge Undertaking 13.7.70.

107 BR/NBR/10/23 Shareholdings in the Tay Bridge Undertaking.

108 NBR/1/17/24 February 1870. BR/NBR/10/11: Letter McLaren to Johnston: 'An error in Wylie's borings. New borings made by Wilson. Pass books of Wylie and one of the older Ower. William had principal charge. Part of borings dates 1866.' The problem with this is that the bridge underwent significant variation in both location and structure between 1866 and 1872, and the older borings might not have related to the current site. Ower was Charles Ower, then an assistant to Bouch, but later partner in an architectural firm in Dundee. Inquiry 16470. In February 1870, he sought recompense for £137 from the Company for the cost of them.

109 *Inquiry* 16497. He had worked with Bouch on the Edinburgh, Leith & Granton Railway, and the bridge across the Forth at Stirling.

110 NAS/GD 266/167/34 and 44.

111 *Inquiry* 16497 and 16515. Paterson had also worked on Edinburgh's Scotland Street tunnel. His assistants were Ralph and Butler.

112 *Dundee Advertiser* 26.9.71.

113 BR/NBR/10/9/ Letter 8.12.78.
114 *Dundee Advertiser* 26.9.71.
115 Thomas, *North British*, p. 138.
116 Ibid. *Dundee Advertiser* 27.10.71.
117 BR/NBR/4/81 Scrapbook. *Dundee Advertiser* 22.9.71. Lord Kinnaird favoured an 18-foot-high, 60-foot-broad arched viaduct running along the dockside, the arches being let as warehouses.
118 *Scotsman* 2.12.71.
119 Evidence of Peter MacPherson, the North British Goods Manager, *Scotsman* 11.5.72.
120 Thomas, *North British*, p. 158.
121 *Dundee Advertiser* 21.11.71.
122 BR/CAL 4/8 Scrapbook: 2.2.72.
123 *Scotsman* 2.12.71.
124 *Scotsman* 13.12.71.
125 *Dundee Courier and Argus* 27.11.71 and 1.12.71.
126 BR/CAL 4/8 Scrapbook.
127 *Railway News* 10.2.72.
128 *Inquiry* 16485.
129 BR/NBR/1/17 12.5.71 It may have reflected the fact that Butler had already brought some plant to site.
130 Dundee Central Library, Lamb Collection 303 (3).

CHAPTER 4 THE LONGEST AND CHEAPEST RAILWAY BRIDGE IN THE WORLD

1 *Inquiry* 16212.
2 Rational analysis implies that it is most improbable.
3 The first bridge had been proposed upstream, crossing by the island of Mugdrum, not far west of Newburgh; the second, designed in November 1864, was slightly closer to Dundee than the final line; the third, was 300 yards upstream of the current site. Bouch Proof of Evidence for the Inquiry NBR/10/10/42, p. 3.
4 NAS/GD/266/21 Bouch to Wieland 28.7.77.
5 ICE *Obituary*, Charles de Bergue, *Minutes of Proceedings Vol 38, Part 2*. Session 1873–4, p. 309.
6 Grothe, *Good Words Journal*, p. 41.
7 His speech at the opening banquet for the Tay Bridge is very revealing.
8 ICE *Obituary*, Albert Grothe. *Minutes of Proceedings, Vol. 198, Part 4*. Session 1913–14, p. 345.
9 *Dundee Advertiser* March 1873 (Lamb Collection LC (303 (4)).
10 *Dundee Advertiser* October 1878 (LC 303 (4)).
11 Dundee City Archives/GD/TD 3/ 10 Beattie precognition, p. 15.
12 DUA/MS 30/12/1 3.2.73. It was stated that Bouch had based his plan upon the Glasgow tramway system without appreciating the difference in topography, street width, etc.
13 DCA/GD/TD 3/10 Beattie precognition.
14 I am indebted to Dr Mal Clark for this information.
15 XXIV, Inquiry Report.

16 Inquiry, p. xxiv. Liquidate and Ascertained Damages is the grandiose title for the penalty for late completion.

17 BR/NBR/10/10/42 Bouch precognition, p. 7.

18 McCullough, *Great Bridge*, pp. 196–208.

19 Quoted in McCullough, *Great Bridge*, p. 197.

20 McCullough, *Great Bridge*, pp. 298–308.

21 E. Gilkes, 'The Tay Bridge', in *Proceedings of the Cleveland Institution of Engineers* 6.11.76 (Middlesbrough, 1876), p. 15.

22 I am grateful to Bill Dow for this.

23 This was Henry Law's view who had also known him in London. *Inquiry* 12687. Beattie regarded him as 'painfully conscientious'. Compare this to Lewis' demonisation of him in *Silvery Tay*. Where he was acting beyond his undoubted competence was the responsibility of Bouch (precognition).

24 *Inquiry* 16623.

25 De Bergue obituary, ICE *Memoirs*, p. 309.

26 BR/NBR/10/27 Report from the Engineer 16.9.73.

27 Information from Dr Mal Clark.

28 *Inquiry* 16528.

29 *Inquiry* 12963.

30 Dundee Central Library, newspaper extracts, Lamb Collection LC 303 (4). BR/NBR/10/9. Bouch to NBR 16.9.73.

31 *Scotsman* 29.3.73.

32 BR/NBR/1/275 Meeting 11.7.70.

33 *Scotsman* 9.12.72.

34 ICE *Obituary* W.H. Barlow, *Minutes of Proceedings, Vol. 151, Part 1*. Session 1902–3, pp. 388–400.

35 BR/NBR/10/10/42, p. 21.

36 BR/FOR/4/9. Report by Pole and Barlow 30 June 1873.

37 *Scotsman* 9.12.72.

38 BR/FOR/1/1 Minutes 3.11.72, 4.11.73, 12.11.73, 4.2.75.

39 ICE *Memoirs*, p. 142.

40 Gilkes, 'The Tay Bridge', following a paper delivered 6.11.76, pp. 12–27.

41 *Inquiry* report, p. 440.

42 *Inquiry* 19597.

43 BR/NBR/10/27.

44 Pers. comm. Mike Chrimes, Librarian, ICE.

45 A. Grothe, *The Tay Bridge: Its Commencement, Progress and Completion* (Dundee, 1878). DUA K Loc 94.1.31 T236.

46 Described variously as the sons of General or Lord Delpratt.

47 Dundee City Archives/GD/TD 3/10 Beattie precognition, p. 6.

48 One of Patterson's assistants was a man called Ralph, and Bouch's two were a Mr Wemyss, and Thomas Peddie.

49 Bouch's time diaries, NAS/GD266/259/1, reveal very few visits to the Tay Bridge site; but it is unclear just how well they were kept up to date.

50 Obituary, *Engineer*, 5.2.97, quoted in D. Smith, ODNB.

51 BR/NBR/10/10/42, pp. 12–13.

52 *Good Words Journal*, p. 44.

53 Dundee City Archives/GD/TD 3/10 Proof of evidence of Frank Beattie.

54 Gilkes, 'The Tay Bridge', address to the Cleveland Institution of Engineers 6.11.76, printed in the *Proceedings* (Middlesbrough, 1876), pp. 12–27.

55 Grothe, 'Tay Bridge', in *Good Words*, p. 103.

56 Grothe, *Good Words*, p. 103.

57 *Inquiry* 19403. When Baker was later asked to recommend an engineer for difficult works in Egypt, he recommended Grothe 'as the man above all others'. *Inquiry* 19405.

58 Rather than of concrete lined with brick, as Henry Law was to state to the Inquiry. It was not the only error of which Law was guilty.

59 P.R. Lewis, *Beautiful Railway Bridge Over the Silvery Tay*, pp. 32, 103.

60 Lewis, *Silvery Tay*, p. 103. This was challenged by Allan Stewart.

61 *Inquiry* 13477. It took the next three days.

62 Grothe, *Good Words*, p. 102; H. Law, report to the Commissioners.

63 *Inquiry* 19530.

64 *Inquiry* 9627.

65 Dundee Central Library, Lamb Collection LC 303 (1).

66 BR/NBR/10/27 Letter 16.9.74.

67 *Scotsman* 6.3.74.

68 Ibid., 1.4.74.

69 *Scotsman* 19.3.74.

70 R.J. Irving, 'The profitability and performance of British Railways 1870–1914', in *Economic History Review*, new series, vol. 31, no. 1 (1978), pp. 46–66.

71 *Inquiry* 5647. Baird.

72 *Inquiry* 5679–81.

73 Dundee City Archives/GD/TD 3/10 Beattie precognition.

74 *Inquiry* 8226. Ferguson.

75 *Inquiry* 6094. Alexander Hampton.

76 *Inquiry* 8777.

77 *Inquiry* 8635–9592.

78 *Inquiry* 7746. Fender.

79 *Inquiry* 9632.

80 Dundee City Archives/GD/TD 3/10 Beattie precognition.

81 Ibid.

82 *Inquiry* 9802. Beattie 10905. Milne.

83 Dundee City Archives/GD/TD 3/10.

84 *Inquiry* 13178.

85 *Inquiry* 9627–10050.

86 *Inquiry* 10963. Milne.

87 *Inquiry* 8160. Ferguson.

88 *Inquiry* 10952. John Gibb's evidence.

89 Law's report, printed as Appendix 3 of the *Inquiry* report, second page.

90 *Inquiry* 11244 –11285.

91 *Inquiry* 10865. A. Milne's evidence.

92 *Inquiry* 10852. A. Milne's evidence.

93 *Inquiry* 11110. Peter Tuite's evidence, 10879 Gibb.

94 *Inquiry* 10946. Milne.

95 Dundee City Archives/GD/TD 3/10.

96 There was quite a contretemps at the *Inquiry* over who had authorised the

increased thickness of the iron columns. Bouch claimed that it was his decision, but the contractors provided compelling evidence to the contrary.

97   *Inquiry* 13741.
98   *Inquiry* 8909. Camphuis.
99   *Inquiry* 5638. Richard Baird.
100 *Inquiry* 5737. James McGowan claimed that the iron 'was the worst he had ever seen'.
101 *Inquiry* 8391. Strachan.
102 *Inquiry* 6337. Hutton.
103 *Inquiry* 8379.
104 *Inquiry* 9276. Camphuis.
105 *Inquiry* 8306. Strachan.
106 *Inquiry*. Peter Tuite's evidence of twenty-six years of experience as a moulder.
107 *Inquiry* 6337. Hutton, 10963; Milne for example.
108 *Inquiry* 11857–11860. Hadland.
109 Letter 30.9.73 and 7.10.73 printed as appendix to the *Inquiry* report.
110 *Inquiry* 12001.
111 *Inquiry* 129. Wingate, 12268; Coburn, 12482; Hinsley, 12404; Hall, 11587. Hadland.
112 *Inquiry* 12425. Thomas Hall.
113 Bouch, Precognition, BR/NBR/10/10/42, p. 39.
114 BR/NBR/1/275. Minutes 30.12.76.
115 *Scotsman* 20.5.76.
116 BR/FOR/1/1 26.8.76.
117 BR/NBR/10/73 600 hours overtime versus 2100 hours ordinary time.
118 BR/NBR/10/8 S. Carew to President Board of Trade, 7.1.80.
119 NBR/10/23.
120 NBR/10/23/ Board Minutes 27.7.76.
121 NBR/10/23 Kippendavie to Bouch 7.7.76.
122 BR/NBR/10/23 Waddell to Bouch 12.5.77.
123 NAS/GD266/188 Letters 29.7.77/4.9.77/11.9.77.
124 BR/NBR/10/23 Gilkes to Kippendavie 7.5.77.
125 BR/NBR/1/275 – meetings 20.12.76, 19.3.77, 26.4.78.
126 NBR/10/27 Noble to Kippendavie 1.3/2.6/8.6/15.6 etc.
127 Gilkes, *Tay Bridge*, p. 26.
128 Dundee City Archives/GD/TD 3/10.
129 BR/NBR/10/11 folio 2. Letter 11 March.
130 BR/NBR/10/23 Gilkes to Kippendavie 7.5.77.
131 *Scotsman* 5.2.77.
132 Dundee City Archives/GD/TD 3/10.
133 BR/NBR/10/11 Beattie to Board of Trade 15.7.80.
134 BR/NBR/10/27 Noble to Bouch 11.4.79.
135 BR/RACS/1/04 Half-yearly report 20.2.77.
136 BR/NBR/10/23 Weiland to Gilkes 11.5.7; Gilkes's reply 26.5.77.
137 Ambrose, *Nothing Like It*, pp. 85ff.
138 *Scotsman* 3.9.77.
139 Dundee Central Library, Lamb Collection LC 15 (17); *Dundee Advertiser* 15.9.77.

140 Dundee Central Library, Lamb Collection LC 303 (6).
141 *Scotsman* 26.9.77.
142 *Dundee Courier and Argus* 10.8.78.
143 *Proceedings* of the Cleveland Institution of Engineers, Session 1876/77 (Middlesbrough), p. 11.

CHAPTER 5 THE ABBREVIATED LIFE OF THE FIRST TAY BRIDGE

1 The payment is not separately identified in the accounts, but Gilkes was paid over £50,000 the following April which may have included it.
2 A. Grothe, *The Tay Bridge* (Dundee, 1878), a record of speeches made at the bridge's opening, p. 111.
3 *Scotsman*, reporting speeches of the Caledonian Railway Company on the opening of the Clyde Bridge, 2 July 1879.
4 *Inquiry* 15963.
5 *Inquiry* 15996.
6 *Inquiry* 16084.
7 Information from Bill Dow.
8 Strathmore to Cox 23.2.77, DUA Cox papers.
9 NAS/GD266/188/1–23 Letter 29.9.77.
10 BR/NBR/10/27 Letter 22.4.78.
11 NAS/GD266/217/283.
12 NAS/GD266/217/2.
13 Ibid., Letter 26.10.79.
14 BR/NBR/10/23.
15 The plan was that the North British would pay £40,000 p.a. and £11,666 would be received from each of the three English companies. The NB's contribution had been calculated as the £10,000 saved from being paid to travel on the Caledonian lines, and £30,000 saved from the costs of operating the Burntisland Ferry. Reported in the *Scotsman* 8.3.78.
16 Reported in the *Scotsman* 8.3.78.
17 BR/NBR/10/27 Letter 22.4.78.
18 BR/NBR/10/9 Letter 20.6.78.
19 Letter 27.6.78 in *Inquiry* xxxvii. BR/NBR/10/9 Letter 22.6.78.
20 BR/NBR/10/9 Letter 22.6.78.
21 NAS/GD 266/188/1–23 Letters June to November 1877. Bouch never replied to Beattie's query as to why he had changed his mind.
22 Ibid., 18.7.78.
23 *Scotsman* 1.6.78; Grothe, *Tay Bridge*, p. 96.
24 Local History Library, *Obituary Book* 1.
25 Grothe, *Tay Bridge*, speech by George Weiland, p. 96.
26 Ibid., p. 109.
27 Ibid., GD266/217/242.
28 *Scotsman* 1.6.78.
29 Dundee Central Library, Lamb Collection DL 216 (68).
30 Dundee Central Library, Lamb Collection 216 (68) and 438 (2).
31 *Inquiry* 9780.
32 H. MacDiarmid, *Scottish Eccentrics* (reprint, New York, 1972), p. 64.
33 MacDiarmid, *Scottish Eccentrics*, pp. 64–5.

34 See *Dundee Obituary Book*, 15.9.1910, p. 75.
35 *William McGonagall Poet: The Book of Lamentations*, John Willocks (Dundee, 1905).
36 W. McGonagall, 'The Autobiography of Sir William Topaz McGonagall' in *More Poetic Gems* (new edn, Dundee, 1968).
37 Willocks, *Book of Lamentations*, p. 18.
38 W. Power, *My Scotland*, quoted in MacDiarmid, *Scottish Eccentrics*, p. 74.
39 Willocks, *Book of Lamentations*, p. 125.
40 NAS/GD266/218 Letter 29.3.79, reply 7.4.79.
41 *Inquiry* 6658. Simpson.
42 *Inquiry* 4646–5370.
43 DUA/17/2/2/2/(7) ii.
44 *Inquiry* 3431.
45 A calendering works gives a beaten, compressed and polished finish to textiles like coarse linen and jute.
46 *Inquiry* 3073–3405.
47 BR/NBR/10/9 Circular from Locomotive Superintendent to all drivers, 4.8.79.
48 *Inquiry* 3839.
49 BR/NBR/1/275 Minutes 1.7.70.
50 J.H. Melville, Falkirk, reported in the *Scotsman* 5.9.78.
51 Irvine Kempt reported in the *Scotsman* 5.9.78.
52 George Cunninghame reported in the *Scotsman* 5.9.78.
53 John Harvey reported in the *Scotsman* 5.9.78.
54 Alexander Thomson, shipowner, Grangemouth: reported in the *Scotsman* 5.9.78.
55 Ibid., Captain John White, Marine Superintendent of the Leith, Hull and Hamburg Shipping Company
56 Ibid., Captain Hamilton of Boston.
57 NBR/FOR/2 Board of Trade Inquiry 1878.
58 *Scotsman* 2.7.79.
59 BR/FOR 1/1 6.8.79.
60 BR/Forth Bridge Prospectus 22.11.79.
61 NAS/ED1/566/6.
62 *Scotsman* 6.9.78; 1.10.78.
63 *Scotsman* 13.10.79.
64 The material included E. Stanhope's report to the House of Commons on *Railway Structures (Use of Steel)* published 23 March 1877 – a committee on which Col. Yolland, William Barlow and Sir John Hawkshaw had sat.
65 Daniel Adamson had published 'The Mechanical and other Properties of iron and mild steel' in French and English for the Iron and Steel Institute.
66 NAS/GD 266/213/1–51,
67 Irving, *Economic History Review*, pp. 46–66.
68 *Scotsman* 26.9.79.
69 BR/CAL 14/4.
70 James Ross, Clerk to Montrose Harbour Board, evidence reported in the *Scotsman* 1.4.79.
71 Ibid., Alexander Copeland, Aberdeen Commercial Company,
72 Ibid., Henry Oakley, General Manager, Great Northern Railway Company.

73 *Inquiry* 15837.

74 *Inquiry* 15798.

75 On 9 May 1878 he wrote to Bouch that the bolts and bracing rivets were 'in a perfect state of security'.

76 *Inquiry Report* xi.

77 *Inquiry* 16004.

78 Allan Stewart disputed that at the Inquiry.

79 *Dundee Courier and Argus* 18.12.79.

80 Ibid., 12.12.79.

81 BR/NBR/10/8 Letter from Durham Magistrate Seaton Carew 7.1.80.

82 He admitted to £35,000 at the Inquiry 17720, but the Durham magistrate gave the figure of £43,000.

83 *Inquiry* 17721.

84 *Dundee Courier and Argus* 3/12/13/15 December 1879.

85 Forth Bridge Railway Company share prospectus. Published *Scotsman* 22.12.79.

86 *The Times* 26.12.79.

87 Robin Lumley has now calculated 83.

88 *Inquiry* 237.

89 *The Times* leader, 30.12.79.

90 T. Fontane, *Across the Tweed*, tr. Brian Battershaw (London, 1965).

91 Ibid., p. 6.

92 I am grateful to Andrea Schwedler for her translation, 2001.

CHAPTER 6 A CHOREOGRAPHED INQUIRY

1 Thornton Wilder, *The Bridge of San Luis Rey* (new edn, London, 1972), pp. 3–4.

2 *Scotsman* 1.1.80.

3 Ibid.

4 *Dundee Evening Telegraph* 31.12.79.

5 Information from Bill Dow. They had simply counted all the weekend tickets in the relevant drawer.

6 *Scotsman* 7.1.80.

7 I am grateful to Ian Flett, Dundee City Archives, for this.

8 *Inquiry* 550.

9 *Dundee Evening Telegraph* 31.1.80.

10 DCA/GD/TD 23.

11 DCA/GD/TD 24/23.

12 BR/NBR/1/22 Meeting of Finance Committee 6.1.81.

13 Dundee Central Library, Lamb Collection LC 303 (4); *Evening Telegraph* 31.12.79.

14 DCA/GD/TD 24/5a.

15 DCA/GD/TD 24/13.

16 Ibid. GD/TD 24/12.

17 *Dundee Courier and Argus* 31.12.79.

18 *Dundee Advertiser* 5.1.80. Rev. A. Inglis.

19 *Dundee Advertiser* 14.1.80.

20 Ibid., 5.1.80.

21 *Herapath's Railway Journal* 3.1.80.
22 *Dundee Advertiser* 27.1.80.
23 BR/NBR/10/8/19 and 23 and 24.
24 BR/NBR/10/8/95 9.2.80.
25 BR/NBR/10/8 7.1.80
26 *Wizard of the North* 30.1.80.
27 BR/NBR/10/11/folio 3. Letter Bouch to Johnston.
28 It met on 10 January 1880.
29 Saturday 3 January 1880.
30 Inquiry 14462. Rothery.
31 He was to end up as a Law Lord and one of the original governors of University College, Dundee.
32 BR/NBR/10/11/2 McLaren to Johnson 8.3.80.
33 DUA/MS 30/8 Barlow to Roddick 1.10.77.
34 Obituary, *Engineer* 11.9.85.
35 Henry Cadogan Rothery, ODNB, G.C. Boase, Rev. E. Metcalfe.
36 I am indebted to Dr Mal Clark for this information.
37 DUA 17/2/9.15.2 (4) i.
38 That is, assuming the contemporary records in the Dundee newspapers were more accurate. Information from Bill Dow. It is certainly the case that the spelling of people's names can differ significantly between the Court record and the original precognition. This book has tended to favour the precognitions since they were taken by careful lawyers and signed by the witnesses.
39 Letter from the Commissioners to Law 22.1.80, printed in the Inquiry Report Appendix 2.
40 ICE *Obituaries* book, p. 362.
41 BR/NBR/10/11 Folio 1. 11.2.80.
42 BR/NBR/10/11 Folio. McLaren to Johnston, 2.3.80.
43 Ibid., McLaren to Johnston 2.3.80.
44 *Dundee Advertiser* 21.1.80.
45 *Scotsman* 10.1.80.
46 BR/NBR/10/11 Folio 1 letter 11.2.80.
47 DUA/17/2/2/ ((1) i and 2/iii) McBeath, not he, had been the inspector of iron, and had indeed condemned many rivets, all of which had been replaced properly. The evidence of Evans and Donegay that rivets holding the tie-bars were either loose or missing was both false and nonsensical. If it had been so, there was nothing to have kept them from falling – and they hadn't fallen. This comment demonstrates the danger that the Inquiry – particularly Rothery – took inexpert unchallenged evidence at face value.
48 DUA 17/2/2/(1) ii) Imperfections were dealt with. Slack nuts, a cracked column and a cracked sole plate were observed by a mechanic/temporary painter John Neilsen. Unusually (for most of the painters had muttered that it was not their business to report anything), he had reported these problems to Noble who had dealt with them. Concluding that the cracked column was an original casting fault or the consequence of pouring concrete rather than a new problem, Noble had bound it with iron hoops, a procedure approved by Bouch.
49 BR/NBR/10/11 Folio 1 Gilkes to Johnston 16.2.80.
50 BR/FOR/1/1 Meetings 21 January, 28 February, 16 June 1880.

51 BR/NBR/10/11 Briefing 1.3.80 Thornton to Balfour.

52 BR/NBR/10/11 Letter 2.3.80.

53 BR/NBR/10/11 Folio 2 McLaren to Johnston 8.3.80.

54 Ibid.

55 BR/NBR/10/11 Letter 3.3.80.

56 DCA/GD/TD 3/10.

57 BR/NBR/10/11 Letter 3.3.80.

58 BR/NBR/10/11 Thornton to Johnston.

59 M. Chrimes, Sir James Brunlees, ODNB.

60 Bouch employed Noble and McBeath as inspectors, Wemyss, Orchar, Meik and Peddie as assistants, and Paterson with two further assistants as resident engineers. He claimed to have spent nine-tenths of his entire bridge fee on his supervisory staff.

61 BR/NBR/10/8/6.

62 Ibid., 19.2.80.

63 *Scotsman* 31.3.80. It is clear from the record of the meeting that the $120,000 was not to pay for any capital work, for that would be charged to the capital account. This sum was to pay for claims, legal and other costs, and expenditure that could only legitimately be called repairs.

64 *Herapath's Railway Journal* 3.1.80.

65 *Herapath's Railway Journal* 3.1.80.

66 *Herapath's Railway Journal* 10.1.80.

67 *Herapath's Railway Journal* 20.3.80.

68 *Scotsman* 31.3.80.

69 *Scotsman* 1.3.80 and 4.3.80.

70 *Scotsman* 15.1.80.

71 NBR/10/11 Folio 2 9.3.80.

72 Ibid., Letter 8.3.80 (2) He added in a further letter: 'There were many things done with which I disapproved, and there were one or two unpleasant incidents which occurred in connection with the thirteen large spans and the fall of two of them in 77.'

73 Folio 2 letter Beattie–Johnston 1.3.80.

74 *Inquiry* 16971.

75 *Inquiry* 17187–17195.

76 NBR 10/11/2 McLaren to Johnston 10.4.80: 'The engine went down again half way to Tayport.'

77 BR/NBR/10/11/2 Letters 21 and 30 April.

78 BR/NBR/10/11/2 Letter 15.4.80.

79 BR/NBR/10/11/2 21.4.80 Armit to Peddie; 27.4.80 Waddell to Johnston.

80 *Inquiry* 17970.

81 *Inquiry* 179141.

82 *Inquiry* 14468. Law said it would have splintered like matchwood.

83 BR/NBR/10/11/2 Letter 4 March.

84 Ibid., Letter 5.3.80.

85 NBR/11/2 McLaren to Johnston 12.4.80. Both of Gilkes's previous firms had his name in the title.

86 BR/NBR/10/11/2 15.4.80 Gilkes to Johntston.

87 Ibid., Johnston to Counsel, April 1880.

88 I am grateful to Dr Mal Clark for this.

89 *Inquiry* 15538.
90 *Inquiry* 14371.
91 *Inquiry* 14570.
92 *Inquiry* 23.4.80.
93 *Inquiry* 14117.
94 *Inquiry* 14795–14812. Bill Dow points out that hollow brick structures are prone to cracking, for unless the bricks and mortar are wholly waterproof, water might pass into the hollow interior, freeze, and crack the structure.
95 *Inquiry* 16412.
96 *Inquiry* 16927: 'I cannot hear'.
97 *Inquiry* 17084.
98 *Inquiry* 17202.
99 *Inquiry* 16707.
100 *Inquiry* 16497–16507.
101 DUA/MS 17/2/2/(1) ii. Young was not called as a witness, and Trayner remained unaware of his evidence. He scarcely needed it.
102 McCullough, *Great Bridge*, chapter 16ff.
103 *Inquiry–Report of the Commissioner of Wrecks*, p. 536.
104 *Inquiry* ibid., p. 551.
105 *Inquiry* ibid., p. 556.
106 *Inquiry* ibid., p. 557.

CHAPTER 7 THE TUMBLING OF BOUCH'S BRIDGES

1 BR/NBR/10/11/2 Telegram Wieland–Johnston 14.5.80.
2 Board meeting 10.5.80.
3 BR/NBR/10/11/2 Walker–Johnston 13.5.80.
4 10/11/2 Walker–Johnston 13.5.80.
5 Ibid., Weiland–Johnston telegram 14.5.80.
6 The repaired bridge would be one mile seven furlongs long, with four central navigation spans seventy-six foot clear above high tide in the navigation channels, reducing to fifty-four feet at the northern end.
7 BR/NBR/10/11/2 Thornton–Johnston 19.5.80.
8 Ibid., 26.5.80.
9 BR/NBR/10/27/4. The slates were from Dinorwic.
10 BR/NBR/10/11/2 Thornton–Johnston 18.5.80. Apologies to John Masefield.
11 BR/NBR/10/11/2 27.4.80.
12 BR/NBR/10/11/2 1.5.80.
13 BR/NBR/0/11/2 Thornton–Johnston 10.5.80.
14 BR/NBR/10/11/2 19.5.80.
15 BR/NBR/10/11/2 17.5.80.
16 BR/NBR/10/11/2 18.5.80.
17 BR/NBR/10/11/2. Thornton–Johnston 10.6.80.
18 Ibid., 18.6.80.
20 DUA MS 17/ 2/2/8A.
21 DUA MS 17P/92.
22 BR/NBR/10/10/33 Law to Johnston 15.7.80.
23 DUA/ MS 17P/92.

24 BR/NBR/10/11/2 Thornton to Johnston 10.6.80.

25 BR/NBR/10/11/2 G.M. Davis to Johnston.

26 BR/NBR/10/11/2 Grothe to Johnston 21.6.80.

27 I am particularly indebted to Dr Mal Clark for this information; and for his analysis of the Inquiry 'The Verdict on the Tay Bridge Disaster: An Error of Judgement by Joseph Chamberlain?'

28 Information from Dr Clark. National Register of Archives (NRA) TI/12888/37 and 41; NRA BT15/20 – and /F893/1882.

29 On 30 June 1880. *Minutes of Proceedings upon A Formal Investigation Directed by the Board of Trade to be held into the Causes of, and Circumstances Attending, the Accident to the Tay Bridge 30 June 1880* (henceforth the *Inquiry*). BR/NBR/10/1 *Reports and Evidence* BR/NBR/10/2.

30 Yolland and Barlow Report. 15th conclusion. They also accepted Grothe's claim that the 'burning-on' of the lugs had only occurred in the temporary columns used for construction.

31 For example, in believing that the collapse had begun at the northern rather than the southern end.

32 *The Times* 5.7.80.

33 *The Times* 5.7.80.

34 *Inquiry* 15041.

35 John Prebble, *The High Girders* (London, 1979), and John Cochrane's opinion.

36 Most commentators – John Thomas, *The Tay Bridge Disaster: New Light on the 1879 Tragedy* (Newton Abbot, 1972) and David Swinfen, *The Fall of the Tay Bridge* (Edinburgh, 1994) – concur with this.

37 W. McGonagall, 'The Tay Bridge Disaster', in *Poetic Gems* (Dundee, 1890).

38 Yolland and Barlow Report, Clause X1.

39 T. Martin and I.A. Macleod, 'The Tay Rail Bridge Disaster', in *Civil Engineering* 1995, vol. 108, apply computer analysis to wind loading to demonstrate that when the train was on the high girders, pressure of a gust at 40mph would have been sufficient to destabilise the bridge. There is no evidence of gusts of that pressure than night. Indeed, P.J.A. Burt in 'The Great Storm and the Fall of the first Tay Bridge', in *Weather*, vol. 59, December 2004, concluded 'the storm which brought down the bridge was not that severe'.

40 Peter Lewis, *Bridge Over the Silvery Tay*; also P.R. Lewis and K. Reynolds, 'Forensic Engineering: A Reappraisal of the Tay Bridge Disaster', in *Interdisciplinary Science Reviews*, 2002, vol. 27, no. 4. This was followed by P.R. Lewis and C. Gagg, 'Aesthetics versus Function: the Fall of the Dee Bridge, 1847', in *Interdisciplinary Science Reviews*, 2004, vol. 29, no. 2 which concluded that the collapse of Robert Stephenson's Dee Bridge occurred through metal fatigue.

41 BR/NBR/10/10 Letter from William Pole FRS and Allan D. Stewart CE 25.2.80.

42 Bouch, Baker, Grothe, Gilkes – all of those judgments had been rejected by posterity save for the lone voice of Bill Dow, to whom I am enormously indebted.

43 Information from Dr Mal Clark.

44 Brunlees: 'the second class carriage must have been stopped by something'. *Inquiry* 15574, 15564.

45 *Inquiry* 14475–7. Lewis demonstrates that in at least one case, the fracture appears to have begun in a blowhole, confirming that poor foundry practices might have played a contributory part.

46 BR/NBR/10/11/2 Correspondence Armit and Waddell with Bouch 27.4.80 and 21.4.80. Bill Dow points out that the Inquiry also ignored evidence of wheel marks across the bars that had been inserted to keep the rails apart after Hutchinson's inspection.

47 BR/NBR/10/11/2 Chalmers to Drummond 2.5.80.

48 *Inquiry* 1477.

49 BR/NBR/10/11 Thornton to Johnston 23.2.80.

50 DUA/MS17/2/2 (ii) Precognition of John Neilson, Mechanic.

51 *Inquiry* 10652.

52 *Inquiry Report* xxxvii.

53 BR/NBR/10/11 Letter 2.7.80.

54 BR/NBR/10/10 Cable, Wieland to Johnston 5.7.80.

55 NBR/10/10 Dickson to Johnston 5.7.80.

56 NBR/10/10 Bouch to Johnston 5.7.80.

57 BR/NBR/10/10 Weiland to Johnston 5.7.80.

58 *Scotsman* 7.7.80.

59 BR/NBR/10/11 Letter Thornton–Johnston 8.7.80.

60 BR/NBR/10/11 8.7.80.

61 BR/NBR/10/11 7.7.80.

62 BR/FOR/1/1 9.7.80 It seems that he did not, and the Board itself had to write to Arrol directly three weeks later to inform him that the contract was to be abandoned. BR/FOR 1/1 Minutes 9.7.80 and 3.8.80.

63 BR/NBR/10/10 Bouch to Johnston 14.7.80.

64 Dr Mal Clark: Q 2203 12.-7/80. G 51. Question Time 15.7.80.

65 *Herapath's Railway Journal*, 10.7.80.

66 *The Times* 14.7.80.

67 BR/NBR/10/10 Dickson to Johnston 16.7.80.

68 BR/NBR/10/10 Walker to Johnston 8. 7.80.

70 Ibid.

71 Committee 20.7.80; *Scotsman* 21.7.80.

72 Reported in the *Scotsman* 22.7.80.

73 *Scotsman* 21.7.80, *Dundee Advertiser* 27.7.80.

74 *Dundee Advertiser*, 28.7.80.

75 *Scotsman* 23.7.80.

76 *Scotsman* 29.7.80.

77 *Dundee Advertiser*, 29.7.80.

78 *Scotsman* 9.8.80.

79 *Scotsman* 9.8.80.

80 Pers. comm. John Rapley.

81 NAS/GD266/253.

82 *Scotsman* 4.11.80.

83 BR/FOR 4/9 Report from W. Barlow and Dr Pole 30.6.73.

84 Deepdale, Forth Bridge and Tay Bridge.

85 *Engineer*, Arrol Obituary, 28.2.1913.

86 NAS/GD 266/240 Time Books.

87 Bouch and Arrol's estates are contained within their ODNB entries.

Cox's wealth, DPL, Local History Library *Obituaries Book*, p. 39.
88 DUA/MS 30/12/1.
89 BR/NBR/10/11 29.7.80.
90 BR/NBR/10/11 10.7.80.
91 Ibid., 6.7.80.
92 I am grateful to Bill Dow for this.
93 BR/NBR/37/3129 letter 10.9.80.
94 *Report on the Railway System of Scotland for the year 1879* quoted in the *Scotsman*.
95 *Scotsman* 24.9.80.
96 *Dundee Advertiser* 30.9.80.
97 BR/NBR/1/22 Works Committee 16.12.80. Directors' meeting 2.3.81; 23.10.80.
98 BR/NBR/1/22 Directors' Meeting 24.6.80.
99 BR/FOR1/1 Directors' Meeting 3.9.80.
100 BR/NBR/1/22 Directors Meeting 28.8.80.
101 BR/FOR/1/1 30.9.81.
102 BR/FOR/4/4 Anonymous report, probably *Engineering*, probably 1881, p. 4.
103 BR/FOR/4/11 Letter 16.8.80.
104 Ibid., Letter Maclay, Murray and Spens 26.8.80.
105 BR/FOR/4/11 £27,000 had been spent on materials to date. Wieland had actually written to Bouch on 29 July asking him to verify that Arrol's money had been authorised. Bouch did not deign to reply.
106 BR/FOR/4/11 Letter 8.3.81.
107 *Scotsman* 23.11.80, BR/FOR/1/1 Directors 13.1.81.
108 BR/FOR/4/11 Letters to Wieland 17.2.81, and in reverse 16.2.81.

CHAPTER 8 PHOENIX IN THE TAY

1 The guaranteeing companies were the Great Northern 18.75%, the Midland 32.5%, the North Eastern 18.75%, and the North British 30%. BR/FOR/1/1 Minute 26.7.82 Meeting on 17 June 1882.
2 BR/FOR/1/1 26.7.1882: also FOR/4/3 Agreement 10.12.1881. They changed from a 'contingent' guaranteed income to the Bridge Company equivalent to a 6% return on the capital needed to bridge the Forth. The rail link between Inverkeithing and Burntisland was transferred to the North British to construct separately.
3 BR/FOR/4/3 Agreement 29.6.81.
4 NAS/GD 266/267 Trustees' Estate records. The discharge was signed on 14.4.81. BR/NBR/1/22.
5 Pers. comm. John Rapley.
6 BR/NBR/1/22 Directors' meetings 11.5.81 and 2.6.81.
7 Obituary, *Engineer*, 28.2.13.
8 BR/NBR/37/3129 Letter 16.9.80.
9 C. Barlow, *The New Tay Bridge* (London, 1889), p. 3.
10 Barlow, 'Tay Viaduct', p. 90.
11 Widening it on one side, widening it on both sides, or building a single line track parallel to the existing as Brunlees had proposed. Barlow, 'Tay Viaduct', p. 89.

12 C. Barlow, 'The Tay Viaduct, Dundee', in *Proceedings of the Institution of Civil Engineers* 8.5.88, p. 90.
13 Ibid., pp. 3–4.
14 *Tay Bridge Guide*, 1887; DPL Lamb Collection LC 304 (7), p. 7.
15 Barlow, 'Tay Viaduct', p. 96.
16 Barlow, *Proc. ICE*, 8.5.88, p. 128.
17 Crawford Barlow, in his account of the construction of the new bridge, calculated the annual payments to the Caledonian at 5% cost of the £570,000 cost of the new bridge.
18 NBR/8/1218/New Tay Bridge, Letter 15.12.80.
19 Technically the Shore Dues book. DUA/MS 17/2/2 (10).
20 GD/TD 27 Letter 25.1.81.
21 TD 26 and TD 3.
22 J.S. Shipway, 'Tay Rail Bridge Centenary: Some Notes', in *Proceedings of the Institution Civil Engineers*, part 1, 1989, 86, Dec. 1089–1109, pp. 1099.
25 Crawford, *New Tay Bridge*, p. 17.
24 DUA/MS 17/2/2/ (140 iii).
25 DUA/MS 17/2/2/ (2 (14) I).
26 *Scotsman* 9.3.82.
27 *Scotsman* 30.6.82.
28 BR/NBR/1/79 Report to shareholders, 2.3.83.
29 Ibid., p. 7.
30 Rather than James Stirling of Kippendale as Crawford Barlow called him.
31 Acceptance speech for the Freedom of Dundee, 4.12.89, *Dundee Year Book 1889*.
32 See, for example, Sir Robert Purvis' *Sir William Arrol* (Edinburgh, 1913) which had been prepared with his assistance.
33 This is based upon the obituary in the *Engineer* 28.2.1913, and his entry by M. Moss in the *Oxford Dictionary of National Biography*.
34 M. Moss, Sir William Arrol, ODNB.
35 *Scotsman* 27.2.80 quoted in A. Murray, *The Forth Railway Bridge* (Edinburgh, 1983), p. 62.
36 Purvis, *Arrol*, p. 31.
37 James Nasmyth, *Autobiography* (S. Smiles (ed.), London 1883), pp. 199–200.
38 J. Ruskin, *On Art and Life* (reprint, Harmondsworth, 2004), p. 14.
39 Barlow, *Tay Bridge*, p. 46.
40 The records are not quite clear on this.
41 Dalmarnock Accident Fund, NAS/GD/1/1057.
42 3rd annual Festival flier. DPL Lamb Collection LC 304 (25).
43 DPL Lamb Collection LC 304 (A).
44 *Tay Bridge Guide*, p. 16.
45 He must have been including the earlier years of construction under Bouch.
46 Speech on receiving the Freedom of Dundee 4.12.89, *Dundee Year Book*, 1889.
47 Quoted in his obituary in the *Engineer* 28.2.1913.
48 The North British was also persuaded to forego its normal deduction of a percentage retention.
49 Barlow, *Proc. ICE*, 8.5.88, p. 127.
50 W. Inglis, 'The Construction of the Tay Viaduct, Dundee', *Proc. ICE* 8.5.88, p. 100.

51 Shipway, *Tay Railway Bridge*, p. 18.
52 Arrol, *Proc. ICE*, 8.5.88 DUA/MS 30/1 (13).
53 *Scotsman* 4.6.87.
54 Inglis, 'Tay Viaduct', p. 130.
55 BR/NBR/1/79 Report to shareholders 4.3.84, 20.8.84, 26.3.85.
56 Inglis, 'Tay Viaduct', p. 103.
57 *Tay Bridge Guide*; Inglis, 'Tay Viaduct', p. 105.
58 Ibid., p.106. D. Hill-Smith, 'Revolutionary methods used to build the new bridge', in the *Courier and Advertiser*, 10.9.1987.
59 The old ones were placed on the outside of the new bridge, and twinned by stronger new girders on the inside. One or two found their way onto the Forth Bridge construction site.
60 Speech on receiving the Freedom of Dundee, *Dundee Year Book*, 1889.
61 Ibid.
62 Inglis, 'Tay Viaduct', *Proc ICE*, 8.5.88. Arrol also paid tribute to Messrs Stuart, Thomson, Turnbull, Campbell and Harris.
63 Purvis, *Arrol, a Memoir* (Edinburgh, 1913), pp. 98–101.
64 Ibid., p. 135.
65 Inglis, 'Tay Viaduct', p. 112.
66 BR/NBR/1/79 Report 6.5.86.
67 Inglis, 'Tay Viaduct', p. 113.
68 *Scotsman* 11.6.87.
69 *Scotsman* 11.6.87.
70 *Scotsman* 14.6.87.
71 *Dundee Advertiser Guide* (Dundee, 1887) DPL Lamb Collection LC 304 (a).
72 J. Leng, *The Tay Bridge*, p. 16.
73 Ibid.
74 Robertson's bicycle shop advertisement in Leng, *Tay Bridge*, p. 17.
75 *Dundee Advertiser* 10.6.87.
76 *Dundee Advertiser* 10.6.87.
77 Pers. comm, M. Chrimes.
78 BR/NBR/1/275 Tay Bridge Undertaking Meeting 26.4.1878.
79 Leng, *Tay Bridge*, p. 16.
80 *Scotsman* 8.3.88.
81 It varied from between 100 to 900 men. Shipway, 'Tay Rail Bridge Centenary', p. 1109.
82 BR/FOR/1/1 Hutchinson's 16th report, 28.1.87.
83 G. Berkley, ICE Vice-President, ICE meeting 8.5.88.
84 DPL, Local History Library *Obituaries* Book, pp. 28–9.
85 Ibid.
86 D. Porter, ONDB.
87 *Dundee Advertiser* 13.12.1906.
88 W. McGonagall, *Poetic Gems* (Dundee, 1890), p. 13.
89 Letter 6.5.91 quoted in D. Phillips, *No Poet's Corner in the Abbey* (Dundee, 1871), p. 191.
90 Phillips, *No Poet's Corner*, p. 206.

CHAPTER 9 CONQUERING THE FORTH

1 F.T. Vischer, quoted in I.B. Whyte, 'A Sensation of Immense Power', in *John Fowler, Benjamin Baker, Forth Bridge* (Stuttgart, 1997), p. 11.
2 BR/FOR/1/1 3.8.81. The Forth Bridge Board would now consist solely of one of its own directors, and nominees of the four guarantor companies.
3 Bouch's had been both curved and on a steep gradient. FOR/1/1 30.9.81.
4 Special permission was obtained from the Board of Trade for the lower members to curve downwards at the sides. FOR 4/3 Harrison, Barlow and Fowler to Board of Trade 9.8.81.
5 FOR 4/3 Harrison, Barlow and Fowler to Board of Trade 9.8.81 Minimum tensile strength 30 tons per square inch: compression 34 tons psi.
6 BR/FOR/1/1 Report 5.11.1881.
7 The changes were to provide vertical steel towers at the centre of each of the bays, acting as anchor to their cantilevers, and broaden the foundations accordingly.
8 The fee was based on 3% on railway works, 5% on the bridge, inclusive of all charges and expenses. 'No additional charge was to be made on any ground whatsoever.' Ibid., 5.11.81. So when Fowler asked for an advance, it was swiftly rejected: not in the agreement.
9 BR/FOR/4/3 W.P. Beale's handwritten comments on the Specification.
10 One of the conditions upon it taking over the Scottish North East in 1866.
11 BR/FOR/4/41 *Nature* 19.10.82, *Engineering* 27.10.82.
12 BR/FOR/1/1 17.2.82.
13 M. Chrimes, ODNB.
14 He had had an illegitimate child by a Welsh girl who had emigrated to Canada. ODNB.
15 Acceptance Speech, Turners' Livery Company, 27.3.90, quoted in the *Scotsman* 28.7.90.
16 Simmons, *The Victorian Railway* (London, 1995), p. 112.
17 Ibid.
18 Baker claimed that Bouch's first Forth River bridge was moved upstream to Charlestown because he 'had not the courage to face a span of 1700 feet, and nothing less is practicable at Queensferry'. Baker, *Forth Bridge*, 1882, p. 6.
19 Speech in Montreal, 1886, quoted by W. Westhofen, *The Forth Bridge* (reprint, Edinburgh, 1989), p. 69.
20 B. Baker, 'Bridging the Firth of Forth'. Lecture to Royal Institution, 20.5.87, p. 8.
21 S. Mackay, *The Forth Bridge* (Edinburgh, 1990), p. 16. The others may have been, by comparison with their photographs in *Industries*, Frederick Wood and Andrew Biggart.
22 Baker, 'Bridging', p. 19.
23 Purvis, *Arrol*, claimed that Fowler had got the idea from a conversation with James Nasmyth, p. 79.
24 Westhofen, *Forth Bridge*, p. 10.
25 Baker, 'Bridging', p. 10.
26 *Engineering, The Forth Bridge*, 1882, p. 5.
27 BR/FOR/1/1 June 1887.

28 NAS/GD/330/295 Fowler to Board 25.11.87.

29 FOR/4/3 20.12.81 – Letter to guaranteeing companies.

30 BR/FOR/4/11 Arrol to Wieland 8.3.81 FOR 1/1 Meetings 4.11.82 and 21.12.82. Also BR/FOR/3/4 Contract. £10,000 would be allowed for materials already on site.

31 FOR/1/1/ Meeting 19.10.82.

32 Ibid.

33 Baker, *Forth Bridge*, pp. 4–5.

34 Baker, 'Bridging the Forth', p. 7.

35 BR/FOR/1/1 15.7.84.

36 Westhofen, *Forth Bridge*, pp. 13, 16, 71.

37 Engineering report BR/FOR/1/1 6.7.85.

38 BR/FOR/1/2 Meeting 14.10.84.

39 *Scientific American*. FOR/4/2 no date, presumed 1887. Baker, 'Bridging', p. 21.

40 *The Times* 26.5.85.

41 Inspector's report: 12.6.83 Temporary works. They wrote that the caissons were being manufactured at Arrol's works in Edinburgh, but must have meant Glasgow.

42 Westhofen, *Forth Bridge*, p. 22.

43 Steel was also supplied by the Steel Company of Scotland at Blochairn, and Dalzell's iron and steel works at Motherwell.

44 Inspector's report: 12.6.83 Permanent works.

45 Hutchinson's quarterly reports usually give a census of the workforce on a particular day. The number never rises over 4000, although Arrol, Baker and newspapers like the *Scotsman* often reach a figure of 4500. The variation may be explained either by some unstated inclusion or exclusion or, more likely, that there were temporary fluctuations between the Board of Trade census days. Equally, it is not certain that the Board of Trade was counting night workers if they were different from day workers.

46 Baker, *Chambers' Journal*, 1.9.88.

47 Ibid., p. 6.

48 Westhofen, *Forth Bridge*, p. 61.

49 Hutchinson, 9th Report. *Scotsman* 31.5.85.

50 Westhofen, *Forth Bridge*, p. 62.

51 10.12.84. Tancred Arrol to Baker.

52 NAS GD/330/295 Agreement from meeting held 29.11.84 at 2 Queen Square: Fowler and Baker, Tancred, Arrol, Falkiner and Phillips. In future, Arrol to have direct personal control of the whole of the works and is to be responsible to the engineers for the economical management of the same. All divided responsibility to cease. A first-rate man experienced in bridge work to be appointed by Arrol as 'contractor's agent' or 'general superintendent of works'. To avoid delay, fortnightly meeting of contractors. Mr Gray responsible under the new post for masonry and concrete and will see that proper materials delivered on time. Mr River for timber, Mr Blackburn for iron staging and caisson work; Mr Moir for putting caissons together; a foreman like Mr McLean to be responsible for fitting caissons with airlocks; Mr More for the Fife skewback; similar for the other two; Mr Aitken for the lower shops; McLean upper shop. Additional drawing offices to be provided;

Biggart head of drawing office; Middleton of the surveys and measurements; Westhofen in association with Biggart to take up in detail the matters connected with the erection of steelwork.

53 *Industries, Forth Bridge* special issue, March 1890.
54 10.2.85 The original contract provided for a maximum of £60,000. The engineer could certify 85% of the plant purchased (allowing it to be purchased through the contract). £30,000 was to be advanced against the final payment which was due six months after completion. £30,000 was for machinery, another £30,000 in the form of releasing half of the retention, and a further £20,000 as a special advance New agreement with Sir Thomas Selby Tancred, Joseph Phillips, Travers H. Falkiner, William Arrol.
55 B. Baker, lecture delivered at the Royal Institution 20.5.87 BR/FOR/4/3.
56 Purvis, *Arrol*, p. 81.
57 Baker, 'Bridging', p. 16. Baker does not explain how they were got out. It cannot have been easy.
58 Westhofen, *Forth Bridge*, p. 26.
59 Purvis, *Arrol*, p. 83.
60 *Industries, Forth Bridge* special issue, p. 10.
61 Westhofen, *Forth Bridge*, p. 27.
62 Baker, *Chambers' Journal*, 1.9.88.
63 Baker, 'Bridging', p. 18.
64 Malcolm Wood, speech to Mechanical Engineers 1887, p. 149.
65 Letter 6.10.90, quoted in Purvis, *Arrol*, pp. 103–4. The context was the railway servants' strike.
66 Baker, 'Bridging the Forth', p. 14.
67 Baker, 'Bridging the Forth', p. 14.
68 *Industries*, Forth Bridge, p. 10 Purvis, *Arrol*, p. 82.
69 BR/FOR/2; *Industries* 20.4.88.
70 *Industries* 20.4.88; Baker, 'Bridging', p. 18.
71 South Queensferry North West. Westhofen, *Forth Bridge*, p. 26.
72 Purvis, *Arrol*, p. 88.
73 Westhofen, *Forth Bridge*, p. 26.
74 BR/FOR/2 *Mechanical World* 28.1.88.
75 Information from Dr Billy Kenefick, pers. comm.
76 Westhofen, *Forth Bridge*, p. 62.
77 BR/FOR/1/1 Engineers' Report 3.7.86.
78 NAS/GD/330/295 Fowler to Arrol 23.9.86.
79 NAS/GD 330/295 Fowler to Arrol 23.9.86.
80 Mr Scott, the Chief Mechanical Engineer, Mr Biggart and other chiefs.
81 NAS/GD 330/295, Fowler to Arrol 30.9.86. Fowler to White Miller, 8.10.86.
82 BR/FOR/1/1/ Meeting 15.2.87.
83 Cutting in BR/FOR/4/41, no date.
84 NAS/GD1/1057 Dalmarnock Accident Fund.
85 Westhofen, *Forth Bridge*, p. 5.
86 Baker, *Chambers' Journal*, 1.9.88.
87 BR/FOR/1/2 Hutchinson 18th report 31.8.87.
88 Baker, 'Bridging the Firth', pp. 26–7.
89 McCullough, *Great Bridge*, p. 506.

90 BR/FOR/1/2 Hutchinson's final report 24.2.90.
91 Forth Bridges Visitor Centre Trust. Research by Val Wilson, 2004.
92 Westhofen, *Forth Bridge*, p. 62.
93 BR/FOR/1/2 Hutchinson 18th and 19th reports 31.8.87 and 29.11.87.
94 BR/FOR/1/2 Hutchinson 23rd 30.1.88
95 *Scotsman* 4.8.87.
96 Ibid., p. 62.
97 Quoted in *Scotsman* 29.9.87. By far the most frequently used doctor was Dr Hunter, who was responsible for south Queensferry and neighbourhood.
98 Arrol letter to *Scotsman* 7.9.87.
99 Baker, 'Bridging the Firth', p. 26.
100 BR/FOR/1/2 Hutchinson final report 6.3.90.
101 BR/FOR/1/1 Meeting June 1887.
102 I am grateful to Jamie Troughton for a sight of this.
103 Westhofen, *Forth Bridge*, p. 64.
104 *Manchester Guardian*, April 1889. FOR/4/2. Date cut off.
105 B. Baker, *Chambers' Journal*, 1.9.88.
106 Baker, 'Bridging', p. 22.
107 *Scotsman* 25.2.86.
108 Baker, 'Bridging', p. 4.
109 RAC(S) 1 March 86, *Scotsman* 12.3.87, BR/FOR/1/2 Hutchinson's 21st report to Board of Trade, 1888.
110 Westhofen, *Forth Bridge*, p. 64.
111 BR/FOR/1/2 Hutchinson's 25th report.
112 Westhofen, *Forth Bridge*, p. 58.
113 *Scotsman* 28.9.89.
114 Westhofen, *Forth Bridge* , pp. 58–9.
115 The Congress was fully covered in the *Scotsman* 29.10.89 –2.11.89 from which this information derives.
116 *Scotsman* 2.11.89.
117 *Scotsman* 1.11.89.
118 Quoted by Benjamin Baker, *Scotsman*, 28.11.89. Also W. Morris, *News from Nowhere* (Harmondsworth, 1984), p. 332.
119 *Industries* 28.2.90.
120 Edinburgh Literary Institute, meeting 27.11.89, *Scotsman* 28.11.89.
121 Waterhouse to Fowler, quoted in Mackay, *Forth Bridge*, pp. 11–12.
122 BR/FOR/1/2 24.2.90.
123 Ibid., p. 63.
124 Westhofen, *Forth Bridge*, p. 63; on 15 October 1889.
125 *The Times* 4.3.80.
126 *Scotsman* 11.6.87.
127 *Scotsman* 5.3.90.
128 *Scotsman* 6.3.90.
129 *The Times* 4.3.90.
130 Quoted in MacKay, *Forth Bridge*, p. 111.
131 *Scotsman* 4.3.90.
132 BR/FOR/1/2 Meeting 23.4.90.
133 BR/FOR/1/2 Meeting 5.2.90.
134 *Scotsman* 3.6.90.

CHAPTER 10 WARFARE SUBLIMATED

1 ASRSS manifesto published in *Scotsman* 9.1.91.
2 *Scotsman* 22.12.90.
3 *Scotsman* 9.1.91.
4 *Scotsman* 21.2.91.
5 BR/CAL/1/152 Meetings of General Managers 1882–8 – and also 1893–7 bound in.
6 I am indebted to John McGregor for pointing this out.
7 National Archives of Scotland, RAC(S) NB Report 17.3.92.
8 National Archives of Scotland, RAC(S)/1 North British Reports to shareholders 1890 –1902.
9 BR/NBR/1/42 Directors' Minutes. It was still meeting on 27.9.95.
10 *The Times* 14.9.95.
11 *Scotsman* 1.8.95.
12 O.S. Nock, *Railway Race to the North* (London, 1976), chapter 4.
13 *Scotsman* 10.8.95.
14 J. Thomas, *The North British Railway*, vol. 2 (Newton Abbot, 1975), p. 45.
15 Thomas, *North British Railway*, vol. 2, p. 46.
16 London & North West Railway Company to the *Glasgow Herald* 24.8.95.
17 *Railway News* 17.8.95. Also BR/GNS/4/9 *Aberdeen Journal* 14.8.95.
18 RAC(S) 1 report to shareholders, 17.3.92.
19 Thomas, *North British*, vol. 2, p. 48.
20 Chairman Midland Railway Company 9.8.95, reported in *Scotsman*.
21 Quoted in *The Times* 22.8.95.
22 *Scotsman* 23.8.95.
23 BR/NBR/8/1063 Oakley to Conacher 22.8.95.
24 *The Times* 1.8.95.
25 Thomas, *North British*, vol. 2, p. 48.
26 BR/GNS/4/9 *London Daily Chronicle* 31.7.95.
27 BR/GNS/4/9 Schedule of Arrivals.
28 *London Daily Chronicle* 31.7.95.
29 *Scotsman* 1.8.95.
30 *Scotsman* 10.8.95.
31 *Daily Free Press* 19.8.95.
32 *Scotsman* 21.8.95.
33 *Aberdeen Journal* 20.8.95.
34 *Scotsman* 22.8.95.
35 Ibid.
36 *Scotsman* 22.8.95, *The Times* 22.8.95.
37 *Aberdeen Journal* 27.8.95.
38 BR/NBR/Memorandum 28.8.95.
39 *Dundee Advertiser* 22.8.95.
40 *Aberdeen Journal* 27.8.95.
41 BR/NBR/8/1063 Wire 22.8.95 Oakley to Conacher.
42 Ibid., Wire Conacher to Oakley 23.8.95
43 *The Times* 23.8.95.
44 *The Times* 24.8.95.
45 BR/NBR/8/1063 letter Conacher – Oakley 26.8.95.

46 NBR 8/1063 Railway Race.
47 Letter Gibb to Conacher, 28.8.95 and Oakley to Conachar 28.8.95
48 *Glasgow Herald* 24.8.95.
49 *Scotsman* 10.8.95.
50 Ibid.
51 Quoted in Nock, *Railway Race*, p. 79.
52 *The Times* 22.8.95.
53 *Standard*, quoted in *Scotsman*, 26.8.95.
54 *The Times* 24.8.95.
55 *The Times* 9.10.95.
56 *Scotsman* 25.9.95.
57 *Building News*, '1875', quoted in C. Meeks, *The Railroad Station* (New Jersey, 1978).
58 J. Simmons, 'Railways, Hotels and Tourism in Great Britain 1839 – 1914' in *Journal of Contemporary History* Vol 19 (1984) pp. 20-222.
59 J. Bruce-Watt, *The Caledonian Hotel* (London, 1983)
60 C. Meeks, *The Railroad Station* (New Jersey, 1978), p. 109.
61 Thomas, *North British 2*, pp. 23-4.
62 *Scotsman* 21.2.91.
63 *The Times* July/August 1890.
64 I am extremely grateful to Donald Cattanach for this information. Pers comm. November 2005.
65 The records show no mention of J. J. Burnet being asked to submit, as stated in Gifford, McWilliam and Walker, *The Buildings of Edinburgh* (London, 1984).
66 BR/NBR/8/1766 Entries for the Station Hotel.
67 Ibid.
68 Ibid.
69 RAC(S) 1 Report to Shareholders 14.3.95.
70 BR/NBR/Hotel &c. Cttee Minutes 21.10.1896. I am grateful to Donald Cattanach for this.
71 Ibid.
72 BR/NBR/8/17/66 Report by General Manager on the New Hotel 15.12.97.
73 Ibid., Hotel Committee Report 13.12.97.
74 Ibid., Waterhouse to Tweeddale 21.12.98.

ENVOI

1 *Daily Chronicle* 25.8.95.
2 *Scotsman* 5.3.90.
3 B. Baker, *The Forth Bridge* (London, 1882), p. 5.
4 That, at least, used to be Scotrail's excuse. Pers. Comm.
5 *Engineering*, 6.11.1914. Caledonian had 1034 miles open to traffic in 1904, the North British had 300 miles more; excluding season ticket holders, the North British carried just under 40 million passengers, the Caledonian about two million fewer. Since the Caledonian carried slightly more goods traffic (implying that its line utilisation was better) its income, at over £4.7 millions, was marginally more than its rival's.
6 DUA/MS30/1/31.
7 *The Times* 4.3.90.

BIBLIOGRAPHY

ABBREVIATIONS

CRC/CAL   Caledonian Railway Company
NAS   National Archives of Scotland
DCA   Dundee City Archives
DPL   Dundee Public Libraries
DUA   Dundee University Archives
E & G   Edinburgh & Glasgow Railway
E & N   Edinburgh & Northern Railway
E, P & D   Edinburgh, Perth & Dundee Railway
FBR   Forth Bridge Railway
ICE   Institution of Civil Engineers
Inquiry   Minutes of the proceedings of the Tay Bridge Inquiry
Lamb Collection Extensive material concerning Dundee history held in the
                 Wellgate Library
NBR   North British Railway
PKCA   Perth and Kinross Council Archives
RIBA   Royal Institute of British Architects

PRIMARY SOURCES

This book is founded principally upon the British Rail archives in the National Archives of Scotland, Edinburgh, supplemented by the excellent material in Dundee – particularly the Lamb Collection in the city's Wellgate Library, and the railway collections in the University Archives. Because the material is so extensive, it has not been thought appropriate to list many of the individual items in the Forth Bridge, Caledonian and North British railways' records. What follows are just the highlights.

MANUSCRIPT

Dundee City Council Archives	GD/TD 21/17	Tay Bridge Disaster Petitions
Dundee University Archives	MS 30	Tay Bridge Collection
	MS 105	Shiell and Small Papers

	MS 105/VI/1	Forth and Tay Bridge Papers
	MS 105/8	Scottish Central Railway Archives
	MS 105/3	Dundee & Perth & Aberdeen Junction Company
	MS 105/11	Dundee & Newtyle Railway
	MS 6/2/7/74	James Cox, *Autobiography*, written probably 1876
	MS 016.624	James Cox, Miscellaneous
	R888	papers of Tay Bridge Material
	K Loc 624.27.449	
	MS 17/11	Thornton Collection
Dundee Central Library		Lamb Collection
Perth and Kinross Archives	PE 19	Railway Papers
National Archives of Scotland	BR/FOR	Forth Bridge Railway
	BR/NBR	North British Railway
	BR/CAL	Caledonian Railway
	GD/266	Papers of Sir Thomas Bouch
	GB234/GD1/569	Miscellaneous documents re Forth Bridge
	BR/NBR/10/10/42	Sir Thomas Bouch, *Proof of Evidence to the Tay Bridge Inquiry*

PRINTED PRIMARY SOURCES

*Minutes of Proceedings upon A Formal Investigation
Directed by the Board of Trade to be held into the
Causes of, and Circumstances Attending,
the Accident to the Tay Bridge
30 June 1880* (henceforth the Inquiry).

	BR/NBR/10/1
Reports and Evidence	BR/NBR/10/2

NEWSPAPERS AND JOURNALS

Aberdeen Journal
Daily Free Press
Dundee Advertiser
Dundee Courier and Argus
Dundee Evening Telegraph
Dundee Obituaries Book, Local History Library, Wellgate
Dundee Year Books
Engineer
Glasgow Herald
Herapath's Railway Journal
Illustrated London News
London Daily Chronicle
North British Railway Study Group Journal

North East Railway Magazine
Railway News
Scotsman
Stirling Observer
The Times
Transport History
Wizard of the North

BOOKS AND PAPERS

Acworth, W.M., *Railways of Scotland* (1890).

Baker, B., *The Forth Bridge* (London, 1882).

Baker, B., 'Bridging the Firth of Forth'. Lecture to Royal Institution, 20.5.1887.

Barlow, C., *The New Tay Bridge* (London, 1889).

Barlow, C. 'The Tay Viaduct, Dundee', in *Proceedings of the Institution of Civil Engineers* 8.5.88.

Bremner, D., *The Industries of Scotland* (Edinburgh, 1869).

Cockburn, H., *Memorials of His Time* (new edn, Edinburgh, 1910).

Evans, D. Morier, *The Commercial Crisis 1847–48* (repr. New York, 1969).

Fontane, T., *Across the Tweed*, tr. Brian Battershaw (London, 1965).

Gilkes, E., 'The Tay Bridge', in *Proceedings of the Cleveland Institution of Engineers* (Middlesbrough, 1876).

Grothe, A., *The Tay Bridge: Its Commencement, Progress and Completion* (Dundee, 1878).

Industries, Special Issue, *The Forth Bridge* (London, 1890).

Inglis, W., 'The Construction of the Tay Viaduct, Dundee', *Proc. ICE* 8.5.88.

Institution of Civil Engineers, *Memoirs*.

Knight, Prof., *A Biographical Sketch with Reminiscences of Sir Thomas Thornton* (Dundee, 1905).

Landale, C., *Report . . . whether it is practical and expedient to construction A RAIL-WAY between the Valley of Strathmore and Dundee* (Dundee, 1825).

Leng, J., *The Tay Bridge Guide* (Dundee, 1887).

Lewin, H.G., *The Railway Mania and its Aftermath*, ed. C.R. Clinker (Newton Abbot, 1968).

McGonagall, W., 'The Autobiography of Sir William Topaz McGonagall' in *More Poetic Gems* (new edn, Dundee, 1968).

McGonagall, W., *The Book of Lamentations,* written by John Willocks, (Dundee, 1905).

Nasmyth, J., *Autobiography*, ed. S. Smiles (London, 1883).

The North British (Tay Bridge) Railway Bill, November 1865.

Phelps, Sir A., *Life and Labours of Mr Brassey* (London, 1876).

Phillipps, P., *The Forth Bridge* (1889).

Purvis, Sir R., *Sir William Arrol* (Edinburgh, 1913).

Ruskin, J., *Unto This Last* (new edn, London, 1926).

Ruskin, J., *On Art and Life* (reprint, Harmondsworth, 2004).

Smiles, S., *Lives of the Engineers – Smeaton and Rennie* (London, 1874).

Smiles, S., *Lives of the Engineers – George and Robert Stephenson* (London, 1879).

Smiles, S., *Self Help* (new edn Bury St Edmunds, 1996).

Westhofen, W., *The Forth Bridge* (London, 1890, reprint, Edinburgh, 1989).

SECONDARY SOURCES

Oxford Dictionary of National Biography	William Arrol
	Peter Barlow
	C.P. Bidder
	Thomas Bouch
	Thomas Brassey
	Isambard Kingdom Brunel
	Sir Marc Brunel
	George Hudson
	Joseph Locke
	Henry Rothery
Institution of Civil Engineers *Memoirs*	William Barlow
	John Cochrane
	James Falshaw
	Edgar Gilkes
	Albert Grothe
	Maj. General Charles Hutchinson
	Henry Law
	Lt Col. William Yolland

Scotland

Brotchie, A.W., *Tramways of the Tay Valley* (Dundee, 1965).

Bruce, W.S., *The Railways of Fife* (Edinburgh, 1980).

Bruce-Watt, J., *The Caledonian Hotel Edinburgh* (London, 1983).

Butt, J., and Ward, J.T., 'The Promotion of the Caledonian Railway Company', in *Transport History*, vol. 3 (1970).

Checkland, O. & S., *Industry and Ethos – Scotland 1832–1914* (Edinburgh, 1989).

Dempster, W.J., *Patrick Matthew and Natural Selection* (Edinburgh, 1983).

Duck, R.W., and Dow, W., 'Side-Scan Sonar Reveals Submerged Remains of the First Tay Railway Bridge', in *Geoarchaeology*, vol. 9, no. 2 (1994).

Ferguson, N., *The Dundee and Newtyle Railway* (Headington, 1995).

Geddes, P., 'Beginnings of a Survey of Edinburgh', in *Scottish Geographical Magazine* (Edinburgh, 1919).

Hill-Smith, D., 'Revolutionary Methods Used to Build the New Bridge', in *Dundee Courier and Advertiser*, 10.9.1987.

Koerte, A. S., *Two Railway Bridges of an Era: Firth of Forth and Firth of Tay* (Basel, 1991).

Mackay, S., *The Forth Bridge* (Edinburgh, 1990).

Marshall, P.F., *The Railways of Dundee* (Headington, 1996).

McGregor, J., *The West Highand Railway* (East Linton, 2005).

McManus, J., 'The Geological Setting of the Bridges of the Lower Tay Estuary with Particular Reference to the Fill of the Buried Channel, *Quarterly Journal of Engineering Geology,* 3 (1970).

Michie, R.C., 'Investment and Railways in Nineteenth-century Scotland', in *Scottish Industrial History*, vol. 5.1. (1982), pp. 45–535.

Miskell, L., 'Civic Leadership and the Manufacturing Elite', in L. Miskell, C.A. Whatley and B. Harris (eds), *Victorian Dundee: Image and Realities* (East Linton, 2000).

Murray, A., *The Forth Railway Bridge: A Celebration* (Edinburgh, 1983).

Nock, O.S., *The North British Railway* (London, 1959).

Nock, O.S., *Caledonian Railway* (London, 1964).

Paxton, R., Kerr, J., McBeth, D., *Our Engineering Heritage* (Edinburgh, 1981).

Phillips, D., *No Poet's Corner in the Abbey* (Dundee, 1871).

Robertson, C.J.A., *The Origins of the Scottish Railway System 1722–1844* (Edinburgh, 1983).

Robertson, C.J.A., 'The Cheap Railway Movement in Scotland: The St Andrews Railway Company', in *Transport History*, vol. 7, no. 1 (1974).

Shipway, J.S., 'Tay Rail Bridge Centenary: Some Notes', in *Proc. ICE*, part 1, 1989.

Steel, G.M., *Dundee's Iron Horses: The Story of a Lost Industry* (Edinburgh, 1974).

Tennant, C., *The Radical Laird* (Kineton, 1970).

Thomas, J., *The North British Railway*, vols 1 and 2 (1975).

Thomas, J., *Forgotten Railways: Scotland* (Newton Abbot, 1976).

Thomas, J., and Turnock, D., *North of Scotland* (Newton Abbot, 1989).

Vallance, H.A., 'The Fife Coast Line', in *The Railway Magazine*, 1953.

Vamplew, W., 'The North British Railway Inquiry of 1866', in *Scottish Industrial History Miscellany* (Edinburgh, 1978).

Vamplew, W., 'Banks and Railway Finance: A Note on the Scottish Experience', in *Transport History*, vol. 4, no. 2 (1971), pp. 166–82.

Whyte, I.B., 'A Sensation of Immense Power', in *John Fowler, Benjamin Baker, Forth Bridge* (Stuttgart, 1997).

England, Europe and America

Construction and railways

Ambrose, S.E., *Nothing Quite Like It in the World: The Men who Built the Transcontinental Railroad 1863–1869* (New York, 2001).

Beaumont, R., *The Railway King* (London, 2002).

Berton, P., *The National Dream* (Toronto, 1970).

Berton, P., *The Last Spike* (Canada, 2001).

Billington, D.P., *The Tower and the Bridge: The New Art of Structural Engineering* (New York, 1983).

Brooke, D., *The Railway Navvy* (Newton Abbot, 1983).

Buchanan, A., *Life and Times of Isambard Kingdom Brunel* (London, 2002).

Burton, A., *On the Rails* (London, 2004).

Carter, E.G., *A Historical Geography of the Railways of the British Isles* (London, 1959).

Carter, I., *Railways and Culture in Britain* (Manchester, 2001).

Coleman, T., *The Railway Navvies* (Harmondsworth, 1968).

Colquhoun, K., *A Thing in Disguise: The Visionary Life of Joseph Paxton* (London, 2003).

Gardner, J., *London Midland Scottish* (1934).

Joby, R.S., *The Railway Builders* (Newton Abbot, 1983).

Kellett, J.R., *The Impact of Railways on Victorian Cities* (London, 1969).

Kingsford, P.W., *Victorian Railwaymen* (Plymouth, 1970).

Lavallée, O., *Van Horne's Road* (Mississauga, 1974).

Lewis, P.R., and Gagg, C., 'Aesthetics versus Function: The Fall of the Dee

Bridge, 1847', in *Interdisciplinary Science Reviews*, vol. 20, no. 2, 2004.

Lloyd, D., and Insall, D., *Railway Station Architecture* (Newton Abbot, 1978).

Maré, E. de, *The Bridges of Britain* (London, 1954).

McCullough, D., *The Great Bridge: The Epic Story of the Building of the Brooklyn Bridge* (New York, 1972).

McKenna, F., *The Railway Workers 1840–1970* (London, 1980).

Meeks, C., *The Railroad Station* (New Jersey, 1978).

Nock, O.S., *The Railway Engineers* (London, 1955).

Nock, O.S., *Railway Race to the North* (London, 1976).

Rolt, L.T.C., *Thomas Telford* (London, Penguin 1979).

Scott, W.J., *The Great Railway Race of 1895* (London, 1895).

Simmons, J., 'Railways, Hotels and Tourism in Great Britain', in *Journal of Contemporary History*, vol. 19 (1984).

Simmons, J., *The Railway in England and Wales*, 4 vols (Leicester, from 1978).

Simmons, J., *The Victorian Railway* (new edn, London, 1995).

Stover, J.F., *Iron road to the West* (New York, 1978).

Vaughan, A., *Railwaymen, Politics and Money* (London, 1997).

Vaughan, A., *Isambard Kingdom Brunel: Engineering Knight Errant* (London, 1991).

The Broader Context

Arnold, A.U., and McCartney, S., *George Hudson: The Rise and Fall of the Railway King* (London, 2004).

Carlyle, T., *Heroes, Hero-worship and the Heroic in History* (London, 1895).

Cootner, P., 'The Role of the Railroads in United States Economic Growth', in *Journal of Economic History*, vol. 23, no. 4 (December, 1963).

Doukas, K.A., *The French Railroads and the State* (New York, 1976).

Evans, A.K.B., and Gough, J.V. (eds), *The Impact of the Railway on Society in Britain* (Aldershot, 2003).

Evans Carter, E.F., *An Historical Geography of the Railways of the British Isles* (London, 1959).

Freeman, M., *Railways and the Victorian Imagination* (New Haven, 1999).

Gourvish, T.R., *Railways and the British Economy 1830–1914* (London, 1980).

Hawke, G.R., *Railways and Economic Growth in England and Wales* (Oxford, 1970).

Irving, R.J., 'The Profitability and Performance of British Railways 1870–1914', in *Economic History Review*, new series, vol. 31, no. 1 (1978).

Morris, R.J., 'Samuel Smiles and the Genesis of Self Help', in *Historical Journal*, 24 (1981).

O'Brien, P., *The New Economic History of the Railways* (London, 1977).

Pollins, H., 'The Marketing of Railway Shares in the First Half of the 19th Century', in *Economic History Review*, vol. 7, no. 2 (1954).

Pollins, H., 'Railway Contractors and the Finance of Railway Development in Britain', in M.C. Reed (ed.), *Railways in the Victorian Economy* (Newton Abbot, 1969).

Reed, M.C. (ed.), *Railways in the Victorian Economy* (Newton Abbot, 1969).

Theories for the Tay Bridge Collapse

Burt, P.J.A., 'The Great Storm and the Fall of the First Tay Bridge', in *Weather*, vol. 59, no. 12 (December, 2004).

Clark, M., 'The Verdict on the Tay Bridge Disaster: An Error of Judgement by Joseph Chamberlain?' (in press).

Dow, W., 'Destined for Disaster', in *Scots Magazine* (December, 1979).

Dow, W., 'The Tay Bridge Collapsed', in *The Broughty Ferry Guide* (December, 1979).

Engineer, 'Historic Accidents and Disasters, no. 1: The Tay Bridge' (July 1941).

Henderson, I., 'The British Approach to Disaster Management: A Fresh Look at the Tay Bridge Disaster, 1879', in *Northern Scotland*, vol. 18 (1998).

Law, J.N.C., 'Sir Thomas Bouch: A Scapegoat?' in *Railway Magazine* (March, 1965).

Lewis, P.R., and Reynolds, K., 'Forensic Engineering: A Reappraisal of the Tay Bridge Disaster', in *Interdisciplinary Science Reviews*, vol. 27, no. 4 (2002).

Lewis, P.R., *Beautiful Railway Bridge Over the Silvery Tay* (Stroud, 2004).

Lewis P.R., and Gagg, C., 'Aesthetics versus Function: The Fall of the Dee Bridge, 1847', in *Interdisciplinary Science Reviews*, vol. 29, no. 2 (2004).

Martin, T.J., and MacLeod, I.A., 'The Tay Rail Bridge Disaster', in *Proc. ICE* (December, 1986).

Martin T., and Macleod, I.A., 'The Tay Rail Bridge Disaster: A Re-appraisal Based on Modern Analysis Methods', in *Civil Engineering*, vol. 108 (1995).

Prebble, J., *The High Girders* (London, 1975).

Swinfen, David, *The Tay Bridge Disaster* (Edinburgh, 1996).

Thomas, John, *The Tay Bridge Disaster: New Light on the 1879 Tragedy* (Newton Abbot, 1972).

PICTURE CREDITS

230	The Institution of Civil Engineers
244	Central Library, Dundee City Council
247	Central Library, Dundee City Council
250	Central Library, Dundee City Council
253	Central Library, Dundee City Council
257	Central Library, Dundee City Council
260	Central Library, Dundee City Council
262	Central Library, Dundee City Council
266	National Archives of Scotland/BRB Residuary Ltd
269	Both – author
270	Author
281	Author
283	Central Library, Dundee City Council
286	Author
291	M.G.A. MacKinnon
298	Central Library, Dundee City Council
302	Author
303	Author
304	National Archives of Scotland/BRB Residuary Ltd
310	Author
322	Author
323	Author

INDEX